TAKING SIDES

Clashing Views in

Health and Society

TENTH EDITION

D0776635

TAKING SIDES

Clashing Views in

Health and Society

TENTH EDITION

Selected, Edited, and with Introductions by

Eileen L. Daniel
State University of New York College at Brockport

Mc
Graw
Hill

Connect
Learn
Succeed™

TAKING SIDES: CLASHING VIEWS IN HEALTH AND SOCIETY, TENTH EDITION

Published by McGraw-Hill, a business unit of The McGraw-Hill Companies, Inc., 1221 Avenue of the Americas, New York, NY 10020. Copyright © 2012 by The McGraw-Hill Companies, Inc. All rights reserved. Previous edition(s) © 2010, 2008, and 2006. Printed in the United States of America. No part of this publication may be reproduced or distributed in any form or by any means, or stored in a database or retrieval system, without the prior written consent of The McGraw-Hill Companies, Inc., including, but not limited to, in any network or other electronic storage or transmission, or broadcast for distance learning.

Some ancillaries, including electronic and print components, may not be available to customers outside the United States.

Taking Sides® is a registered trademark of the McGraw-Hill Companies, Inc.
Taking Sides is published by the **Contemporary Learning Series** group within the McGraw-Hill Higher Education division.

1 2 3 4 5 6 7 8 9 0 DOC/DOC 1 0 9 8 7 6 5 4 3 2 1

MHID: 0-07-805023-5
ISBN:978-0-07-805023-7
ISSN: 1094-7531

Managing Editor: *Larry Loeppke*
Senior Developmental Editor: *Jade Benedict*
Senior Permissions Coordinator: *Lenny J. Behnke*
Senior Marketing Communications Specialist: *Mary Klein*
Lead Project Manager: *Jane Mohr*
Design Coordinator: *Brenda J. Rolwes*
Cover Graphics: *Rick D. Noel*
Buyer: *Nicole Baumgartner*
Media Project Manager: *Sridevi Palani*
Compositor: MPS Limited, a Macmillan Company
Cover Image: Close-Up of Pills, Pregnant Woman Using Exercise Ball, Scientist Examining Corn, Businesswoman: © Getty Images RF

www.mhhe.com

Editors/Academic Advisory Board

TAKING SIDES: Clashing Views in HEALTH AND SOCIETY

Tenth Edition

EDITOR

Eileen L. Daniel
State University of New York College at Brockport

ACADEMIC ADVISORY BOARD MEMBERS

Editors/Academic Advisory Board continued

Editors/Academic Advisory Board continued

Preface

This book contains 42 articles arranged in 21 *pro* and *con* pairs. Each pair addresses a controversial issue in health and society, expressed in terms of a question in order to draw the lines of debate more clearly.

Most of the questions that are included here relate to the health topics of modern concern, such as managed care, abortion, and drug use and abuse. The authors of these articles take strong stands on specific issues and provide support for their positions. Although we may not agree with a particular point of view, each author clearly defines his or her stand on the issues.

This book is divided into six parts, each containing related issues. Each issue is preceded by an *introduction,* which sets the stage for the debate, gives historical background on the subject, and provides a context for the controversy. Each issue concludes with a *postscript,* which offers a summary of the debate and some concluding observations and suggests further readings on the subject. The postscript also raises further points since most of the issues have more than two sides. At the back of the book is a listing of all the *contributors to this volume,* which gives information on the physicians, professors, journalists, theologians, and scientists whose views are debated here.

Taking Sides: Clashing Views in Health and Society, 10th Edition is a tool to encourage critical thought on important health issues. Readers should not feel confined to the views expressed in the articles. Some readers may see important points on both sides of an issue and may construct for themselves a new and creative approach, which may incorporate the best of both sides or provide an entirely new vantage point for understanding.

Changes to This Edition The tenth edition of *Taking Sides: Clashing Views in Health and Society* includes some important changes from previous editions. For other issues, I have kept the topic from the seventh edition but have replaced one or both of the selections in order to make the topic more current or more clearly focus the controversy. As a result, there are a total of 7 new issues and 14 new articles. The introductions and postscripts have been revised and updated.

Supplements An *Instructor's Manual with Test Questions* (both multiple-choice and essay) is available through the publisher for instructors using *Taking Sides* in the classroom. Also available is a general guidebook, *Using Taking Sides in the Classroom,* which discusses teaching techniques and methods for integrating the pro–con approach of *Taking Sides* into any classroom setting.

Acknowledgments Special thanks to John, Diana, and Jordan. Also, thanks to my colleagues at the State University of New York College at Brockport for all their helpful contributions. I was also assisted in preparing this edition by the valuable suggestions from the adopters of *Taking Sides* who filled out comment cards and questionnaires. Many of their recommendations were incorporated into this edition. Finally, I appreciate the assistance of the staff at Dushkin/McGraw-Hill.

Eileen L. Daniel
State University of New York College at Brockport

Contents In Brief

Contents

UNIT 1   THE HEALTH CARE INDUSTRY   1

Physicians for a National Health Program argue that single-payer financing is the only way to ensure that all Americans would be covered for all needed medical services. Physician and director of the Clinical Bioethics Department at the U.S. National Institutes of Health Ezekiel Emanuel opposes the proposed adoption of a single-payer system of national health insurance in the United States on the basis that it would not fix the present health care problems.

Professor of bioethics Peter Singer believes that the costs of the current health care in the United States make systematic rationing critical. Writer James Ridgeway argues that health care should be treated as a human right instead of a profit-making opportunity.

Paul Antony, chief medical officer at the Pharmaceutical Research and Manufacturers of America (PhRMA), claims that direct-to-consumer advertising of prescription medications has been beneficial to American patients and is a powerful tool in educating consumers and improving their health. Professors Marc-André Gagnon and Joel Lexchin argue that drug companies spend almost twice as much on advertising to consumers as they do on research and development.

UNIT 2   HEALTH AND SOCIETY   61

Issue 4.   Are We Winning the War on Cancer?   62

YES: **John R. Seffrin**, from "Winning the War on Cancer: Public Health or Public Policy Challenge?" *Vital Speeches of the Day* (September 2006)   *64*

NO: **Reynold Spector**, from "The War on Cancer: A Progress Report for Skeptics," *Skeptical Inquirer* (January/February 2010)   *70*

American Cancer Society president John R. Seffrin claims we are winning the war against cancer and that it is possible to eliminate the disease as a major public health problem. Physician and professor of medicine Reynold Spector argues that the gains made against cancer have been limited and that overall there has been very little progress in the war on cancer.

Issue 5.   Should Marijuana Be Legalized for Medicinal Purposes?   82

YES: **Kevin Drum**, from "The Patriot's Guide to Legalization," *Mother Jones* (July/August 2009)   *84*

NO: **Christian Science Monitor Editorial Board**, from "Legalize Marijuana? Not So Fast," *The Christian Science Monitor* (May 22, 2009)   *89*

Kevin Drum contends that medical marijuana is now legal in more than a dozen states without any serious problems or increased usage. The editorial board of *The Christian Science Monitor* maintains that the drug can lead to dependence and can cause lung damage and other health concerns.

Issue 6.   Should Doctors Prescribe Drugs Based on Race?   95

YES: **Sally Satel**, from "I Am a Racially Profiling Doctor," *The New York Times Magazine* (May 5, 2002)   *97*

NO: **Gregory Michael Dorr and David S. Jones**, from "Facts and Fiction: BiDil and the Resurgence of Racial Medicine," *Journal of Law, Medicine & Ethics* (Fall 2008)   *102*

Physician Sally Satel believes it important to note a patient's race and to treat accordingly because many diseases and treatment responses cluster by race and ethnicity. Professors Gregory Michael Dorr and David Jones argue that there is risk to using race and ethnicity to select treatment options.

Issue 7.   Should Embryonic Stem Cell Research Be Permitted?   112

Professor Jeffrey Hart contends there are many benefits to stem cell research and that a ban on funded cloning research is unjustified. Writer Ramesh Ponnuru argues that a single-celled human embryo is a living organism that directs its own development and should not be used for experimentation.

UNIT 3   MIND-BODY RELATIONSHIP   123

Alan I. Leshner, director of the National Institute on Drug Abuse at the National Institutes of Health, believes that addiction to drugs and alcohol is not a behavioral condition but a treatable disease. Psychiatrist Sally L. Satel counters that labeling addiction a chronic and relapsing brain disease is propaganda and that most addicts are the instigators of their own addiction.

Writer Gregg Easterbrook believes men and women who practice in any of the mainstream faiths enjoy better health and that lack of religious involvement does have a negative effect on mortality. Author Michael Shermer contends that intercessory prayer offered by strangers on the health and recovery of patients undergoing coronary bypass surgery is ineffective. He also addresses flaws in studies showing a relationship between prayer and health.

UNIT 4   SEXUALITY AND GENDER ISSUES   161

Science writer Phyllida Brown maintains that even a small amount of alcohol can damage a developing fetus and cites new research indicating that even small amounts of alcohol consumed during pregnancy may be harmful. Journalist Julia Moskin argues that there are almost no studies on the effects of moderate drinking during pregnancy and that small amounts of alcohol are unlikely to have much effect.

Pharmacist John Menges believes that it is his right to refuse to dispense any medication designed to end a human life. Attorney R. Alta Charo argues that health care professionals who protect themselves from the moral consequences of their actions may do so at their patients' risk.

The late Cynthia Dailard, a senior public policy associate at the Guttmacher Institute, argued that universal vaccination was needed because virtually all cases of cervical cancer are linked to the human papillomavirus. Most infected people are unaware of their infection, which is linked to nearly 10,000 cases of cervical cancer. Professors Gail Javitt, Deena Bertowitz, and Lawrence Gostin believe that mandating the cervical cancer vaccine raises significant legal, ethical, and social concerns. They are also concerned about the long-term safety and effectiveness of the vaccine.

Ian Gentles, vice president of the deVeber institute for Bioethics and Social Research in Ontario, maintains that there is a causal connection between abortion and increased risk of suicide. Senior editor and author Emily Bazelon counters that the psychological risks posed by abortion are no greater than the risk of carrying an unwanted pregnancy to term.

Physician and Director of Pittsburgh Cancer Institute Ronald B. Herberman maintains that radio frequency radiation associated with cell phones is a potential health risk factor for users, especially children. Physicist Bernard Leikind argues that there is no plausible mechanism by which cell phone radiation can cause cancer.

Carl Bloice and Conn Hallinan maintain that rising global temperatures will increase mosquito-borne diseases, asthma, and heat stroke. Indur Goklany argues that rising global temperatures are not responsible for increased illnesses and deaths.

Author Pat Thomas believes that breastfeeding is the best and healthiest way to feed infants and children and that formula manufacturers are promoting their products at the expense of babies and children. *The Atlantic* editor Hanna Rosin claims the data on the benefits of breastfeeding are inconclusive and suggests a more relaxed approach to the issue.

Authors Henry I. Miller and Gregory Conko defend biotechnology used in genetically modifying crops and foods and believe they bring many advantages. Reporter Mark Schapiro argues that the impact of genetically engineered products include the emergence of potential allergens that could trigger reactions in humans, the rising resistance of pests to the Bt toxin, and the crossing of new genes into wild relatives.

Samuel H. Preston maintains that obesity negatively affects a person's longevity and has become a major public health problem for Americans. Law professor and writer Paul Campos disagrees and claims that the health consequences of obesity are not as dire as some health officials claim.

Correlation Guide

The *Taking Sides* series presents current issues in a debate-style format designed to stimulate student interest and develop critical thinking skills. Each issue is thoughtfully framed with an issue summary, an issue introduction, and a postscript. The pro and con essays—selected for their liveliness and substance—represent the arguments of leading scholars and commentators in their fields.

Taking Sides: Clashing Views in Health and Society, 10/e is an easy-to-use reader that presents issues on important topics such as *health insurance, drug testing,* and *government regulation in health care.* For more information on *Taking Sides* and other *McGraw-Hill Contemporary Learning Series* titles, visit www.mhhe.com/cls.

This convenient guide matches the issues in **Taking Sides: Clashing Views in Health and Society, 10/e** with the corresponding chapters in two of our best-selling McGraw-Hill Health textbooks by Insel/Roth and Payne et al.

Taking Sides: Health and Society, 10/e	Core Concepts in Health, 12/e by Insel/Roth	Understanding Your Health, 12/e by Payne et al.
Issue 1: Should the United States Adopt a Single-Payer Plan to Fund National Health Insurance?	**Chapter 15:** Conventional and Complementary Medicine	**Chapter 18:** Becoming an Informed Health Care Consumer
Issue 2: Should Health Care Be Rationed in the United States?	**Chapter 15:** Conventional and Complementary Medicine	**Chapter 18:** Becoming an Informed Health Care Consumer
Issue 3: Should Prescription Drugs Be Advertised Directly to Consumers?	**Chapter 7:** The Use and Abuse of Psychoactive Drugs	**Chapter 7:** Making Decisions About Drug Use **Chapter 18:** Becoming an Informed Health Care Consumer
Issue 4: Are We Winning the War on Cancer?	**Chapter 15:** Conventional and Complementary Medicine	**Chapter 11:** Living with Cancer
Issue 5: Should Marijuana Be Legalized for Medicinal Purposes?	**Chapter 7:** The Use and Abuse of Psychoactive Drugs	**Chapter 7:** Making Decisions About Drug Use
Issue 6: Should Doctors Prescribe Drugs Based on Race?	**Chapter 7:** The Use and Abuse of Psychoactive Drugs	**Chapter 7:** Making Decisions About Drug Use **Chapter 18:** Becoming an Informed Health Care Consumer
Issue 7: Should Embryonic Stem Cell Research Be Permitted?		

(Continued)

Taking Sides: Health and Society, 10/e	Core Concepts in Health, 12/e by Insel/Roth	Understanding Your Health, 12/e by Payne et al.
Issue 8: Should Addiction to Drugs Be Labeled a Brain Disease?	**Chapter 1:** Taking Charge of Your Health **Chapter 7:** The Use and Abuse of Psychoactive Drugs	**Chapter 7:** Making Decisions About Drug Use
Issue 9: Do Religion and Prayer Benefit Health?	**Chapter 3:** Psychological Health	**Chapter 2:** Achieving Psychological Health
Issue 10: Is It Necessary for Pregnant Women to Completely Abstain From All Alcoholic Beverages?	**Chapter 5:** Sexuality, Pregnancy, and Childbirth **Chapter 8:** Alcohol and Tobacco	**Chapter 16:** Managing Your Fertility
Issue 11: Should Pro-Life Health Providers Be Allowed to Deny Prescriptions on the Basis of Conscience?	**Chapter 3:** Psychological Health **Chapter 5:** Sexuality, Pregnancy, and Childbirth	**Chapter 16:** Managing Your Fertility
Issue 12: Should the Cervical Cancer Vaccine for Girls Be Compulsory?	**Chapter 5:** Sexuality, Pregnancy, and Childbirth	**Chapter 13:** Preventing Infectious Diseases
Issue 13: Is There a Post-Abortion Syndrome?	**Chapter 3:** Psychological Health **Chapter 5:** Sexuality, Pregnancy, and Childbirth	**Chapter 3:** Managing Stress
Issue 14: Do Ultrathin Models and Actresses Influence the Onset of Eating Disorders?	**Chapter 11:** Weight Management	**Chapter 6:** Maintaining a Healthy Weight
Issue 15: Is There a Valid Reason for Routine Male Circumcision?	**Chapter 13:** Immunity and Infection	**Chapter 13:** Preventing Infectious Diseases
Issue 16: Is There a Link Between Vaccination and Autism?	**Chapter 13:** Immunity and Infection **Chapter 14:** Environmental Health	**Chapter 13:** Preventing Infectious Diseases **Chapter 20:** The Environment and Your Health
Issue 17: Do Cell Phones Cause Cancer?	**Chapter 14:** Environmental Health	**Chapter 20:** The Environment and Your Health
Issue 18: Will Global Warming Negatively Impact Human Health?	**Chapter 14:** Environmental Health	**Chapter 20:** The Environment and Your Health
Issue 19: Is Breastfeeding the Best Way to Feed Babies?	**Chapter 5:** Sexuality, Pregnancy, and Childbirth	**Chapter 17:** Becoming a Parent
Issue 20: Is It Safe to Consume Genetically Engineered Foods?	**Chapter 9:** Nutrition Basics **Chapter 14:** Environmental Health	**Chapter 5:** Understanding Nutrition and Your Diet
Issue 21: Does Obesity Cause a Decline in Life Expectancy?	**Chapter 11:** Weight Management	**Chapter 6:** Maintaining a Healthy Weight

Topic Guide

T his topic guide suggests how the selections in this book relate to the subjects covered in your course. You may want to use the topics listed on these pages to search the web more easily.

Addiction

8. Should Addiction to Drugs Be Labeled a Brain Disease?

Alcohol

10. Is It Necessary for Pregnant Women to Completely Abstain from All Alcoholic Beverages?

Behavior change

13. Is There a Post-Abortion Syndrome?
14. Do Ultrathin Models and Actresses Influence the Onset of Eating Disorders?

Beliefs

9. Do Religion and Prayer Benefit Health?
11. Should Pro-Life Health Providers Be Allowed to Deny Prescriptions on the Basis of Conscience?
15. Is There a Valid Reason for Routine Infant Male Circumcision?

Breastfeeding

19. Is Breastfeeding the Best Way to Feed Babies?

Cancer

4. Are We Winning the War on Cancer?
12. Should the Cervical Cancer Vaccine for Girls Be Compulsory?
17. Do Cell Phones Cause Cancer?

Consumer health

3. Should Prescription Drugs Be Advertised Directly to Consumers?
20. Is It Safe to Consume Genetically Engineered Foods?

Controversies

1. Should the United States Adopt a Single-Payer Plan to Fund National Health Insurance?
7. Should Embryonic Stem Cell Research Be Permitted?
9. Do Religion and Prayer Benefit Health?
14. Do Ultrathin Models and Actresses Influence the Onset of Eating Disorders?
16. Is There a Link Between Vaccination and Autism?
17. Do Cell Phones Cause Cancer?
20. Is It Safe to Consume Genetically Engineered Foods?

Depression

13. Is There a Post-Abortion Syndrome?

Drugs

3. Should Prescription Drugs be Advertised Directly to Consumers?
5. Should Marijuana Be Legalized for Medicinal Purposes?
6. Should Doctors Prescribe Drugs Based on Race?
11. Should Pro-Life Health Providers Be Allowed to Deny Prescriptions on the Basis of Conscience?

Eating disorders

14. Do Ultrathin Models and Actresses Influence the Onset of Eating Disorders?

Environmental health hazards

17. Do Cell Phones Cause Cancer?
18. Will Global Warming Negatively Impact Human Health?

(Continued)

Food safety

20. Is It Safe to Consume Genetically Engineered Foods?

Gender issues

1. Should the United States Adopt a Single-Payer Plan to Fund National Health Insurance?
12. Should the Cervical Cancer Vaccine for Girls Be Compulsory?
14. Do Ultrathin Models and Actresses Influence the Onset of Eating Disorders?

Health behavior

10. Is It Necessary for Pregnant Women to Completely Abstain from All Alcoholic Beverages?
14. Do Ultrathin Models and Actresses Influence the Onset of Eating Disorders?

Health care issues

1. Should the United States Adopt a Single-Payer Plan to Fund National Health Insurance?
2. Should Health Care Be Rationed in the United States?
10. Is It Necessary for Pregnant Women to Completely Abstain from All Alcoholic Beverages?
11. Should Pro-Life Health Providers Be Allowed to Deny Prescriptions on the Basis of Conscience?

Health and teens

12. Should the Cervical Cancer Vaccine for Girls Be Compulsory?

Marijuana

5. Should Marijuana Be Legalized for Medicinal Purposes?

Mental health

8. Should Addiction to Drugs Be Labeled a Brain Disease?

9. Do Religion and Prayer Benefit Health?
13. Is There a Post-Abortion Syndrome?

Nutrition

20. Is It Safe to Consume Genetically Engineered Foods?

Obesity

21. Does Obesity Cause a Decline in Life Expectancy?

Pregnancy

10. Is It Necessary for Pregnant Women to Completely Abstain from All Alcoholic Beverages?

Research

7. Should Embryonic Stem Cell Research Be Permitted?

Sexually transmitted diseases

12. Should the Cervical Cancer Vaccine for Girls Be Compulsory?

Tobacco and health

8. Should Addiction to Drugs Be Labeled a Brain Disease?

Vaccination

12. Should the Cervical Cancer Vaccine for Girls Be Compulsory?
16. Is There a Link Between Vaccination and Autism?

Viruses

12. Should the Cervical Cancer Vaccine for Girls Be Compulsory?

Women and gender issues

14. Do Ultrathin Models and Actresses Influence the Onset of Eating Disorders?

Introduction

Dimensions and Approaches to the Study of Health and Society

What Is Health?

Traditionally, being healthy meant being absent of illness. If an individual did not have a disease, then he or she was considered healthy. The overall health of a nation or specific population was determined by data measuring illness, disease, and death rates. Today, this rather negative view of assessing individual health, and health in general, is hanging. A healthy person is one who is not only free from disease but also fully well.

Being well, or wellness, involves the interrelationship of many dimensions of health: physical, emotional, social, mental, and spiritual. This multifaceted view of health reflects a holistic approach, which includes individuals taking responsibility for their own well-being.

Our health and longevity are affected by the many choices we make every day: medical reports tell us that if we abstain from smoking, drugs, excessive alcohol, fat, and cholesterol consumption and get regular exercise, our rates of disease and disability will significantly decrease. These reports, while not totally conclusive, have encouraged many people to make positive lifestyle changes. Millions of people have quit smoking, alcohol consumption is down, and more and more individuals are exercising regularly and eating low-fat diets. Although these changes are encouraging, many people who have been unable or unwilling to make these changes are left feeling worried and/or guilty over continuing their negative health behaviors.

But disagreement exists among the experts about the exact nature of positive health behaviors, which causes confusion. For example, some scientists claim that overweight Americans should make efforts to lose weight, even if it takes many tries. Many Americans have unsuccessfully tried to lose weight by eating a low-fat diet, although the experts debate which is best: a low-fat, high-carbohydrate diet or a low-carbohydrate diet, which includes ample protein and fat. Other debatable issues include whether or not people utilize conventional medicine or seek out alternative therapies.

Health status is also affected by society and government. Societal pressures have helped pass smoking restrictions in public places, mandatory safety belt legislation, and laws permitting condom distribution in public schools. The government plays a role in the health of individuals as well, although it has failed to provide minimal health care for any low-income Americans.

Unfortunately, there are no absolute answers to many questions regarding health and wellness issues. Moral questions, controversial concerns, and individual perceptions of health matters all can create opposing views. As you evaluate the issues in this book, you should keep an open mind toward both sides. You may not change your mind regarding the morality of abortion or the limitation of health care for the elderly or mentally handicapped, but you will still be able to learn from the opposing viewpoint.

The Health Care Industry

The issues in this book are divided into six units. The first deals with the health care industry. The topics addressed in this unit include a debate about whether or not the United States should adopt a single-payer plan to fund national health insurance. In the United States, approximately 40 million Americans have no health insurance; there has been resurgence in infectious diseases, such as TB, and antibiotic-resistant strains of bacterial infections, which threaten thousands of Americans, all put pressure on the current system along with AIDS, diabetes, and other chronic diseases. Those enrolled in government programs such as Medicaid often find few, if any, physicians who will accept them as patients since reimbursements are so low and the paperwork is so cumbersome. On the other hand, Americans continue to live longer and longer, and for most of us, the health care available is among the best in the world. Issue 2 deals with whether or not health care should be rationed. Although many Americans agree that there are some situations in which limited health care dollars should be rationed, it is unclear by whom or how these decisions should be made. Other issue in this unit addresses the debate over the value of direct marketing pre-scription drugs. Although many lifesaving medications have been developed in recent years, they come at a high price. Should consumers pay for the advertising of drugs to enrich pharmaceutical companies?

Health and Society

Unit 2 introduces current issues related to health from a societal perspective. This unit addresses the controversial issues of the role of race in the treatment and study of disease, the debate over the "war" on cancer, should marijuana be legalized for medicinal purposes, and should embryonic stem cell research be allowed. This technology offers the potential to cure or treat diseases such as Parkinson's, multiple sclerosis, and others. Although there are pros and cons to the use of stem cells, ethical and moral questions also arise. Finally, the issues of health care, medical treatment, and race are addressed. As scientists develop the ability to genetically "map" the human body, the role of race has surfaced. This particular issue addresses prescription drugs specifically designed for African Americans.

Mind-Body Relationship

Unit 3 discusses two important issues related to the relationship between mind and body. Millions of Americans use and abuse the drugs that alter their minds and affect their bodies. These drugs range from illegal substances, such as crack cocaine and opiates, to the widely used legal drugs, alcohol and tobacco. Increasingly, prescription drugs obtained either legally or not are becoming substances of abuse. Use of these substances can lead to physical and psychological addiction and the related problems of family dysfunction, reduced worker productivity, and crime. Are addictions within the control of individuals who abuse drugs? Or are they an actual disease of the brain that needs treatment? A second issue in this unit discusses the role of spirituality in the prevention and treatment of disease. Many studies have found that religion and prayer play a role in recovery from sickness. Should health providers encourage spirituality for their patients? Does prayer really help to prevent a disease and hasten recovery from illnesses?

Sexuality and Gender Issues

There is much advice given to pregnant women to help ensure they have healthy babies. Research indicates that women who avoid drugs, alcohol, and tobacco reduce the risk of complications. If a pregnant woman does not consume any alcohol, her child will not be born with fetal alcohol syndrome. For some women, however, avoiding alcohol during pregnancy is particularly difficult, and they question whether or not it is safe to have a moderate amount of alcohol. For years, physicians and other health providers have cautioned that even one drink consumed at the wrong time could negatively affect the outcome of the pregnancy. This obviously created much concern for women, especially those who drank before they knew they were pregnant. The two articles debate the issue of the safety of alcohol consumption during pregnancy.

The abortion issue continues to cause major controversy. More restrictions have been placed on the right to abortion as a result of the political power wielded by the pro-life faction. Pro-choice followers, however, argue that making abortion illegal again will force many women to obtain dangerous "back alley" abortions. One controversial issue relating to abortion is whether or not women suffer from post-abortion syndrome. This topic is addressed from two very different perspectives.

Other issues debate the conscience clause relative to health providers and whether or not the cervical cancer vaccine for girls should be mandatory. Should pro-life doctors and pharmacists have the right to refuse to prescribe and/or dispense birth control or morning-after pills if their beliefs and conscience do not support the use of these drugs? Two new articles are debates over the role, if any, ultrathin models and actresses play in the onset of eating disorders. On one side, researchers claim that the promotion of an ultrathin ideal body produces an environment that favors eating disorders. The other side argues that eating disorders predate the ultrathin ideal. Also in this unit is an argument over the validity of routine male circumcision.

Public Health Issues

Debate continues over fundamental matters surrounding many health concerns. Topics addressed in this unit include issues related to a possible link between immunizations and autism and the ongoing debate over the health impacts of global warming. Although most scientists believe global warming is occurring and the results can negatively impact health, there are dissenting viewpoints.

The threat of bioterrorism has resurrected the risk of smallpox, thought to be eradicated in the late 1970s. Should all parents be forced to have their children immunized against smallpox, which carries certain risks? At the turn of the century, millions of American children developed childhood diseases, such as tetanus, polio, measles, and pertussis (whooping cough). Many of these children died or became permanently disabled because of these illnesses. Today, vaccines exist to prevent all of these conditions; however, not all children receive their recommended immunizations. Some do not get vaccinated until the schools require them, and others are allowed exemptions. More and more, parents are requesting exemptions for some or all vaccinations based on fears over their safety and/or their effectiveness. The pertussis vaccination seems to generate the biggest fears. Reports of serious injury to children following the whooping cough vaccination (usually given in a combination of diphtheria, pertussis, and tetanus, or DPT) have convinced many parents to forgo immunization. As a result, the rates of measles and pertussis have been climbing after decades of decline. Is it safer to be vaccinated than to risk getting the disease? Is there a relationship between vaccination and the development of autism? Is the research linking the two valid? Also included in this unit are the health issues linked to breastfeeding. Is it the best way to feed babies? What about women who are unable to nurse their babies? Two authors disagree on this concern. Finally, the topic of a theoretical relationship between cell phone usage and cancer is addressed. As the number of cell phones continues to rise, questions about their safety are raised.

Consumer Health Issues

Unit 6 introduces questions about particular issues related to choices about health issues. The questions here include (1) Is it safe to consume genetically engineered foods? (2) Does obesity cause a decline in life expectancy?

As Americans grow increasingly overweight, the most effective means of weight control continues to be debated. Along with that debate is the controversy over how dangerous it is to be overweight or obese. And is it true that being overweight or obese will actually shorten one's life?

Will the many debates presented in this book ever be resolved? Some issues may resolve themselves because of the availability of resources. For instance, health care rationing in the United States, as it is in the United Kingdom, may be legislated simply because there are increasingly limited resources to go around. An overhaul of the health care system to provide care for all while keeping costs down seems inevitable, as most Americans agree that the system should be changed. Other controversies may require the test of time for resolution. The debates over the health effects of global warming and the long-term benefits of medical marijuana may also take years to be fully resolved.

Other controversies may never resolve themselves. There may never be a consensus over the right of health providers to be allowed to deny care based on their beliefs, the abortion issue, rationing health care, or the cancer–cell phone connection. This book will introduce you to many ongoing controversies on a variety of sensitive and complex health-related topics. To have a good grasp of one's own viewpoint, it is necessary to be familiar with and understand the points made by the opposition.

Internet References . . .

The National Committee for Quality Assurance

The National Committee for Quality Assurance's Web page features an HMO accreditation status list that is updated monthly. It also provides accreditation summary reports on a number of HMO plans and other consumer information on managed care plans.

http: //www.ncqa.org

Prescription Drugs: The Issue

A profile of prescription drugs, including a look at the interest groups behind the issue and the campaign contributions they made based on records..

http://www.opensecrets.org

United States Census Bureau Health Insurance Data

Census Bureau data on health insurance coverage status and type of coverage by age, sex, gender, race, Hispanic origin, state, and other characteristics.

http://www.census.gov/hhes/www/hlthins/hlthins.html

The Health Care Industry

*T*he United States currently faces many challenging health problems, including lack of universal health insurance for all its citizens. Unlike other major industrialized nations, we do not have a single-payer plan to fund national health insurance. Also included in this unit is the issue of the need to ration health care and the issue of direct marketing of prescription drugs to Americans. For more than 20 years, drug companies have advertised prescription medications on television, in newspapers and magazines, and online. Does this benefit the consumer or the pharmaceutical manufacturers?

- Should the United States Adopt a Single-Payer Plan to Fund National Health Insurance?
- Should Health Care Be Rationed in the United States?
- Should Prescription Drugs Be Advertised Directly to Consumers?

ISSUE 1

Should the United States Adopt a Single-Payer Plan to Fund National Health Insurance?

YES: Physicians for a National Health Program, from "Proposal of the Physicians' Working Group for Single-Payer National Health Insurance" (2006). http://www.pnhp.org/

NO: Ezekiel J. Emanuel, from "The Problem with Single-Payer Plans," *Hastings Center Report* (January–February 2008)

ISSUE SUMMARY

YES: Physicians for a National Health Program argue that single-payer financing is the only way to ensure that all Americans would be covered for all needed medical services.

NO: Physician and director of the Clinical Bioethics Department at the U.S. National Institutes of Health Ezekiel Emanuel opposes the proposed adoption of a single-payer system of national health insurance in the United States on the basis that it would not fix the present health care problems.

Many Americans have perceived serious wrongs with the current health care system. In general, these concerns are (1) increasing health care access to the uninsured, (2) gaining the ability to keep one's health insurance when one changes or loses a job, and (3) controlling the escalating costs of health care. In addition, America is the only developed country in the world which lacks universal health care sponsored by the government.

Health care in the United States is not handled by a single payer but by various unrelated agencies and organizations and through a number of programs, including private insurance, government-supported Medicaid for the needy, and Medicare for the elderly. Currently there are between 35 and 40 million people—about 16 percent of the population—who do not have any health insurance and who do not qualify for government-sponsored programs. These people must often do without any medical care or suffer financial catastrophe if illness occurs. In "Health Care in USA a Shame" (*USA Today,* March 22, 2007), the authors question whether we as a nation are willing to do what's necessary to provide coverage for all Americans.

In addition to the number of uninsured people, America's health care is the most expensive in the world. The United States spends more on health care than any other nation, about $2,600 per capita. The share of the national output of wealth, the gross domestic product (GDP), expended by the United States on health is 14 percent and rising. Yet the United States has a lower life expectancy, higher infant mortality, and a higher percentage of low birth weight infants than Canada, Japan, or most western European nations. It is also estimated that 18,000 people die every year from preventable diseases just because they lack health insurance. The uninsured also live a less healthy life and die younger than those with health insurance.

While there is a need for universal coverage, there is not a universal agreement that a single-payer system supported by the government is the best solution. The American Medical Association, among others, believes that government-sponsored universal coverage would discourage hospital expansions, reduce or eliminate thousands of jobs in the insurance industry, reduce physicians' fees, and stifle innovation. Other concerns would be longer waits for health care, possible rationing, and the creation of a new bureaucracy.

One solution to America's lack of universal health care coverage has been the shift to managing care through various plans, such as health maintenance organizations (HMOs). HMOs are organizations that provide health care in return for prefixed payments. Most HMOs provide care through a network of doctors and hospitals that their members must use in order to be covered. Currently, more than 50 million workers—70 percent of the nation's eligible employees—now have health care through some type of managed care. The rise in managed care is related to employer efforts to reduce health care benefit costs. There are cost savings, but consumer groups and physicians worry that managed care will move medical decisions from doctors to accountants. One other option would be to make health insurance mandatory, forcing Americans to purchase coverage. Those without means would be able to get government support. There are both proponents and opponents to this solution as well as universal coverage and HMOs.

While politicians and health providers debate the issues, we continue to have a fragmented health care system. In the following selections, Physicians for a National Health Program argue that single-payer financing is the only way to ensure that all Americans would be covered for all needed medical services. Ezekiel Emanuel, physician and director of the Clinical Bioethics Department at the U.S. National Institutes of Health, opposes the proposed adoption of a single-payer system of national health insurance in the U.S. on the basis that it would not fix the present health care problems.

Proposal of the Physicians' Working Group for Single-Payer National Health Insurance

"Health care is an essential safeguard of human life and dignity, and there is an obligation for society to ensure that every person be able to realize this right."

—Cardinal Joseph Bernardin

Introduction

U.S. health care is rich in resources. Hospitals and sophisticated equipment abound; even many rural areas boast well-equipped facilities. Most physicians and nurses are superbly trained; dedication to patients is the norm. Our research output is prodigious. And we fund health care far more generously than any other nation.

Yet despite medical abundance, care is too often meager because of the irrationality of the present health care system. Over 39 million Americans have no health insurance whatsoever, including 33% of Hispanics, 21% of African-Americans and Asians, and 11% of non-Hispanic Whites. Many more—perhaps most of us—are underinsured. The world's richest health care system is unable to assure such basics as prenatal care and immunizations, and we trail most of the developed world on such indicators as infant mortality and life expectancy. Even the well-insured may find care compromised when HMOs deny them expensive medications and therapies. For patients, fear of financial ruin often amplifies the misfortune of illness.

For physicians, the gratifications of healing give way to anger and alienation in a system that treats sick people as commodities and doctors as investors' tools. In private practice we waste countless hours on billing and bureaucracy. For the uninsured, we avoid procedures, consultations, and costly medications. In HMOs we walk a tightrope between thrift and penuriousness, under the surveillance of bureaucrats who prod us to abdicate allegiance to patients, and to avoid the sickest, who may be unprofitable. In academia, we watch as the scholarly traditions of openness and collaboration give way to secrecy and assertions of private ownership of vital ideas; the search for knowledge displaced by a search for intellectual property.

For seven decades, opponents have blocked proposals for national health insurance, touting private sector solutions. Their reforms over the past quarter century have emphasized market mechanisms, endorsed the central role of private insurers, and nourished investor-ownership of care. But vows of greater efficiency, cost control, and consumer responsiveness are unfulfilled; meanwhile the ranks of the uninsured have swelled. HMOs, launched as health care's bright hope, have raised Medicare costs by billions, and fallen to the basement of public esteem. Investor-owned hospital chains, born of the promise of efficiency, have been wracked by scandal; their costs high, their quality low. And drug firms, which have secured the highest profits and lowest taxes of any industry, price drugs out of reach of those who need them most.

Many in today's political climate propose pushing on with the marketization of health care. They would shift more public money to private insurers; funnel Medicare through private managed care; and further fray the threadbare safety net of Medicaid, public hospitals and community clinics. These steps would fortify investors' control of care, squander additional billions on useless paperwork, and raise barriers to care still higher.

It is time to change fundamentally the trajectory of America's health care—to develop a comprehensive National Health Insurance (NHI) program for the United States.

Four principles shape our vision of reform.

1. Access to comprehensive health care is a human right. It is the responsibility of society, through its government, to assure this right. Coverage should not be tied to employment. Private insurance firms' past record disqualifies them from a central role in managing health care.
2. The right to choose and change one's physician is fundamental to patient autonomy. Patients should be free to seek care from any licensed health care professional.
3. Pursuit of corporate profit and personal fortune have no place in caregiving and they create enormous waste. The U.S. already spends enough to provide comprehensive health care to all Americans with no increase in total costs. However, the vast health care resources now squandered on bureaucracy (mostly due to efforts to divert costs to other payers or onto patients themselves), profits, marketing, and useless or even harmful medical interventions must be shifted to needed care.
4. In a democracy, the public should set overall health policies. Personal medical decisions must be made by patients with their caregivers, not by corporate or government bureaucrats.

We envision a national health insurance program (NHI) that builds upon the strengths of the current Medicare system. Coverage would be extended to all age groups, and expanded to include prescription medications and long term care. Payment mechanisms would be structured to improve efficiency and assure prompt reimbursement, while reducing bureaucracy and cost shifting. Health planning would be enhanced to improve the availability of resources and minimize wasteful duplication. Finally, investor-owned facilities would be phased out. In each section we present a key feature of the proposal followed by the rationale for our approach.

Coverage

A single public plan would cover every American for all medically-necessary services including: acute, rehabilitative, long term and home care, mental health, dental services, occupational health care, prescription drugs and supplies, and preventive and public health measures. Boards of expert and community representatives would assess which services are unnecessary or ineffective, and exclude them from coverage. As in the Medicare program, private insurance duplicating the public coverage would be proscribed. Patient co-payments and deductibles would also be eliminated.

Abolishing financial barriers to care is the *sine qua non* of reform. Only a single comprehensive program, covering rich and poor alike, can end disparities based on race, ethnicity, social class and region that compromise the health care of the American people. A single payer program is also key to minimizing the complexity and expense of billing and administration.

Private insurance that duplicates the NHI coverage would undermine the public system in several ways. (1) The market for private coverage would disappear if the public coverage were fully adequate. Hence, private insurers would continually lobby for underfunding of the public system. (2) If the wealthy could turn to private coverage, their support for adequate funding of NHI would also wane. Why pay taxes for coverage they don't use? (3) Private coverage would encourage doctors and hospitals to provide two classes of care. (4) A fractured payment system, preserving the chaos of multiple claims data bases, would subvert quality improvement efforts, e.g. the monitoring of surgical death rates and other patterns of care. (5) Eliminating multiple payers is essential to cost containment. Public administration of insurance funds would save tens of billions of dollars each year. Our private health insurers and HMOs now consume 13.6 percent of premiums for overhead, while both the Medicare program and Canadian NHI have overhead costs below 3 percent. Our multiplicity of insurers forces U.S. hospitals to spend more than twice as much as Canadian hospitals on billing and administration, and U.S. physicians to spend about 10 percent of their gross incomes on excess billing costs. Only a true single payer system would realize large administrative savings. Perpetuating multiple payers—even two—would force hospitals to maintain expensive cost accounting systems to attribute costs and charges to individual patients and payers. In the U.K., market-based reforms that fractured hospital payment have swollen administrative costs.

Co-payments and deductibles endanger the health of the sick poor, decrease use of vital inpatient medical services as much as unnecessary ones, discourage preventive care, and are unwieldy and expensive to administer. Canada has few such charges, yet health costs are lower than in the U.S. and have risen more slowly.

Instead of the confused and often unjust dictates of insurance companies, a greatly expanded program of clinical effectiveness research would guide decisions on covered services and drugs, as well as on capital allocation.

Payment for Hospital Services

The NHI would pay each hospital a monthly lump sum to cover all operating expenses—that is, a global budget. The hospital and the NHI would negotiate the amount of this payment annually, based on past expenditures, previous financial and clinical performance, projected changes in levels of services, wages and input costs, and proposed new and innovative programs. Hospitals would not bill for services covered by the NHI. Hospitals could not use any of their operating budget for expansion, profit, excessive executives' incomes, marketing, or major capital purchases or leases. Major capital expenditures would come from the NHI fund, but would be appropriated separately based upon community needs. Investor-owned hospitals would be converted to not-for-profit status, and their owners compensated for past investment.

Global budgeting would simplify hospital administration and virtually eliminate billing, freeing up substantial resources for enhanced clinical care. Prohibiting the use of operating funds for major capital purchases or profit would eliminate the main financial incentive for both excessive interventions (under fee-for-service payment) and skimping on care (under capitated or DRG systems), since neither inflating revenues nor limiting care could result in institutional gain. Separate and explicit appropriation of capital funds would facilitate rational health care planning. These methods of hospital payment would shift the focus of hospital administration away from lucrative services that enhance the "bottom line" and toward providing optimal clinical services in accord with patients' needs.

Ezekiel J. Emanuel

➡ **NO**

The Problem with Single-Payer Plans

Many liberals in America dream about single-payer plans. Even if they acknowledge that a single-payer plan cannot be enacted, they still think it the best reform. Another proposal may be politically necessary to achieve universal coverage, but it would be a compromise, a fall-back. Single payer is the ideal.

This is wrong. Even in theory, single payer is not the best reform option. Here's the problem: while it proposes the most radical reform of the health care financing system, it is conservative, even nostalgic, when it comes to the broken delivery system. It retains and solidifies the nineteenth century, fragmented, fee-for-service delivery system that provides profligate and bad quality care.

❧

Reform of the American health care system needs to address problems with both the financing and the delivery systems. As proponents of single-payer systems note, the financing system is inequitable, inefficient, and unsustainable. There are now forty-seven million uninsured Americans, about 70 percent of whom are in families with full-time workers. Wealthy individuals receive much higher tax breaks than the poor, and insurance premiums are a larger percent of wages for those working at low wages and in small businesses. Many working poor and lower middle class Americans pay taxes to support Medicaid and SCHIP, yet are excluded from these programs. The employer-based and individual market parts of the financing system are inefficient because they have huge administrative costs, especially related to insurance underwriting, sales, and marketing. The government part of the finance system is inefficient because it fails to address key policy issues, fraud, and—for Medicaid—complex determinations of eligibility. Over the past three decades, health care costs have risen 2–4 percent over growth in the overall economy. Medicaid is now the largest part of state budgets, forcing states to cut other programs.

But the delivery system is also fraught with problems. First, it is badly fragmented. Currently, 75 percent of physicians practice in groups of eight or less. Of the one billion office visits each year, one-third are to solo practitioners, and one-third are to groups of four or fewer physicians. On average, each year Medicare beneficiaries see seven different physicians, who are financially, clinically, and administratively uncoordinated.

From *Hastings Center Report*, vol. 38, no. 1, January/February 2008, pp. 38–41. Copyright © 2008 by The Hastings Center. Reprinted by permission.

A second problem is that the delivery system is structured for acute care, but the contemporary need is for chronic care. Over 133 million Americans have chronic conditions, and among Americans sixty-five and older, 75 percent have two or more chronic conditions, and 20 percent have five chronic conditions. Consequently, 70 percent of health care costs are devoted to patients with chronic conditions.

Also, the care that the system delivers is of much poorer quality than Americans realize. Use of unproven, non-beneficial, marginal, or harmful services is common. The list of offending interventions that are paid for and widely used but either unproven or of marginal benefit to patients is vast— IMRT and proton beam for early prostate cancer, CT and MRI angiograms, Epogen for chemotherapy induced anemia, Erbitux and Avastin for colorectal cancer, and drug-eluting stents for coronary artery disease. Stanford researchers recently showed that between 15 and 20 percent of prescriptions are written for indications for which there is absolutely no published data supporting their use.[1] The Dartmouth studies on variation in practices demonstrate that for many interventions, more services are not better. For instance, heart attack patients in Miami receive vastly more care than similar patients in Minnesota at 2.45 times the cost, yet have slightly worse outcomes.[2]

⋯⟨◉⟩⋯

In the context of reforming the American health care system, "single payer" has come to be associated with three key reforms: *a single national plan* for all Americans, *reduced administrative costs,* and *negotiated prices* for hospitals and physicians and perhaps for health care goods and services, such as drugs. Single-payer plans have two huge advantages.

First, single-payer plans clearly provide for universal health care coverage. Unlike Massachusetts-style individual mandate reform proposals, single-payer plans do not achieve 95 percent or 97 percent coverage, but true 100 percent coverage for all Americans.

Second, single-payer plans enhance the efficiency of the health care financing system by eliminating the wasteful costs of insurance underwriting, sales, and marketing. This could save between $60 and $100 billion. Similarly, a single-payer plan with a formulary and negotiated prices would be able to reduce drug costs. McKinsey Global Institute has estimated that bringing drug costs in the United States down to those of other developed countries would save the U.S. system $57 billion.[3] This is a huge and real savings, enough to cover all the uninsured and probably expand the range of covered services to include dental care and other items.

The problem with single-payer plans is that they have an assortment of serious structural problems. To wit:

Institutionalized Fee-for-Service

Single-payer plans would preserve the dysfunctional delivery system. We know two things about how to reform the delivery system. First, because no one yet has the secret formula for delivering the best quality health care, a real reform of the financing system needs to foster innovation in delivery and then measure the delivery system to find out what changes improve quality. Second, while the overall contours of reform are unknown, there is a clear need for better integration and coordination of care. Integration requires three *I*'s—infrastructure, information, and incentives. Better delivery of care needs an infrastructure that coordinates doctors, hospitals, home health care agencies, and other providers administratively, fiscally, and clinically. They need to share information easily. And there have to be incentives for this coordination. It will not happen spontaneously.

The problem is that a single-payer approach uses fee-for-service reimbursement to entrench the existing delivery system. Retaining and institutionalizing the fee-for-service payment model would quash the ability to integrate care. Solo practitioners or small groups would have no incentive—financial or otherwise—for integration and coordination of care across providers.

Also, single-payer reform is hostile to the very organizations that have the financial and administrative capacity to build the infrastructure and information systems for the coordinated care delivery systems: insurance companies and health plans. If there is to be an infrastructure for integration of services, information-sharing, and incentives for collaboration, some organization has to develop and implement it. Call it what you will, that organization would look a lot like a health insurance company. (Some might argue that the Veterans Affairs health system is a single-payer system that does a great job of coordinating and integrating care. True, but it covers only thirteen million people. In essence, the VA is a big health plan, like Kaiser. There is no way a single administrative body can efficiently coordinate care for three hundred million people.) In the current system, the financial incentives for health insurance companies lead to perverse behaviors, such as avoiding sick patients. But single-payer plans eliminate not only their problems, but also their potential benefits.

Deceptive Administrative Savings

There is no doubt that a single-payer system would produce huge administrative savings, but low administrative costs should not be confused with low total health care costs.

Very low administrative costs in Medicare create an opening for fraud and abuse. The last assessment by the Inspector General of the Department of Health and Human Services occurred in 1996. At that time, the IG estimated that Medicare made about $23.2 billion in improper payments due to insufficient or absent documentation, incorrect billing, billing for excluded services, and other problems. In 1996, Medicare spent about $200 billion. Thus, fraud was over 10 percent of total Medicare costs. (I leave it to you to imagine why the government has not repeated this assessment in the past decade.) True, the Canadian single-payer system does not report high levels of fraud and abuse, but Canada is not the United States. Canada's population is about one-tenth that of the United States, and Canadians believe in good government.

Furthermore, a plan covering all Americans would be much larger than Medicare. It would have to process more than one billion physician visits, forty million hospitalizations, and 3.7 billion prescriptions each year. This would require sophisticated information technology, but that technology would be a major administrative cost, and keeping it updated could be politically difficult. As we have seen in the IRS and the FBI, there is great aversion to spending money on major IT upgrades.

Finally, monitoring the quality of care delivered to patients also constitutes an administrative expense. It is an administrative burden to systematically assess whether new technologies like cancer genetic fingerprints are in fact beneficial, whether new surgical procedures really lead to longer life, and whether new ways of preparing patients for surgery and handling intravenous lines reduce infections and hospital days.

Nothing would absolutely prohibit single-payer plans from spending more money on administration to detect fraud, improve computerization, address payment issues, and assess quality. Nothing, that is, but a strong ideological commitment to keeping administrative expenses very, very low. The war cry for single-payer plans is very low administrative costs, but repeatedly touting this advantage creates a line in the sand. Indeed, it may exacerbate the inflexibility of a single-payer plan. Because of its size, any agency administering a single-payer plan would have a built-in tendency toward inertia. Further, striving to keep administrative costs low would translate into hiring fewer people to manage the system. Fewer people would mean less expertise for addressing problems and less time to search for creative solutions. This is a prescription for inflexibility and lack of innovation.

Ineffective Cost-Control Strategies

Efficiency savings from reduced administrative costs or cheaper drug prices should not be confused with controlling costs overall. Efficiencies, such as reducing administrative waste, are one-time savings. *Controlling costs* means reducing the increase in medical spending year after year. Single-payer plans use the savings from efficiencies to extend coverage to the uninsured and expand covered services without raising the total amount spent on health care. But these one-time savings do not attack the fundamental forces that drive health care cost inflation. Unless there is some mechanism to control those pressures, the one-time savings would be used up in a few years, and overall health care spending would go higher and higher. How can single-payer plans respond to this health care inflation?

There are three possible approaches. One is to "constrain the supply": use the national health plan's control to constrain the introduction and deployment of technology. A single-payer plan could decide to limit the number of MRI scanners, for example. Indeed, in the Physicians' Working Group proposal, the national health plan would negotiate with hospitals on capital expansion and could easily limit how many hospitals can build facilities for MRI scanners or new specialized surgical suites.[4] This strategy creates queuing for access to the technology. As every major country trying this has learned, queuing creates huge public resentment. People on the waiting list get furious at the central administration. Americans, especially the upper middle class, are unlikely to tolerate it.

Constraining supply also promotes gaming of the system and inequality. When technology is limited, patients—and physicians—try to jump the queue.

Physicians are not great at creating priority lists based on medical need. Particularly when they have their own practices, their obligation is to their individual patients, not to ensuring that other physicians' patients get care and not to promoting the overall health of the population.

Countries that have tried this approach have found, not surprisingly, that such gaming tends to favor well-off patients. In many facets of life, well-off people have learned how to come out on top in situations where there are limits. Limits on health care technology gives them one more setting in which their greater gaming skills can be deployed. A study in Winnipeg, Canada, showed that although all Canadians were legally entitled to the same services, the well-off had substantially better access to high technology services that were constrained.[5]

A second approach, a variant of "constrain the supply," is a "low prices and fees" approach. As the only organization paying physicians, hospitals, drug companies, and other health providers, a national health plan would have a huge incentive to squeeze down on fees. This would keep costs down, and since providers would have no one else to turn to, they would have limited recourse.

The United States government uses this low-price approach in Medicaid and Medicare. To save money, every so often Congress or the Medicare administrators roll back the fees paid to hospitals, physicians, and others. Then, just as predictably, those groups scream that they are going broke and lobby Congress to increase the fees. And so the see-saw goes on—prices rolled back and then increased after lobbying. This does not end up saving much, in part because how much is paid out depends not only on the fee or price but also on the volume—on how much is done. So one way physicians respond to lower fees is to ramp up volume; they see a lot of patients for shorter and shorter times. This is easily done because for many diseases there are no data on how often patients should be seen in the physician's office. And it is exactly how Canadian health insurance administrators kept fees low.

The British National Health Service used to do exactly what the Physicians' Working Group wants to do: It paid hospitals a fixed price for operating expenses and controlled capital expenditures to limit expansion and the purchase of new technologies. The result: the hospitals put off maintenance and began falling apart. They put off cleaning and became filthy. They could not buy new equipment or adapt quickly to changes in medical practice. Eventually, even the stiff-upper-lip British rebelled. The British National Health Service reversed course and recently gave hospitals the ability to make their own decisions, including decisions to raise funds or float bonds to expand or buy new technologies.

Both "constrain the supply" and "low prices and fees" are centralized, micromanaging cost control techniques. You do not have to be a die-hard capitalist to think they are bad techniques. Most left-leaning economists agree that it is better to develop incentives and let the market control costs than to have government set prices or supply.

The third approach to cost control in a single-payer system is that adopted by Medicare in the United States: do nothing, and just pay whatever bill comes in. Let the costs go through the roof. The crisis will come later—after the current administrators and politicians are long gone. This is probably why a

New York Times editorial said, "Even in fantasy, no one has yet come up with a way to pay for Medicare."[6]

These three options are what most single-payer systems in the world have done. None works, and all have long-term consequences.

Politicized Decision-Making

As Michael Millenson, a health policy consultant, remarks, when single-payer advocates think about who would run the national health plan, they think of Ted Kennedy. But, he asks, what if the head were Dick Cheney? Medicare reveals what is likely to happen if we have a single-payer plan. Every Medicare decision is subject to political pressure from somewhere. When Medicare tries to lower hospital fees or equalize payments, hospitals pressure their representatives and senators for increases in payments. Patient advocacy groups lobby to have Medicare pay for their favorite technology or treatment. Drug companies use campaign contributions—and patient advocacy groups—to prevent a Medicare formulary and forbid price negotiations that might limit their profits. The result is that Medicare decisions are made slowly, and rarely on their merits. No federal administrative agency can be completely free of political influence. But single-payer reform plans tend to ignore the importance of administrative independence.

The ideal reform must address not only the inequitable, inefficient, and unsustainable financing system, but also the fragmented delivery system. And it must develop a plan that creates an accountable and innovative delivery system overseen by a (relatively) independent agency that can make hard administrative choices.

References

1. D.C. Radley, S.N. Finkelstein, and R.S. Stafford, "Off-Label Prescribing among Office-Based Physicians," *Archives of Internal Medicine* 166, no. 9 (2006): 1021–26.

2. E.S. Fisher, D.E. Wennberg, T.A. Stukel, and D.J. Gottlieb, "Variations in the Longitudinal Efficiency of Academic Medical Centers." *Health Affairs* Web exclusive, October 7, 2004, http://content.healthaffairs.org/cgi/content/full/hlthaff.var.19/DC3.

3. C. Angrisano, D. Farrell, B. Kocher, M. Laboissiere, and S. Parker, "Accounting for the Cost of Health Care in the United States" (The McKinsey Global Institute, 2004), http://www.mckinsey.com/mgi/reports/pdfs/healthcare/MGI_US_HC_fullreport.pdf.

4. "Proposal of the Physicians' Working Group for Single-Payer National Health Insurance" (Physicians for a National Health Program, 2006), http://www.pnhp.org/publications/proposal_of_the_physicians_working_group_for_singlepayer_national_health_insurance.php.

5. D.A. Alter, A.S. Basinski, E.A. Cohen, and C.D. Naylor, "Fairness in the Coronary Angiography Queue," *Canadian Medical Association Journal* 161, no. 7 (1999): 813–17.

6. "Talking Deficits," *New York Times* opinion, May 23, 2004.

POSTSCRIPT

Should the United States Adopt a Single-Payer Plan to Fund National Health Insurance?

Since millions of Americans have no health insurance, many solutions have been proposed. They include the development of a single-payer plan universal health insurance sponsored by the government, further development of health maintenance organizations, and mandatory requirements to purchase health insurance. As the only industrialized country without universal coverage, it is clear that for individuals without insurance, health care is spotty, often sub-standard, unavailable, or not cost efficient. Ezekiel Emanuel and Victor Fuchs have proposed a voucher plan that offers universal coverage ("How to Cure US Health Care," *Fortune,* November 13, 2006). The authors recommend that every American under 65 receive a voucher that funds a core benefits package offered by qualified health plans. The vouchers would be funded by a tax that would replace the current billions spent on employment-based health care and Medicaid. They believe the voucher system would benefit the economy because the private sector would be relieved of the huge amount it spends on health care. The states would no longer have the burden of Medicaid, and the new system would address rising health care expenses. The plan would be under pressure to deliver care as efficiently as possible thus saving additional money.

Plans like the Emanuel/Fuchs vouchers seem to address the issue of universal access and rising health care costs. Why then does change not take place, and what are the obstacles to reform? One problem appears to be acceptance of the status quo. There are many individuals and organizations who are quite happy with the current system. The second barrier comes from groups who want change in the system, but they don't necessarily want the same changes. Some want better access and coverage for certain demographic groups while others want more resources directed at particular diseases or a focus on certain areas such as rural or urban health. Still others demand more preventive care and health education. While there is often support for change in the health care system, there are many single-issue constituencies that prevent real comprehensive reform.

For information on single-payer plans and other issues related to the American health care system, see "Learning to Care about Health Care" (*American Spectator,* July/August 2008). Author Philip Klein urges conservatives to encourage free-market solutions instead of allowing the government to develop a single-payer plan. Mark E. Kitow in "Confronting the Fear Factor" (*Benefits Quarterly,* Fall 2007) maintains that since their introduction following

World War II, single-payer health care systems have not worked well. He believes a more feasible alternative lies in providing a safety net for individuals who truly need care without tearing down the current system of supply and demand. Robert Kuttner disagrees and argues that our fragmented system does not keep costs down nor provide optimal care. He maintains a single-payer system would encourage public health measures and efficient use of medical services (*New England Journal of Medicine*, February 7, 2008).

ISSUE 2

Should Health Care Be Rationed in the United States?

YES: **Peter Singer**, from "Why We Must Ration Health Care," *The New York Times* (July 15, 2009)

NO: **James Ridgeway**, from "Meet the Real Death Panels" *Mother Jones* (July/August 2010)

ISSUE SUMMARY

YES: Professor of bioethics Peter Singer believes that the costs of the current health care in the United States make systematic rationing critical.

NO: Writer James Ridgeway argues that health care should be treated as a human right instead of a profit-making opportunity.

There are different types of health care rationing in the United States. Rationing is defined as restricting or limiting health care services or supplies to only those individuals who can afford to pay. Currently about one-sixth of the U.S. population is either too poor to pay for health care services or does not qualify for government-supported programs such as Medicaid. Rationing, however, is based not only on ability to pay, but also on employment benefits, age, preexisting medical conditions, and even lifestyle. Should health care benefits cover expensive treatments such as liver transplants to chronic alcoholics? More than 40 million Americans have no health insurance, while others are denied coverage based on preexisting health problems. Government programs for the poor such as Medicaid also ration coverage by income levels, while health maintenance organizations restrict access and coverage for certain procedures and drugs.

Because of their high health care utilization, there is talk of rationing health care for those older than 65 years. In 1980, 11 percent of the U.S. population was older than 65 years, but they utilized about 29 percent ($219 billion) of the total American health care expenditures. By the beginning of the new millennium, the percentage of the population older than 65 years had risen to 12 percent, which consumed 31 percent of total health care expenditures, or $450 billion. It has been projected that by the year 2040, people older than 65 years will represent 21 percent of the population and consume 45 percent of all health care expenditures.

Medical expenses at the end of life appear to be particularly high in relation to other health care costs. Studies have shown that nearly one-third of annual Medicare costs are for the beneficiaries who die that year. Expenses for dying patients increase significantly as death nears, and payments for health care during the last weeks of life make up 40 percent of the medical costs for the entire last year of life. Some studies have shown that up to 50 percent of the medical costs incurred during a person's entire life are spent during their last year!

Overall, as health care costs for Americans of all ages rise, there will be consequences of not controlling these costs. As Peter Singer states, "Rationing health care means getting value for the billions we are spending by setting limits on which treatments should be paid for from the public purse. If we ration, we would not be writing blank checks to pharmaceutical companies for the patented drugs, nor paying for whatever procedures doctors choose to recommend. When public funds subsidize health care or provide it directly, it is crazy not to try to get value for the money. The debate over health care reform in the United States should start from the promise that some form of health care rationing is both inescapable and desirable. Then we can ask, What is the best way to do it?" Although Singer is an advocate for rational rationing, others such as James Ridgeway believe that we need to make our system more efficient so we can economically provide health care services to all Americans, not just to those who can pay.

In the first selection, Peter Singer argues that it is critical that we adopt some type of systematic rationing as the costs of health care continue to rise. In the second selection, James Ridgeway maintains that health care must be appropriate, not rationed. He stresses that health care is a basic right of all humans and should not be viewed as an opportunity to make a profit.

YES ⤶

Peter Singer

Why We Must Ration Health Care

Y ou have advanced kidney cancer. It will kill you, probably in the next year or two. A drug called Sutent slows the spread of the cancer and may give you an extra six months, but at a cost of $54,000. Is a few more months worth that much?

If you can afford it, you probably would pay that much, or more, to live longer, even if your quality of life wasn't going to be good. But suppose it's not you with the cancer but a stranger covered by your health-insurance fund. If the insurer provides this man—and everyone else like him—with Sutent, your premiums will increase. Do you still think the drug is a good value? Suppose the treatment cost a million dollars. Would it be worth it then? Ten million? Is there any limit to how much you would want your insurer to pay for a drug that adds six months to someone's life? If there is any point at which you say, "No, an extra six months isn't worth that much," then you think that health care should be rationed.

In the current U.S. debate over *health care reform*, "rationing" has become a dirty word. Meeting last month with five governors, *President Obama* urged them to avoid using the term, apparently for fear of evoking the hostile response that sank the Clintons' attempt to achieve reform. In a *Wall Street Journal* op-ed published at the end of last year with the headline "Obama Will Ration Your Health Care," Sally Pipes, C.E.O. of the conservative Pacific Research Institute, described how in Britain the national health service does not pay for drugs that are regarded as not offering good value for money, and added, "Americans will not put up with such limits, nor will our elected representatives." And the Democratic chair of the Senate Finance Committee, Senator *Max Baucus*, told CNSNews in April, "There is no rationing of health care at all" in the proposed reform.

Remember the joke about the man who asks a woman if she would have sex with him for a million dollars? She reflects for a few moments and then answers that she would. "So," he says, "would you have sex with me for $50?" Indignantly, she exclaims, "What kind of a woman do you think I am?" He replies: "We've already established that. Now we're just haggling about the price." The man's response implies that if a woman will sell herself at any price, she is a prostitute. The way we regard rationing in health care seems to rest on a similar assumption, that it's immoral to apply monetary considerations to saving lives—but is that stance tenable?

Health care is a scarce resource, and all scarce resources are rationed in one way or another. In the United States, most health care is privately financed, and so most rationing is by price: you get what you, or your employer, can afford to insure you for. But our current system of employer-financed health insurance exists only because the federal government encouraged it by making the premiums tax deductible. That is, in effect, a more than $200 billion government subsidy for health care. In the public sector, primarily *Medicare, Medicaid* and hospital emergency rooms, health care is rationed by long waits, high patient copayment requirements, low payments to doctors that discourage some from serving public patients and limits on payments to hospitals.

The case for explicit health care rationing in the United States starts with the difficulty of thinking of any other way in which we can continue to provide adequate health care to people on Medicaid and Medicare, let alone extend coverage to those who do not now have it. Health-insurance premiums have more than doubled in a decade, rising four times faster than wages. In May, Medicare's trustees warned that the program's biggest fund is heading for insolvency in just eight years. Health care now absorbs about one dollar in every six the nation spends, a figure that far exceeds the share spent by any other nation. According to the *Congressional Budget Office*, it is on track to double by 2035.

President Obama has said plainly that America's health care system is broken. It is, he has said, by far the most significant driver of America's long-term debt and deficits. It is hard to see how the nation as a whole can remain competitive if in 26 years we are spending nearly a third of what we earn on health care, while other industrialized nations are spending far less but achieving health outcomes as good as, or better than, ours.

Rationing health care means getting value for the billions we are spending by setting limits on which treatments should be paid for from the public purse. If we ration we won't be writing blank checks to pharmaceutical companies for their patented drugs, nor paying for whatever procedures doctors choose to recommend. When public funds subsidize health care or provide it directly, it is crazy not to try to get value for money. The debate over health care reform in the United States should start from the premise that some form of health care rationing is both inescapable and desirable. Then we can ask, What is the best way to do it?

Last year Britain's National Institute for Health and Clinical Excellence gave a preliminary recommendation that the National Health Service should not offer Sutent for advanced kidney cancer. The institute, generally known as NICE, is a government-financed but independently run organization set up to provide national guidance on promoting good health and treating illness. The decision on Sutent did not, at first glance, appear difficult. NICE had set a general limit of £30,000, or about $49,000, on the cost of extending life for a year. Sutent, when used for advanced kidney cancer, cost more than that, and research suggested it offered only about six months extra life. But the British media leapt on the theme of penny-pinching bureaucrats sentencing sick people to death. The issue was then picked up by the U.S. news media and by those lobbying against health care reform in the United States. An article in *The New York Times* last December featured Bruce Hardy, a kidney-cancer patient whose wife, Joy, said, "It's hard to know that there is something out there that could help but they're saying you can't have it because of cost." Then she asked the classic question: "What price is life?"

Last November, Bloomberg News focused on Jack Rosser, who was 57 at the time and whose doctor had told him that with Sutent he might live long enough to see his 1-year-old daughter, Emma, enter primary school. Rosser's wife, Jenny, is quoted as saying: "It's immoral. They are sentencing him to die." In the conservative monthly *The American Spectator,* David Catron, a health care consultant, describes Rosser as "one of NICE's many victims" and writes that NICE "regularly hands down death sentences to gravely ill patients." Linking the British system with Democratic proposals for reforming health care in the United States, Catron asked whether we really deserve a health care system in which "soulless bureaucrats arbitrarily put a dollar value on our lives." (In March, NICE issued a final ruling on Sutent. Because of how few patients need the drug and because of special end-of-life considerations, it recommended that the drug be provided by the National Health Service to patients with advanced kidney cancer.)

There's no doubt that it's tough—politically, emotionally, and ethically—to make a decision that means that someone will die sooner than they would have if the decision had gone the other way. But if the stories of Bruce Hardy and Jack Rosser lead us to think badly of the British system of rationing health care, we should remind ourselves that the U.S. system also results in people going without life-saving treatment—it just does so less visibly. Pharmaceutical manufacturers often charge much more for drugs in the United States than they charge for the same drugs in Britain, where they know that a higher price would put the drug outside the cost-effectiveness limits set by NICE. American patients, even if they are covered by Medicare or Medicaid, often cannot afford the copayments for drugs. That's rationing too, by ability to pay.

Dr. Art Kellermann, associate dean for public policy at Emory School of Medicine in Atlanta, recently wrote of a woman who came into his emergency room in critical condition because a blood vessel had burst in her brain. She was uninsured and had chosen to buy food for her children instead of spending money on her blood-pressure medicine. In the emergency room, she received excellent high-tech medical care, but by the time she got there, it was too late to save her.

A *New York Times* report on the high costs of some drugs illustrates the problem. Chuck Stauffer, an Oregon farmer, found that his prescription-drug insurance left him to pay $5,500 for his first 42 days of Temodar, a drug used to treat brain tumors, and $1,700 a month after that. For Medicare patients drug costs can be even higher, because Medicare can require a copayment of 25 percent of the cost of the drug. For Gleevec, a drug that is effective against some forms of leukemia and some gastrointestinal tumors, that one-quarter of the cost can run to $40,000 a year.

In Britain, everyone has health insurance. In the U.S., some 45 million do not, and nor are they entitled to any health care at all, unless they can get themselves to an emergency room. Hospitals are prohibited from turning away anyone who will be endangered by being refused treatment. But even in emergency rooms, people without health insurance may receive less health care than those with insurance. Joseph Doyle, a professor of economics at the Sloan School of Management at *M.I.T.*, studied the records of people in Wisconsin who were injured in severe automobile accidents and had no choice but to go to the hospital. He estimated that those who had no health insurance received 20 percent less care and had a death rate 37 percent higher than those with health insurance. This difference held up even when those without health insurance were compared with those without *automobile insurance,* and with those on Medicaid—groups with whom they share some characteristics that might affect treatment. The lack of insurance seems to be what caused the greater number of deaths.

When the media feature someone like Bruce Hardy or Jack Rosser, we readily relate to individuals who are harmed by a government agency's decision to limit the cost of health care. But we tend not to hear about—and thus don't identify with—the particular individuals who die in emergency rooms because they have no health insurance. This "identifiable victim" effect, well documented by psychologists, creates a dangerous bias in our thinking. Doyle's figures suggest that if those Wisconsin accident victims without health insurance had received equivalent care to those with it, the additional health care would have cost about $220,000 for each life saved. Those who died were on average around 30 years old and could have been expected to live for at least another 40 years; this means that had they survived their accidents, the cost per extra year of life would have been no more than $5,500—a small fraction of the $49,000 that NICE recommends the British National Health Service should be ready to pay to give a patient an extra year of life. If the U.S. system spent less on expensive treatments for those who, with or without the drugs, have at most a few months to live, it would be better able to save the lives of more people who, if they get the treatment they need, might live for several decades.

Estimates of the number of U.S. deaths caused annually by the absence of universal health insurance go as high as 20,000. One study concluded that in the age group 55 to 64 alone, more than 13,000 extra deaths a year may be attributed to the lack of insurance coverage. But the estimates vary because Americans without health insurance are more likely, for example, to smoke than Americans with health insurance, and sorting out the role that the lack of insurance plays is difficult. Richard Kronick, a professor at the School of Medicine at the *University of California, San Diego,* cautiously concludes from his own study that there is little evidence to suggest that extending health insurance to all Americans would have a large effect on the number of deaths in the United States. That doesn't mean that it wouldn't; we simply don't know if it would.

In any case, it isn't only uninsured Americans who can't afford treatment. President Obama has spoken about his mother, who died from ovarian cancer in 1995. The president said that in the last weeks of her life, his mother "was spending too much time worrying about whether her health insurance would cover her bills"—an experience, the president went on to say, that his mother shared with millions of other Americans. It is also an experience more common in the United States than in other developed countries. A recent Commonwealth Fund study led by Cathy Schoen and Robin Osborn surveyed adults with chronic illness in Australia, Canada, France, Germany, the Netherlands, New Zealand, the United Kingdom and the United States. Far more Americans reported forgoing health care because of cost. More than half (54 percent) reported not filling a prescription, not visiting a doctor when sick, or not getting recommended care. In comparison, in the United Kingdom the figure was 13 percent, and in the Netherlands, only 7 percent. Even among Americans with insurance, 43 percent reported that cost was a problem that had limited the treatment they received. According to a 2007 study led by David Himmelstein, more than 60 percent of all bankruptcies are related to illness, with many of these specifically caused by medical bills, even among those who have health insurance. In Canada the incidence of bankruptcy related to illness is much lower.

When a *Washington Post* journalist asked Daniel Zemel, a Washington rabbi, what he thought about federal agencies putting a dollar value on human life, the rabbi cited a Jewish teaching explaining that if you put one human life on one side of a scale, and you put the rest of the world on the other side, the scale is balanced equally. Perhaps that is how those who resist health care rationing think. But we already put a dollar value on human life. If the Department of Transportation, for example, followed rabbinical teachings it would exhaust its entire budget on road safety. Fortunately the department sets a limit on how much it is willing to pay to save one human life. In 2008 that limit was $5.8 million. Other government agencies do the same. Last year the *Consumer Product Safety Commission* considered a proposal to make mattresses less likely to catch fire. Information from the industry suggested that the new standard would cost $343 million to implement, but the Consumer Product Safety Commission calculated that it would save 270 lives a year—and since it valued a human life at around $5 million, that made the new standard a good value. If we are going to have consumer-safety regulation at all, we need some idea of how much safety is worth buying. Like health care bureaucrats, consumer-safety bureaucrats sometimes decide that saving a human life is not worth the expense. Twenty years ago, the *National Research Council,* an arm of the *National Academy of Sciences,* examined a proposal for installing seat belts in all school buses. It estimated that doing so would save, on average, one life per year, at a cost of $40 million. After that, support for the proposal faded away. So why is it that those who accept that we put a price on life when it comes to consumer safety refuse to accept it when it comes to health care?

Of course, it's one thing to accept that there's a limit to how much we should spend to save a human life, and another to set that limit. The dollar value that bureaucrats place on a generic human life is intended to reflect social values, as revealed in our behavior. It is the answer to the question "How much are you willing to pay to save your life?"—except that, of course, if you asked that question of people who were facing death, they would be prepared to pay almost anything to save their lives. So instead, economists note how much people are prepared to pay to reduce the risk that they will die. How much will people pay for air bags in a car, for instance? Once you know how much they will pay for a specified reduction in risk, you multiply the amount that people are willing to pay by how much the risk has been reduced, and then you know, or so the theory goes, what value people place on their lives. Suppose that there is a 1 in 100,000 chance that an air bag in my car will save my life, and that I would pay $50—but no more than that—for an air bag. Then it looks as if I value my life at $50 × 100,000, or $5 million.

The theory sounds good, but in practice it has problems. We are not good at taking account of differences between very small risks, so if we are asked how much we would pay to reduce a risk of dying from 1 in 1,000,000 to 1 in 10,000,000, we may give the same answer as we would if asked how much we would pay to reduce the risk from 1 in 500,000 to 1 in 10,000,000. Hence multiplying what we would pay to reduce the risk of death by the reduction in risk lends an apparent mathematical precision to the outcome of the calculation—the supposed value of a human life—that our intuitive responses to the questions cannot support. Nevertheless this approach to setting a value on a human life is at least closer to what we really believe—and to what we should believe—than dramatic pronouncements about the infinite value of every human life, or the suggestion that we cannot distinguish between the value of a single human life and the value of a million human lives, or even of the rest of the world. Though such feel-good claims may have some symbolic value in particular circumstances, to take them seriously and apply them—for instance, by leaving it to chance whether we save one life or a billion—would be deeply unethical.

Governments implicitly place a dollar value on a human life when they decide how much is to be spent on health care programs and how much on other public goods that are not directed toward saving lives. The task of health care bureaucrats is then to get the best value for the resources they have been allocated. It is the familiar comparative exercise of getting the most bang for your buck. Sometimes that can be relatively easy to decide. If two drugs offer the same benefits and have similar risks of side effects, but one is much more expensive than the other, only the cheaper one should be provided by the public health care program. That the benefits and the risks of side effects are similar is a scientific matter for experts to decide after calling for submissions and examining them. That is the bread-and-butter work of units like NICE. But the benefits may vary in ways that defy straightforward comparison. We need a common unit for measuring the goods achieved by health care. Since we are talking about comparing different goods, the choice of unit is not merely a scientific or economic question but an ethical one.

As a first take, we might say that the good achieved by health care is the number of lives saved. But that is too crude. The death of a teenager is a greater tragedy than the death of an 85-year-old, and this should be reflected in our priorities. We can accommodate that difference by calculating the number of life-years saved, rather than simply the number of lives saved. If a teenager can be expected to live another 70 years, saving her life counts as a gain of 70 life-years, whereas if a person of 85 can be expected to live another 5 years, then saving the 85-year-old will count as a gain of only 5 life-years. That suggests that saving one teenager is equivalent to saving 14 85-year-olds. These are, of course, generic teenagers and generic 85-year-olds. It's easy to say, "What if the teenager is a violent criminal and the 85-year-old is still working productively?" But just as emergency rooms should leave criminal justice to the courts and treat assailants and victims alike, so decisions about the allocation of health care resources should be kept separate from judgments about the moral character or social value of individuals.

Health care does more than save lives: it also reduces pain and suffering. How can we compare saving a person's life with, say, making it possible for someone who was confined to bed to return to an active life? We can elicit people's values on that too. One common method is to describe medical conditions to people—let's say being a quadriplegic—and tell them that they can choose between 10 years in that condition or some smaller number of years without it. If most would prefer, say, 10 years as a quadriplegic to 4 years of nondisabled life, but would choose 6 years of nondisabled life over 10 with quadriplegia, but have difficulty deciding between 5 years of nondisabled life or 10 years with quadriplegia, then they are, in effect, assessing life with quadriplegia as half as good as nondisabled life. (These are hypothetical figures, chosen to keep the math simple, and not based on any actual surveys.) If that judgment represents a rough average across the population, we might conclude that restoring to nondisabled life two people who would otherwise be quadriplegics is equivalent in value to saving the life of one person, provided the life expectancies of all involved are similar.

This is the basis of the quality-adjusted life-year, or QALY, a unit designed to enable us to compare the benefits achieved by different forms of health care. The QALY has been used by economists working in health care for more than 30 years to compare the cost-effectiveness of a wide variety of medical procedures and, in some countries, as part of the process of deciding which medical treatments will be paid for with public money. If a reformed U.S. health care system explicitly accepted rationing, as I have argued it should, QALYs could play a similar role in the U.S.

Some will object that this discriminates against people with disabilities. If we return to the hypothetical assumption that a year with quadriplegia is valued at only half as much as a year without it, then a treatment that extends the lives of people without disabilities will be seen as providing twice the value of one that extends, for a similar period, the lives of quadriplegics. That clashes with the idea that all human lives are of equal value. The problem, however, does not lie with the concept of the quality-adjusted life-year, but with the judgment that, if faced with 10 years as a quadriplegic, one would prefer a shorter lifespan without a disability. Disability advocates might argue that such judgments, made by people without disabilities, merely reflect the ignorance and prejudice of people without disabilities when they think about people with disabilities. We should, they will very reasonably say, ask quadriplegics themselves to evaluate life with quadriplegia. If we do that, and we find that quadriplegics would not give up even one year of life as a quadriplegic in order to have their disability cured, then the QALY method does not justify giving preference to procedures that extend the lives of people without disabilities over procedures that extend the lives of people with disabilities.

This method of preserving our belief that everyone has an equal right to life is, however, a double-edged sword. If life with quadriplegia is as good as life without it, there is no health benefit to be gained by curing it. That implication, no doubt, would have been vigorously rejected by someone like *Christopher Reeve,* who, after being paralyzed in an accident, campaigned for more research into ways of overcoming spinal-cord injuries. Disability advocates, it seems, are forced to choose between insisting that extending their lives is just as important as extending the lives of people without disabilities, and seeking public support for research into a cure for their condition.

The QALY tells us to do what brings about the greatest health benefit, irrespective of where that benefit falls. Usually, for a given quantity of resources, we will do more good if we help those who are worst off, because they have the greatest unmet needs. But occasionally some conditions will be both very severe and very expensive to treat. A QALY approach may then lead us to give priority to helping others who are not so badly off and whose conditions are less expensive to treat. I don't find it unfair to give the same weight to the interests of those who are well off as we give to those who are much worse off, but if there is a social consensus that we should give priority to those who are worse off, we can modify the QALY approach so that it gives greater weight to benefits that accrue to those who are, on the QALY scale, worse off than others.

The QALY approach does not even try to measure the benefits that health care brings in addition to the improvement in health itself. Emotionally, we feel that the fact that Jack Rosser is the father of a young child makes a difference to the importance of extending his life, but his parental status is irrelevant to a QALY assessment of the health care gains that Sutent would bring him. Whether decisions about allocating health care resources should take such personal circumstances into account isn't easy to decide. Not to do so makes the standard inflexible, but taking personal factors into account increases the scope for subjective—and prejudiced—judgments.

The QALY is not a perfect measure of the good obtained by health care, but its defenders can support it in the same way that *Winston Churchill* defended democracy as a form of government: it is the worst method of allocating health care, except for all the others. If it isn't possible to provide everyone with all beneficial treatments, what better way do we have of deciding what treatments people should get than by comparing the QALYs gained with the expense of the treatments?

Will Americans allow their government, either directly or through an independent agency like NICE, to decide which treatments are sufficiently cost-effective to be provided at public expense and which are not? They might, under two conditions: first, that the option of private health insurance remains available, and second, that they are able to see, in their own pocket, the full cost of not rationing health care.

Rationing public health care limits free choice if private health insurance is prohibited. But many countries combine free national health insurance with optional private insurance. Australia, where I've spent most of my life and raised a family, is one. The U.S. could do something similar. This would mean extending Medicare to the entire population, irrespective of age, but without Medicare's current policy that allows doctors wide latitude in prescribing treatments for eligible patients. Instead, Medicare for All, as we might call it, should refuse to pay where the cost per QALY is extremely high. (On the other hand, Medicare for All would not require more than a token copayment for drugs that are cost-effective.) The extension of Medicare could be financed by a small income-tax levy, for those who pay income tax—in Australia the levy is 1.5 percent of taxable income. (There's an extra 1 percent surcharge for those with high incomes and no private insurance. Those who earn too little to pay income tax would be carried at no cost to themselves.) Those who want to be sure of receiving every treatment that their own privately chosen physicians recommend, regardless of cost, would be free to opt out of Medicare for All as long as they can demonstrate that they have sufficient private health insurance to avoid becoming a burden on the community if they fall ill. Alternatively, they might remain in Medicare for All but take out supplementary insurance for health care that Medicare for All does not cover. Every American will have a right to a good standard of health care, but no one will have a right to unrationed health care. Those who opt for unrationed health care will know exactly how much it costs them.

One final comment. It is common for opponents of health care rationing to point to Canada and Britain as examples of where we might end up if we get "socialized medicine." On a blog on Fox News earlier this year, the conservative writer John Lott wrote, "Americans should ask Canadians and Brits—people who have long suffered from rationing—how happy they are with central government decisions on eliminating 'unnecessary' health care." There is no particular reason that the United States should copy the British or Canadian forms of universal coverage, rather than one of the different arrangements that have developed in other industrialized nations, some of which may be better. But as it happens, last year the Gallup organization did ask Canadians and Brits, and people in many different countries, if they have confidence in "health care or medical systems" in their country. In Canada, 73 percent answered this question affirmatively. Coincidentally, an identical percentage of Britons gave the same answer. In the United States, despite spending much more, per person, on health care, the figure was only 56 percent.

James Ridgeway

→ **NO**

Meet the Real Death Panels

*H**ealth care* reform is done, but the battle over "entitlement reform" is just beginning—and already, deficit hawks are suggesting that geezers like me need to pull the plug on ourselves for the good of society. Are they looking out for future generations—or just the bonuses of *health care* execs?

There's a certain age at which you cease to regard your own death as a distant hypothetical and start to view it as a coming event. For me, it was 67—the age at which my father died. For many Americans, I suspect it's 70—the age that puts you within striking distance of our average national life expectancy of 78.1 years. Even if you still feel pretty spry, you suddenly find that your roster of doctor's appointments has expanded, along with your collection of daily medications. You grow accustomed to hearing that yet another person you once knew has dropped off the twig. And you feel more and more like a walking ghost yourself, invisible to the younger people who push past you on the subway escalator. Like it or not, death becomes something you think about, often on a daily basis.

Actually, you don't think about death, per se, as much as you do about dying—about when and where and especially how you're going to die. Will you have to deal with a long illness? With pain, immobility, or dementia? Will you be able to get the *care* you need, and will you have enough money to pay for it? Most of all, will you lose control over what life you have left, as well as over the circumstances of your death?

These are precisely the preoccupations that the right so cynically exploited in the debate over *health care* reform, with that ominous talk of Washington bean counters deciding who lives and dies. It was all nonsense, of course—the worst kind of political scare tactic. But at the same time, supporters of *health care* reform seemed to me too quick to dismiss old people's fears as just so much paranoid foolishness. There are reasons why the death-panel myth found fertile ground—and those reasons go beyond the gullibility of half-senile old farts.

While politicians of all stripes shun the idea of *health care rationing* as the political third rail that it is, most of them accept a premise that leads, one way or another, to that end. Here's what I mean: Nearly every other industrialized country recognizes *health care* as a human right, whose costs and benefits are shared among all citizens. But in the United States, the leaders of both political parties along with most of the "experts" persist in treating *health care* as a commodity that is purchased, in one way or another, by those who can afford it. Conservatives embrace this notion as the perfect expression of the all-powerful market; though they make a great show of recoiling from the term, in practice they are endorsing *rationing* on the basis of wealth. Liberals, including supporters of President Obama's *health care* reform, advocate subsidies, regulation, and other modest measures to give the less fortunate a little more buying power. But as long as *health care* is viewed as a product to be bought and sold, even the most well-intentioned reformers will someday soon have to come to grips with *health care rationing*, if not by wealth then by some other criteria.

In a country that already spends more than 16 percent of each GDP dollar on *health care*, it's easy to see why so many people believe there's simply not enough of it to go around. But keep in mind that the rest of the industrialized world manages to spend between 20 and 90 percent less per capita and still rank higher than the US in overall *health care* performance. In 2004, a team of researchers including Princeton's Uwe Reinhardt, one of the nation's best known experts on *health* economics, found that while the US spends 134 percent more than the median of the world's most developed nations, we get less for our money—fewer physician visits and hospital days per capita, for example—than our counterparts in countries like Germany, Canada, and Australia. (We do, however, have more MRI machines and more cesarean sections.)

Where does the money go instead? By some estimates, administration and insurance profits alone eat up at least 30 percent of our total *health care* bill (and most of that is in the private sector—Medicare's overhead is around 2 percent). In other words, we don't have too little to go around—we overpay for what we get, and we don't allocate our spending where it does us the most good. "In most [medical] resources we have a surplus," says Dr. David Himmelstein, cofounder of Physicians for a National *Health* Program. "People get large amounts of *care* that don't do them any good and might cause them harm [while] others don't get the necessary amount."

Looking at the numbers, it's pretty safe to say that with an efficient *health care* system, we could spend a little less than we do now and provide all Americans with the most spectacular *care* the world has ever known. But in the absence of any serious challenge to the *health-care*-as-commodity system, we are doomed to a battlefield scenario where Americans must fight to secure their share of a "scarce" resource in a life-and-death struggle that pits the rich against the poor, the insured against the uninsured—and increasingly, the old against the young.

For years, any push to improve the nation's finances—balance the budget, pay for the bailout, or help stimulate the economy—has been accompanied by rumblings about the greedy geezers who resist entitlement "reforms" (read: cuts) with their unconscionable demands for basic *health care* and a hedge against destitution. So, too, today: Already, President Obama's newly convened deficit commission looks to be blaming the nation's fiscal woes not on tax cuts, wars, or bank bailouts, but on the burden of Social Security and Medicare. (The commission's co-chair, former Republican senator Alan Simpson, has declared, "This country is gonna go to the bow-wows unless we deal with entitlements.")

Old people's anxiety in the face of such hostile attitudes has provided fertile ground for Republican disinformation and fearmongering. But so has the vacuum left by Democratic reformers. Too often, in their zeal to prove themselves tough on "waste," they've allowed connections to be drawn between two things that, to my mind, should never be spoken of in the same breath: death and cost.

Dying Wishes

The death-panel myth started with a harmless minor provision in the *health* reform bill that required Medicare to pay in case enrollees wanted to have conversations with their own doctors about "advance directives" like *health care* proxies and living wills. The controversy that ensued, thanks to a host of right-wing commentators and Sarah Palin's Facebook page, ensured that the advance-planning measure was expunged from the bill. But the underlying debate didn't end with the passage of *health care* reform, any more than it began there. For if *rationing* is inevitable once you've ruled out reining in private profits, the question is who should be denied *care,* and at what point. And given that no one will publicly argue for withholding cancer treatment from a seven-year-old, the answer almost inevitably seems to come down to what we spend on people—old people—in their final years.

As far back as 1983, in a speech to the *Health* Insurance Association of America, a then-57-year-old Alan Greenspan suggested that we consider "whether it is worth it" to spend so much of Medicare's outlays on people who would die within the year. (Appropriately, Ayn Rand called her acolyte "the undertaker"—though she chose the nickname because of his dark suits and austere demeanor.)

Not everyone puts the issue in such nakedly pecuniary terms, but in an April 2009 interview with *The New York Times Magazine,* Obama made a similar point in speaking of end-of-life *care* as a "huge driver of cost." He said, "The chronically ill and those toward the end of their lives are accounting for potentially 80 percent of the total *health care* bill out here."

The president was being a bit imprecise. Those figures are actually for Medicare expenditures, not the total *health care* tab, and more important, lumping the dying together with the "chronically ill"—who often will live for years or decades—makes little sense. But there is no denying that end-of-life *care* is expensive. Hard numbers are not easy to come by, but studies from the 1990s suggest that between a quarter and a third of annual Medicare expenditures go to patients in their last year of life, and 30 to 40 percent of those costs accrue in the final month. What this means is that around one in ten Medicare dollars—some $50 billion a year—are spent on patients with fewer than 30 days to live.

Pronouncements on these data usually come coated with a veneer of compassion and concern: How terrible it is that all those poor dying old folks have to endure aggressive treatments that only delay the inevitable; all we want to do is bring peace and dignity to their final days! But I wonder: If that's really what they're worried about, how come they keep talking about money?

At this point, I ought to make something clear: I am a big fan of what's sometimes called the "right to die" or "death with dignity" movement. I support everything from advance directives to assisted suicide. You could say I believe in one form of *health care rationing*: the kind you choose for yourself. I can't stand the idea of anyone—whether it's the government or some hospital administrator or doctor or Nurse Jackie—telling me that I must have some treatment I don't want, any more than I want them telling me that I can't have a treatment I do want. My final wish is to be my own one-member death panel.

A physician friend recently told me about a relative of hers, a frail 90-year-old woman suffering from cancer. Her doctors urged her to have surgery, followed by treatment with a recently approved cancer medicine that cost $5,000 a month. As is often the case, my friend said, the doctors told their patient about the benefits of the treatment, but not about all the risks—that she might die during the surgery or not long afterward. They also prescribed a month's supply of the new medication, even though, my friend says, they must have known the woman was unlikely to live that long. She died within a week. "Now," my friend said, "I'm carrying around a $4,000 bottle of pills."

Perhaps reflecting what economists call "supplier-induced demand," costs generally tend to go up when the dying have too little control over their *care*, rather than too much. When geezers are empowered to make decisions, most of us will choose less aggressive—and less costly—treatments. If we don't do so more often, it's usually because of an overbearing and money-hungry *health care* system, as well as a culture that disrespects the will of its elders and resists confronting death.

Once, when I was in the hospital for outpatient surgery, I woke up in the recovery area next to a man named George, who was talking loudly to his wife, telling her he wanted to leave. She soothingly reminded him that they had to wait for the doctors to learn the results of the surgery, apparently some sort of exploratory thing. Just then, two doctors appeared. In a stiff, flat voice, one of them told George that he had six months to live. When his wife's shrieking had subsided, I heard George say, "I'm getting the fuck out of this place." The doctors sternly advised him that they had more tests to run and "treatment options" to discuss. "Fuck that," said George, yanking the IV out of his arm and getting to his feet. "If I've got six months to live, do you think I want to spend another minute of it here? I'm going to the Alps to go skiing."

I don't know whether George was true to his word. But not long ago I had a friend, a scientist, who was true to his. Suffering from cancer, he anticipated a time when more chemotherapy or procedures could only prolong a deepening misery, to the point where he could no longer recognize himself. He prepared for that time, hoarding his pain meds, taking *care* to protect his doctor and pharmacist from any possibility of legal retribution. He saw some friends he wanted to see, and spoke to others. Then he died at a time and place of his choosing, with his family around him. Some would call this euthanasia, others a sacrilege. To me, it seemed like a noble end to a fine life. If freedom of choice is what makes us human, then my friend managed to make his death a final expression of his humanity.

My friend chose to forgo medical treatments that would have added many thousands of dollars to his *health care* costs—and, since he was on Medicare, to the public expense. If George really did spend his final months in the Alps, instead of undergoing expensive surgeries or sitting around hooked up to machines, he surely saved the *health care* system a bundle as well. They did it because it was what they wanted, not because it would save money. But there is a growing body of evidence that the former can lead to the latter—without any *rationing* or coercion.

One model that gets cited a lot these days is La Crosse, Wisconsin, where Gundersen Lutheran hospital launched an initiative to ensure that the town's older residents had advance directives and to make hospice and palliative *care* widely available. A 2008 study found that 90 percent of those who died in La Crosse under a physician's *care* did so with advance directives in place. At Gundersen Lutheran, less is spent on patients in their last two years of life than nearly any other place in the US, with per capita Medicare costs 30 percent below the national average. In a similar vein, Oregon, in 1995, instituted a two-page form called Physician Orders for Life-Sustaining Treatment; it functions as doctor's orders and is less likely to be misinterpreted or disregarded than a living will. According to the Dartmouth Atlas of *Health Care,* a 20-year study of the nation's medical costs and resources, people in Oregon are less likely to die in a hospital than people in most other states, and in their last six months, they spend less time in the hospital. They also run up about 50 percent less in medical expenditures.

It's possible that attitudes have begun to change. Three states now allow what advocates like to call "aid-in-dying" (rather than assisted suicide) for the terminally ill. More Americans than ever have living wills and other advance directives, and that can only be a good thing: One recent study showed that more than 70 percent of patients who needed to make end-of-life decisions at some point lost the capacity to make these choices, yet among those who had prepared living wills, nearly all had their instructions carried out.

Here is the ultimate irony of the deathpanel meme: In attacking measures designed to Promote advance directives, conservatives were attacking what they claim is their core value—the individual right to free choice.

The QALY of Mercy

A wonkier version of the reform-equals-*rationing* argument is based less on panic mongering about Obama's secret euthanasia schemes and more on the implications of something called "comparative effectiveness research." The practice got a jump start in last year's stimulus bill, which included $1.1 billion for the Federal Coordinating Council for Comparative Effectiveness Research. This is money to study what treatments work best for which patients. The most obvious use of such data would be to apply the findings to Medicare, and the effort has already been attacked as the first step toward the government deciding when it's time to kick granny to the curb. Senate minority leader Mitch McConnell (R-Ky.) has said that Obama's support for comparative effectiveness research means he is seeking "a national *rationing* board."

Evidence-based medicine, in itself, has absolutely nothing to do with age. In theory, it also has nothing to do with money—though it might, as a byproduct, reduce costs (for example, by giving doctors the information they need to resist pressure from drug companies). Yet the desire for cost savings often seems to drive comparative effectiveness research, rather than the other way around. In his *Time Magazine* interview last year, Obama said, "It is an attempt to say to patients, you know what, we've looked at some objective studies concluding that the blue pill, which costs half as much as the red pill, is just as effective, and you might want to go ahead and get the blue one."

Personally, I don't mind the idea of the government promoting the blue pill over the red pill, as long as it really is "just as effective." I certainly trust the government to make these distinctions more than I trust the insurance companies or pharma reps. But I want to know that the only target is genuine waste, and the only possible casualty is profits.

There's nothing to give me pause in the *health care* law's comparative effectiveness provision, which includes $500 million a year for comparative effectiveness research. The work is to be overseen by the nonprofit Patient-Centered Outcomes Research Institute, whose 21-member board of governors will include doctors, patient advocates, and only three representatives of drug and medical-device companies.

Still, there's a difference between comparative effectiveness and comparative cost effectiveness—and from the latter, it's a short skip to outright cost-benefit analysis. In other words, the argument sometimes slides almost imperceptibly from comparing how well the blue pill and the red pill work to examining whether some people should be denied the red pill, even if it demonstrably works better.

The calculations driving such cost-benefit analyses are often based on something called QALYs—quality-adjusted life years. If a certain cancer drug would extend life by two years, say, but with such onerous side effects that those years were judged to be only half as worth living as those of a healthy person, the QALY is 1.

In Britain, the National *Health* Service has come close to setting a maximum price beyond which extra QALYs are not deemed worthwhile. In assessing drugs and treatments, the NHS's National Institute for *Health* and Clinical Excellence usually approves those that cost less than 20,000 pounds per QALY (about $28,500), and most frequently rejects those costing more than 30,000 pounds (about $43,000).

It's not hard to find examples of comparative effectiveness research—complete with QALYs—that hit quite close to home for almost anyone. Last year I was diagnosed with atrial fibrillation, a disturbance in the heart rhythm that sometimes leads to blood clots, which can travel to the brain and cause a stroke. My doctor put me on warfarin (brand name Coumadin), a blood-thinning drug that reduces the chances of forming blood clots but can also cause internal bleeding. It's risky enough that when I go to the dentist or cut myself shaving, I have to watch to make sure it doesn't turn into a torrent of blood. The levels of warfarin in my bloodstream have to be frequently checked, so I have to be ever mindful of the whereabouts of a hospital with a blood lab. It is a pain in the neck, and it makes me feel vulnerable. I sometimes wonder if it's worth it.

It turns out that several comparative effectiveness studies have looked at the efficacy of warfarin for patients with my heart condition. One of them simply weighed the drug's potential benefits against its dangerous side effects, without consideration of cost. It concluded that for a patient with my risk factors, warfarin reduced the chance of stroke a lot more than it increased the chance that I'd be seriously harmed by bleeding. Another study concluded that for a patient like me, the cost per QALY of taking warfarin is $8,000— cheap, by most standards.

Prescription drug prices have more than doubled since the study was done in 1995. But warfarin is a relatively cheap generic drug, and even if my cost per QALY was $15,000 or $20,000, I'd still pass muster with the NHS. But if I were younger and had fewer risk factors, I'd be less prone to stroke to begin with, so the reduction in risk would not be as large, and the cost per QALY would be correspondingly higher about $370,000. Would I still want to take the drug if I were, say, under 60 and free of risk factors? Considering the side effects, probably not. But would I want someone else to make that decision for me?

Critics of the British system say, among other things, that the NHS's cost-per-QALY limit is far too low. But raising it wouldn't resolve the deeper ethical question: Should anyone but the patient get to decide when life is not worth living? The Los Angeles Times' Michael Hiltzik, one of the few reporters to critically examine this issue, has noted that "healthy people tend to overestimate the effect of some medical conditions on their sufferers' quality of life. The hale and hearty, for example, will generally rate life in a wheelchair lower than will the wheelchair-bound, who often find fulfillment in ways 'healthier' persons couldn't imagine."

Simone de Beauvoir wrote that fear of aging and death drives young people to view their elders as a separate species, rather than as their future selves: "Until the moment it is upon us old age is something that only affects other people." And the more I think about the subject, the more I am sure of one thing: It's not a good idea to have a 30-year-old place a value on my life.

Whose Death Is it Anyway?

Probably the most prominent advocate of age-based *rationing* is Daniel Callahan, cofounder of a bioethics think tank called the Hastings Center. Callahan's 1987 book, *Setting Limits: Medical Goals in an Aging Society,* depicted old people as "a new social threat," a demographic, economic, and medical "avalanche" waiting to happen. In a 2008 article, Callahan said that in evaluating Medicare's expenditures, we should consider that "there is a duty to help young people to become old people, but not to help the old become still older indefinitely . . . One may well ask what counts as 'old' and what is a decently long lifespan? As I have listened to people speak of a 'full life,' often heard at funerals, I would say that by 75–80 most people have lived a full life, and most of us do not feel it a tragedy that someone in that age group has died (as we do with the death of a child)." He has proposed using "age as a specific criterion for the allocation and limitation of *care*," and argues that after a certain point, people could justifiably be denied Medicare coverage for life-extending treatments.

You can see why talk like this might make some old folks start boarding up their doors. (It apparently, however, does not concern Callahan, who last year at age 79 told *The New York Times* that he had just had a life-saving seven-hour heart procedure.) It certainly made me wonder how I would measure up.

So far, I haven't cost the system all that much. I take several different meds every day, which are mostly generics. I go to the doctor pretty often, but I haven't been in the hospital overnight for at least 20 years, and my one walk-in operation took place before I was on Medicare. And I am still working, so I'm paying in as well as taking out.

But things could change, perhaps precipitously. Since I have problems with both eyesight and balance, I could easily fall and break a bone, maybe a hip. This could mean a hip replacement, months of therapy, or even long-term immobility. My glaucoma could take a turn for the worse, and I would face a future of near blindness, with all the associated costs. Or I could have that stroke, in spite of my drug regimen.

I decided to take the issue up with the Australian philosopher Peter Singer, who made some waves on this issue with a *New York Times* op-ed published last year, titled "Why We Must Ration *Health Care*." Singer believes that *health care* is a scarce resource that will inevitably be limited. Better to do it through a public system like the British NHS, he told me, than covertly and inequitably on the private US model. "What you are trying to do is to get the most value for the money from the resources you have," he told me.

In the world he imagines, I asked Singer over coffee in a Manhattan café, what should happen if I broke a hip? He paused to think, and I hoped he wouldn't worry about hurting my feelings. "If there is a good chance of restoring mobility," he said after a moment, "and you have at least five years of mobility, that's significant benefit." He added, "Hip operations are not expensive." A new hip or knee runs between $30,000 and $40,000, most of it covered by Medicare. So for five years of mobility, that comes out to about $7,000 a year—less than the cost of a home-*care* aide, and exponentially less than a nursing home.

But then Singer turned to a more sobering thought: If the hip operation did not lead to recovery of mobility, then it might not be such a bargain. In a much-cited piece of personal revelation, Obama in 2009 talked about his grandmother's decision to have a hip replacement after she had been diagnosed with terminal cancer. She died just a few weeks later. "I don't know how much that hip replacement cost," Obama told the *Times Magazine*. "I would have paid out of pocket for that hip replacement just because she's my grandmother." But the president said that in considering whether "to give my grandmother, or everybody else's aging grandparents or parents, a hip replacement when they're terminally ill . . . you just get into some very difficult moral issues."

Singer and I talked about what choices we ourselves might make at the end of our lives. Singer, who is 63, said that he and his wife "know neither of us wants to go on living under certain conditions. Particularly if we get demented. I would draw the line if I could not recognize my wife or my children. My wife has a higher standard—when she couldn't read a novel. Yes, I wouldn't want to live beyond a certain point. It's not me anymore." I'm 10 years older than Singer, and my own advance directives reflect similar choices. So it seems like neither one of us is likely to strain the public purse with our demands for expensive and futile life-prolonging *care*.

You can say this is all a Debbie Downer, but people my age know perfectly well that these questions are not at all theoretical. We worry about the time when we will no longer be able to contribute anything useful to society and will be completely dependent on others. And we worry about the day when life will no longer seem worth living, and whether we will have the courage—and the ability—to choose a dignified death. We worry about these things all by ourselves we don't need anyone else to do it for us. And we certainly don't need anyone tallying up QALYs while our overpriced, underperforming private *health care* system adds a few more points to its profit margin.

Let it Bleed

What happened during the recent *health care* wars is what military strategists might call a "bait-and-bleed" operation: Two rival parties are drawn into a protracted conflict that depletes both their forces, while a third stands on the sidelines, its strength undiminished. In this case, Republicans and Democrats alike have shed plenty of blood, while the clever combatant on the sidelines is, of course, the *health care* industry.

In the process, *health care* reform set some unsettling precedents that could fuel the phony intergenerational conflict over *health care* resources. The final reform bill will help provide coverage to some of the estimated 46 million Americans under 65 who live without it. It finances these efforts in part by cutting Medicare costs—some $500 billion over 10 years. Contrary to Republican hysteria, the cuts so far come from all the right places—primarily from ending the tip-offs by insurers who sell government-financed "Medicare Advantage" plans. The reform law even manages to make some meaningful improvements to the flawed Medicare prescription drug program and preventive *care*. The legislation also explicitly bans age-based *health care rationing*.

Still, there are plenty of signs that the issue is far from being put to rest. Congress and the White House wrote into the law something called the Independent Payment Advisory Board, a presidentially appointed panel that is tasked with keeping Medicare's growth rate below a certain ceiling. Office of Management and Budget director Peter Orszag, the economics wunderkind who has made Medicare's finances something of a personal project, has called it potentially the most important aspect of the legislation: Medicare and Medicaid, he has said, "are at the heart of our long-term fiscal imbalance, which is the motivation for moving to a different structure in those programs." And then, of course, there's Obama's deficit commission: While the president says he is keeping an open mind when it comes to solving the deficit "crisis," no one is trying very hard to pretend that the commission has any purpose other than cutting Social Security, Medicare, and probably Medicaid as well.

Already, the commission is working closely with the Peter G. Peterson Foundation, headed by the billionaire businessman and former Nixon administration official who has emerged as one of the nation's leading "granny bashers"—deficit hawks who accuse old people of bankrupting the country.

In the end, of course, many conservatives are motivated less by deficits and more by free-market ideology: Many of them want to replace Medicare as it now exists today with a system of vouchers, and place the emphasis on individual savings and tax breaks. Barring that, Republicans have proposed a long string of cuts to Medicaid and Medicare, sometimes defying logic—by, for example, advocating reductions in in-home *care,* which can keep people out of far more expensive nursing homes.

The common means of justifying these cuts is to attack Medicare "waste." But remember that not only are Medicare's administrative costs less than one-sixth of those of private insurers, Medicare pays doctors and hospitals less (20 and 30 percent, respectively) than private payment rates; overall, Medicare pays out less in annual per capita benefits than the average large employer *health* plan, even though it serves an older, sicker population.

That basic fact is fully understood by the *health care* industry. Back in January 2009, as the nation suited up for the health care wars, the Lewin Group—a subsidiary of the *health* insurance giant United *Health*—produced an analysis of various reform proposals being floated and found that the only one to immediately reduce overall *health care* costs (by $58 billion) was one that would have dramatically expanded Medicare.

Facts like these, however, have not slowed down the granny bashers. In a February op-ed called "The Geezers' Crusade," commentator David Brooks urged old people to willingly submit to entitlement cuts in service to future generations. Via Social Security and Medicare, he argued, old folks are stealing from their own grandkids.

I'm as public spirited as the next person, and I have a Gen X son. I'd be willing to give up some expensive, life-prolonging medical treatment for him, and maybe even for the good of humanity. But I'm certainly not going to do it so some WellPoint executive can take another vacation, so Pfizer can book $3 billion in annual profits instead of $2 billion, or so private hospitals can make another campaign contribution to some gutless politician.

Here, then, is my advice to anyone who suggests that we geezers should do the right thing and pull the plug on ourselves: Start treating *health care* as a human right instead of a profit-making opportunity, and see how much money you save. Then, by all means, get back to me.

POSTSCRIPT

Should Health Care Be Rationed in the United States?

In October 1986, Dr. Thomas Starzl of Pittsburgh, Pennsylvania, transplanted a liver into a 76-year-old woman at a cost of more than $200,000. Soon after that, Congress ordered organ transplantation to be covered under Medicare, which ensured that a greater number of older persons would receive this benefit. At the same time these events were taking place, a government campaign to contain medical costs was under way, with health care for the elderly targeted.

Not everyone agrees with this means of cost cutting. In "Public Attitudes about the Use of Chronological Age as a Criterion for Allocating Health Care Resources," *The Gerontologist* (February 1993), the authors report that the majority of older people surveyed accept the withholding of life-prolonging medical care from the hopelessly ill, but that few would deny treatment on the basis of age alone. Two publications that express opposition to age-based health care rationing are "Health Care Rationing: Goodwill to All?" *Social Research* (vol. 64, Spring 2007) and "Who Should We Treat: Rights, Rationing and Resources in the NHS," *Journal of Medical Ethics* (vol. 33, March 2007).

Currently, about 40 million Americans have no medical insurance and are at risk of being denied basic health care services. At the same time, the federal government pays most of the health care costs of the elderly. Although it may not meet the needs of all older people, the amount of medical aid that goes to the elderly is greater than that for any other demographic group, and the elderly have the highest disposable income.

Most Americans have access to the best and most expensive medical care in the world. As these costs rise, some difficult decisions may have to be made regarding the allocation of these resources. As the population ages and more health care dollars are spent on care during the last years of life, medical services for the elderly or the dying may become a natural target for reduction to balance the health care budget. Additional readings on this subject include "On the Road to Rationing," *USA Today* (January 7, 2011) and "The Real Meaning of Rationing," *JAMA* (November 24, 2011). In "Rationing Health Care: Should Life-Style Be Used as a Criterion," *Journal of Cardiology* (August 2010), the authors discuss whether or not to restrict certain health treatments to those who may smoke, drink excessively, or are obese. See also: "Rationing," *PT in Motion* (February 2010); "Health Economics in Public Health," *American Journal of Preventive Medicine* (March 2009); "Ethics and Public Health Emergencies: Encouraging Responsibility," *American Journal of Bioethics* (April 2007); "Funding Decisions in Chronically Sick

Individuals," *British Journal of Nursing* (March 9, 2006); "Dare We Use the Word (Gasp)—'Rationing'?" *Healthcare Financial Management* (May 2004); "Putting a Value on Health," *The Atlantic Monthly* (January/February 2004); "Managed Care Organizations and the Rationing Problem," *The Hastings Center Report* (January/February 2003); and "Medicine, Public Health, and the Ethics of Rationing," *Perspectives in Biology and Medicine* (Winter 2002).

ISSUE 3

Should Prescription Drugs Be Advertised Directly to Consumers?

YES: Paul Antony, from "PhRMA Chief Medical Officer Testifies on DTC Advertising," http://www.phrma.org/

NO: Marc-André Gagnon and Joel Lexchin, from "The Cost of Pushing Pills: A New Estimate of Pharmaceutical Promotion Expenditures in the United States," *PLoS Medicine* (January 2008)

ISSUE SUMMARY

YES: Paul Antony, chief medical officer at the Pharmaceutical Research and Manufacturers of America (PhRMA), claims that direct-to-consumer advertising of prescription medications has been beneficial to American patients and is a powerful tool in educating consumers and improving their health.

NO: Professors Marc-André Gagnon and Joel Lexchin argue that drug companies spend almost twice as much on advertising to consumers as they do on research and development.

Prescription drug spending continues to grow at a faster pace than any other component of health care in the United States, and it is expected to continue for at least the next several years. The nation's prescription drug bill has been rising 14–18 percent a year and is expected to exceed more than $168 billion in 2012.

There are two primary reasons drug spending has increased: higher use and a higher average cost per prescription. Research indicates that each year, drug spending will account for 18–25 percent of overall health care spending. Prescription drug costs have increased from less than 10 percent of total health care costs to more than 15 percent of the total health care bill—and could approach 20 percent of total health care costs in the future. There are several key drivers of these cost increases, which include the significant increase in the elderly population over the next decade. People tend to use more drugs as they grow older to treat chronic conditions and, on average, tend to use drugs that cost more. Also, interestingly, the thresholds for determining diabetes and high cholesterol were recently lowered. As a result, more than 38 million additional people fell under the guidelines for prescription drug treatment. Although this should have a long-term, positive impact on patients' health, the short-term impact on drug spending is significant.

Costs for prescription drugs continue to escalate to allow pharmaceutical companies to recoup costs for advertising and research and development. Drug companies have invested heavily in advertising directly to consumers for the latest heartburn, allergy, arthritis, erectile dysfunction, or pain medication, to name a few. This has led to a nation of consumers entering their doctors' offices with a particular brand name drug in mind that they think will cure their ailment.

In 1977, regulations were liberalized by the Food and Drug Administration, allowing direct-to-consumer advertising of prescription drugs. Although legal, the practice remains controversial and may influence the way doctors prescribe drugs. At an estimated annual cost of $2.5 billion, pharmaceutical advertising on television and in the popular press has made drug companies and their brands household names. Recent analysis from the managed care industry has shown that prescriptions written for the top 50 most heavily advertised drugs rose nearly 25 percent, compared with 4.3 percent for all other drugs combined. Drug manufacturing, a $122 billion industry, is becoming more dependent on advertising to sell their products.

In addition to advertising expenditures, the drug companies claim they must heavily spend on research and development to bring new, better drugs to market. More new drugs are being released, with additional drugs in clinical trials. In 2000, the Food and Drug Administration approved 27 new drugs plus many improved or enhanced versions of existing drugs. Currently, more than 1,000 drugs are in the pipeline. The pharmaceutical companies claim that it costs an average of $800 million to bring a new drug to market. Critics claim that much of the research and development needed to bring a drug to market is supported by taxpayers via support by the federal government. A study by the National Institute for Health Care Management Foundation found, however, that two-thirds of the prescription drugs recently approved by the Food and Drug Administration were modified or enhanced versions of existing drugs. Only 15 percent of the approved drugs were both new and improved over existing medications.

Although it is clear that drug prices have risen dramatically, there are some positive effects to this trend to consider as many key drugs will lose their patent protection in the next couple of years, providing an opportunity to switch to generics. Although the initial cost of the generic alternatives for some of these drugs may be expensive, it does provide for a more competitive environment. In addition, some of the drugs being introduced will significantly improve the health of patients. Patients who continue to comply with drug therapies may improve their health for the long term. However, the role of direct advertising costs remains an issue from both an economic and a moral perspective.

In the following selections, Paul Antony claims direct-to-consumer advertising has been a benefit to American patients and has had a powerful impact on the education of consumers and their health improvement. Marc-André Gagnon and Joel Lexchin argue that the pharmaceutical industry continues to spend an inordinate amount of money on direct patient advertising and that this money should be earmarked toward research and development of better, more effective medications.

YES ↵

Paul Antony

PhRMA Chief Medical Officer Testifies on DTC Advertising

Washington, D.C. (September 29, 2005)—PhRMA Chief Medical Officer Paul Antony testified before Congress today at a hearing held by the U.S. Senate Special Committee on Aging on direct-to-consumer advertising and submitted the following written statement:

Mr. Chairman, Ranking Member Kohl and Members of the Committee, on behalf of the Pharmaceutical Research and Manufacturers of America (PhRMA), I am pleased to appear at this hearing today on direct-to-consumer (DTC) advertising. I am Paul Antony, M.D., Chief Medical Officer at PhRMA.

DTC advertising has been proven to be beneficial to American patients. And, continuing regulatory oversight by the FDA helps ensure that the content of DTC advertising informs and educates consumers about medical conditions and treatment options. PhRMA and its member companies have a responsibility to ensure that ads comply with FDA regulations. We take that job seriously. We want to continue to be a valuable contributor to improving public health.

DTC Advertising can be a powerful tool in educating millions of people and improving health. Because of DTC advertising, large numbers of Americans are prompted to discuss illnesses with their doctors for the first time. Because of DTC advertising, patients become more involved in their own health care decisions, and are proactive in their patient–doctor dialogue. Because of DTC advertising, patients are more likely to take their prescribed medicines.

PhRMA's Guiding Principles on Direct-to-Consumer Advertisements About Prescription Medicines

PhRMA and its member companies have long understood the special relationship we have with the patients [who] use our innovative medicines. Despite the very positive role DTC advertising plays in educating patients about health issues and options, over the years, we have heard the concerns expressed about DTC advertising—that some ads may oversell benefits and undersell risks; that some ads may lead to inappropriate prescribing; that some patients may not

From *PhRMA.org*, September 29, 2005. Pharmaceutical Research and Manufacturers of America (PhRMA).

be able to afford the advertised medicines; and that some ads may not be appropriate for some audiences. Some doctors have also complained that drug companies launch advertising campaigns without helping to educate doctors in advance. Although actual practice and data on the effects of DTC advertising differ from these concerns, PhRMA recognized our obligation to act. On July 29, 2005, PhRMA's Board of Directors unanimously approved Guiding Principles on Direct-to-Consumer Advertisements About Prescription Medicines. These principles help ensure that DTC advertising remains an important and powerful tool to educate patients while at the same time addressing many of the concerns expressed about DTC advertising over the past few years.

First, PhRMA member companies take their responsibility to fully comply with FDA advertising regulations very seriously. Our advertising is already required to be accurate and not misleading; it can only make claims supported by substantial evidence; it must reflect the balance between risks and benefits; and it must be consistent with FDA-approved labeling. However, patients, health care providers, and the general public expect us to do more than just meet our exacting legal obligations, and our Guiding Principles do go further.

Our principles recognize that at the heart of our companies' DTC communications efforts is patient education. This means that DTC communications designed to market a medicine should responsibly educate patients about a medicine, including the conditions for which it may be prescribed. DTC advertising should also foster responsible communications between patients and health care professionals to help the patient achieve better health and a better appreciation of a medicine's known benefits and risks. Specifically, the Principles state that risk and safety information should be designed to achieve a balanced presentation of both risks and benefits associated with the advertised medicines.

Our Guiding Principles recognize that companies should spend appropriate time educating health care professionals about a new medicine before it is advertised to patients. That way, providers will be prepared to discuss the appropriateness of a given medication with a patient.

Current law provides that companies must submit their DTC television advertisements to FDA upon first use for FDA's review at its discretion. Companies that sign onto these Guiding Principles agree to submit all new DTC television ads to the FDA before releasing these ads for broadcast, giving the Agency an opportunity to review consistent with its priorities and resources. Companies also commit to informing FDA of the earliest date the advertisement is set to air. Should new information concerning a previously unknown safety risk be discovered, companies commit to work with FDA to "responsibly alter or discontinue a DTC advertising campaign."

In addition, the Principles encourage companies to include, where feasible, information about help for the uninsured and underinsured in their DTC communications. Our member companies offer a host of programs that can assist needy patients with their medicines.

The Principles also recognize that ads should respect the seriousness of the health condition and medicine being advertised and that ads employing humor or entertainment may not be appropriate in all instances.

As a result of concerns that certain prescription drug ads may not be suitable for all viewing audiences, the Guiding Principles state that, "DTC television and print advertisements should be targeted to avoid audiences that are not age appropriate for the messages involved."

Signatory companies are committed to establishing their own internal processes to ensure compliance with the Guiding Principles and to broadly disseminate them internally and to advertisers. In addition, PhRMA's Board unanimously approved the creation of an office of accountability to ensure the public has an opportunity to comment on companies' compliance with these Principles. The office of accountability will be responsible for receiving comments from the general public and from health care professionals regarding DTC ads by any company that publicly states it will follow the principles. The PhRMA office of accountability will provide to these companies any comment that is reasonably related to compliance with the Principles. Periodic reports will be issued by the PhRMA office of accountability to the public regarding the nature of the comments. Each report will also be submitted to the FDA.

PhRMA's Board also agreed to select an independent panel of outside experts and individuals to review reports from the office of accountability after one year and evaluate overall trends in the industry as they relate to the Principles. The panel will be empowered to make recommendations in accordance with the Principles. The Principles will go into effect in January 2006.

We believe these Principles will help patients and health care professionals get the information they need to make informed health care decisions.

The Value of DTC Advertising
Informing and Empowering Consumers

Surveys indicate that DTC advertising makes consumers aware of new drugs and their benefits, as well as risks and side effects with the drugs advertised. They help consumers recognize symptoms and seek appropriate care. According to an article in the New England Journal of Medicine, DTC advertising is concentrated among a few therapeutic categories. These are therapeutic categories in which consumers can recognize their own symptoms, such as arthritis, seasonal allergies, and obesity; or for pharmaceuticals that treat chronic diseases with many undiagnosed sufferers, such as high cholesterol, osteoporosis, and depression.

DTC advertising gets patients talking to their doctors about conditions that may otherwise have gone undiagnosed or undertreated. For example, a study conducted by RAND Health and published in the New England Journal of Medicine found that nearly half of all adults in the United States fail to receive recommended health care. According to researchers on the RAND study, "the deficiencies in care . . . pose serious threats to the health of the American public that could contribute to thousands of preventable deaths in the United States each year." The study found underuse of prescription medications in seven of the nine conditions for which prescription medicines were the recommended treatment. Conditions for which underuse was found include asthma, cerebrovascular disease, congestive heart failure, diabetes, hip fracture, hyperlipidemia, and hypertension. Of those seven conditions for which RAND found underuse of recommended prescription medicines, five are DTC advertised.

The Rand Study, as well as other studies, highlight the underuse of needed medications and other healthcare services in the U.S.

- According to a nationally representative study of 9,090 people aged 18 and up, published in JAMA, about 43 percent of participants with recent major depression are getting inadequate therapy.
- A 2004 study published in the Archives of Internal Medicine, found that, "In older patients, failures to prescribe indicated medications, monitor medications appropriately, document necessary information, educate patients, and maintain continuity are more common prescribing problems than is use of inappropriate drugs."
- A May/June 2003 study published in the Journal of Managed Care Pharmacy, which examined claims data from 3 of the 10 largest health plans in California to determine the appropriateness of prescription medication use based upon widely accepted treatment guidelines, found that "effective medication appears to be underused." Of the four therapeutic areas of study—asthma, CHF, depression, and common cold or upper respiratory tract infections—asthma, CHF, and depression were undertreated. The researchers concluded that "the results are particularly surprising and disturbing when we take into account the fact that three of the conditions studied (asthma, CHF, and depression) are known to produce high costs to the healthcare system."
- According to a study released in May 2005 by the Stanford University School of Medicine, among patients with high cholesterol in moderate and high-risk groups, researchers found fewer than half of patient visits ended with a statin recommendation. Based on the findings, the researchers say physicians should be more aggressive in investigating statin therapy for patients with a high or moderate risk of heart disease, and that patients should ask for their cholesterol levels to be checked regularly.

Increasing Communication Between the Doctor and Patient

A vast majority of patients (93 percent) who asked about a drug reported that their doctor "welcomed the questions." Of patients who asked about a drug, 77 percent reported that their relationship with their doctor remained unchanged as a result of the office visit, and 20 percent reported that their relationship improved. In addition, both an FDA survey of physicians (from a random sample of 500 physicians from the American Medical Association's database) and a survey by the nation's oldest and largest African-American medical association, found that DTC advertisements raise disease awareness and bolster doctor-patient ties.

The doctor-patient relationship is enhanced if DTC advertising prompts a patient to talk to his doctor for the first time about a previously undiscussed condition, to comply with a prescribed treatment regimen, or to become aware of a risk or side effect that was otherwise unknown. A 2002 Prevention Magazine survey found that 24.8 million Americans spoke with their doctor about a medical condition for the first time as a result of seeing a DTC advertisement. Similarly, the FDA patient survey on DTC advertising found that nearly one in five patients reported speaking to a physician about a condition for the first time because of a DTC ad.

PhRMA and its member companies believe it is vital that patients, in consultation with their doctors, make decisions about treatments and medicines. Prescribing decisions should be dominated by the doctor's advice. While our member companies direct a large majority of their promotional activities toward physicians, such promotion in no way guarantees medicines will be prescribed.

According to a General Accounting Office report, of the 61.1 million people (33 percent of adults) who had discussions with their physician as a result of a DTC advertisement in 2001, only 8.5 million (5 percent of adults) actually received a prescription for the product, a small percentage of the total volume of prescriptions dispensed. Indeed, an FDA survey of physicians revealed that the vast majority of physicians do not feel pressure to prescribe. According to the survey, 91 percent of physicians said that their patients did not try to influence treatment courses in a way that would have been harmful and 72 percent of physicians, when asked for prescription for a specific brand name drug, felt little or no pressure to prescribe a medicine.

De-Stigmatizing Disease

DTC advertising also encourages patients to discuss medical problems that otherwise may not have been discussed because it was either thought to be too personal or that there was a stigma attached to the disease. For example, a Health Affairs article examined the value of innovation and noted that depression medications, known as selective serotonin reuptake inhibitors (SSRIs), that have been DTC advertised, have led to significant treatment expansion. Prior to the 1990's, it was estimated that about half of those persons who met a clinical definition of depression were not appropriately diagnosed, and many of those diagnosed did not receive clinically appropriate treatment. However, in the 1990's with the advent of SSRIs, treatment has been expanded. According to the article, "Manufacturers of SSRIs encouraged doctors to watch for depression and the reduced stigma afforded by the new medications induced patients to seek help." As a result, diagnosis and treatment for depression doubled over the 1990's.

Utilization and DTC Advertising

According to reports and studies, there is no direct relationship between DTC advertising and the price growth of drugs. For example, in comments to the FDA in December 2003, the FTC stated, "[DTC advertising] can empower consumers to manage their own health care by providing information that will help them, with the assistance of their doctors, to make better informed decisions about their treatment options. . . . Consumer[s] receive these benefits from DTC advertising with little, if any, evidence that such advertising increases prescription drug prices." Notably, since January 2000, the CPI component that tracks prescription medicines [has] been in line with overall medical inflation.

The FTC comments referenced above also note, "DTC advertising accounts for a relatively small proportion of the total cost of drugs, which reinforces the view that such advertising would have a limited, if any, effect on price." Likewise, a study by Harvard University and the Massachusetts Institute of Technology and published by the Kaiser Family Foundation found that DTC advertising accounts for less than 2 percent of the total U.S. spending for prescription medicines.

One study in the American Journal of Managed Care looked at whether pharmaceutical marketing has led to an increase in the use of medications by patients with marginal indications. The study found that high-risk individuals were receiving lipid-lowering treatment "consistent with evidence-based practice guidelines" despite the fact that "a substantial portion of patients continue to remain untreated and undertreated. . . ." The study concluded that "greater overall use did not appear to be associated with a shift towards patients with less CV [cardiovascular] risk."

Pharmaceutical utilization is increasing for reasons other than DTC advertising. As the June 2003 study of DTC advertising commissioned by the Kaiser Family Foundation found, "[O]ur estimates indicate that DTCA is important, but not the primary driver of recent growth [in prescription drug spending]."

Other reasons pharmaceutical utilization is increasing, include:

- Improved Medicines—Many new medicines replace higher-cost surgeries and hospital care. In 2004 alone, pharmaceutical companies added 38 new medicines and over the last decade, over 300 new medicines have become available for treating patients. These include important new medicines for some of the most devastating and costly diseases, including: AIDS, cancer, heart disease, Alzheimer's, and diabetes. According to a study prepared for the Department of Health and Human Services, "[n]ew medications are not simply more costly than older ones. They may be more effective or have fewer side effects; some may treat conditions for which no treatment was available."
- New Standards of Medical Practice Encouraging Greater Use of Pharmaceuticals—Clinical standards are changing to emphasize earlier and tighter control of a range of conditions, such as diabetes, hypertension and cardiovascular disease. For example, new recommendations from the two provider groups suggest that early treatment, including lifestyle changes and treatment with two or more types of medications, can significantly reduce the risk of later complications and improve the quality of life for people with type 2 diabetes.
- Greater Treatment of Previously Undiagnosed and Untreated Conditions—According to guidelines developed by the National Heart, Lung, and Blood Institute's National Cholesterol Education Program (NCEP) Adult Treatment Panel (ATP), approximately 36 million adults should be taking medicines to lower their cholesterol, a number that has grown from 13 million just 8 years ago.

- Aging of America—The aging of American translates into greater reliance on pharmaceuticals. For example, congestive heart failure affects an estimated 2 percent of Americans age[d] 40 to 59, more than 5 percent of those aged 60 to 69, and 10 percent of those [aged] 70 or more.

While some assume that DTC advertising leads to increased use of newer medicines rather than generic medicines, generics represent just over 50 percent of all prescriptions (generics are historically not DTC advertised). In contrast, in Europe, where DTC advertising is prohibited, the percentage of prescriptions that are generic is significantly lower. Likewise, it is worth noting that while broadcast DTC has been in place since 1997, the rate of growth in drug cost increases has declined in each of the last 5 years and in 2004 was below the rate of growth in overall health care costs.

Economic Value of DTC Advertising

Increased spending on pharmaceuticals often leads to lower spending on other forms of more costly health care. New drugs are the most heavily advertised drugs, a point critics often emphasize. However, the use of newer drugs tends to lower all types of non-drug medical spending, resulting in a net reduction in the total cost of treating a condition. For example, on average replacing an older drug with a drug 15 years newer increases spending on drugs by $18, but reduces overall costs by $111.

The Tufts Center for the Study of Drug Development reports that disease management organizations surveyed believe that increased spending on prescription drugs reduces hospital inpatient costs. "Since prescription drugs account for less than 10 percent of total current U.S. health care spending, while inpatient care accounts for 32 percent, the increased use of appropriate pharmaceutical therapies may help moderate or reduce growth in the costliest component of the U.S. health care system," according to Tufts Center Director Kenneth I. Kaitin.

Opponents also compare the amount of money spent by drug companies on marketing and advertising to the amount they spend on research and development of new drugs. However, in 2004, pharmaceutical manufacturers spent an estimated $4.15 billion on DTC advertising, according to IMS Health, compared to $49.3 billion in total R&D spending by the biopharmaceutical industry, according to Burrill & Company. PhRMA members alone spent $38.8 billion on R&D in 2004.

Conclusion

DTC advertising provides value to patients by making them aware of risks and benefits of new drugs; it empowers patients and enhances the public health; it plays a vital role in addressing a major problem in this country of undertreatment and underdiagnosis of disease; encourages patients to discuss medical problems with their health care provider that may otherwise not be discussed due to a stigma being attached to the disease; and encourages patient compliance with physician-directed treatment regimens.

Given the progress that continues to be made in society's battle against disease, patients are seeking more information about medical problems and potential treatments. The purpose of DTC advertising is to foster an informed conversation about health, disease and treatments between patients and their health care practitioners. Our Guiding Principles are an important step in ensuring patients and health care professionals get the information they need to make informed health care decisions.

This concludes my written testimony. I would be happy to answer any questions or to supply any additional material by Members or Committee Staff on this or any other issue.

**Marc-André Gagnon and
Joel Lexchin**

 **NO**

The Cost of Pushing Pills: A New Estimate of Pharmaceutical Promotion Expenditures in the United States

In the late 1950s, the late Democratic Senator Estes Kefauver, Chairman of the United States Senate's Anti-Trust and Monopoly Subcommittee, put together the first extensive indictment against the business workings of the pharmaceutical industry. He laid three charges at the door of the industry: (1) Patents sustained predatory prices and excessive margins; (2) Costs and prices were extravagantly increased by large expenditures in marketing; and (3) Most of the industry's new products were no more effective than established drugs on the market. Kefauver's indictment against a marketing-driven industry created a representation of the pharmaceutical industry far different than the one offered by the industry itself. As Froud and colleagues put it, the image of life-saving "researchers in white coats" was now contested by the one of greedy "reps in cars." The outcome of the struggle over the image of the industry is crucial because of its potential to influence the regulatory environment in which the industry operates.

Fifty years later, the debate still continues between these two depictions of the industry. The absence of reliable data on the industry's cost structures allows partisans on both sides of the debate to cite figures favorable to their own positions. The amount of money spent by pharmaceutical companies on promotion compared to the amount spent on research and development is at the heart of the debate, especially in the United States. A reliable estimate of the former is needed to bridge the divide between the industry's vision of research-driven, innovative, and life-saving pharmaceutical companies and the critics' portrayal of an industry based on marketing-driven profiteering.

IMS, a firm specializing in pharmaceutical market intelligence, is usually considered to be the authority for assessing pharmaceutical promotion expenditures. The US General Accounting Office, for example, refers to IMS numbers in concluding that "pharmaceutical companies spend more on research and development initiatives than on all drug promotional activities." Based on the data provided by IMS, the Pharmaceutical Research and Manufacturers of America (PhRMA), an American industrial lobby group for research-based

From *PLoS Medicine*, January 2008, Public Library of Science.

pharmaceutical companies, also contends that pharmaceutical firms spend more on research and development (R&D) than on marketing: US$29.6 billion on R&D in 2004 in the US as compared to US$27.7 billion for all promotional activities.

In this paper, we make the case for the need for a new estimate of promotional expenditures. We then explain how we used proprietary databases to construct a revised estimate and finally, we compare our results with those from other data sources to argue in favor of changing the priorities of the industry.

The Case for a New Estimate of Pharmaceutical Promotion

There are many concerns about the accuracy of the IMS data. First, IMS compiles its information through surveys of firms, creating the possibility that companies may systematically underestimate some of their promotional costs to enhance their public image. Second, IMS does not include the cost of meetings and talks sponsored by pharmaceutical companies featuring either doctors or sales representatives as speakers.

The number of promotional meetings has increased dramatically in recent years, going from 120,000 in 1998 to 371,000 in 2004. In 2000, the top ten pharmaceutical companies were spending just under US$1.9 billion on 314,000 such events. Third, IMS does not include the amount spent on phase IV "seeding" trials, trials designed to promote the prescription of new drugs rather than to generate scientific data. In 2004, 13.2% (US$4.9 billion) of R&D expenditures by American pharmaceutical firms was spent on phase IV trials. Almost 75% of these trials are managed solely by the commercial, as opposed to the clinical, division of biopharmaceutical companies, strongly suggesting that the vast majority of these trials are done just for their promotional value.

Finally, IMS data seem inconsistent with estimates based on the information in the annual reports of pharmaceutical companies. For example, in an accounting study based on the annual reports of ten of the largest global pharmaceutical firms, Lauzon and Hasbani showed that between 1996 and 2005, these firms globally spent a total of US$739 billion on "marketing and administration." In comparison, these same firms spent US$699 billion in manufacturing costs, US$288 billion in R&D, and had a net investment in property and equipment of US$43 billion, while receiving US$558 billion in profits.

Annual reports, however, have their own limitations. First, pharmaceutical firms are multinational and diversified; their annual reports provide no information on how much they spend on pharmaceutical marketing, as compared to the marketing of their non-pharmaceutical products, and they do not provide information about how much is spent on marketing specifically in the US. Second, annual reports merge the categories of "marketing" and "administration," without delineating the relative importance of each. Finally, "marketing" is a category that includes more than just promotion; it also includes the costs of packaging and distribution. In terms of offering a more precise estimate of overall expenditures on pharmaceutical promotion in the US, annual reports are thus far from satisfactory.

In the absence of any collection of information on promotional spending by government or any other noncommercial source, the market research company IMS has long been the only source of such information, which it gains by surveying pharmaceutical firms. Since 2003, however, the market research company CAM has been providing comprehensive information on promotion expenditures by surveying doctors instead of firms. (In July 2005, CAM was merged into the Cegedim Group, another market research company.) We chose to compare IMS data to those produced by CAM in order to provide a more accurate estimate of promotional spending in the US. Other proprietary sources of data do not break down promotional expenditures into different categories and therefore were not used in our comparison.

Methods

According to its Web site (http://www.imshealth.com/), IMS provides business intelligence and strategic consulting services for the pharmaceutical and health care industries. It is a global company established in more than 100 countries. IMS gathers data from 29,000 data suppliers at 225,000 supplier sites worldwide. It monitors 75% of prescription drug sales in over 100 countries, and 90% of US prescription drug sales. It tracks more than 1 million products from more than 3,000 active drug manufacturers. IMS data for 2004 were obtained from its Web site for the amount spent on: visits by sales representatives (detailing), samples, direct-to-consumer advertising, and journal advertising.

The Cegedim Web site (http://www. cegedim-crm.com/index.php?id=12) describes CAM as a global company dedicated to auditing promotional activities of the pharmaceutical industry, established in 36 countries worldwide. CAM annually surveys a representative sample of 2,000 primary care physicians and 4,800 specialists in a variety of specialties in selected locations in the US. From CAM's newsletter, we obtained access to data from CAM for the same promotion categories as from IMS. In addition, CAM provided figures for the amount of spending on company-sponsored meetings, e-promotion, mailings, and clinical trials.

We used 2004 as the comparison year because it was the latest year for which information was available from both organizations. We focused on the US because it is the only country for which information is available for all important promotional categories. The US is also, by far, the largest market for pharmaceuticals in the world, representing around 43% of global sales and global promotion expenditures.

We asked both CAM and IMS about the procedures that they used to collect information on different aspects of promotion. Based on the answers we received, we determined the relevant figures for expenditures for samples and detailing. Each author independently decided on which values should be used, based on an understanding of the methods that the companies used to collect the information and the limitations of those methods. Differences were resolved by consensus.

We queried CAM and IMS about the estimated value of unmonitored promotional expenditures. IMS did not provide an answer to this question. In order to validate its estimates, CAM relies on a validation committee that includes representatives from various pharmaceutical firms, including Merck, Pfizer, Bristol-Myers Squibb, Eli Lilly, Aventis, Sanofi-Synthelabo, AstraZeneca, and Wyeth. Under a confidentiality agreement, the firms supply CAM with internal data related to their detailing activity and promotional costs in the US. Through the validation committee, CAM can thus compare totals obtained through its own audits with the firms' internal data about their promotional budgets in order to evaluate if all promotion has been properly audited through its physician surveys. As a result of this comparison, CAM's validation committee considers that about 30% of promotional spending is not accounted for in its figures. CAM is unable to provide an exact breakdown of unmonitored promotion, but it believes that around 10% is due to incomplete disclosure and omissions by surveyed physicians and the remaining 20% comes from a combination of promotion directed at categories of physicians that are not surveyed, unmonitored journals in which pharmaceutical promotion appears, and possibly unethical forms of promotion. We adjusted total expenditures to account for this unreported 30%.

Results

For 2004, CAM reported total promotional spending in the US of US$33.5 billion, while IMS gave the figure of US$27.7 billion for the same year. Both CAM and IMS cited the media intelligence company CMR as the source for the amount spent on direct-to-consumer advertising (US$4 billion), and they also gave the same figure for journal advertising (US$0.5 billion).

There were two major differences between the two sets of figures: the amounts spent on detailing and the amounts spent on samples. IMS estimated the amount spent on detailing at US$7.3 billion versus US$20.4 billion for CAM, and while IMS gave a retail value of US$15.9 billion for samples, CAM estimated a wholesale value of US$6.3 billion.

Using the IMS figure of US$15.9 billion for the retail value of samples, and adding the CAM figures for detailing and other marketing expenses after correcting for the 30% estimate of unaccounted promotion, we arrived at US$57.5 billion for the total amount spent in the US in 2004, more than twice what IMS reported (see Table 1).

Discussion

Our revised estimate for promotional spending in the US is more than twice that from IMS. This number compares to US$31.5 billion for domestic industrial pharmaceutical R&D (including public funds for industrial R&D) in 2004 as reported by the National Science Foundation.

However, even our revised figure is likely to be incomplete. There are other avenues for promotion that would not be captured by either IMS or CAM, such as ghostwriting and illegal off-label promotion. Furthermore, items

Table 1

Pharmaceutical Marketing Expenditures in the United States in 2004: Data from IMS, CAM, and Our New Estimate

Type of Promotion	IMS (US$ Billions)	CAM (US$ Billions)	New Estimate (US$ Billions)	Percent of Total of New Estimate
Samples	15.9	6.3	15.9 (IMS)	27.7
Detailing	7.3	20.4	20.4 (CAM)	35.5
DTCA (data provided by CMR)	4	4	4 (CMR)	7
Meetings	nd	2	2 (CAM)	3.5
E-promotion, mailing, clinical trials	nd	0.3	0.3 (CAM)	0.5
Journal advertising	0.5	0.5	0.5 (CAM/IMS)	0.9
Unmonitored promotion (estimate[a])	nd	14.4	14.4 (CAM)	25
Total	**27.7**	**47.9**	**57.5**	**100**

[a]Includes incomplete disclosure and omissions by surveyed physicians, promotion to unaudited physician categories, promotion in unmonitored journals, and could possibly include unethical forms of promotion funded out of the firms' marketing budget. See text for details about this category.
DTCA, direct-to-consumer advertising; nd, no data
doi:10.1371/journal.pmed.0050001.t001

with promotional potential such as "seeding trials" or educational grants might be included in other budgets and would not be seen in the confidential material provided to CAM's validation committee.

IMS and CAM data were used for comparison purposes for a number of reasons: data from both were publicly available, both operate on a global scale and are well regarded by the pharmaceutical industry, both break down their information by different categories of promotion, and, most importantly, they use different methods for gathering their data, thereby allowing us to triangulate on a more accurate figure for each category.

Methodological differences between the ways that IMS and CAM collect data will affect the values for promotional spending depending on the category being considered. Because of the problematic nature of some data from each firm, we believe that the most precise picture of industry spending can be obtained by selectively using both sets of figures.

CAM compiles its data on the value of detailing and samples through systematic surveys of primary care providers and specialists and by estimating an average cost for each visit by a sales representative according to the type of physician. By contrast, IMS compiles its data on the value of detailing through surveys of firms, while its data on samples are obtained by monitoring products directly from manufacturers.

There is a significant discrepancy between the two sets of data in the cost of detailing: US$7.3 billion for IMS and US$20.4 billion for CAM. This difference can be explained by the fact that CAM offers a more complete data set since it includes in the average cost of a call (a sales representative's visit to a physician) not only the "cost to field the rep" (salary and benefits of the representative and the transportation cost) but also the costs for the area and regional managers, the cost of the training, and the cost of detail aids such as brochures and advertising material. By contrast, in reporting the cost of detailing IMS only considers the "cost to field the rep." Furthermore, relying on physician-generated data to estimate the amount spent on detailing is likely to give a more accurate figure than using figures generated by surveying firms. Companies may not report some types of detailing, for example, the use of sales representatives for illegal off-label promotion, whereas doctors are not likely to distinguish between on- and off-label promotion and would report all encounters with sales representatives.

In the case of samples, there is also a large difference between the IMS (US$15.9 billion) and CAM (US$6.3 billion) estimates. CAM estimates the amount spent on samples by multiplying the number of samples declared by physicians with their wholesale value. The latter is determined by using the average wholesale price (AWP), which is the amount set by manufacturers and used by Medicare in the US to determine reimbursement. CAM then divides that amount in half to account for the fact that samples are frequently given out in small dosage forms. CAM admits, however, that the amount for samples is understated because, when physicians fill out their survey, any quantity of samples of the same product left during a call is considered to be only one sample unit. CAM's calculations also rely on the AWP, which has been criticized for not taking into account the various discounts and rebates that are negotiated between manufacturers and purchasers.

IMS provides exact figures for the retail value for samples by monitoring 90% of all pharmaceutical transactions and by tracking products directly from manufacturers. This method for calculating the value of samples is much more direct than CAM's and therefore is likely to be subject to less error.

Using the wholesale value for samples, the CAM figure would be appropriate if we were arguing that the money spent on samples should go to another activity such as R&D. However, we have used the retail value of samples because this is consistent with companies' reporting of drugs they donate. As these are both categories of products that are being distributed without a charge to the user, it is inconsistent for donations to be reported in terms of retail value and samples in terms of wholesale value.

We believe that it is appropriate to correct for unmonitored promotion and that the figure we used is a reliable estimate. The 30% correction factor is based on a direct comparison that CAM is able to make between the data it collects through its surveys and the amount reported by companies.

There are other ways of combining the data that we have presented, but with the exception of choosing the lower amounts for detailing and samples and ignoring the 30% for unmonitored promotion, all of them yield a higher figure than the one from IMS. Some examples of alternative estimates follow: using the CAM estimate for the wholesale value of samples and the 30% adjustment, the total amount would be US$47.9 billion; without the

30% adjustment CAM's estimate is US$33.5 billion. Adding the figures for the categories that IMS does not cover (meetings, e-promotion, mailing, clinical trials) boosts its estimate to US$31 billion; using the lower figures for detailing and samples plus the CAM amounts for the other categories and applying the 30% adjustment gives an amount of US$29.1 billion. Therefore, the actual amount could range from a low of US$27.7 billion to a high of US$57.5 billion. Our analysis shows, however, that the figure of US$57.5 billion is the most appropriate one when using the most relevant figures for each category of promotional spending.

Excluding direct-to-consumer advertising, CAM considers that around 80% of the remaining promotion is directed towards physicians, with 20% of this figure going to pharmacists. (IMS does not provide any comparable values.) With about 700,000 practicing physicians in the US in 2004, we estimate that with a total expenditure of US$57.5 billion, the industry spent around US$61,000 in promotion per physician. As a percentage of US domestic sales of US$235.4 billion, promotion consumes 24.4% of the sales dollar versus 13.4% for R&D.

Our new estimate of total promotion costs and promotion as a percentage of sales is broadly in line with estimates of promotional or marketing spending from other sources. The annual reports of Novartis distinguish "marketing" from "administration." Marcia Angell extrapolates from this annual report to the entire industry and calculates a figure of US$54 billion spent on pharmaceutical promotion in the US in 2001. As a proportion of sales, she estimates 33% is spent on marketing. Using similar methodology, the Office of Technology Assessment derived an estimate for marketing costs in the US by extrapolating from the cost structure of Eli Lilly. The Office of Technology Assessment considers that firms spend around 22.5% of their sales on marketing. Based on United Nations Industrial Development Organization estimates, a report from the Organization for Economic Cooperation and Development estimated that, in 1989, pharmaceutical firms globally spent 24% of their sales on marketing, but few details of the methodology used were provided, making it impossible to verify the accuracy of the estimate. Finally, in 2006 Consumers International surveyed 20 European pharmaceutical firms to obtain more information about their exact expenditures on drug promotion. Among the 20 firms contacted, only five agreed to provide separate figures for marketing, which ranged from 31% to 50% of sales depending on the firm.

The results are also consistent with data on the share of revenue allocated to "marketing and administration" according to annual reports of large pharmaceutical companies, if we consider that the largest part of "marketing and administration" is devoted to promotion. Lauzon and Hasbani found that 33.1% of revenues was allocated to "marketing and administration," similar to the 31% reported by the Centers for Medicare and Medicaid Services and the 27% from Families USA.

The value of our estimate over these others is that it is not based on extrapolating from annual reports of firms that are both diversified and multinational. Our estimate is driven by quantifiable data from highly reliable sources and concerns only the promotion of pharmaceutical products in the

US. The derivation of our figure is thus transparent and can form the basis for a vigorous debate.

Conclusion

From this new estimate, it appears that pharmaceutical companies spend almost twice as much on promotion as they do on R&D. These numbers clearly show how promotion predominates over R&D in the pharmaceutical industry, contrary to the industry's claim. While the amount spent on promotion is not in itself a confirmation of Kefauver's depiction of the pharmaceutical industry, it confirms the public image of a marketing-driven industry and provides an important argument to petition in favor of transforming the workings of the industry in the direction of more research and less promotion.

POSTSCRIPT

Should Prescription Drugs Be Advertised Directly to Consumers?

Although new prescription drugs may save lives, it can also be argued that the pharmaceutical industry, via advertising to consumers and physicians, has increased the demand for its products and the costs of drugs. Television advertisements for heartburn medicine imply that overeating is not a problem if one takes the right pill. Shifting to a healthier lifestyle may help many Americans avoid and reduce their need for costly prescription medications. Also, advertising may divert money away from research, and may influence physicians' prescribing practices. In "Who Are the Opinion Leaders? The Physicians, Pharmacists, Patients, and Direct-to-Consumer Prescription Drug Advertising, *Journal of Health Communication* (September 2010), Lee discusses the popular perception that physicians prescribe requested drugs to patients influenced by prescription drug advertising seen on television or in magazines. In "Consumer Responses to Coupons in Direct-to-Consumer Advertising of Prescription Drugs," *Health Marketing Quarterly* (December 2009), the authors determined that coupons for prescription drugs in newspapers, in magazines, or online had an impact on drugs requested by patients when visiting their physicians. For an overview of the advertising issue, see "A Decade of Controversy: Balancing Policy with Evidence in the Regulation of Prescription Drug Advertising," *American Journal of Public Health* (January 2010).

There appears to be a drug war in America. Rapidly escalating prescription costs from advertising and other issues are affecting the most vulnerable among us—the elderly. The lack of a pharmacy benefit in Medicare coverage plus the rising costs of medications causes too many seniors to make tough choices: their prescription drugs or other necessities such as food. Some states including Maine, Florida, and Michigan have taken on the drug companies to lower the cost of prescription medications. The industry has vowed to fight the states on every front. More states are ready to address the problem of rising drug prices under the Medicaid program and a battle may be looming. See "A New Prescription," *Economist* (February 24, 2007); "GOP's Medicare Drug Bill Caters to Special Interests," *USA Today* (February 17, 2005); and "War on Drug Prices: States Are Taking Up the Fight to Reduce Prescription Drug Costs," *State Legislatures* (March 2002).

Some American consumers are also fighting back. They are traveling to Mexico and Canada in search of lower prices. Others are asking for generic versions of their medications and also requesting double dosage pills and splitting them. Often, the larger dose pills have a lower unit cost. Still others are shopping online, by mail, or through prescription drug groups. Although all these techniques may save money, critics of the pharmaceutical industry assert the real problem is that the drug companies' rising profits, monopolies on patented drugs, high advertising costs, and political contributions all play a role in high prescription costs. For further reading on the subject, see "Exporting Drug Prices," *Reason* (May 2007); "United States Prescription Drug Crisis," *Journal of Legal Medicine* (December 2006) "Cross-Border Headache," *Economist* (January 15, 2005); "Uninsured Should Be Able to Buy Prescription Drugs from Canada," *The Orlando Sentinel* (January 5, 2005); and "Undue Influence: Regulation of the Pharmaceutical Industry," *The American Prospect* (August 13, 2001).

Internet References . . .

American Cancer Society

This site offers tips on staying healthy and preventing cancer, a resource for support and treatment, and research into cancer prevention and treatment.

http://www.cancer.org

National Organization for the Reform of Marijuana Laws (norml)

You can find information about marijuana, FAQs, legalization, media, and legal issues.

http://norml.org/

NIH Guide: NIH Policy on Reporting Race and Ethnicity Data

This site offers information on the National Institutes of Health's policy on the use of subjects in medical research.

http://grants.nih.gov/grants/guide/notice-files/NOT-OD-01-053.html

National Bioethics Advisory Commission: Publications

Data on bioethical issues including stem cell research.

http://www.bioethics.gov/

Health and Society

*P*ublic policy and medical ethics have not always kept pace with rapidly growing technology and scientific advances. This unit discusses some of the issues relating to the role of health concerns and society and includes selections that address cancer research and treatment. Are we truly making progress against this disease? As more and more states are legalizing marijuana for medicinal purposes, what are the ramifications? The final two issues in this unit include the role of race in prescribing medications by physicians and whether or not embryonic stem research should be permitted.

- Are We Winning the War on Cancer?
- Should Marijuana Be Legalized for Medicinal Purposes?
- Should Doctors Prescribe Drugs Based on Race?
- Should Embryonic Stem Cell Research Be Permitted?

ISSUE 4

Are We Winning the War on Cancer?

YES: **John R. Seffrin,** from "Winning the War on Cancer: Public Health or Public Policy Challenge?" *Vital Speeches of the Day* (September 2006)

NO: **Reynold Spector,** from "The War on Cancer: A Progress Report for Skeptics," *Skeptical Inquirer* (January/February 2010)

ISSUE SUMMARY

YES: American Cancer Society president John R. Seffrin claims we are winning the war against cancer and that it is possible to eliminate the disease as a major public health problem.

NO: Physician and professor of medicine Reynold Spector argues that the gains made against cancer have been limited and that overall there has been very little progress in the war on cancer.

Cancer is a group of diseases characterized by uncontrolled cellular growth, invasion that intrudes on and destroys nearby tissues, and may metastasize or spread to other locations in the body via blood or lymph. The malignant characteristics of cancers differentiate them from benign growths or tumors, which do not invade or metastasize. Fortunately, most cancers can be treated with drugs or chemotherapy, surgery, and/or radiation. The outcome of the disease is based on the type of cancer, for example, lung or breast, and the extent of disease. Although cancer affects people of all ages, and a few types of cancer are actually more common in children, most cancer risks increase with age. Cancer rates are increasing as more people live longer and lifestyles change such as increased smoking occur in the developing world.

Most cancers have an environmental link, with 90–95 percent of cases attributed to environmental factors and 5–10 percent due to heredity. Typical environmental factors that contribute to cancer deaths include diet and obesity (30–35 percent), smoking and tobacco use (25–30 percent), infectious agents (15–20 percent), and ionizing and nonionizing radiation (up to 10 percent). The remaining may be caused by stress, lack of exercise, and some environmental pollutants. Cancer prevention is related to those active measures that decrease the incidence of the disease. Since the vast majority of cancer risk factors are environmental or lifestyle-related, cancer is largely a preventable disease. Individuals who avoid tobacco, maintain a healthy weight, eat a diet rich in fruits and vegetables, exercise, use alcohol in moderation, take measures to prevent the transmission of sexually transmitted diseases, and avoid exposure to air pollution are likely to significantly reduce their risks of the disease.

Cancer's reputation is a deadly one. In reality, about half of the patients receiving treatment for invasive cancer will not survive the disease or the treatment. The survival rate, however, can vary significantly by the type of cancer, ranging from basically all patients surviving to almost no patients surviving. Predicting either short-term or long-term survival is challenging and depends on a variety of factors. The most important factors are the type of cancer and the patient's age and overall health. Medically frail patients suffering simultaneously from other illnesses have lower survival rates than otherwise healthy patients. Despite strong social pressure to maintain an upbeat, optimistic attitude or act like a determined "fighter" to "win the battle," research has not shown that personality traits have a connection to survival.

In 1971, the then president Richard Nixon signed the National Cancer Act of 1971. The goal of the act was to find a cure for cancer by increased research to improve the understanding of cancer biology and the development of more effective treatments such as targeted drug therapies. The act is also viewed as the beginning of the war on cancer and the vow to end the disease for good. Despite significant progress in the treatment of certain forms of cancer, the disease in general remains a major cause of death 40 years after this effort began, leading to a perceived lack of progress and to new legislation aimed at augmenting the original National Cancer Act of 1971. New research directions, in part based on the results of the Human Genome Project, hold promise for a better understanding of the hereditary factors underlying cancer and the development of new diagnostics, treatments, preventive measures, and early detection ability.

In the following selections, American Cancer Society President John R. Seffrin claims we are winning the war against cancer and that it is possible to eliminate the disease as a major public health problem. Physician and professor of medicine Reynold Spector argues that the gains made against cancer have been limited and that overall there has been very little progress in the war on cancer.

YES ⬅

John R. Seffrin

Winning the War on Cancer: Public Health or Public Policy Challenge?

Ladies and gentlemen—we are winning!

For the first time—we can today state that we are winning the war on cancer.

What is even more—we now know essentially what it will take to finish the job—that is eliminating cancer as a major public health problem—first here in the US and then worldwide. Indeed, the progress made in our understanding of the cancer problem is so great—so substantial—that we find ourselves in a very different place—and in a very different situation—than when the American Cancer Society was founded in 1913 or even when the National Cancer Act was passed in 1971.

Today, we know more about cancer than ever before. We understand many of its causes. We know how to prevent it, and, we increasingly know how to cure it, especially in its early stages. Despite this significant growth in the knowledge base, we have not succeeded in stemming the growing burden of cancer. The gap between what is and what could be in cancer control and cancer care is the single most important issue facing the cancer community in the world today.

So it is in this context that I would like to share with you these four facts of life or new realities which form the core of my message today.

1. For the first time, we know what it will take to win the war on cancer, based on evidence.
2. We can eliminate cancer as a major health problem in the US in this century, if we do the right things.
3. However, if we fail to intervene—if we fail to do the right things, cancer will become the leading cause of death in the US by 2018 and eventually, likely, the leading cause of death in the world.
4. So the conquest of the world's most feared disease is a question of choice, priority, resources, and resolve, not luck or a magic bullet or a single miracle cure.

While the hopeful side of cancer has never been more hopeful—and the prospects for saving and improving lives are truly extraordinary—we do have our work cut out for us.

From *Vital Speeches of the Day*, September 2006.

Science alone, public health alone, or public policy alone cannot get us to where we need to be to realize this very possible dream. It will take all three and a lot of commitment and collaboration to make it happen. And as I speak, the cancer burden is actually getting worse—not better—and cancer will kill more people in the world this year than HIV/AIDS, tuberculosis, and malaria combined.

Perhaps ironically, in the last 60 years, science has made remarkable progress toward unraveling the mystery of cancer. But so much of what we know about cancer is not being adequately translated into what we do about cancer.

As a result, if current trends persist, by 2020, the number of new cancer cases worldwide will grow to 15 million and the number of deaths will double to as many as 12 million. An estimated 70 percent of these deaths will occur in developing countries, which are least prepared to address their growing cancer burdens.

With recent advances in our understanding of cancer, these are people whose lives need not be lost. They continue to experience unnecessary suffering and death not because we don't know how to prevent it or detect it early or treat it, but because we refuse to ensure that all people in all nations—including our own—have equal access to lifesaving cancer advances.

That's why this July the American Cancer Society is doing something that hasn't been done before—bringing together two world conferences that have rarely been held in the same year, and never in the same country—the World Cancer Congress and the 13th World Conference on Tobacco OR Health.

These two conferences will bring together over 5,500 participants from more than 130 countries: oncologists, public health leaders, tobacco control advocates, cancer association leaders, health ministries, and journalists. These meetings will reach across the entire breadth of cancer control and cancer care to focus energy and attention not just on talking about the cancer problem, but on identifying and sharing practical solutions that can make a lifesaving difference in communities around the world now.

Why is it so critical to unite the global cancer and tobacco control communities? Because, if your aim is to solve the cancer problem, the two are inseparable. The world is on a collision course if we fail to take action against the scourge of tobacco. Indeed, it's a train wreck not waiting to happen! Indeed, it's already happening and its repercussions will have a public health and economic impact unlike any we have ever experienced before.

As the only consumer product proven to kill more than half of its regular users, tobacco will be responsible for 4.9 million deaths worldwide this year alone. Today, that burden is almost evenly shared by industrialized and developing nations, but the trend is rapidly changing to the developing countries of the world.

If we fail to act to prevent this tragedy in the making, the consequences will most certainly be dire and destabilizing. As a direct result of tobacco use, at current rates, 650 million people alive today will eventually die, half of whom are now children. Half of these people will die in middle age—when they are most productive for their economies, their communities, and their families.

In the last century, tobacco use killed 100 million people. If left unchecked, tobacco use will kill more than one billion people in this century, and if we let it happen, it will be the worst case of avoidable loss of life in world history. Yet, we know with comprehensive, concerted action, we can eliminate the global scourge of tobacco and save hundreds of millions of lives within the next few decades, if we do the right things.

Let's take the United States as an example. We have enjoyed many resounding victories against Big Tobacco that are making a real difference toward the ultimate bottom line—lives saved. More than 2,200 communities nationwide have enacted smoke-free laws that are protecting the health of millions of Americans. In fact, tomorrow the Surgeon General will release the first report in 20 years focusing on secondhand smoke, and we expect it to confirm the public health and economic benefits of clean indoor air laws.

However, as smoking rates decline in the US and many other industrialized nations, the tobacco industry has dramatically stepped up its efforts in emerging markets. Because tobacco kills the majority of its customer base, the industry must persuade millions of people to become new smokers each year just to break even. In the largely unrestricted markets of the developing world, that means that no one is immune to the industry's tactics, especially the most vulnerable people of all—children.

Fortunately, thanks to the rigorous educational, scientific, and advocacy efforts of dedicated tobacco control activists worldwide, many nations are taking a stand against tobacco by supporting the world's first global public health treaty—the World Health Organization Framework Convention on Tobacco Control (FCTC). This treaty's evidence-based interventions have been proven to work in diverse cultures around the world.

The treaty hits the tobacco companies where they live by restricting their insidious and immoral marketing tactics. It gives nations—particularly the low-income nations the tobacco companies have targeted as their most promising markets—powerful new tools to protect their citizens from the tobacco industry's deception.

The US is to be commended for supporting adoption of the treaty, but our nation's role in this arena has been halted because we have so far refused to ratify it. As of June 20, 2006, 131 countries already have ratified the treaty, making it the most rapidly embraced treaty in UN history. Why are we lagging behind? The United States ratification and effective implementation of the treaty is essential to turning the tide of the global tobacco pandemic. To that end, I have urged President Bush to send the treaty to the Senate for ratification. And since many of the ratifying countries will be represented at the upcoming conferences, we will use that opportunity to bring pressure to bear on the administration and the US Senate to promptly join the rest of the world in ratifying the treaty. When ratified and implemented, we know from experience and evidence that human suffering will be reduced and lives will be saved.

In addition to taking immediate action against tobacco, there are three actions I believe it will take to eliminate cancer as a major public health problem at the earliest possible time.

First, we must accelerate discovery by redoubling and balancing our cancer research portfolio. Thanks to decades of well-funded, peer-reviewed research, cancer research has gone from a good bet to a sure bet. Remarkable achievements such as the mapping of the human genome make new cancer cures virtually inevitable, if we do the right things—and that is fully fund NIH and its National Cancer Institute. Further progress is guaranteed if research funding keeps pace. Landmark discoveries such as cancer vaccines and better and more targeted therapies are inevitable (assumed), but only if we fuel the engines of discovery. And we know that's what the American tax-payer and voter wants us to do!

And we must, at the same time, balance our research portfolio to include applied behavioral research, psychosocial and translational research, and evidence-based prevention interventions. If we redouble and balance cancer research efforts, the number of lives we could improve and save is unlimited over time. Unfortunately, funding for the NIH—the worldwide leader among cancer research institutions—is in jeopardy. If we fail to continue stoking the engines of research, we will effectively renege on our nation's commitment to the American people. And that's wrong!

Second, we must promote and elevate prevention into public policy and standard practice nationwide. One example of the enormous potential of prevention is cervical cancer. In nations like ours, where screening tests are available and early detection is standard practice, screening and follow-up treatment has reduced cervical cancer deaths by as much as 80 percent. And yet, despite these advances in prevention, in many parts of the world, cervical cancer is still a leading cause of cancer death in women.

As you know, recent FDA approval of the HPV vaccine, the first vaccine targeted specifically to preventing cancer, is one of the most important advances in women's health in recent decades. Successful global implementation of an effective HPV vaccine offers a truly unprecedented opportunity to prevent millions of deaths and dramatically reduce the world's cancer burden. The challenge is to make such advances available to every woman who needs them.

This is typical of the challenge facing cancer control advocates worldwide. Science has given us the tools to save lives, but our medical care and political systems are not equipped to deliver on those advances, which brings me to the third action.

Thirdly, we must drive delivery of state-of-the-art cancer care and control at the community level. In places where public health organizations, governments, and the private sector have worked together to drive delivery at the community level, there have been impressive results. With state-of-the-art cancer care, as many as 75 percent of cancer patients could survive long-term. Today, tragically, nowhere near this many will receive treatment that fully takes advantage of what science has taught us.

Access to the means for the attainment and preservation of health is a basic human need and right and should not be thought of as a privilege for just the few.

If we fail to do the right things, it will not only result in an otherwise avoidable public health catastrophe, but also an economic missed opportunity. For example, here in the US, a 20% reduction in cancer mortality will yield a

10 trillion dollar value to the American people, according to a study done by Kevin M. Murphy and Robert H. Topel entitled The Economic Value of Medical Research.

Because cancer tends to strike and kill in the prime of one's life, its human and economic impact is difficult to exaggerate. Truly, a nation's very competitiveness in the future will be tied to how healthy its citizens are.

So the underlying key to achieving each of these goals is advocacy. Cancer is as much a political and public policy issue as it is a medical and public health issue. Remarkable advances in prevention, early detection, and treatment virtually guarantee lower incidence and mortality rates—if they are available to everyone who needs them.

That means our most pressing challenge is to make cancer a policy priority—to educate lawmakers, governments, and civic leaders about the urgency of cancer control and inspire their commitment to enact public policies that will make cancer advances available to all people everywhere.

Obviously, this is an enormously complicated task, but we need only look to advocacy successes here in the United States to see the remarkable, lifesaving potential of public policy solutions to the world's public health problems.

Let me cite one contemporary example. Recently, the American Cancer Society Cancer Action Network (ACS CAN)—the Society's sister 501(c)4 advocacy organization—took action against the small business health care legislation known as "Health Insurance Marketplace Modernization and Affordability Act," or S. 1955, which would have effectively gutted state laws that require health insurers to cover lifesaving cancer screenings and treatments.

Working with our partners—AARP and the American Diabetes Association—ACS CAN launched a multi-media advertising campaign that received an immediate, strong response from grassroots volunteers. More than 170,000 emails poured into US Senate offices and nearly 10,000 calls came in from constituents requesting to be connected to the target Senate offices. I'm proud to report that our collaborative efforts were successful. On May 12, the bill was stopped in the US Senate.

But, although we've made extraordinary progress, we still have a long way to go.

That's why ACS CAN is planning to bring 10,000 energetic advocates representing every congressional district in the country to Capitol Hill this September 19 and 20 for Celebration on the Hill to meet with their elected officials and participate in activities on the National Mall with an important message: "We care about cancer, and we will be heard. We will do our part, but you must do yours. And we will not take 'no' for an answer." Cancer survivors don't take life and health for granted—and they vote with their feet and voices as well as their ballots.

Our ability to make a difference in the lives of people touched by cancer increases exponentially when we help pass laws and establish public policies that secure investments in research and prevention, and access to quality health care.

Ultimately, the challenge for all of us will be to do what we can to redouble our efforts in pursuit of our common cancer-fighting agenda. This means we must have the courage to share, the courage to take responsible, bold risks, and the courage to persevere. In other words, we must have the courage to transform what is into what could be.

In conclusion, I leave you with the following truth: When the American Cancer Society was founded in 1913, a diagnosis of cancer was a virtual death sentence only to be preceded by an often protracted period of pain and suffering. Due to an indefatigable commitment to research and intervention at the community level, cancer has been transformed and is today potentially the most preventable and most curable of the major life-threatening diseases facing humankind.

We now have the knowledge and know-how to turn that potentiality into reality, if we do the right things. And may God speed that day.

Thank you.

Reynold Spector

➡ **NO**

The War on Cancer: A Progress Report for Skeptics

In 1971, President Nixon and Congress declared war on cancer. Since then, the federal government has spent well over $105 billion on the effort. What have we gained from that huge investment? David Nathan, a well-known professor and administrator, maintains in his book *The Cancer Treatment Revolution* (Wiley, 2007) that we have made substantial progress. However, he greatly overestimates the potential of the newer so-called "smart drugs." Researchers Psyrri and De Vita (2008) also claim important progress. However, they cherry-pick the cancers with which there has been some progress and do not discuss the failures. Moreover, they only discuss the last decade rather than a more balanced view of 1950 or 1975 to the present.

On the other hand, Gina Kolata pointed out in *The New York Times* that the cancer death rate, adjusted for the size and age of the population, has decreased by only 5 percent since 1950. She argues that there has been very little overall progress in the war on cancer.

In this article, I will focus on adult cancer, since child cancer makes up less than 1 percent of all cancer diagnosed. I will then place the facts in proper perspective after an overview of the epidemiology, diagnosis, and treatment (especially with smart drugs) of adult cancer in the United States.

The Cancer Facts

Summary statistics show that the war on cancer has not gone well. This is in marked contrast to death rates from stroke and cardiovascular disease (adjusted for the age and size of the population), which have fallen by 74 percent and 64 percent, respectively, from 1950 through 2006; and by 60 percent and 52 percent, respectively, from 1975 through 2006. These excellent results against stroke and heart disease are mainly due to improvements in drug therapy, especially the control of high blood pressure to prevent stroke and the use of statins, aspirin, beta blockers, calcium channel blockers, and ACE inhibitors (now all generic) to prevent and treat heart disease. Cancer therapy is clearly decades behind. However, these data conceal a great deal of useful information and do not provide guidance on how to make progress against cancer.

Figure 1

U.S. Mortality, 2006

Rank	Cause of Death	No. of Deaths	% of All Deaths
1.	Heart Diseases	631,636	26.0
2.	Cancer	559,888	23.1
3.	Cerebrovascular Diseases	137,119	5.7
4.	Chronic Lower Respiratory Diseases	124,583	5.1
5.	Accidents (unintentional injuries)	121,599	5.0
6.	Diabetes Mellitus	72,449	3.0
7.	Alzheimer Disease	72,432	3.0
8.	Influenza & Pneumonia	56,326	2.3
9.	Nephritis*	45,344	1.9
10.	Septicemia	34,234	1.4

*Includes nephrotic syndrome and nephrosis.
Sources: U.S. Mortality Data 2006, National Health and Statistics, Centers for Disease Control and Prevention, 2009

Methodological Issues

To understand the issues, we must describe a few statistical traps and define our terms (see table 1). For example, there are several types of detection bias. First, if one discovers a malignant tumor very early and starts therapy immediately, even if the therapy is worthless, it will appear that the patient lives longer than a second patient (with an identical tumor) treated with another worthless drug if the cancer in the second patient was detected later. Second, detection bias can also occur with small tumors, especially of the breast and prostate, that would not harm the patient if left untreated but can lead to

Table 1

Critical Terms Defined in the Text

1. Cancer—three kinds: local, regional, distant (metastatic)
2. Carcinoma (cancer) in situ—e.g., ductal carcinoma of the breast (DCIS)
3. Slow cancers—e.g., prostate, breast
4. Cancer treatments: surgery, chemotherapy, radiation therapy
5. Partial response
6. Complete response
7. Cure
8. Median survival, one/five-year survival

Figure 2

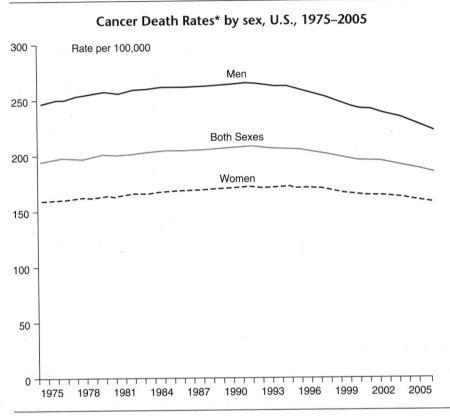

Cancer Death Rates* by sex, U.S., 1975–2005

*Age-adjusted to the U.S. 2000 standard population.

Sources: U.S. Mortality Data 2006, National Health and Statistics, Centers for Disease Control and Prevention, 2008

unnecessary and sometimes mutilating therapy. Another type is publication bias, whereby positive studies (especially those funded by the pharmaceutical industry) tend to be published while negative studies do not.

What is cancer? Cancer is a large group of diseases characterized by the uncontrolled growth and spread of abnormal cells locally, regionally, and/or distantly (metastatically). A carcinoma (cancer) in situ is a small cancer that has not invaded the local tissue. Some cancers grow very slowly, and the patient may survive for ten years or more with minimal treatment. Other cancers (e.g., lung and pancreas) grow quickly and, even today, kill more than half of the patients in less than one year (see table 2). The therapy for cancer is generally surgery, if possible, and/or chemotherapy and/or radiation therapy. Chemotherapy aims to kill the cancer cells, but most chemotherapeutic drugs are nonspecific and also kill sensitive normal cells, especially in the intestine and bone marrow. Radiation therapy is also nonspecific. In chemotherapy

Table 2

Common Cancers Current Death and Survival Statistics (American Cancer Society 2009)

Cancer Origin	Percent of Cancer Deaths	One-Year Survival (%)	Five-Year Survival (%)
Lung	28	41	15
Colon/Rectum	9	83	64
Breast	8	>95	89
Pancreas	6	24	5
Prostate	5	*	*
Leukemia	4	**	51
Lymphoma	4	82	68
Liver	3	†	<10
Other	33	‡	‡

*Survival statistics for prostate cancer are very misleading since they include many treated cancers that would not have harmed (or killed) the patient (see test).

**Leukemia is a heterogenous group of diseases. The five-year survival figure is an average of all types.

†Liver cancer is a rapidly fatal disease in which treatment is ineffective.

‡Other cancers are so heterogenous that the reader should consult the American Cancer Society (2009) for specific data.

and radiation therapy, a partial response is defined as shrinkage of the tumor in each dimension by 50 percent; a complete response means no detectable tumor, but this does not necessarily mean a "cure." Many complete responses are only transitory. Median survival is the length of time in which one-half of the patients in a cohort die.

What Do We Know About Cancer?

The "causes" of cancer are shown in table 3, though there is still much we don't know. For example, we do not know exactly how smoking causes cancer; in most cases, we do not know how "acquired" mutations cause cancer. In some cancers, there are more than five hundred identifiable genetic abnormalities—no one knows which one(s), if any, is "causative." The importance of epigenetic changes is currently speculative. It is quite possible that there is a completely unknown causal mechanism in many cancers.

The diagnosis of cancer today is relatively straightforward with imaging techniques (x-ray, CAT, MRI, PET) and biopsies that are subjected to routine histology, electron microscopy, and immunological techniques.

Table 3

Examples of Probable or Definite Causes of Cancer
(American Cancer Society 2009)

1. External Factors
   a. Tobacco
   b. Chemicals (e.g., asbestos, benzene, alcohol)
   c. Radiation
   d. Infections, organisms (e.g., hepatitis B, papilloma virus, *Helicobacter*)
   e. Hormone replacement therapy with estrogen
2. Inernal Factors
   a. Genetic mutations
      1) inherited
      2) acquired
   b. Hormones (e.g., estrogen)
   c. Immune disorders (e.g., AIDS)
   d. Epigenetic changes
   e. Obesity

Table 4

Criteria for Utility of Cancer Therapy
(Fojo and Grady 2009)

1. Meaningful prolongation of life or cure (mortality)
2. Improvement of quality of life (symptoms)
3. Value of treatment (compared to cost)

Cancer Therapy

To have a reasonable discussion of cancer therapy, we need to agree on the objectives of therapy, as shown in table 4. Everyone agrees that meaningful prolongation of life, preferably complete surgical removal of the tumor and cure, is a high priority. The treatment should also improve the quality of life. But, as is well known, many chemotherapeutic and radiation regimens cause mild to devastating—even fatal—side effects. Nathan (2007) compares conventional chemotherapy to "carpet-bombing," an extreme but realistic metaphor. Finally, the results of a cost-benefit analysis must be reasonable. (In some cases, justifiably and importantly, chemotherapy and/or radiation and/or other drugs are used as palliative measures exclusively to counter symptoms from the disease [e.g., pleural effusions in the chest cavity or bone pain] or from the treatments [e.g., vomiting, mucositis, low white blood counts, heart failure, nerve damage, diarrhea, and/or inflammation of the bladder]). In the final analysis, what counts are the criteria in table 4. Partial or even complete remissions, unless they prolong life and/or improve the overall quality of life at a reasonable cost, are scientifically interesting but of little use to the patient.

Currently there are a few metastatic cancers that can sometimes be cured with chemotherapy and/or radiation therapy, but unfortunately these cures make up a very small percentage of the whole cancer problem. These cancers include testicular cancer, choriocarcinoma, Hodgkin's and non-Hodgkin's lymphoma, leukemia, and rare cases of breast and ovarian cancer. A few cancers can be made into chronic diseases that require daily treatment, e.g., chronic myelogenous leukemia.

Returning to table 2, lung cancer, the most common cancer, is a devastating disease; if the surgeon cannot totally remove it, the diagnosis is grim. In fact, about 60 percent of lung cancer patients are dead within one year of diagnosis with the best available therapy, and only 15 percent survive five years.

There has been some progress in the death rate from colorectal cancer, especially in women. This is mainly due to earlier diagnosis and surgical therapy.

Cancer of the breast is often a slow cancer and has a five- to ten-year median survival rate with just surgical therapy. There has been a modest decline in death rates from breast cancer since 1975. It is worth noting that currently, if the breast cancer is metastatic, five-year survival is only 27 percent. However, breast cancer presents a serious dilemma. Early detection of invasive breast cancer by screening is good; however, about 62,000 cases of ductal carcinoma in situ (DCIS) are also discovered every year. In greater than 50 percent of these women, especially older women, these lesions will not progress and do not need treatment. However, it is difficult to predict who will not need therapy, so the American Cancer Society (2009) recommends all patients with DCIS undergo therapy—generally breast surgery. Thus, more than thirty thousand patents annually are unnecessarily treated. We need to figure out which DCIS are harmless in order to avoid unnecessary treatment. On balance, I feel that breast cancer screening has a small but positive net benefit.

Pancreatic cancer is devastating (see table 2), and little progress has been made against it since 1975. Pancreatic cancer is very challenging because the tumors are surrounded by dense fibrous connective tissue with few blood vessels. Because of this, it is difficult to deliver drugs to pancreatic tumors. Moreover, this explains in part why chemotherapy is so ineffective for pancreatic cancer (see table 2). Better animal models are needed.

Prostate cancer mortality has declined slightly since 1975 with an unexplained increase in the mid-1990s. But prostate cancer therapy also presents a serious quandary. At autopsy, approximately 30 percent (or more) of men have cancer foci in their prostate glands, yet only 1 to 2 percent of men die of prostate cancer. Thus less than 10 percent of prostate cancer patients require treatment. This presents a serious dilemma: whom should the physician treat? Moreover, recently, two large studies of prostate cancer screening with prostate specific antigen (PSA) have seriously questioned the utility of screening. In one study, the investigators had to screen over a thousand men before they saved one life. This led to about fifty "false positive" patients who often underwent surgery and/or radiation therapy unnecessarily. The second study, conducted in the United States, was negative, i.e., no lives were saved due to the screening, but many of the screening-positive patients with prostate cancer were treated. Welch and Albertson (2009) and Brawley (2009) estimate that more than a million men in the U.S. have been unnecessarily treated for prostate cancer between 1986 and 2005, due to over-diagnostic PSA screening tests. In the end, screening for prostate cancer will not be useful until methods are developed to determine which prostate cancers detected by screening will harm the patient. Many men—especially elderly ones—with a histological diagnosis of prostate cancer elect "watchful waiting" with no therapy, a rational strategy.

There are many other things we do not understand about cancer—even on a phenomenological level. For example, in the United States, the incidence and death rates from cancer of the stomach have fallen dramatically since 1930. The reason for this is unknown but may be due to changes in food preservation; it is not due to treatment.

Smart Drugs

David Nathan (2007) extols the virtues and potential of the new "smart drugs." Smart drugs are defined as drugs that focus on a particular vulnerability of the cancer; they are not generalized but rather specific toxins. But the *Journal of the American Medical Association* reports that 90 percent of the drugs or biologics approved by the FDA in the past four years for cancer (many of them smart drugs) cost more than $20,000 for twelve weeks of therapy, and many offer a survival benefit of only two months or less. Let us take bevacizumab (Avastin), the ninth largest selling drug in America ($4.8 billion in 2008), costing about $8,000 per month per patient. Bevacizumab, a putative smart drug, is an intravenous man-made antibody that blocks the action of vascular endothelial growth factor (VEFG). It sometimes works because tumors (and normal tissues) release VEFG to facilitate small blood vessel in-growth into the tumor. These small blood vessels "nourish" the tumor (or normal tissue). The idea is to "starve" the growing tumor with once or twice monthly intravenous injections of bevacizumab.

The FDA has approved bevacizumab for the cancers listed in table 5. Since the median survival of colorectal cancer is eighteen months, bevacizumab therapy would cost about $144,000 (in such a patient) for four months prolongation of survival. In the other cancers in table 4, there is no prolongation of survival. Moreover, bevacizumab can have terrible side effects, including gastrointestinal perforations, serious bleeding, severe hypertension, clot formation, and delayed wound healing. By the criteria in table 4, bevacizumab is at best a marginal drug. It only slightly prolongs life, demonstrable only in colorectal cancer, has serious side effects, and is very expensive.

Bevacizumab is frequently cited as an example of the so-called newer smart drugs. But by interfering with small blood vessel growth throughout the body, it is a nonspecific toxin—and hence has serious side effects. It is not so different from the older non-specific chemotherapy.

The use of bevacizumab and similar drugs raises another issue. According to Gina Kolata, 60 to 80 percent of oncologists' revenue comes from infusion

Table 5

Bevacizumab (Avastin)—Utility

Cancer	Evidence for Prolongation of Life; time*
Bowel/Rectum	Yes, four months (median survival) with other drugs
Lung	No +
Breast	No
Kidney	No
Glioblastoma (Brain)	No

*Compared to randomized control (if available).

+"No" means a lack of a statistically significant prolongation.

of anti-cancer drugs in their offices. Many believe that such economic incentives are the reason for the substantial overuse of expensive chemotherapeutic drugs. However, it is very difficult to document the extent of the overuse of cancer chemotherapy. Does it make sense to employ such expensive drugs that do not prolong life (see table 5) and have such serious side effects? Moreover, although VEGF and bevacizumab are interesting science, there has been gross exaggeration of bevacizumab's clinical utility in the press (see tables 4 and 5).

So why does the U.S. Food and Drug Administration (FDA) approve bevacizumab (and other drugs) that do not improve longevity and/or the quality of life (see table 5)? The answer is that bevacizumab coupled with other drugs can cause partial remissions, "stabilization" of the cancer, or "lack of progression" for several months. However, this often does not lead to prolongation of life in most of the cancers in table 5. Moreover, many patients pay a heavy price in terms of side effects and cost. It is also worth noting that several European national regulatory authorities do not accept the utility of some of these smart drugs and do not license them for sale in their countries. In agreement with the Europeans, scientists at the U.S. National Cancer Institute are urging the oncology community, regulators, and the public to set limits on the use and pricing of such marginal drugs. They view the current situation as unsustainable.

Why Has the War on Cancer Failed?

As documented above, unlike the successes against heart disease and stroke, the war on cancer, after almost forty years, must be deemed a failure with a few notable exceptions. Why? Is it because cancer is an incredibly tough problem, or are there other explanations? In table 6, I have listed six reasons for the failure, although there is little doubt that effective, safe therapy of the various cancers is a difficult problem.

Table 6

Why Has the War on Cancer Failed?

1. We don't understand the cause/pathogenesis in most case of cancer—smoking is an obvious phenomenological exception.
2. Most treatments (except surgery) are nonspecific cell killers and not "smart."
3. Clinical trials and the grant system don't foster innovation—need reform.
4. Screening for useful drugs against cancer cells has not worked.
5. Animal models of cancer are often inadequate—e.g., pancreatic cancer as described in this article.
6. Unproductive "facts" in research come and go.

Where Should We Go from Here?

In my view the principal problem is that we just do not understand the causes of most cancers. We don't even know if the problem is genetic or epigenetic or something totally unknown. In theory, problems 2 through 6 in table 6 are all correctable with political and scientific will and more knowledge. Even though we know cancer of the lung is caused by cigarette smoking, we do not know the mechanism, and (except for surgery) we do not know how to meaningfully intervene (see table 2). The pharmaceutical industry cannot make real progress until we understand the mechanisms and molecular causes of cancer so that industrial, academic, and governmental scientists have rational targets for intervention. We will make no progress if there are five hundred or more genetic abnormalities in a single cancer cell. Where would one begin?

What Should We Do Now?

We can still do a lot even today (see table 7). Smoking and hormone replacement therapy are a cause of lung and breast cancer, respectively, and should be stopped or minimized. For hepatitis B (which causes over 50 percent of liver cancer) and papilloma virus (which causes almost all cervical cancer and some anal and mouth cancers), we can vaccinate with vaccines that are essentially 100 percent effective. *Helicobacter* (the probable cause of some stomach cancer) can be easily eliminated with antibiotics. Prophylactic finasteride and tamoxifen (both generic) can decrease prostate and breast cancer, respectively (in high risk patients). We must also decrease alcohol intake (liver and esophageal cancer) and obesity. Obesity is associated with increased cancer risk but the mechanism, if causal, is obscure.

   We can screen for cervical, colorectal, and breast cancer, although the value of breast cancer screening is not clear (due to overdiagnosis), as I discussed above. However, in my view, the benefit of breast cancer screening slightly outweighs the harm. For example, if DCIS treatment could be rationalized and provided only to those who need it, breast cancer screening would

Table 7

The Way Forward

1. Prevention (cancer prevented)
   a. Stop smoking (lung; others)
   b. Minimize hormone replacement therapy (breast)
   c. Vaccines
      1) Hepatitis B (liver)
      2) Papilloma virus (cervical, anal, penis)
   d. Eliminate *Helicobacter* with antibiotics (stomach)
   e. Prevent contracting AIDS (sarcoma)
   f. Chemoprophylaxis
      3) finasteride (prostate)
      4) tamoxifen (high risk breast)
   g. Decrease alcohol (liver, esophagus)
   h. Decrease obesity (many types)
2. Screening for
   a. Cervical cancer
   b. Colorectal cancer
   c. Breast cancer
3. More knowledge of cancers' causes and better animal models
4. Better drugs—once appropriate targets identified

then be unarguably useful. All attempts to screen for lung cancer, even in smokers, have so far been futile.

If all these recommendations were followed, we could cut cancer deaths in half. Moreover, with better mechanistic understanding of cancer, we could make truly "smart" drugs, as has been done in recent years for atherosclerosis (heart attacks), hypertension (strokes), gastrointestinal diseases (ulcers), and AIDS—with truly remarkable results. Let us hope cancer is next.

POSTSCRIPT

Are We Winning the War on Cancer?

Although many diseases have similar or worse outcomes, cancer is generally more feared than heart disease or diabetes. Cancer is regarded as a disease that must be "battled" and a "war" on cancer has been declared. Fighting or military-like descriptions are often used to address cancer's human effects, and they emphasize the need for the patient to take immediate, decisive actions himself or herself, rather than to delay, ignore, or rely on others caring for him or her.

Forty years ago, talk therapy to change a patient's outlook on life was a relatively popular alternative cancer treatment. It was based on the idea that cancer was caused by a negative personality or attitude. People with a "cancer personality"—depressed, repressed, self-hating, and unable to express their emotions—were believed to have developed cancer through their personality and/or their attitudes. This theory allowed society to blame the victim for having developed cancer or having prevented its cure by their negative attitude and personality. It also increased patients' anxieties as they incorrectly believe that natural emotions of sadness, anger, or fear either gave them the disease or prevented them from being cured. The author Susan Sontag helped promote this idea in her book *Illness as Metaphor* written in 1978 while recovering from treatment for breast cancer. Although the idea of personality causing cancer has not been supported by research, the belief that thinking positively will increase survival, especially among breast cancer patients, is common. An article "Invited Commentary: Personality as a Causal Factor in Cancer Risk and Mortality—Time to Retire a Hypothesis?" in the *American Journal of Epidemiology* (2010) reports findings from a large-scale study of the value of two personality dimensions, neuroticism and extraversion, for cancer risk and life expectancy. Overall, no relationship was found between personality and cancer onset or survival. The authors question whether it is time for the field to move on from considering a role for personality in cancer to more promising and modifiable factors.

For further information on the progress of the war on cancer, see "Declining Death Rates Reflect Progress Against Cancer," *PLoS ONE* (2010). The article discusses the success of the "war on cancer" initiated in 1971. The authors found that death rate for all cancers combined in men showed a net decline of 21 percent and 11 percent from the 1990 and 1970 rates, respectively. Similarly, the all-cancer death rate in women showed a net decline of 12 percent and 6 percent from the 1991 and 1970 rates, respectively. These decreases since 1990–91 translate to preventing of 561,400 cancer deaths in men and 205,700 deaths in women. The decrease in death rates from all cancers involved all ages and racial/ethnic groups. The positive change in cancer death rates since 1990 resulted mostly from reductions in smoking, increased screening allowing early detection of several cancers, and improvements in treatment for specific cancers. Although much overall progress has been made in cancer treatment and prevention, lung cancer remains a difficult disease to treat with generally poor prognoses. In "Lung Cancer: Progress in Diagnosis, Staging and Therapy," *Respirology* (January 2010), the authors indicate that lung cancer remains one of the greatest medical challenges with nearly 1.5 million new cases world-wide each year and a growing tobacco epidemic in the developing world. The value of screening for early disease is not yet established and trials to see if mortality can be improved as a result are in progress. For further reading, see "Two Decades of Declining Cancer Mortality: Progress with Disparity," *Annual Review of Public Health* (2010). In this article, the authors claim that despite considerable progress in preventing and treating cancer, disparities in cancer mortality persist across different races and social classes. Because all the factors that account for declining cancer trends are related to social class, and because of large social class disparities in cancer risk factors, there will likely be a widening gap in cancer deaths among those in lower socioeconomic groups in the future.

Also see the following: "Breast Cancer—A Voyage into Hearts and Minds," *Psychologist* (February 2011); "Cancer," *Time* (February 14, 2011); "Fighting Cancer Takes on a New Dimension," *Chronicle of Philanthropy* (January 13, 2011); and "Not Just an Illness of the Rich," *Scientific American* (March 2011).

ISSUE 5

Should Marijuana Be Legalized for Medicinal Purposes?

YES: **Kevin Drum**, from "The Patriot's Guide to Legalization," *Mother Jones* (July/August 2009)

NO: **Christian Science Monitor Editorial Board**, from "Legalize Marijuana? Not So Fast," *The Christian Science Monitor* (May 22, 2009)

ISSUE SUMMARY

YES: Kevin Drum contends that medical marijuana is now legal in more than a dozen states without any serious problems or increased usage.

NO: The editorial board of *The Christian Science Monitor* maintains that the drug can lead to dependence and can cause lung damage and other health concerns.

$\mathbf{A}$t one time, there were no laws in the United States regulating the use or sale of drugs, including marijuana. Rather than by legislation, their use was regulated by religious teaching and social custom. As society grew more complex and more heterogeneous, the need for more formal regulation of drug sales, production, and use developed.

Attempts at regulating patent medications through legislation began in the early 1900s. In 1920, Congress, under pressure from temperance organizations, passed an amendment prohibiting the manufacture and sale of all alcoholic beverages. From 1920 until 1933, the demand for alcohol was met by organized crime, who either manufactured it illicitly or smuggled it into the United States. The government's inability to enforce the law, as well as increasing violence, finally led to the repeal of prohibition in 1933.

Many years later, in the 1960s, drug usage again began to worry many Americans. Heroin abuse had become epidemic in urban areas, and many middle-class young adults had begun to experiment with marijuana and LSD by the end of the decade. Cocaine also became popular first among the middle class and later among inner-city residents. More recently, crack houses, babies born with drug addictions, and drug-related crimes and shootings are the images of a new epidemic of drug abuse.

Many of those who believe illicit drugs are a major problem in America, however, are usually referring to hard drugs, such as cocaine and heroin. Soft drugs like marijuana, though not legal, are not often perceived as a major threat to the safety and well-being of citizens. Millions of Americans have tried marijuana and did not become addicted. The drug has also been used illegally by those suffering from AIDS, glaucoma, and cancer to alleviate their symptoms and to stimulate their appetites. Should marijuana be legalized as a medicine, or is it too addictive and dangerous? In California, Proposition 215 was passed in the November 1996 ballot. A similar measure was passed in Arizona. These initiatives convinced voters to relax current laws against marijuana use for medical and humane reasons. Several other states followed and legalized marijuana for medicinal purposes.

Opponents of these recent measures argue that marijuana use has been steadily rising among teenagers and that this may lead to experimentation with hard drugs. There is concern that if marijuana is legal via a doctor's prescription, the drug will be more readily available. There is also concern that the health benefits of smoking marijuana are overrated. For instance, among glaucoma sufferers, in order to achieve benefits from the drug, patients would literally have to be stoned all the time. Unfortunately, the efficacy of marijuana is unclear because, as an illicit drug, studies to adequately test it have been thwarted by drug control agencies.

Although marijuana's effectiveness in treating the symptoms of disease is unclear, is it actually dangerous and addictive? Scientists contend that the drug can negatively affect cognition and motor function. It can also have an impact on short-term memory and can interfere with perception and learning. Physical health effects include lung damage. Until recently, scientists had little evidence that marijuana was actually addictive. Although heavy users did not seem to experience actual withdrawal symptoms, studies with laboratory animals given large doses of THC, the active ingredient in marijuana, suffered withdrawal symptoms similar to those of rodents withdrawing from opiates.

Not all researchers agree, however, that marijuana is dangerous and addictive. The absence of well-designed, long-term studies on the effects of marijuana use further complicates the issue, as does the current potency of the drug. Growers have become more skilled about developing strains of marijuana with high concentrations of THC. Today's varieties may be three to five times more potent than the pot used in the 1960s. Much of the data are unclear, but what is known is that young users of the drug are likely to have problems learning. In addition, some users are at risk for developing dependence.

In the following selections, Kevin Drum states that there are no proven studies to support the view that marijuana prohibition is justified. The editors of *The Christian Science Monitor* argue that marijuana causes many physical and psychological effects, particularly to adolescents.

YES ⬋

Kevin Drum

The Patriot's Guide to Legalization

Have you ever looked at our marijuana policy? I mean really looked at it?

When we think of the drug war, it's the heavy-duty narcotics like heroin and cocaine that get most of the attention. And why not? That's where the action is. It's not marijuana that is sustaining the Taliban in Afghanistan, after all. When Crips and Bloods descend into gun battles in the streets of Los Angeles, they're not usually fighting over pot. The junkie who breaks into your house and steals your Blu-ray player isn't doing it so he can score a couple of spliffs.

No, the marijuana trade is more genteel than that. At least, I used to think it was. Then, like a lot of people, I started reading about the open warfare that has erupted among the narcotraffickers in Mexico and is now spilling across the American border. Stories of drugs coming north and arsenals of guns going south. Thousands of people brutally murdered. Entire towns terrorized. And this was a war not just over cocaine and meth, but marijuana as well.

And I began to wonder: Maybe the war against pot is about to get a lot uglier. After all, in the 1920s, Prohibition gave us Al Capone and the St. Valentine's Day Massacre, and that was over plain old whiskey and rum. Are we about to start paying the same price for marijuana?

If so, it might eventually start to affect me, too. Indirectly, sure, but that's more than it ever has before. I've never smoked a joint in my life. I've only seen one once, and that was 30 years ago. I barely drink, I don't smoke, and I don't like coffee. When it comes to mood altering substances, I live the life of a monk. I never really cared much if marijuana was legal or not.

But if a war is breaking out over the stuff, I figured maybe I should start looking at the evidence on whether marijuana prohibition is worth it. Not the spin from the drug czar at one end or the hemp hucksters at the other. Just the facts, as best as I could figure them out. So I did. Here's what I found.

In 1972, the report of the National Commission on Marihuana and Drug Abuse urged that possession of marijuana for personal use be decriminalized. A small wave of states followed this recommendation, but most refused; in Washington, President Carter called for eliminating penalties for small-time possession, but Congress stonewalled. And that's the way things have stayed since the late '70s. Some states have decriminalized, most haven't, and possession is still a criminal offense under federal law. So how has that worked out?

I won't give away the ending just yet, but one thing to know is this: On virtually every subject related to cannabis (an inclusive term that refers to both the sativa and indica varieties of the marijuana plant, as well as hashish, bhang, and other derivatives), the evidence is ambiguous. Sometimes even mysterious. So let's start with the obvious question.

Does decriminalizing cannabis have any effect at all? It's remarkably hard to tell—in part because drug use is faddish. Cannabis use among teens in the United States, for example, went down sharply in the '80s, bounced back in the early '90s, and has declined moderately since. Nobody really knows why.

We do, however, have studies that compare rates of cannabis use in states that have decriminalized vs. states that haven't. And the somewhat surprising conclusion, in the words of Robert MacCoun, a professor of law and public policy at the University of California-Berkeley, is simple: "Most of the evidence suggests that decriminalization has no effect."

But decriminalization is not legalization. In places that have decriminalized, simple possession is still illegal; it's just treated as an administrative offense, like a traffic ticket. And production and distribution remain felonies. What would happen if cannabis use were fully legalized?

No country has ever done this, so we don't know. The closest example is the Netherlands, where possession and sale of small amounts of marijuana is de facto legal in the famous coffeehouses. MacCoun and a colleague, Peter Reuter of the University of Maryland, have studied the Dutch experience and concluded that while legalization at first had little effect, once the coffeehouses began advertising and promoting themselves more aggressively in the 1980s, cannabis use more than doubled in a decade. Then again, cannabis use in Europe has gone up and down in waves, and some of the Dutch increase (as well as a later decrease, which followed a tightening of the coffeehouse laws in the mid-'90s) may have simply been part of those larger waves.

The most likely conclusion from the overall data is that if you fully legalized cannabis, use would almost certainly go up, but probably not enormously. MacCoun guesses that it might rise by half—say, from around 15 percent of the population to a little more than 20 percent. "It's not going to triple," he says. "Most people who want to use marijuana are already finding a way to use marijuana."

Still, there would be a cost. For one thing, a much higher increase isn't out of the question if companies like Philip Morris or R.J. Reynolds set their finest minds on the promotion of dope. And much of the increase would likely come among the heaviest users. "One person smoking eight joints a day is worth more to the industry than fifty people each smoking a joint a week," says Mark Kleiman, a drug policy expert at UCLA. "If the cannabis industry were to expand greatly, it couldn't do so by increasing the number of casual users. It would have to create and maintain more chronic zonkers." And that's a problem. Chronic use can lead to dependence and even long-term cognitive impairment. Heavy cannabis users are more likely to be in auto accidents. There have been scattered reports of respiratory and fetal development problems. Still, sensible regulation can limit the commercialization of pot, and compared to other illicit drugs (and alcohol), its health effects are fairly mild.

Even a 50 percent increase in cannabis use might be a net benefit if it led to lower rates of use of other drugs.

So would people just smoke more and drink less? Maybe. The generic term for this effect in the economics literature is "substitute goods," and it simply means that some things replace other things. If the total demand for transportation is generally steady, an increase in sales of SUVs will lead to a decrease in the sales of sedans. Likewise, if the total demand for intoxicants is steady, an increase in the use of one drug should lead to a decrease in others.

Several years ago, John DiNardo, an economist now at the University of Michigan, found a clever way to test this via a natural experiment. Back in the 1980s, the Reagan administration pushed states to raise the drinking age to 21. Some states did this early in the decade, some later, and this gave DiNardo the idea of comparing data from the various states to see if the Reagan policy worked.

He found that raising the drinking age did lead to lower alcohol consumption; the effect was modest but real. But then DiNardo hit on another analysis—comparing cannabis use in states that raised the drinking age early with those that did it later. And he found that indeed, there seemed to be a substitution effect. On average, among high school seniors, a 4.5 percent decrease in drinking produced a 2.4 percent increase in getting high.

But what we really want to know is whether the effect works in the other direction: Would increased marijuana use lead to less drinking? "What goes up should go down," DiNardo told me cheerfully, but he admits that in the absence of empirical evidence this hypothesis depends on your faith in basic economic models.

Some other studies are less encouraging than DiNardo's, but even if the substitute goods effect is smaller than his research suggests—if, say, a 30 percent increase in cannabis use led to a 5 or 10 percent drop in drinking—it would still be a strong argument in favor of legalization. After all, excessive drinking causes nearly 80,000 deaths per year in the United States, compared to virtually none for pot. Trading alcohol consumption for cannabis rise might be a pretty attractive deal.

But what about the gateway effect? This has been a perennial bogeyman of the drug warriors. Kids who use pot, the TV ads tell us, will graduate to ecstasy, then coke, then meth, and then—who knows? Maybe even talk radio.

Is there anything to this? There are two plausible pathways for the gateway theory. The first is that drug use of any kind creates an affinity for increasingly intense narcotic experiences. The second is that when cannabis is illegal, the only place to get it is from dealers who also sell other stuff.

The evidence for the first pathway is mixed. Research in New Zealand, for example, suggests that regular cannabis use is correlated with higher rates of other illicit drug use, especially in teenagers. A Norwegian study comes to similar conclusions, but only for a small segment of "troubled" teenagers. Other research, however, suggests that these correlations aren't caused by gateway effects at all, but by the simple fact that kids who like drugs do drugs. All kinds of drugs.

The second pathway was deliberately targeted by the Dutch when they began their coffeehouse experiment in the '70s in part to sever the connection of cannabis with the illicit drug market. The evidence suggests that it worked: Even with cannabis freely available, Dutch cannabis use is currently about average among developed countries and use of other illicit drugs is about average, too. Easy access to marijuana, outside the dealer network for harder drugs, doesn't seem to have led to greater use of cocaine or heroin.

So, to recap: Decriminalization of simple possession appears to have little effect on cannabis consumption. Full legalization would likely increase use only moderately as long as heavy commercialization is prohibited, although the effect on chronic users might be more substantial. It would increase heroin and cocaine use only slightly if at all, and it might decrease alcohol consumption by a small amount. Which leads to the question:

Can we still afford prohibition? The consequences of legalization, after all, must be compared to the cost of the status quo. Unsurprisingly, this too is hard to quantify. The worst effects of the drug war, including property crime and gang warfare, are mostly associated with cocaine, heroin, and meth. Likewise, most drug-law enforcement is aimed at harder drugs, not cannabis; contrary to conventional wisdom, only about 44,000 people are currently serving prison time on cannabis charges—and most of those are there for dealing and distribution, not possession.

Still, the University of Maryland's Reuter points out that about 800,000 people are arrested for cannabis possession every year in the United States. And even though very few end up being sentenced to prison, a study of three counties in Maryland following a recent marijuana crackdown suggests that a third spend at least one pretrial night in jail and a sixth spend more than ten days. That takes a substantial human toll. Overall, Harvard economist Jeffrey Miron estimates the cost of cannabis prohibition in the United States at $13 billion annually and the lost tax revenue at nearly $7 billion.

So what are the odds of legalization? Slim. For starters, the United States, along with virtually every other country in the world, is a signatory to the 1961 Single Convention on Narcotic Drugs (and its 1988 successor), which flatly prohibits legalization of cannabis. The only way around this is to unilaterally withdraw from the treaties or to withdraw and then reenter with reservations. That's not going to happen.

At the federal level, there's virtually no appetite for legalizing cannabis either. Though public opinion has made steady strides, increasing from around 20 percent favoring marijuana legalization in the Reagan era to nearly 40 percent favoring it today, the only policy change in Washington has been Attorney General Eric Holder's announcement in March that the Obama administration planned to end raids on distributors of medical marijuana. (Applications for pot dispensaries promptly surged in Los Angeles County.)

The real action in cannabis legalization is at the state level. More than a dozen states now have effective medical marijuana laws, most notably California. Medical marijuana dispensaries are dotted all over the state, and it's common knowledge that the "medical" part is in many cases a thin fiction. Like the Dutch coffeehouses, California's dispensaries are now a de facto legal distribution network that severs the link between cannabis and other illicit drugs for a significant number of adults (albeit still only a fraction of total users). And the result? Nothing. "We've had this experiment for a decade and the sky hasn't fallen," says Paul Armentano, deputy director of the National Organization for the Reform of Marijuana Laws. California Assemblyman Tom Ammiano has even introduced a bill that would legalize, tax, and regulate marijuana; it has gained the endorsement of the head of the state's tax collection agency, which informally estimates it could collect $1.3 billion a year from cannabis sales. Still, the legislation hasn't found a single cosponsor, and isn't scheduled for so much as a hearing.

Which is too bad. Going into this assignment, I didn't care much personally about cannabis legalization. I just had a vague sense that if other people wanted to do it, why not let them? But the evidence suggests pretty clearly that we ought to significantly soften our laws on marijuana. Too many lives have been mined and too much money spent for a social benefit that, if not zero, certainly isn't very high.

And it may actually happen. If attitudes continue to soften; if the Obama administration turns down the volume on anti-pot propaganda; if medical dispensaries avoid heavy commercialization; if drug use remains stable; and if emergency rooms don't start filling up with drug-related traumas while all this is happening, California's experience could go a long way toward destigmatizing cannabis use. That's a lot of ifs.

Still, things are changing. Even GOV icon Arnold Schwarzenegger now says, "I think it's time for a debate." That doesn't mean he's in favor of legalizing pot fight this minute, but it might mean we're getting close to a tipping point. Ten years from now, as the flower power generation enters its 70s, you might finally be able to smoke a fully legal, taxed, and regulated joint.

A footnoted version of this article is at motherjones.com/patriots-guide-to-legalization.

 **NO**

Legalize Marijuana? Not So Fast

Backers serve up a timely batch of arguments, but their latest reasons are half-baked.

The American movement to legalize marijuana for regular use is on a roll. Or at least its backers say it is.

They point to California Gov. Arnold Schwarzenegger, who said in early May that it's now time to debate legalizing marijuana—though he's personally against it. Indeed, a legislative push is on in his state (and several others, such as Massachusetts and Nevada) to treat this "soft" drug like alcohol—to tax and regulate its sale, and set an age restriction on buyers.

Several recent polls show stepped-up public support for legalization. This means not only lifting restrictions on use ("decriminalization"), but also on supply—production and sales. The Obama administration, meanwhile, says the US Drug Enforcement Agency will no longer raid dispensaries of medical marijuana—which is illegal under federal law—in states where it is legal.

The push toward full legalization is a well-organized, Internet-savvy campaign, generously funded by a few billionaires, including George Soros. It's built on a decades-long, step-by-step effort in the states. Thirteen states have so far decriminalized marijuana use (generally, the punishment covers small amounts and involves a fine). And 13 states now allow for medical marijuana.

Paul Armentano, deputy director of the National Organization for the Reform of Marijuana Laws (NORML), recently told a Monitor reporter that three reasons account for the fresh momentum toward legalization: 1) the weak economy, which is forcing states to look for new revenue; 2) public concern over the violent drug war in Mexico; and 3) more experience with marijuana itself.

If there is to be a debate, let's look at these reasons, starting with experience with marijuana.

A Harmless Drug?

Supporters of legalization often claim that no one has died of a pot overdose, and that it has beneficial effects in alleviating suffering from certain diseases.

True, marijuana cannot directly kill its user in the way that alcohol or a drug like heroin can. And activists claim that it may ease symptoms for certain patients—though it has not been endorsed by the major medical associations representing those patients, and the Food and Drug Administration disputes its value.

Rosalie Pacula, codirector of the Rand Drug Policy Research Center, poses this question: "If pot is relatively harmless, why are we seeing more than 100,000 hospitalizations a year" for marijuana use?

Emergency-room admissions where marijuana is the primary substance involved increased by 164 percent from 1995 to 2002—faster than for other drugs, according to the Drug Abuse Warning Network.

Research results over the past decade link frequent marijuana use to several serious mental health problems, with youth particularly at risk. And the British Lung Foundation finds that smoking three to four joints is the equivalent of 20 tobacco cigarettes.

While marijuana is not addictive in the way that a drug like crack-cocaine is, heavy use can lead to dependence—defined by the same criteria as for other drugs. About half of those who use pot daily become dependent for some period of time, writes Kevin Sabet, in the 2006 book, "Pot Politics"—and 1 in 10 people in the US who have ever used marijuana become dependent at some time (about the same rate as alcohol). Dr. Sabet was a drug policy adviser in the past two presidential administrations.

He adds that physicians in Britain and the Netherlands—both countries that have experience with relaxed marijuana laws—are seeing withdrawal symptoms among heavy marijuana users that are similar to those of cocaine and heroin addicts. This has been confirmed in the lab with monkeys.

Today's marijuana is also much more potent than in the hippie days of yesteryear. But that doesn't change what's always been known about even casual use of this drug: It distorts perception, reduces motor skills, and affects alertness. When combined with alcohol (not unusual), or even alone, it worsens the risk of traffic accidents.

Would Legalization Take the Violence Out of the Mexican Drug War?

NORML likes to point out that marijuana accounts for the majority of illicit drug traffic from Mexico. End the illicit trafficking, and you end the violence. But that volume gives a false impression of marijuana's role in crime and violence, says Jonathan Caulkins, a professor at Carnegie Mellon and a drug-policy adviser in the US and Australia.

It's the dollars that count, and the big earners—cocaine, methamphetamine, heroin—play a much larger role in crime and violence. In recent years, Mexico has become a major cocaine route to the US. That's what's fanning the violence, according to Dr. Caulkins, so legalizing marijuana is unlikely to quiet Mexico's drug war.

Neither are America's prisons stuffed with users who happened to get caught with a few joints (if that were the case, a huge percentage of America's college students—an easy target—would be behind bars). Yes, there are upward of 700,000 arrests on marijuana charges each year, but that includes repeat arrests, and most of those apprehended don't go to jail. Those who do are usually large-scale offenders.

Only 0.7 percent of inmates in state and federal prisons are in for marijuana possession (0.3 percent counting first-time offenders only, according to a 2002 US Justice Department survey). In federal prisons, the median amount of marijuana for those convicted of possession is 115 pounds—156,000 marijuana cigarettes.

Can Marijuana Rescue State Coffers?

The California legalization bill proposes a $50/ounce tax on marijuana. The aim is to keep pot as close to the black-market price as possible while still generating an estimated $1.3 billion in income for this deficit-challenged state.

But the black market can easily undercut a $50 tax and shrink that expected revenue stream. Just look at the huge trade in illegal cigarettes in Canada to see how taxing can spur a black market (about 30 percent of tobacco bought in Canada is illegal).

A government could attempt to eliminate the black market altogether by making marijuana incredibly cheap (Dr. Pacula at the RAND Organization says today's black market price is about four times what it would be if pot were completely legalized). But then use would skyrocket and teens (though barred) could buy it with their lunch money.

Indeed, legalizing marijuana is bound to increase use simply because of availability. Legalization advocates say "not so" and point to the Netherlands and its legal marijuana "coffee shops." Indeed, after the Dutch de facto legalized the drug in 1976, use stayed about the same for adults and youth. But it took off after 1984, growing by 300 percent over the next decade or so. Experts attribute this to commercialization (sound like alcohol?), and also society's view of the drug as normal—which took a while to set in.

Now the Dutch are finding that normalization has its costs—increased dependence, more dealers of harder drugs, and a flood of rowdy "drug tourists" from other countries. The Dutch "example" should be renamed the Dutch "warning."

As America has learned with alcohol, taxes don't begin to cover the costs to society of destroyed families, lost productivity, and ruined lives—and regulators still have not succeeded in keeping alcohol from underage drinkers.

No one has figured out what the exact social costs of legalizing marijuana would be. But ephemeral taxes won't cover them—nor should society want to encourage easier access to a drug that can lead to dependency, has health risks, and reduces alertness, to name just a few of its negative outcomes.

Why legalize a third substance that produces ill effects, when the US has such a poor record in dealing with the two big "licits"—alcohol and tobacco?

Parents Need to Resist Peer Pressure Too

Legalization backers say the country is at a tipping point, ready to make the final big leap. They hope that a new generation of politicians that has had experience with marijuana will be friendly to their cause.

But this new generation is also made up of parents. Do parents really want marijuana to become a normal part of society—and an expectation for their children?

Maybe parents thought they left peer pressure behind when they graduated from high school. But the push to legalize marijuana is like the peer pressure of the schoolyard. The arguments are perhaps timely, but they don't stand up, and parents must now stand up to them.

They must let lawmakers know that legalization is not OK, and they must carry this message to their children, too. Disapproval, along with information on risk, are the most important factors in discouraging marijuana and cocaine use among high school seniors, according to the University of Michigan's "Monitoring the Future" project on substance abuse.

Parents must make clear that marijuana is not a harmless drug—even if they personally may have emerged unscathed.

And they need to teach the life lesson that marijuana does not really solve personal challenges, be they stress, relationships, or discouragement.

In the same way, a search for joy and satisfaction in a drug is misplaced.

The far greater and lasting attraction is in a life rooted in moral and spiritual values—not in a haze, a daze, or a munchie-craze.

Today's youth are tomorrow's world problem solvers—and the ones most likely to be affected if marijuana is legalized. Future generations need to be clear thinkers. For their sakes, those who oppose legalizing marijuana must become vocal, well-funded, and mainstream—before it's too late.

POSTSCRIPT

Should Marijuana Be Legalized for Medicinal Purposes?

Recent laws in several states legalizing marijuana for medicinal purposes make many people nervous. The majority of Americans are against making marijuana completely legal even if prescribed to individuals who have legitimate medicinal need for the drug. A compromise might be to decriminalize marijuana, making it neither strictly legal nor illegal. If decriminalized, there would be no penalty for personal or medical use or possession, although there would continue to be criminal penalties for sale for profit and distribution to minors. Marijuana has been decriminalized in a few states, but it is illegal in most of the country.

Although decriminalization appeals to many, in early 1992, the Drug Enforcement Administration published a document stating that the federal government was justified in its continued prohibition of marijuana for medicinal purposes. The report indicated that too many questions surrounded the effectiveness of medicinal marijuana. See "Medical Marijuana on Trial," *The New York Times* (March 29, 2005) and "The Right Not to Be in Pain: Using Marijuana for Pain Management," *The Nation* (February 3, 2003). The effectiveness of marijuana as therapy for cancer patients and AIDS patients continues to be debated, but the Center on Addiction and Substance Abuse of Columbia University maintains that recent research suggests that the drug is addictive and can wreck the lives of users, particularly teenagers. They argue that legalizing marijuana would undermine the impact of drug education and increase usage. An article in *The American Nurse* (May/June 2010) addresses this issue in "Exploring the Science of Medical Marijuana."

Other articles that debate the safety and legality of marijuana include "Legalization Would Stem Marijuana Boom," *The Christian Science Monitor* (March 18, 2005); "Legalize Marijuana Medicine," *Progressive* (December 2004); "Reefer Rx: Marijuana as Medicine," *Harvard Health Letter* (September 2004); "Medicinal Grass," *Reason* (January 2005); "Pot Shots," *Science News* (October 7, 2004); "Federal Foolishness and Marijuana," *The New England Journal of Medicine* (January 30, 1997); "The War Over Weed," *Newsweek* (February 3, 1997); "Prescription Drugs," *Reason* (February 1997); "Marijuana: Useful Medicine or Dangerous Drug?" *Consumers' Research Magazine* (May 1997); "Moving Marijuana," *Reason* (May 1998); "Bad News for Pot Smokers; Ounce for Ounce, a British Study Says, Marijuana Does More Damage Than Tobacco," *The Report Newsmagazine* (December 16, 2002); "Cannabis Use among Teens May Lead to Addiction," *Alcoholism & Drug Abuse Weekly* (April 14, 2003);

"High Road: Is Marijuana a 'Gateway'?" *Reason* (March 2003). In the following article, marijuana is discussed in a risk versus benefit format: "How Marijuana Got Mainstreamed? Well, No. But the Latest Research Suggests the Health Risk from Occasional Use Is Mild, and It Might Ease Certain Ills," *Time* (November 22, 2010).

ISSUE 6

Should Doctors Prescribe Drugs Based on Race?

YES: Sally Satel, from "I Am a Racially Profiling Doctor," *The New York Times Magazine* (May 5, 2002)

NO: Gregory Michael Dorr and David S. Jones, from "Facts and Fiction: BiDil and the Resurgence of Racial Medicine," *Journal of Law, Medicine & Ethics* (Fall 2008)

ISSUE SUMMARY

YES: Physician Sally Satel believes it important to note a patient's race and to treat accordingly because many diseases and treatment responses cluster by race and ethnicity.

NO: Professors Gregory Michael Dorr and David Jones argue that there is risk to using race and ethnicity to select treatment options.

In 2005, the Food and Drug Administration approved the first "ethnic drug," called BiDil. The drug, intended to treat congestive heart failure, was designed for African Americans only. The drug was touted as a means to improve the health of African Americans, a community historically underserved by the American medical complex. In 1998, former President Bill Clinton committed the country to a goal of eliminating health disparities among racial and ethnic minority populations by the year 2010. The government's plan was to maintain the progress on overall health of the American people while equalizing health care in six propriety areas, including infant mortality, cancer screening and management, cardiovascular disease, diabetes, HIV/AIDS, and adult and child immunizations. This commitment, known as the *Race and Health Initiative*, emphasizes key areas that represent a major burden of disease that are highly preventable if appropriate interventions are taken.

Infant death rates among racial minorities are above the national average. The greatest disparity exists for black Americans, whose infant death rate is more than twice that of white Americans. Cancer and cardiovascular deaths too are higher among racial and ethnic groups, especially blacks. Diabetes death rates were nearly two and a half times higher in black and Native American populations, and nearly two times higher among Latinos than whites. Similarly, AIDS has had a disproportionate impact on racial and ethnic minority groups in the United States. Nearly 75 percent of the estimated 40,000 annual HIV infections are among blacks and Latinos. Racial disparities also exist for childhood and adult vaccination rates.

The causes of these differences appear to be a complex mixture of biology, environment, culture, and socioeconomic status. Many racial disparities in health status generally do not reflect biologically determined causes but rather a group's living circumstances, access to health care, and cultural factors such as disenfranchisement with the health care system. There are, however, genetic differences that do affect drug responses and existence of certain diseases.

Several population-based genetic studies have determined that there are racial differences in the way people metabolize certain medications and respond to treatment. There appear to be many genetic variants affecting drug responses which should enable health practitioners to prescribe medications and therapies accordingly. Race may play a role in the cause of disease as well. Racially based genetic coding might prove important because some diseases appear in certain groups of people and may be both racially and genetically linked, for example, cystic fibrosis and Tay-Sachs disease.

The subject of medical research and race is, however, related to past abuses and the risk of abuses in the future. Tuskegee, Alabama, will be forever linked in America's memory due to the Tuskegee Syphilis Study. In the counties surrounding this small southern community, the U.S. Public Health Service ran a 40 year study, from 1932 until 1972, of "untreated syphilis in the male Negro," while telling the men in the study that they were being "treated" for their "bad blood." The outcry over the study, which affected approximately 399 African American men with the disease and 201 controls, led to a lawsuit, Senate hearings, a federal investigation, and new rules about informed consent. It has also generated rumors, a presidential apology, a common topic for Institutional Review Boards, and a National Bioethics Institute.

In the following selections, physician Sally Satel believes it important to note a patient's race and to treat accordingly because many diseases and treatment responses cluster by race and ethnicity. Professors Gregory Michael Dorr and David Jones argue that there is risk to using race and ethnicity to select treatment options.

YES ↵

Sally Satel

I Am a Racially Profiling Doctor

In practicing medicine, I am not colorblind. I always take note of my patient's race. So do many of my colleagues. We do it because certain diseases and treatment responses cluster by ethnicity. Recognizing these patterns can help us diagnose disease more efficiently and prescribe medications more effectively. When it comes to practicing medicine, stereotyping often works.

But to a growing number of critics, this statement is viewed as a shocking admission of prejudice. After all, shouldn't all patients be treated equally, regardless of the color of their skin? The controversy came to a boil last May in *The New England Journal of Medicine*. The journal published a study revealing that enalapril, a standard treatment for chronic heart failure, was less helpful to blacks than to whites. Researchers found that significantly more black patients treated with enalapril ended up hospitalized. A companion study examined carvedilol, a beta blocker; the results indicated that the drug was equally beneficial to both races.

These clinically important studies were accompanied, however, by an essay titled "Racial Profiling in Medical Research." Robert S. Schwartz, a deputy editor at the journal, wrote that prescribing medication by taking race into account was a form of "race-based medicine" that was both morally and scientifically wrong. "Race is not only imprecise but also of no proven value in treating an individual patient," Schwartz wrote. "Tax-supported trolling . . . to find racial distinctions in human biology must end."

Responding to Schwartz's essay in *The Chronicle of Higher Education*, other doctors voiced their support. "It's not valid science," charged Richard S. Cooper, a hypertension expert at Loyola Medical School. "I challenge any member of our species to show where this kind of analysis has come up with something useful."

But the enalapril researchers were doing something useful. Their study informed thousands of doctors that, when it came to their black patients, one drug was more likely to be effective than another. The study may have saved some lives. What's more useful than that?

Almost every day at the Washington drug clinic where I work as a psychiatrist, race plays a useful diagnostic role. When I prescribe Prozac to a patient who is African-American, I start at a lower dose, 5 or 10 milligrams instead of the usual 10-to-20 milligram dose. I do this in part because clinical experience and pharmacological research show that blacks metabolize antidepressants more slowly than Caucasians and Asians. As a result, levels of the medication can build up and make side effects more likely. To be sure, not every African-American is a slow metabolizer of antidepressants; only 40 percent are. But the risk of provoking side effects like nausea, insomnia or fuzzy-headedness in a depressed person—someone already terribly demoralized who may have been reluctant to take medication in the first place—is to worsen the patient's distress and increase the chances that he will flush the pills down the toilet. So I start all black patients with a lower dose, then take it from there.

In my drug-treatment clinic, where almost all of the patients use heroin by injection, a substantial number of them have hepatitis C, an infectious blood-borne virus that now accounts for 40 percent of all chronic liver disease. The standard treatment for active hepatitis C is an antiviral-drug combination of alpha interferon and ribavirin. But for some as yet undiscovered reason, African-Americans do not respond as well as whites to this regimen. In white patients, the double therapy reduces the amount of virus in the blood by over 90 percent after six months of treatment. In blacks, the reduction is only 50 percent. As a result, my black patients with hepatitis C must be given a considerably less reassuring prognosis than my white patients.

Without a doubt, there are many medical situations in which race is irrelevant. In an operation to repair a broken leg, for example, a patient's race doesn't matter. But there are countless situations in which the race factor should be considered. My colleague Ronald W. Dworkin, an anesthesiologist in a Baltimore-area hospital, takes race into account when performing one of his most important activities: intubation, the placement of a breathing tube down a patient's windpipe. During intubation, he says, black patients tend to salivate heavily, which can cause airway complications. As a precautionary measure, Dworkin gives many of his black patients a drying agent. "Not every black person fits this observation," he concedes, "but there is sufficient empirical evidence to make every anesthesiologist keep this danger in the back of his or her mind." The day I spoke with him, Dworkin attended a hysterectomy in a middle-aged Asian woman. "Asians tend to have a greater sensitivity to narcotics," he says, "so we always start with lower doses. They run the risk of apnea"—the cessation of breathing—"if we do not."

Could doctors make a diagnosis for and treat a patient properly if they did not know his race? "Most of the time," says Jerome P. Kassirer, a professor of medicine at Yale and Tufts. "But knowing that detail early on helps me make educated guesses more efficiently."

Kassirer, the former editor of *The New England Journal of Medicine*, is a renowned diagnostician. He is legendary among trainees for what he can tell about a case from just a few facts. He gave an example from a recent morning report, the daily session in which young doctors describe to senior physicians the most vexing cases admitted to the hospital the previous night. During one report, the resident began: "The patient is a 45-year-old Asian male who came to the emergency room complaining of 'feeling weak and wobbly in my legs' after drinking two bottles of beer." Kassirer stopped her right there. "Here's what I infer from that information," he said. "First, we know that sudden weakness can be caused by a low concentration of potassium in the blood, and we know that Asian males have an unusual propensity for a rare condition in which low potassium causes temporary paralysis. We know that these paralytic attacks are sometimes brought on by alcohol."

Of course, the patient could have been suffering from some other muscular or neurological disease, and Kassirer instructed the trainees to consider those as well. But in this case the patient's potassium was low, and the diagnosis was correct—and confirmed within 24 hours by simply observing the patient. Thanks to racial profiling, the Asian patient was spared an uncomfortable and costly work-up—not to mention the worry that he might have something like Lou Gehrig's disease.

"Rather than casting our net broadly, doctors quickly focus on a problem by recognizing patterns that have clinical significance," Kassirer says. "Typically, the clinician generates an initial hypothesis merely from a patient's age, sex, appearance, presenting complaints—and race."

All of these examples fly in the face of what we are increasingly told about race and biology: namely, that the two have nothing to do with each other. When the preliminary sequence of the human genome was announced in June 2000, many felt the verdict was conclusive. Race, it was said, was an arbitrary, nefarious biological fiction. Scholars heralded the finding of the Human Genome Project that 99.9 percent of the human genetic complement is the same in everyone, regardless of race, as proof that race is biologically meaningless. Some prominent scientists said the same. J. Craig Venter, the geneticist whose company played a key role in mapping the human genome, proclaimed, "There is no basis in the genetic code for race."

What does it really mean, though, to say that 99.9 percent of our content is the same? In practical terms it means that the DNA of any two people will differ in one out of every 1,000 nucleotides, the building blocks of individual genes. With more than three billion nucleotides in the human genome, about three million nucleotides will differ among individuals. This is hardly a small change; after all, mutation of a single one can cause the gene within which it is embedded to produce an altered protein or enzyme. It may seem counterintuitive, but the 0.1 percent of human genetic variation is a medically meaningful fact.

Not surprisingly, many human genetic variations tend to cluster by racial groups—that is, by people whose ancestors came from a particular geographic region. Skin color itself is not what is at issue—it's the evolutionary history indicated by skin color. In Africa, for example, the genetic variant for sickle cell anemia cropped up at some point in the gene pool and was passed on to descendants; as a result, the disease is more common among blacks than whites. Similarly, Caucasians are far more likely to carry the gene mutations that cause multiple sclerosis and cystic fibrosis.

Admittedly, race is a rough marker. A black American may have dark skin—but her genes may well be a complex mix of ancestors from West Africa, Europe and Asia. No serious scientist, in fact, believes that genetically pure populations exist. Yet an imprecise clue is better than no clue at all.

Jay N. Cohn, a professor of medicine at the University of Minnesota, explains that skin color and other physical features can be a diagnostic surrogate for the genetic differences that influence disease and response to treatment. "Physical appearance, including skin color, is now the only way to distinguish populations for study," he says. "You'd have to use a blindfold to keep a physician from paying attention to obvious differences that may and should influence diagnosis and treatment!" Lonnie Fuller, a professor emeritus at Morehouse School of Medicine, says: "Drugs can stay in the body longer when their metabolism in the liver is slower. We know this can vary by race, and doctors should keep it in mind."

Recognizing that our one-size-fits-all approach to medicine has serious flaws, some doctors are urging research into the development of racially targeted drugs. In March 2001, the Food and Drug Administration allowed the testing of a drug called BiDil in about 600 black subjects who will participate in the African-American Heart Failure Trial, the largest clinical trial ever to focus exclusively on African-Americans.

In previous studies including both white and black patients, BiDil provided a selective benefit for the black subjects. White subjects did no better on average than those given a placebo. The leading explanation for this disparity revolves around the molecule nitric oxide, a chemical messenger that helps regulate the constriction of blood vessels, an important mechanical dynamic in the control of blood pressure. High blood pressure contributes to and worsens heart failure because it makes the heart pump harder to overcome peripheral resistance in the arteries. BiDil acts by dilating blood vessels and replenishing local stores of nitric oxide. For unexplained reasons, blacks are more likely than whites to have nitric oxide insufficiency.

To be sure, a small percentage of blacks with high blood pressure do not have low nitric oxide activity. And the fact that BiDil's intended use relies on a crude predictor of drug response—"a poor man's clue" is how one scientist described race—is something its developers at the University of Minnesota School of Medicine readily acknowledge. Nevertheless, in the sometimes cloudy world of medicine, a poor man's clue is all you've got. Perhaps that's why members of the Congressional Black Caucus voiced support for the clinical trial. So did the Association of Black Cardiologists, which is helping recruit patients for the trial. B. Waine Kong, the organization's head officer, put it simply: "It is in the name of science that we participate."

Doctors look forward to the day when they can, in good conscience, be colorblind. Researchers predict that it will eventually be common practice for doctors to generate a "genomic profile" of every patient—a precise analysis of a person's genetic makeup—so that decisions about therapies can be based on subtle characteristics of the patient's enzyme and receptor biology. At that point, racial profiling by doctors won't be necessary. Until then, however, group identity at least offers a starting point.

A high level of sensitivity about race is understandable in view of eugenics programs in early 20th-century America and ethnic cleansing abroad. The memory of the Tuskegee syphilis study, in which hundreds of rural blacks were never told they had the disease nor offered penicillin for it, still haunts the U.S. Public Health Service, the agency that conducted the study. Other scholars have expressed the worry that genetic differences among races could become the only explanation for the health disparities among them—allowing interest in examining social and economic factors to dwindle.

Indeed, the public seems to have embraced the idea of colorblind medicine. "In the last decade, many Americans have urged that the concept of race be abandoned, purged from our public discourse, rooted out of medicine and exiled from science," writes Troy Duster, a sociologist at N.Y.U.

But in this case, the public is wrong. As rough a biological classification as race may be, doctors must not be blind to its clinical implications. So much of medicine is a guessing game—and race sometimes provides an invaluable clue. As citizens, we can celebrate our genetic similarity as evidence of our spiritual kinship. As doctors and patients, though, we must realize that it is not in patients' best interests to deny the reality of differences.

Gregory Michael Dorr
and David S. Jones

→ **NO**

Facts and Fictions: BiDil and the Resurgence of Racial Medicine

In a 2002 cover article in the *New York Times Magazine,* psychiatrist Sally Satel proudly asserted "I Am a Racial Profiling Doctor."[1] When she treats African Americans in her Washington, D.C. clinic, she starts them on lower doses of fluoxetine because, she claimed, 40% of them are slow metabolizers of antidepressants. Citing other examples of racial differences in disease and therapeutics, Satel defended her politically incorrect position: "When it comes to practicing medicine, stereotyping often works." She called on her readers to accept her vision of race-based medical practice.

Another episode suggests that Satel's vision might face a skeptical audience. In a 2005 episode of the popular television drama "House M.D.," a doctor gave an African American patient a race-specific treatment for heart disease.[2] When the patient returned for follow up, having not filled the prescription, the misanthropic Dr. House pushed him to accept the medication. The patient refused: "I'm not buying into no racist drug, okay? . . . My heart's red, your heart's red. And it don't make no sense to give us different drugs."

These two visions, seemingly fact and fiction, frame the dramatic debate that has emerged over the past ten years about race-based therapeutics. Much of the controversy (and presumably the episode of "House") has been motivated by BiDil, the first drug approved by the Food and Drug Administration (FDA) for a race-specific indication: the treatment of heart failure in people who self-identify as black. The idea that different races, or, more generally, that people of different backgrounds should be treated differently is an ancient one in medicine, dating back at least to the Hippocratic authors of ancient Greece. In this country physicians have long assumed that different races, even people from different regions, experienced diseases differently and required distinctive therapeutics.[3] As recently as the 1940s, physicians debated whether or not treatments for tuberculosis would work as well in American Indians as they did in whites.[4]

The traditional enthusiasm for racial therapeutics dissipated somewhat in the decades after World War II, for at least two reasons. First, rapid developments in biomedical science, and especially in pharmacology, bolstered the hope that science could provide powerful medications that would work in every patient with a specific disease. Second, old notions of race gave way to a new consensus

From *Journal of Law, Medicine & Ethics,* Fall 2008, pp. 443–448. Copyright © 2008 by American Society of Law, Medicine & Ethics. Reprinted by permission.

that human beings are fundamentally similar, whatever their superficial racial appearances. This sentiment received its most public endorsement in June 2000 when former President Bill Clinton celebrated the completion of the first phase of the Human Genome Project: "I believe one of the great truths to emerge from this triumphant expedition inside the human genome is that in genetic terms, all human beings, regardless of race, are more than 99.9% the same."[5]

However, interest in race-specific therapeutics never disappeared completely. In the 1940s and 1950s, medical researchers described a series of racial variations in drug response, most famously the increased incidence of hemolytic anemia seen in black soldiers given malaria prophylaxis during World War II. Continuing work documented countless racial differences, from inconsequential to life-threatening.[6] This was especially true in the realm of cardiac therapeutics, where researchers had long argued that the pathophysiological mechanisms of heart disease differed between black and white Americans.[7] If the disease processes differed from race to race, then therapeutics should differ as well.

It was in this setting—long traditions of racial therapeutics, increasing discomfort with old notions of race, and lingering evidence of physiological differences between races—that BiDil emerged. Few were surprised that it reinvigorated old tensions and controversies in American medicine and society. When the FDA approved BiDil in June 2005, it sparked intense debate among physicians, academics, civil rights advocates, media pundits, and the general public. To explore these debates, the Center for the Study of Diversity in Science, Technology, and Medicine at the Massachusetts Institute of Technology hosted a conference, "Race, Pharmaceuticals, and Medical Technology," in April 2006. We sought to investigate a series of central questions: What evidence exists that the causes of disease vary significantly between different racial and ethnic groups? Should treatment decisions be based on the race and ethnicity of patients? Should other group-specific medications be developed? How does this new impulse towards race-based medicine compare with America's checkered history of abusive biomedical experimentation on minority populations?

Since these questions reflected old tensions in medicine made newly relevant by growing concerns with health inequalities, the advent of genomic technology, and the intensification of pharmaceutical marketing, we believed that an interdisciplinary conference would make valuable contributions to scholarship and health policy. The following essays represent faith rewarded. Produced initially for this conference, and then reworked as events have unfolded over subsequent years, these essays represent a range of perspectives on the dilemmas posed by racial therapeutics, as well as some possible answers. To define some common ground, this essay reviews BiDil's history and justifications. It then introduces the other essays, suggesting connections between them, and brings the BiDil story forward to the present.

BiDil's Complicated Course

On June 23, 2005, the FDA approved BiDil as a race-specific treatment for heart failure.[8] Unlike most drugs that appear before the FDA, BiDil is not *sui generis*. Instead, it is a compound of two existing generic drugs, combined into a single pill. These drugs, hydralazine and isosorbide dinitratre (H/I), were previously approved by the FDA for the treatment of hypertension and angina, respectively. Many physicians have prescribed them for off-label use in cases of heart failure, regardless of the patient's race, since the 1980s.

H/I are both vasodilators, which explains their utility in treating hypertension. Researchers discovered their efficacy in heart failure through two cooperative drug trials sponsored by the U.S. Veteran's Administration: the Vasodilator Heart Failure Trials (V-HeFT) I and II. V-HeFT I (1980 to 1985) showed H/I to be an effective treatment for heart failure. V-HeFT II (1986–1991) tested H/I against an angiotensin-converting enzyme (ACE) inhibitor and found the ACE inhibitor to be a superior treatment. ACE inhibitors subsequently became the standard of care for heart failure, although doctors continued to prescribe H/I to patients who did not tolerate ACE therapy.

In 1987, even as V-HeFT II was underway, cardiologist Jay Cohn, the lead V-HeFT investigator, applied for a patent on a "method of reducing mortality associated with congestive heart failure using hydralazine and isosorbide dinitrate." Cohn obtained this patent for the "method" of treating heart failure with H/I in 1989, without any mention of race specificity in H/I's efficacy. Cohn and others formulated a single pill of combined H/I, filing to trademark the new pill as BiDil in 1992. Cohn licensed the intellectual property rights to his method patent, and thus to BiDil, to a North Carolina company called Medco. Medco obtained the trademark for BiDil in 1995 and sought FDA approval for the combination method the following year. In 1997 the FDA rejected Medco's application, arguing that the statistics from the V-HeFT trials were too inconclusive to support approval. Nevertheless, a number of cardiologists on the FDA review panel noted their belief in BiDil's efficacy, and said they would prescribe it. These panelists suggested that Medco conduct an appropriately designed clinical trial of BiDil and reapply. Facing a 25% loss in stock value after the FDA rejection, Medco balked at another clinical trial and allowed BiDil's intellectual property rights to revert to Cohn.

Cohn, together with cardiologist Peter Carson, reanalyzed the original V-HeFT data, paying special attention to racial correlations. In 1999 Carson published "Racial Differences to Therapy for Heart Failure: Analysis of the Vasodilator Heart Failure Trials."[9] The salutary response to H/I of the 49 African American men in V-HeFT I convinced Cohn and Carson of BiDil's race-specific action. They applied for a new, race-specific patent on BiDil that was granted by the U.S. Patent and Trademark Office in 2002. The first non-race-specific methods patent for BiDil expired in 2007. This second, race-specific patent extended monopoly control over BiDil until 2020.

The same month that Carson's article appeared, NitroMed, a small pharmaceutical company focused on bringing BiDil and similar products to market, announced its acquisition of the intellectual property rights to BiDil from Cohn. In March of 2001, NitroMed picked up where Medco left off, beginning an FDA-approved, double-blind, placebo-controlled study to investigate BiDil's race specificity, the African-American Heart Failure Trial (A-HeFT). NitroMed enrolled approximately 1,000 people who "self-identified as black (defined as of African descent)" and hoped to demonstrate that BiDil was more effective than the placebo in treating heart failure in African Americans. In the summer of 2004, researchers halted A-HeFT prematurely: analysis of the initial data revealed 43% decreased mortality rate among patients on BiDil compared to those on placebo. To deny BiDil to study participants receiving placebos seemed unethical in the face of these dramatic results. The *New England Journal of Medicine* reported the A-HeFT results, in a paper co-authored by Jay Cohn and Peter Carson among others (including Keith Ferdinand, who also contributes to this volume), in November.[10]

Many patients, clinicians, and media outlets responded to the announcement of BiDil's apparently race-specific effectiveness with great fanfare. BiDil seemed, to many observers, to offer a "magic bullet" therapy for heart failure in African Americans. Given the glaring health disparities between black and white Americans, especially in cardiovascular morbidity and mortality, BiDil seemed revolutionary. If the study's results were accurate, and BiDil had a race-specific action, then the new formula of H/I might offer to increase individual survival and lower health disparities—implicitly increasing social justice in health care—in one stroke. Optimistic predictions about BiDil's clinical, social, and economic significance abounded. Financial analysts speculated that, if NitroMed received a race-specific approval for BiDil from the FDA, then the company could expect profits in excess of $825 million per year as some 750,000 African American heart failure patients switched to the new therapy.[11] Between July and December 2004 the value of NitroMed stock quadrupled.

Yet even as these glowing forecasts appeared, critics of BiDil emerged (including Jonathan Kahn and Susan Reverby of this issue). Skeptics questioned the design of the V-HeFT study, the analysis of the data, NitroMed's motivations in developing a hybrid compound rather than a novel drug, and worried about the larger implications of race-specific medicine.[12] Amidst a rising debate, the FDA's Advisory Council met to consider the promise and perils of BiDil in June 2005. The council evaluated the statistical studies behind BiDil's application and heard testimony from both supporters and critics. Although A-HeFT demonstrated the efficacy of BiDil in African Americans, it did not enroll any other populations and, as a result, it provided no data about race specificity. NitroMed's claim of race specificity continued simply to rely on Cohn and Carson's reanalysis of the V-HeFT data, which the FDA had deemed unconvincing in 1997. Meanwhile, Cohn himself had asserted that BiDil would work in people regardless of race. Despite this ambiguous picture, on June 23 the FDA approved BiDil as a medication specifically indicated for use in self-identified blacks.[13]

BiDil's approval cleared the way for NitroMed to begin marketing the drug. By the fall of 2005, BiDil ads featuring African American models began to appear in medical and popular journals. Shortly thereafter, the drug went on sale. By March of 2006, however, the predicted landslide of prescriptions had not materialized. In fact, NitroMed's Chief Executive Officer and Chief Business Officer both resigned as reports broke that the company had suffered a $108 million loss in the preceding year. Analysts claimed that BiDil's projected profits failed to materialize for two reasons: first, insurers were not reimbursing for BiDil because its less costly generic components, hydralazine and isosorbide dinitrate, were readily available; and second, NitroMed had failed to field an adequately large marketing force to popularize the drug.[14]

From Conference to Journal and Beyond

News of BiDil's disappointing launch hit just before our conference "Race, Pharmaceuticals, and Medical Technology" began. Yet it did not diminish the passion of debates among the scholars and the audience. Officials from NitroMed attended the conference and criticized its organizers for failing to invite a company representative to participate. Working with Keith Ferdinand, one of the authors of A-HeFT, and a local director of the NAACP, NitroMed officials led a spirited defense of the drug, its testing, and its clinical and social salience. They were met in lively debate by skeptics like Kahn and George Ellison who acknowledged that BiDil clearly works but remained unconvinced that its race specificity had been adequately documented.[15]

We hope that this collection of papers offers a nuanced analysis of these difficult social and scientific questions. Considering race-based medicine from numerous disciplinary perspectives—law, history, medicine, epidemiology, anthropology, and science studies—the papers converge on a number of inter-related themes. We have arranged them into four groups.

The first group of papers from George Ellison, Keith Ferdinand, Richard Tutton, and Jennifer Hamilton addresses pharmacogenetics from the stand-point of "evidence-based medicine," broadly construed. Ellison and his co-authors introduce the problem by critiquing the evidence on which claims of BiDil's race specific efficacy is based—both the trials that led to its approval, as well as the justification of that decision recently published by the FDA. Arguing that there actually is no credible evidence of race specificity, they identify both some of the factors that might have influenced the FDA's decision and the potential problems set by this precedent. Keith Ferdinand, one of the few A-HeFT authors without a monetary stake in NitroMed or BiDil, acknowledges these limitations but responds with a compelling pragmatic argument. Whether or not there is a race-specificity to BiDil's actions, it clearly does work in African Americans. The controversies should not prevent it from being used, along with all other possible treatments, to overcome the unequal burden of heart disease in African Americans.

Tutton and his co-authors move from statistical methods to investiga-tors' expectations, and how those expectations shape the design, conduct, and interpretation of biomedical experiments. Interviewing pharmacogeneti-cists, Tutton and his colleagues document how researchers' views of race as an analytic category colors their research conduct, and their beliefs about the prospect of race remaining as a meaningful biomedical construct. Taking up a parallel case, Hamilton examines the racial implications of the first large-scale investigation of human genetic variation, the International Haplotype Map (HapMap) Project. As geneticists use "geographical ancestry" as a category for analyzing the 0.1% genetic variation among humans, they risk, by their very methodology, reinscribing traditional ethno-racial categories in genetic biology—potentially revivifying and reifying the prejudices long associated with these categories. Read together, these four papers limn the broad contours of the debate about race and pharmaceutical development at the level of researchers, clinicians, and biostatisticians.

Widening the focus from the clinical and experimental Susan Reverby, Timothy Caulfield, Osagie Obasogie, and Wen Hua Kuo's essays place the results of evidence-based medical research in their broader social context. Reverby, who testified about BiDil before the FDA, juxtaposes BiDil's development and approval to the notorious United States Public Health Service's "Study of Untreated Syphilis in the Male Negro," the so-called "Tuskegee Experiment." According to Reverby, BiDil operates, in the shadow of Tuskegee, as a cultural artifact in three ways: first, as an acknowledgment that race influences biomedicine by acting as a "useful proxy" for underlying genetic causes; second, as a promise that, once technology improves, race will dissolve as a relevant analytic biomedical construct; and, third, as a guarantee that, until the abandonment of race and/or the solution of health disparities, something tangible is being done to rectify past abuses and present inequity. These tensions appeared clearly in media discussions of BiDil, as revealed by Caulfield and Harry's systematic analysis of newspaper coverage of the drug. Although the media is often critiqued for oversimplifying genetic technology and reifying race, Caulfield and Harry found healthy skepticism about race and biology, as well as nuanced discussions of the possible roles of race-based pharmaceutical in American society.

Appreciating the realities of market economics, racism, and efforts to increase social justice, Obasogie posits extending a legal doctrine—"strict scrutiny" of racial categories—to biomedical research. The United States Supreme Court has ruled that any legal recognition of race must withstand the most stringent analysis, establishing an unquestionably "rational relationship" between the use of race and a constitutional end, or else race is disallowed. Can a similarly strict standard be devised for and applied to biomedical research? Even if a strict scrutiny cognate is devised, Kuo's essay reminds us that an American standard may not attract sufficient support to govern international pharmaceutical development. Exploring the invocations of race at the International Conference on Harmonisation of Technical Requirements for Registration of Pharmaceuticals for Human Use between 1993 and 1999, Kuo highlights the conundrum created when Western notions of "race" collided with Japanese ideas of *minzoku*. In this case, conflicting cultural understandings of race's clinical relevance confounded efforts to standardize drug trials worldwide, impeding the ability of Western pharmaceutical companies to introduce their products into Asian markets. These four essays interrogate the social and cultural implications of racialized pharmaceutical development, suggesting historical, contemporary, and future ramifications of racial medicine.

In the third group of papers, Patricia Barton, Susan Smith, and Nadav Davidovitch relate three historical case studies of racial medicine. Barton analyzes how British military surgeons evaluated the racial implications of quinine therapy during the Raj. Explaining quinine's perceived differential effectiveness among Englishmen, Bengalis, and Rajputs presented a research question that might simultaneously clarify anti-malarial therapy and justify the colonial order's racial hierarchy. Smith recounts the American military's chemical weapons experiments during World War II, in which physicians predicted differential responses of white, black, Puerto Rican, and Japanese skin to mustard gas. Despite failing to document inter-group differences, these experiments did little to change attitudes about biological difference or curtail racialized research. Davidovitch and Avital Margalit chronicle the ethnic issues surrounding Israel's use of mass irradiation to control ringworm among North African immigrants, particularly analyzing the efforts of the government and survivors to control the memory of this episode. Perhaps counterintuitive from today's perspective, the use of ethnically inflected therapies by a population once subjected to the most extreme form of "racial medicine" points to the power of difference to influence action. These three essays document the ubiquity and durability of racial medicine in the Western world, suggesting the inextricably intertwined nature of science and social culture. We are left to ponder whether race-neutral science is possible in a society dogged by racial bias.

In a partial answer to the question "Whither race, research, and medicine?" the final essays from Anne Pollock and Dorothy Roberts ask readers to reconceptualize race and reconsider its influence on the development and marketing of pharmaceuticals. Pollock, too, offers reflections on how pharmaceuticals interact with notions of socio-political identity, taking the development of anti-hypertensive thiazides as a case study. An older, proven therapy, thiazides have been invoked in new debates about the possible evolutionary pressures the middle passage exerted on Africans and, by extension, their African American progeny. At the same time, thiazides have been touted as the best therapy for hypertension, especially efficacious in blacks. Thus, thiazides serve as a marker for African American identity—invoked by multiple parties to multifarious ends. Pollock reminds us that racialized medicines are not simply products of the pharmaceutical companies, but are themselves productive of new, evolving concepts of race and identity. Roberts also underscores the imbricated nature of race as a biomedical construct and a social identity, highlighting the socio-political implications of continuing to use race as a proxy for genetic information. Rather than focus on researchers and their caveats about using race as a category of analysis, Roberts considers the impact of race-based and racially inflected research on the public discourse about race and social justice. In her opinion, the current uses of race in biomedical research confuse attempts to develop an anti-racist agenda, simultaneously endangering African Americans' socio-economic status and justifying "colorblind" social policies that avoid dealing with underlying structural inequities. Only by attending to pharmaceuticals' ability to influence identity, Roberts and Pollock imply, can we hope to control the social implications of racialized medicine.

Racial medicine has returned from history's dustbin to today's examination room and tomorrow's front page. BiDil's economic prospects, which peaked soon after its approval by the FDA, crashed by March of 2006, and have remained dismal ever since. Nevertheless, belief in the drug's necessity and efficacy—stemming in large part from its ability to shape socio-political identity and its promise as an agent for increasing social justice—led the NAACP's Boston chapter to launch a campaign protesting Medicaid's refusal to provide reimbursement to patients prescribed BiDil. At the same time, news that NitroMed donated $1.5 million to the NAACP raised the specter of a quid pro quo, with the social justice organization recast in the unlikely role as industry flack, drummer for pharmaceutical sales.[16] Although other "race-based" drugs have yet to follow BiDil's complicated course from prospect to prescription, a series of other race-based treatments have proliferated, from vitamins to hair- and skin-care products. The Patent and Trademark Office has also seen an upsurge in race-based patent submissions, so more products will surely follow. Meanwhile, NitroMed's experience has spawned an unanticipated form of "copy-cat" drug development: methods-patent protected compounds of two generic drugs being released as a "new" drug. This strategy emphasizes pharmaceutical companies' attention to the bottom line, promising more "new" and expensive drugs, and fewer truly novel medications developed in the name of greater therapeutic benefits.

Whether race-based medicine will continue its resurgence as a temporary way-stop on the path to individualized pharmacogenomic therapy remains to be seen. As this collection of essays suggests, however, the ramifications of BiDil's development, approval, and marketing have had far-reaching effects that will continue into the foreseeable future.

References

1. S. Sate, "I Am a Racial Profiling Doctor: Illness Isn't Colorblind. So Why Is It Taboo for Doctors to Take Note of a Patient's Race?" *New York Times Magazine,* May 5, 2002, pp. 56–58, at 58.

2. M. Witten, "Humpy Dumpty," *House MD, Fox* Television, aired September 27, 2005. . . . I learned of this episode in L. Braun, A. Fausto-Sterling, D. Fullwiley, E. M. Hammonds, A. Nelson, W. Quivers, S. M. Reverby, and A. E. Shields, "Racial Categories in Medical Practice: How Useful Are They?" *PLoS Medicine* 4, no. 9 (September 2007): 1423–1428, at 1423.

3. J. H. Warner, "The Idea of Southern Medical Distinctiveness: Medical Knowledge and Practice in the Old South," in J. W. Leavitt and R. L. Numbers, eds., *Sickness and Health in America,* 2nd ed. (Madison: University of Wisconsin Press, 1985): 53–70.

4. D. S. Jones, *Rationalizing Epidemics: Meanings and Uses of American Indian Mortality Since 1600* (Cambridge: Harvard University Press, 2004): at 177.

5. W. J. Clinton, "Remarks on the Completion of the First Survey of the Entire Human Genome Project," June 26, 2000, National Archives and Records Administration. . . .

6. W. Kalow, H. W. Goedde, and D. P. Agarwal, ed., *Ethnic Differences in Reactions to Drugs and Xenobiotics* (New York: Alan R. lass, Inc., 1986).

7. A. Pollock, "Medicating Race: Heart Disease and Durable Preoccupations with Difference," Ph.D. Dissertation, Massachusetts Institute of Technology, 2007; see also the article by Keith C. Ferdinand in this issue.

8. This history largely follows the narrative outlined in J. Kahn, "How a Drug Becomes Ethnic," *Yale Journal of Health Policy, Law, and Ethics* 4, no. 1 (2004): 1–46.

9. P. Carson et al., "Racial Differences in Response to Therapy for Heart Failure: Analysis of the Vasodilator-Heart Failure Trials," *Journal of Cardiac Failure* 5, no. 3 (1999): 178–187.

10. A. L. Taylor et al., "Combination of Isosorbide Dinitrate and Hydralazine in Blacks with Heart Failure," *New England Journal of Medicine* 351, no. 20 (November 11, 2004): 2049–2057.

11. S. Saul, "2 Officials Quit among Slow Sales of Heart Drug for African Americans," *New York Times,* March 22, 2006.

12. J. Kahn, "How a Drug Becomes 'Ethnic': Law, Commerce, and the Production of Racial Categories in Medicine," *Yale Journal of Health Policy, Law, and Ethics* 4, no. 1 (2004): 1–46; P. Sankar and J. Kahn, "BiDil: Race Medicine or Race Marketing?" *Health Affairs,* Web exclusive (October 11, 2005): W5-455-W5-463; J. Kahn, "BiDil: False Promises," *GeneWatch* 18, no. 6 (2005): e-version; J. Kahn, "Exploiting Race in Drug Development: BiDil's Interim Model of Pharmacogenomics," *Social Studies of Science* (forthcoming 2008).

13. D. Gallene, "Heart Pill Intended Only for Blacks Sparks Debate," *Los Angles Times,* June 16, 2005.

14. See Saul, *supra* note 11.

15. In 2007, the Center for the Study of Diversity hosted a conference entitled "The Business of Race and Science." Even though we steered clear of BiDil when accepting papers, BiDil again dominated the discussions. Defenders of BiDil suggested that social scientists, by casting doubt on the biological validity of the concept of race, had enabled the Center for Medicare and Medicaid Studies to withhold reimbursement for BiDil. From their perspective, we seemed to want to kill black people by denying them access to a beneficial drug. For a discussion of this exchange and its rhetoric, see Pollock, *supra* note 7, at 306–311.

16. K. J. Winstein, "NAACP Presses U.S. on Heart Drug," *Wall Street Journal,* January 25, 2007.

POSTSCRIPT

Should Doctors Prescribe Drugs Based on Race?

Race continues to be a contentious issue among medical researchers and practitioners Recent discoveries linking gene variants as the cause of disease have also complicated the issue. In more complex illnesses, the role of race is not as clear as other biological, environmental, cultural, social, and economic factors that affect disease. It appears that a mutation of a single gene is sufficient and necessary to cause some diseases in specific populations and not in others, possibly justifying the research and development into race-specific drugs such as BiDil. BiDil, a combination in a single pill of two generic drugs, has been used for more than a decade to treat heart failure in people of all races and ethnicities. Critics argue that no strong evidence exists to indicate the drug's actions are better or different in African Americans. While the jury is still out on BiDil, research continues into the development of other race-specific drugs. Further readings include "Race in a Bottle" (*Scientific American*, August 2007) and "BiDil for Heart Failure in Black Patients: The US Food and Drug Administrative Perspective" (*Annals of Internal Medicine*, January 2, 2007).

While appropriate treatment for minority patients is a laudable goal, many researchers believe lack of quality basic care is more salient. See "Race, Gender, and Mortality in Adults ≥65 Years of Age with Incident Heart Failure (from the Cardiovascular Health Study)" in the *American Journal of Cardiology* (April, 2009). In "Unequal Treatment in the ER," Josh Fischman discusses a study that found that African American men with chest pain are 25 to 30 percent less likely to receive tests such as a chest X-ray to detect a heart attack than white males with the same symptoms (*U.S. News & World Report*, February 12, 2007). Other articles that address the issue of disparity in health care, as opposed to disease incidence, include the following: "Impact of Health Service Use on Racial Differences in Mortality among the Elderly" (*Research on Aging*, May 2007); "Influence of Race on Inpatient Treatment Intensity at the End of Life" (*Journal of General Internal Medicine*, March 2007); "Disparities in Antidepressant Treatment in Medical Elderly Diagnosed with Depression" (*Journal of the American Geriatrics Society*, March 2005); "Racial and Ethnic Health Disparities and the Unfinished Civil Rights Agenda" (*Health Affairs*, March/April 2005); "Association of Race/Ethnicity with Emergency Department Wait Times" (*Pediatrics*, March 2005); "National Hispanic Conference Focuses on Disparities in Health Care" (*Managed Healthcare Info*, August 26, 2002); "Racial and Ethnic Disparities in the Receipt of Cancer Treatment" (*Journal of the National Cancer Institute*, March 6, 2002); and "Racist Health Care?" (*Florida Law Review*, July 1997).

ISSUE 7

Should Embryonic Stem Cell Research Be Permitted?

YES: Jeffrey Hart, from "NR on Stem Cells: The Magazine Is Wrong," *National Review* (April 19, 2004)

NO: Ramesh Ponnuru, from "NR on Stem Cells: The Magazine Is Right," *National Review* (April 19, 2004)

ISSUE SUMMARY

YES: Professor Jeffrey Hart contends there are many benefits to stem cell research and that a ban on funded cloning research is unjustified.

NO: Writer Ramesh Ponnuru argues that a single-celled human embryo is a living organism that directs its own development and should not be used for experimentation.

Research using human stem cells could one day lead to cures for diabetes, restore mobility to paralyzed individuals, and may offer treatment for diseases such as Alzheimer's and Parkinson's. It may be possible for humans to regenerate body parts, or create new cells to treat disease. Stem cells, which have the potential to develop into many different cell types, serve as a type of repair system for the body. They can theoretically divide without limit to replenish other cells as long as the person or animal is alive. When a stem cell divides, each new cell has the potential to either remain a stem cell or become another type of cell with a more specialized function, such as a brain or blood cell.

Two important characteristics of stem cells differentiate them from other types of cells. One, they are unspecialized cells that renew themselves for long periods through cell division. Two, under certain conditions, they can be become cells with special functions, such as heart cells or the insulin-producing cells of the pancreas. Researchers mainly work with two kinds of stem cells from animals and humans: embryonic stem cells and adult stem cells, which have different functions and characteristics. Scientists learned different ways to get or derive stem cells from early rodent embryos over 20 years ago.

Detailed study of the biology of mouse stem cells led to the discovery, in 1998, of how to isolate stem cells from human embryos and grow the cells in the lab. The embryos used in these studies were created for infertility purposes through in vitro fertilization procedures and when no longer needed for that purpose, they were donated for research with the informed consent of the donor.

Researchers have hypothesized that embryonic stem cells may, at some point in the future, become the basis for treating diseases such as Parkinson's disease, diabetes, and heart disease. Scientists need to study stem cells to learn about their important properties and what makes them different from specialized cell types. As researchers discover more about stem cells, it may become possible to use the cells not just in cell-based therapies but also for screening new drugs and preventing birth defects.

Researching stem cells will allow scientists to understand how they transform into the array of specialized cells that make us human. Some of the most serious medical conditions, such as cancer and birth defects, are due to events that occur somewhere in this process. A better understanding of normal cell development will allow scientists to understand and possibly correct the errors that cause these conditions. Another potential application of stem cells is making cells and tissues for medical therapies. A type of stem cell, pluripotents, offers the possibility of a renewable source of replacement cells and tissues to treat a myriad of diseases, conditions, and disabilities including Parkinson's and Alzheimer's diseases, spinal cord injury, stroke, burns, heart disease, diabetes, and arthritis.

At present, no research on human embryos can be supported by government money. The Bush administration did not support embryonic stem cell research, which they believed to be experimentation on potential human life. As a result, researchers must rely on funding from business, private foundations, and other sources. Although the potential for stem cells is great, there is not universal support for this research. In the following selections, Jeffrey Hart, a senior editor at *National Review,* contends that there are many benefits to stem cell research and that a federal ban on funded experimentation is unjustified. Ramesh Ponnuru argues that stem cell research is amoral because it involves the use of human embryos.

YES

Jeffrey Hart

NR on Stem Cells:
The Magazine Is Wrong

NATIONAL REVIEW has consistently taken a position on stem-cell research that requires some discussion here. Three editorials early this year were based on the assertion that a single fertilized cell is a "human being." This premise—and the conclusions drawn from it—require challenge on conservative grounds, as they have never been approved by American law or accepted as common convention.

The first 2004 editorial appeared in the January 26 issue, and made a series of assertions about recent legislation in New Jersey. It included the notion that it is now "possible" to create a human embryo there—through cloning—that, at age eight months, could be sold for research. But this dystopian fantasy could become fact in no American jurisdiction.

In the March 8 NR we read another editorial; this one achieved greater seriousness. Still, it called for a "new law" that "would say that human beings, however small and young, may not be treated instrumentally and may not be deliberately destroyed."

In all of the editorials, we are asked to accept the insistent dogma that a single fertilized cell is a "human being, however small and young," and is not to be "deliberately destroyed."

This demand grates—because such "human beings" are deliberately destroyed all the time, and such "mass homicide" arouses no public outcry. In fact, there are about 100,000 fertilized cells now frozen in maternity clinics. These are the inevitable, and so deliberate, by-products of in vitro fertilization, accepted by women who cannot conceive children naturally. No wonder there has been no outcry: Where reality shows medical waste that would otherwise lie useless, NR's characterization of these frozen embryos as "small and young" makes one think of the Gerber baby.

The entire NR case against stem-cell research rests, like a great inverted pyramid, on the single assertion that these cells are "human beings"—a claim that is not self-evidently true. Even when the naked eye is aided by a microscope, these cells—"zygotes," to use the proper terminology—do not look like human beings. That resemblance does not emerge even as the zygote grows into the hundred-cell organism, about the size of a pinhead, called a "blastocyst." This is the level of development at which stem cells are produced: The researcher is not interested in larger embryos, much less full-blown, for-sale fetuses.

I myself have never met anyone who bites into an apple, gazes upon the seeds there, and sees a grove of apple trees. I think we must conclude, if we are to use language precisely, that the single fertilized cell is a *developing* or *potential* human being—many of which are destroyed during in vitro fertilization, and even in the course of natural fertilization. But just as a seed—a *potential* apple tree—is no orchard, a *potential* child is not yet a human being.

There is more to this matter than biology: In question is NR's very theory of—and approach to—politics. Classic and valuable arguments in this magazine have often taken the form of Idea (or paradigm) versus Actuality. Here are a few such debates that have shaped the magazine, a point of interest especially to new readers.

Very early in NR's history, the demand for indisputably conservative candidates gave way to William F. Buckley Jr.'s decisive formulation that NR should prefer "the most conservative electable candidate." WFB thus corrected his refusal to vote for Eisenhower, who was at least more conservative than Stevenson. Senior editor James Burnham, a realist, also voted for Ike; in his decision, Actuality won out.

In the 1956 crisis in Hungary, Burnham's profoundly held Idea about the necessity for Liberation in Europe contrasted with Eisenhower's refusal, based on Actuality, to intervene in a landlocked nation where Soviet ground and air superiority was decisive. But later on, Burnham, choosing Actuality over the Idea, saw much sooner than most conservatives that Nixon's containment and "Vietnamization" could not work in South Vietnam, which was a sieve. The "peace" that was "at hand" in 1972 was the peace of the grave.

A final example: In the late 1960s, senior editor Brent Bozell's theoretical demand for perfect Catholic morality—argued in a very fine exchange with another senior editor, Frank Meyer—was rejected by NR.

Thus the tension between Idea and Actuality has a long tradition at NR, revived by this question of stem cells. Ultimately, American constitutional decision-making rests upon the "deliberate consent" of a self-governing people. Such decision-making by consensus usually accords no participant everything he desires, and thus is non-utopian. Just try an absolute, ideological ban on in vitro fertilization, for example, and observe the public response.

In fact, an editorial (NR, August 6, 2001) has held that even in vitro fertilization is hard to justify morally. Understandably, NR has soft-pedaled this opinion: The magazine's view that a single cell is a "human being" has never been expressed in or embraced by American law. It represents an absolutization of the "human being" claim for a single cell. It stands in contradiction to the "deliberate sense" theory NR has heretofore espoused. And, at this very moment, it is being contradicted in the Actual world of research practice.

Recently, for instance, a Harvard researcher produced 17 stem-cell "lines" from the aforementioned leftover frozen cells. The researcher's goal is not homicide, of course, but the possible cure of dreadful diseases. It seems to me that the prospect of eliminating horrible, disabling ailments justifies, morally, using cells that are otherwise doomed. Morality requires the weighing of results, and the claim to a "right to life" applies in both directions. Those lifting that phrase from the Declaration of Independence do not often add "liberty and the pursuit of happiness," there given equal standing as "rights"—rights that might be more widely enjoyed in the wake of stem-cell advances.

As I said earlier, the evolution of NR as a magazine that matters has involved continuing arguments between Idea and Actuality. Here, the Idea that a single fertilized cell is a human being, and that destroying one is a homicide, is not sustainable. That is the basis—the only basis—for NR's position thus far on stem-cell research. Therefore NR's position on the whole issue is unsustainable.

Buckley has defined conservatism as the "politics of reality." That is the strength of conservatism, a Burkean strength, and an anti-utopian one. I have never heard a single cytologist affirming the proposition that a single cell is a "human being"; here, Actuality will prevail, as usual.

In recommending against federal funding for most stem-cell research, President Bush stated that 60 lines of stem cells that already exist are adequate for current research. The National Institutes of Health has said that this is incorrect. There are in fact 15 lines, and these are not adequate even for current research. The president was misinformed. But Actuality is gaining ground nonetheless: Harvard University has recently announced the formation of a $100 million Harvard Stem Cell Institute. And Harvard physicians are conducting community-education programs to counter misinformation (Reuters, March 3): "Scientists at Harvard University announced on Wednesday that they had created 17 batches of stem cells from human embryos in defiance of efforts by President Bush to limit such research. 'What we have done is to make use of previously frozen human fertilized eggs that otherwise were going to be discarded,' [Dr. Douglas] Melton told reporters in a telephone briefing."

Not unexpectedly, and after losing one of its top scientists in the field to Cambridge (England), the University of California, Berkeley, announced that it was pursuing stem-cell research. Other UCs also made such announcements, and California state funding has been promised. It is easy to see that major research universities across the nation—and in any nation that can afford them—will either follow or lose their top scientists in this field. Experience shows that it is folly to reject medical investigation, a folly the universities and private-sector researchers will be sure to avoid.

Weak in theory, and irrelevant in practice, opposition to stem-cell research is now an irrelevance across the board; on this matter, even the president has made himself irrelevant. All this was to be expected: The only surprise has been the speed with which American research is going forward. It is pleasant to have the private sector intervene, as at Harvard, not to mention the initiatives of the states. In practical terms, this argument is over. *National Review* should not make itself irrelevant by trying to continue it.

Ramesh Ponnuru

NO

NR on Stem Cells:
The Magazine Is Right

NATIONAL REVIEW does not oppose stem-cell research. It approves of research on stem cells taken from adult somatic cells, or from umbilical cords. It opposes stem-cell research only when obtaining those cells destroys embryonic human beings, whether these beings are created through cloning, in vitro fertilization, or the old-fashioned way. Jeff Hart challenges NR's stance for three reasons: He disputes the idea that single-celled human embryos are human beings, he questions the prudence of advancing that idea, and he thinks the humanitarian goal of the research justifies the means.

Professor Hart starts his argument by noting that American law has never treated the single-celled embryo as a human being. This is true. But it never treated it as anything else, either. What would American law have had to say about the embryo in 1826, or, for that matter, in 1952?

The single-celled human embryo is neither dead nor inanimate. It is a living organism, not a functional part of another organism, and it directs its own development, according to its genetic template, through the embryonic, fetal, infant, and subsequent stages of development. (The terms "blastocyst," "adolescent," and "newborn" denote stages of development in a being of the same type, not different types of beings.) It is a *Homo sapiens,* not a member of some other species—which is why it is valuable to scientists in the first place. Strictly speaking, it is not even an "it": It has a sex.

"Even when the naked eye is aided by a microscope," writes Professor Hart, early embryos "do not look like human beings." Actually, they look *exactly* like human beings—the way human beings look at that particular stage of development. We all looked like that, at that age. Professor Hart believes that science can open up whole worlds of knowledge and possibility to us. He should be willing to entertain the possibility that among the insights we have gained is the revelation that human beings at their beginnings look like nothing we have ever seen before.

Professor Hart notes that many embryos die naturally. And so? Infant mortality rates have been very high in some societies; old people die all the time. That does not mean it is permissible to kill infants or old people.

I should also comment about the New Jersey law that makes it legally possible to create a human embryo through cloning, develop it through the fetal stage, and sell it for research purposes at eight months. Professor Hart writes that "this dystopian fantasy could become fact in no American jurisdiction." Sadly, this is untrue: In most American jurisdictions, no law on the books would prevent this scenario from taking place.

In the past, scientists have been quite interested in doing research on aborted fetuses. Right now, the early embryo is a hotter research subject. But neither Professor Hart nor I can rule out the possibility that research on cloned fetuses will be thought, in a few years, to hold great promise. If scientists want to conduct such research, the only legal obstacles will be the statutes of those states that have banned human cloning—the very laws that NR favors. New Jersey has brought this dystopia one step closer.

It would be possible for Professor Hart to concede that the history of a body begins with its conception—that we were all once one-celled organisms, in the sense that "we" were never a sperm cell and an egg cell—while still claiming that it would have been morally defensible to destroy us at that time. Our intrinsic moral worth came later, he might argue: when we developed sentience, abstract reasoning, relationships with others, or some other distinguishing attribute. According to this viewpoint, human beings as such have no intrinsic right to life; many human beings enjoy that right only by virtue of qualities they happen to possess.

The implications of this theory, however, extend beyond the womb. Infants typically lack the immediately exercisable capacity for abstract mental reasoning, too—which is how Peter Singer and others have justified infanticide. It is impossible to identify a non-arbitrary point at which there is "enough" sentience or meaningful interaction to confer a right to life. It is also impossible to explain why some people do not have basic rights more or less than other people depending on how much of the accidental quality they possess. In other words, the foundation of human equality is destroyed as soon as we suggest that private actors may treat some members of the human species as though they were mere things. The claim in the Declaration of Independence that "all men are created equal" becomes a self-evident lie.

Life comes before liberty and the pursuit of happiness in that declaration, and at no point is it suggested that liberty includes a right to kill, or that happiness may be pursued through homicide. Morality often "requires the weighing of results," as Professor Hart writes. But we would not kill one five-year-old child for the certain prospect of curing cancer, let alone the mere possibility—because the act would be intrinsically immoral. Or would we? Professor Hart writes that it is "folly to reject medical investigation." So much for restrictions on human experimentation.

Apple seeds are not a grove of trees. An infant is not an adult, either, just a potential adult, but that doesn't mean you can kill it. Professor Hart objects to the use of the words "young" and "small" to characterize the entities whose destruction we are debating. Since the argument for terminating them turns precisely on their having 100 cells or fewer (they're small), and on their not yet having advanced to later stages of human development (they're young), it's hard to see his point.

Let me turn now to the question of the politics of Actuality. NR is, in principle, against the intentional destruction of human embryos. But we have been quite mindful of political circumstances. As Professor Hart notes, we have not said much about regulating the practices of fertility clinics. (He faults us for both running wild with ideas and prudently declining to do so; also, freezing something is not the same as destroying it.) Prudence has kept us from urging the president to fight for a ban on all research that destroys human embryos. We have principally asked for two things: a ban on governmental funding of such research, and a ban on human cloning—even suggesting a simple moratorium on cloning as a compromise. We are not calling, to pursue one of Professor Hart's analogies, for an invasion of Hungary here. But neither are we suggesting that we are indifferent to the Soviet domination of Eastern Europe.

Our position on cloning is not that of some political fringe: It is the position of President Bush. It is the position of the House of Representatives, which has twice voted to ban human cloning. It is a position that, depending on the wording of the poll question, somewhere between one-third and two-thirds of the public shares. It is the position of the governments of Canada and Germany. NR has fought lonelier battles.

We are sometimes told that, in a pluralistic society in which many people have different views about such matters as the moral status of the human embryo, we cannot impose public policies that assume the correctness of some views over others. I cannot agree. Some people will not accept the justice of a ban on cloning for research; few policies command the full assent of all people of good will. But disagreement about the requirements of justice is no excuse for failing to do it.

POSTSCRIPT

Should Embryonic Stem Cell Research Be Permitted?

Many scientists believe that human embryonic stem cell research could one day lead to a cure for a variety of diseases that plague humans. While a cure for diabetes, cancer, Parkinson's, and other diseases would greatly benefit humanity, many believe that it is amoral to use human embryos for this purpose. These individuals believe that every human being begins as a single-cell zygote, and develops into an embryo, fetus, and then is born. To destroy the embryonic stem cell is to destroy a potential life, which many cannot justify. The Bush administration has supported these beliefs and enacted a moratorium on federal funding for embryonic stem cell research.

In "Distinctly Human: The When, Where & How of Life's Beginnings," John Collins Harvey (*Commonweal*, February 8, 2002) asserts that the human embryo is a living human being from the moment of conception. As such, it should never be used as an object or considered as a means to an end. It should not be killed so that parts of it can be used for the benefit of another person. That sentiment is echoed by William Sanders in "Embryology: Inconvenient Facts" (*First Things*, December 2004), who believes that adult human stem cells have been proven to have great value in the invention of new and better medical treatments but the value of embryonic stem cells is theoretical and cannot justify killing an embryo. In "Many Say Adult Stem Cell Reports Overplayed" (*Journal of the American Medical Association*, 2001), the value of adult stem cells is debated. See also: "Ignore the Ethics of Stem Cell Research and They'll Pass You By" (*National Catholic Reporter*, June 16, 2004); "Human Embryonic Stem Cells and Respect for Life" (*Journal of Medical Ethics*, 2000); "Science Unstemmed" (*The American Spectator*, February 2005); "No to Embryonic Stem Cells" (*Southern Medical Journal*, December 2006); and "The Stem Cell Debate" (*American*, November 13, 2006).

For a different viewpoint, see "The Gift of a Cure" (*U.S. News & World Report*, May 21, 2007); "More Political Science" (*Newsweek*, January 22, 2007); "Adult Stem Cells Won't Do" (*New Scientist*, March 10, 2007); "Research and Destroy: How the Religious Right Promotes Its Own 'Experts' to Combat Mainstream Science" (*The Washington Monthly*, October 2004); "Researchers Make the Case for Human Embryonic Stem Cell Research" (*The Journal of the American Medical Association*, August 18, 2004); "Embryonic Stem Cell Research: The Case For" (*National Medicine*, 2001); and "Stem Cells: Science, Policy, and Ethics" (*The Journal of Clinical Investigation*, November 2004). Also see "Human Stem Cell Research: The Mission to Change Federal Policy" (*JDRF*, Fall 2004). This article supports stem cell research to benefit diabetics. "Stem Cells to Fix the Heart" (*Fortune*, November 29, 2004) addresses the use of stem cells to repair damaged hearts and suggests that in the future, there will be no need for heart transplants with the use of embryonic stem cells.

For an overview of stem cell research, see "Stem Cells—Hope and Reality" (*Total Health*, January/February 2007); "An Overview of Stem Cell Research and Regulatory Issues" (*Mayo Clinic Proceedings*, 2003); "Stem Cells—A Beginner's Guide" (*Social Alternatives*, Summer 2003); and "Demystifying Stem Cells" (*The Saturday Evening Post*, November/December 2004).

Internet References . . .

Ethics in Medicine: Spirituality and Medicine

This site offers insight into the doctor's involvement in his or her patient's spiritual beliefs. Issues addressed include taking a "spiritual history" of the patient, the importance of attending to spirituality in medicine, and what role the physician's personal beliefs should play in the doctor–patient relationship.

http://depts.washington.edu/bioethx/topics/spirit.html

National Institutes of Health: National Institute on Drug Abuse

Offers information on drug abuse directed at a variety of constituents: professionals, researchers, teachers, parents, students, and young adults.

http://www.drugabuse.gov/nidahome.html

Web of Addictions

The Web of Addictions site is dedicated to providing accurate information about alcohol and other drug addictions. The site was developed to provide data about drugs of abuse and to provide a resource for teachers, students, and others who needed factual information about abused drugs.

http://www.well.com/user/woa

Mind-Body Relationship

*H*umans have long sought to extend life, eliminate disease, and prevent sickness. In modern times, people depend on technology to develop creative and innovative ways to improve health. However, as cures for diseases such as AIDS, cancer, and heart disease continue to elude scientists and doctors, many people question whether or not modern medicine has reached a plateau in improving health. As a result, over the last decade, an emphasis has been placed on prevention as a way to maintain wellness. Prayer is a way many individuals attempt to prevent and control illness.

- Should Addiction to Drugs Be Labeled a Brain Disease?
- Do Religion and Prayer Benefit Health?

ISSUE 8

Should Addiction to Drugs Be Labeled a Brain Disease?

YES: Alan I. Leshner, from "Addiction Is a Brain Disease," *Issues in Science and Technology* (Spring 2001)

NO: Sally L. Satel, from "The Fallacies of No-Fault Addiction," *The Public Interest* (Winter 1999)

ISSUE SUMMARY

YES: Alan I. Leshner, director of the National Institute on Drug Abuse at the National Institutes of Health, believes that addiction to drugs and alcohol is not a behavioral condition but a treatable disease.

NO: Psychiatrist Sally L. Satel counters that labeling addiction a chronic and relapsing brain disease is propaganda and that most addicts are the instigators of their own addiction.

There are many different theories about why some individuals become addicted to alcohol or other drugs. Historically, drug and alcohol dependency has been viewed as either a disease or a moral failing. In more recent years, other theories of addiction have been developed, including behavioral, genetic, sociocultural, and psychological theories.

The view that drug addiction and alcoholism are moral failings maintains that abusing drugs is voluntary behavior that the user chooses to do. Users choose to overindulge in such a way that they create suffering for themselves and others. American history is marked by repeated and failed government efforts to control this abuse by eliminating drug and alcohol use with legal sanctions, such as the enactment of Prohibition in the late 1920s and the punishment of alcoholics and drug users via jail sentences and fines. However, there seem to be several contradictions to this behavioral model of addiction. Addiction may be a complex condition that is caused by multiple factors, including environment, biology, and other factors. It is not totally clear that addiction is voluntary behavior. And from a historical perspective, punishing alcoholics and drug addicts has been ineffective.

In the United States today, the primary theory for understanding the causes of addiction is the disease model rather than the moral model. Borrowing from the modern mental health movement, addiction as a disease has been promoted by mental health advocates who tried to change the public's perception of severe mental illness. Diseases like bipolar disorder and schizophrenia were defined as the result of brain abnormalities rather than environmental factors or poor parenting. Likewise, addiction was not a moral weakness but a brain disorder that could be treated. In 1995, the National Institute of Drug Addiction (NIDA) supported the idea that drug addiction was a type of brain disorder. Following NIDA's support, the concept of addiction as a brain disease has become more widely accepted.

This model has been advocated by the medical and alcohol treatment communities as well as self-help groups such as Alcoholics Anonymous and Narcotics Anonymous. The disease model implies that addiction is not the result of voluntary behavior or lack of self-control; it is caused by biological factors, which are treatable. Although there are somewhat different interpretations of this theory, it generally refers to addiction as an organic brain syndrome with biological and genetic origins rather than voluntary and behavioral origins.

Alan Leshner believes that taking drugs causes changes in neurons in the central nervous system that compel the individual to use drugs. These neurological changes, which are not reversible, force addicts to continue to take drugs. Psychiatrist Sally Satel disagrees. She believes that most addicts are not innocent victims of chronic disease but individuals who are responsible for their illness and recovery.

YES ↵
Alan I. Leshner

Addiction Is a Brain Disease

The United States is stuck in its drug abuse metaphors and in polarized arguments about them. Everyone has an opinion. One side insists that we must control supply, the other that we must reduce demand. People see addiction as either a disease or as a failure of will. None of this bumpersticker analysis moves us forward. The truth is that we will make progress in dealing with drug issues only when our national discourse and our strategies are as complex and comprehensive as the problem itself.

A core concept that has been evolving with scientific advances over the past decade is that drug addiction is a brain disease that develops over time as a result of the initially voluntary behavior of using drugs. The consequence is virtually uncontrollable compulsive drug craving, seeking, and use that interferes with, if not destroys, an individual's functioning in the family and in society. This medical condition demands formal treatment.

We now know in great detail the brain mechanisms through which drugs acutely modify mood, memory, perception, and emotional states. Using drugs repeatedly over time changes brain structure and function in fundamental and long-lasting ways that can persist long after the individual stops using them. Addiction comes about through an array of neuroadaptive changes and the laying down and strengthening of new memory connections in various circuits in the brain. We do not yet know all the relevant mechanisms, but the evidence suggests that those long-lasting brain changes are responsible for the distortions of cognitive and emotional functioning that characterize addicts, particularly including the compulsion to use drugs that is the essence of addiction. It is as if drugs have highjacked the brain's natural motivational control circuits, resulting in drug use becoming the sole, or at least the top, motivational priority for the individual. Thus, the majority of the biomedical community now considers addiction, in its essence, to be a brain disease: a condition caused by persistent changes in brain structure and function.

This brain-based view of addiction has generated substantial controversy, particularly among people who seem able to think only in polarized ways. Many people erroneously still believe that biological and behavioral explanations are alternative or competing ways to understand phenomena, when in fact they are complementary and integratable. Modern science has taught that it is much too simplistic to set biology in opposition to behavior or to pit

From *California Society of Addiction Medicine Legislative Day Information Book,* February 1, 2006, pp. 92–98. Published by the National Institute on Drug Abuse.

willpower against brain chemistry. Addiction involves inseparable biological and behavioral components. It is the quintessential biobehavioral disorder.

Many people also erroneously still believe that drug addiction is simply a failure of will or of strength of character. Research contradicts that position. However, the recognition that addiction is a brain disease does not mean that the addict is simply a hapless victim. Addiction begins with the voluntary behavior of using drugs, and addicts must participate in and take some significant responsibility for their recovery. Thus, having this brain disease does not absolve the addict of responsibility for his or her behavior, but it does explain why an addict cannot simply stop using drugs by sheer force of will alone. It also dictates a much more sophisticated approach to dealing with the array of problems surrounding drug abuse and addiction in our society.

The Essence of Addiction

The entire concept of addiction has suffered greatly from imprecision and misconception. In fact, if it were possible, it would be best to start all over with some new, more neutral term. The confusion comes about in part because of a now archaic distinction between whether specific drugs are "physically" or "psychologically" addicting. The distinction historically revolved around whether or not dramatic physical withdrawal symptoms occur when an individual stops taking a drug; what we in the field now call "physical dependence."

However, 20 years of scientific research has taught that focusing on this physical versus psychological distinction is off the mark and a distraction from the real issues. From both clinical and policy perspectives, it actually does not matter very much what physical withdrawal symptoms occur. Physical dependence is not that important, because even the dramatic withdrawal symptoms of heroin and alcohol addiction can now be easily managed with appropriate medications. Even more important, many of the most dangerous and addicting drugs, including methamphetamine and crack cocaine, do not produce very severe physical dependence symptoms upon withdrawal.

What really matters most is whether or not a drug causes what we now know to be the essence of addiction: uncontrollable, compulsive drug craving, seeking, and use, even in the face of negative health and social consequences. This is the crux of how the Institute of Medicine, the American Psychiatric Association, and the American Medical Association define addiction and how we all should use the term. It is really only this compulsive quality of addiction that matters in the long run to the addict and to his or her family and that should matter to society as a whole. Compulsive craving that overwhelms all other motivations is the root cause of the massive health and social problems associated with drug addiction. In updating our national discourse on drug abuse, we should keep in mind this simple definition: Addiction is a brain disease expressed in the form of compulsive behavior. Both developing and recovering from it depend on biology, behavior, and social context.

It is also important to correct the common misimpression that drug use, abuse, and addiction are points on a single continuum along which one slides back and forth over time, moving from user to addict, then back to occasional user, then back to addict. Clinical observation and more formal research studies support the view that, once addicted, the individual has moved into a different state of being. It is as if a threshold has been crossed. Very few people appear able to successfully return to occasional use after having been truly addicted. Unfortunately, we do not yet have a clear biological or behavioral marker of that transition from voluntary drug use to addiction. However, a body of scientific evidence is rapidly developing that points to an array of cellular and molecular changes in specific brain circuits. Moreover, many of these brain changes are common to all chemical addictions, and some also are typical of other compulsive behaviors such as pathological overeating.

Addiction should be understood as a chronic recurring illness. Although some addicts do gain full control over their drug use after a single treatment episode, many have relapses. Repeated treatments become necessary to increase the intervals between and diminish the intensity of relapses, until the individual achieves abstinence.

The complexity of this brain disease is not atypical, because virtually no brain diseases are simply biological in nature and expression. All, including stroke, Alzheimer's disease, schizophrenia, and clinical depression, include some behavioral and social aspects. What may make addiction seem unique among brain diseases, however, is that it does begin with a clearly voluntary behavior—the initial decision to use drugs. Moreover, not everyone who ever uses drugs goes on to become addicted. Individuals differ substantially in how easily and quickly they become addicted and in their preferences for particular substances. Consistent with the biobehavioral nature of addiction, these individual differences result from a combination of environmental and biological, particularly genetic, factors. In fact, estimates are that between 50 and 70 percent of the variability in susceptibility to becoming addicted can be accounted for by genetic factors.

Over time the addict loses substantial control over his or her initially voluntary behavior, and it becomes compulsive. For many people these behaviors are truly uncontrollable, just like the behavioral expression of any other brain disease. Schizophrenics cannot control their hallucinations and delusions. Parkinson's patients cannot control their trembling. Clinically depressed patients cannot voluntarily control their moods. Thus, once one is addicted, the characteristics of the illness—and the treatment approaches—are not that different from most other brain diseases. No matter how one develops an illness, once one has it, one is in the diseased state and needs treatment.

Moreover, voluntary behavior patterns are, of course, involved in the etiology and progression of many other illnesses, albeit not all brain diseases. Examples abound, including hypertension, arteriosclerosis and other cardiovascular diseases, diabetes, and forms of cancer in which the onset is heavily influenced by the individual's eating, exercise, smoking, and other behaviors.

Addictive behaviors do have special characteristics related to the social contexts in which they originate. All of the environmental cues surrounding initial drug use and development of the addiction actually become "conditioned" to that drug use and are thus critical to the development and expression of addiction. Environmental cues are paired in time with an individual's initial drug use experiences and, through classical conditioning, take on conditioned stimulus properties. When those cues are present at a later time, they elicit anticipation of a drug experience and thus generate tremendous drug craving. Cue-induced craving is one of the most frequent causes of drug use relapses, even after long periods of abstinence, independently of whether drugs are available.

The salience of environmental or contextual cues helps explain why reentry to one's community can be so difficult for addicts leaving the controlled environments of treatment or correctional settings and why aftercare is so essential to successful recovery. The person who became addicted in the home environment is constantly exposed to the cues conditioned to his or her initial drug use, such as the neighborhood where he or she hung out, drug-using buddies, or the lamppost where he or she bought drugs. Simple exposure to those cues automatically triggers craving and can lead rapidly to relapses. This is one reason why someone who apparently overcame drug cravings while in prison or residential treatment could quickly revert to drug use upon returning home. In fact, one of the major goals of drug addiction treatment is to teach addicts how to deal with the cravings caused by inevitable exposure to these conditioned cues.

Implications

Understanding addiction as a brain disease has broad and significant implications for the public perception of addicts and their families, for addiction treatment practice, and for some aspects of public policy. On the other hand, this biomedical view of addiction does not speak directly to and is unlikely to bear significantly on many other issues, including specific strategies for controlling the supply of drugs and whether initial drug use should be legal or not. Moreover, the brain disease model of addiction does not address the question of whether specific drugs of abuse can also be potential medicines. Examples abound of drugs that can be both highly addicting and extremely effective medicines. The best-known example is the appropriate use of morphine as a treatment for pain. Nevertheless, a number of practical lessons can be drawn from the scientific understanding of addiction.

It is no wonder addicts cannot simply quit on their own. They have an illness that requires biomedical treatment. People often assume that because addiction begins with a voluntary behavior and is expressed in the form of excess behavior, people should just be able to quit by force of will alone. However, it is essential to understand when dealing with addicts that we are dealing with individuals whose brains have been altered by drug use. They need drug addiction treatment. We know that, contrary to common belief, very few addicts actually do just stop on their own. Observing that there are very few heroin addicts in their 50s or 60s, people frequently ask what happened to those who were heroin addicts 30 years ago, assuming that they must have quit on their own. However, longitudinal studies find that only a very small fraction actually quit on their own. The rest have either been successfully treated, are currently in maintenance treatment, or (for about half) are dead. Consider the example of smoking cigarettes: Various studies have found that between 3 and 7 percent of people who try to quit on their own each year actually succeed. Science has at last convinced the public that depression is not just a lot of sadness; that depressed individuals are in a different brain state and thus require treatment to get their symptoms under control. The same is true for schizophrenic patients. It is time to recognize that this is also the case for addicts.

The role of personal responsibility is undiminished but clarified. Does having a brain disease mean that people who are addicted no longer have any responsibility for their behavior or that they are simply victims of their own genetics and brain chemistry? Of course not. Addiction begins with the voluntary behavior of drug use, and although genetic characteristics may predispose individuals to be more or less susceptible to becoming addicted, genes do not doom one to become an addict. This is one major reason why efforts to prevent drug use are so vital to any comprehensive strategy to deal with the nation's drug problems. Initial drug use is a voluntary, and therefore preventable, behavior.

Moreover, as with any illness, behavior becomes a critical part of recovery. At a minimum, one must comply with the treatment regimen, which is harder than it sounds. Treatment compliance is the biggest cause of relapses for all chronic illnesses, including asthma, diabetes, hypertension, and addiction. Moreover, treatment compliance rates are no worse for addiction than for these other illnesses, ranging from 30 to 50 percent. Thus, for drug addiction as well as for other chronic diseases, the individual's motivation and behavior are clearly important parts of success in treatment and recovery.

Implications for treatment approaches and treatment expectations. Maintaining this comprehensive biobehavioral understanding of addiction also speaks to what needs to be provided in drug treatment programs. Again, we must be careful not to pit biology against behavior. The National Institute on Drug Abuse's recently published Principles of Effective Drug Addiction Treatment provides a detailed discussion of how we must treat all aspects of the individual, not just the biological component or the behavioral component. As with other brain diseases such as schizophrenia and depression, the data show that the best drug addiction treatment approaches attend to the entire individual, combining the use of medications, behavioral therapies, and attention to necessary social services and rehabilitation. These might include such services as family therapy to enable the patient to return to successful family life, mental health services, education and vocational training, and housing services.

That does not mean, of course, that all individuals need all components of treatment and all rehabilitation services. Another principle of effective addiction treatment is that the array of services included in an individual's treatment plan must be matched to his or her particular set of needs. Moreover, since those needs will surely change over the course of recovery, the array of services provided will need to be continually reassessed and adjusted.

What to do with addicted criminal offenders. One obvious conclusion is that we need to stop simplistically viewing criminal justice and health approaches as incompatible opposites. The practical reality is that crime and drug addiction often occur in tandem: Between 50 and 70 percent of arrestees are addicted to illegal drugs. Few citizens would be willing to relinquish criminal justice system control over individuals, whether they are addicted or not, who have committed crimes against others. Moreover, extensive real-life experience shows that if we simply incarcerate addicted offenders without treating them, their return to both drug use and criminality is virtually guaranteed.

A growing body of scientific evidence points to a much more rational and effective blended public health/public safety approach to dealing with the addicted offender. Simply summarized, the data show that if addicted offenders are provided with well-structured drug treatment while under criminal justice control, their recidivism rates can be reduced by 50 to 60 percent for subsequent drug use and by more than 40 percent for further criminal behavior. Moreover, entry into drug treatment need not be completely voluntary in order for it to work. In fact, studies suggest that increased pressure to stay in treatment—whether from the legal system or from family members or employers—actually increases the amount of time patients remain in treatment and improves their treatment outcomes.

Findings such as these are the underpinning of a very important trend in drug control strategies now being implemented in the United States and many foreign countries. For example, some 40 percent of prisons and jails in this country now claim to provide some form of drug treatment to their addicted inmates, although we do not know the quality of the treatment provided. Diversion to drug treatment programs as an alternative to incarceration is gaining popularity across the United States. The widely applauded growth in drug treatment courts over the past five years—to more than 400—is another successful example of the blending of public health and public safety approaches. These drug courts use a combination of criminal justice sanctions and drug use monitoring and treatment tools to manage addicted offenders.

Updating the Discussion

Understanding drug abuse and addiction in all their complexity demands that we rise above simplistic polarized thinking about drug issues. Addiction is both a public health and a public safety issue, not one or the other. We must deal with both the supply and the demand issues with equal vigor. Drug abuse and addiction are about both biology and behavior. One can have a disease and not be a hapless victim of it.

We also need to abandon our attraction to simplistic metaphors that only distract us from developing appropriate strategies. I, for one, will be in some ways sorry to see the War on Drugs metaphor go away, but go away it must. At some level, the notion of waging war is as appropriate for the illness of addiction as it is for our War on Cancer, which simply means bringing all forces to bear on the problem in a focused and energized way. But, sadly, this concept has been badly distorted and misused over time, and the War on Drugs never became what it should have been: the War on Drug Abuse and Addiction. Moreover, worrying about whether we are winning or losing this war has deteriorated to using simplistic and inappropriate measures such as counting drug addicts. In the end, it has only fueled discord. The War on Drugs metaphor has done nothing to advance the real conceptual challenges that need to be worked through.

I hope, though, that we will all resist the temptation to replace it with another catchy phrase that inevitably will devolve into a search for quick or easy-seeming solutions to our drug problems. We do not rely on simple metaphors or strategies to deal with our other major national problems such as education, health care, or national security. We are, after all, trying to solve truly monumental, multidimensional problems on a national or even international scale. To devalue them to the level of slogans does our public an injustice and dooms us to failure.

Understanding the health aspects of addiction is in no way incompatible with the need to control the supply of drugs. In fact, a public health approach to stemming an epidemic or spread of a disease always focuses comprehensively on the agent, the vector, and the host. In the case of drugs of abuse, the agent is the drug, the host is the abuser or addict, and the vector for transmitting the illness is clearly the drug suppliers and dealers that keep the agent flowing so readily. Prevention and treatment are the strategies to help protect the host. But just as we must deal with the flies and mosquitoes that spread infectious diseases, we must directly address all the vectors in the drug-supply system.

In order to be truly effective, the blended public health/public safety approaches advocated here must be implemented at all levels of society—local, state, and national. All drug problems are ultimately local in character and impact, since they differ so much across geographic settings and cultural contexts, and the most effective solutions are implemented at the local level. Each community must work through its own locally appropriate antidrug implementation strategies, and those strategies must be just as comprehensive and science-based as those instituted at the state or national level.

The message from the now very broad and deep array of scientific evidence is absolutely clear. If we as a society ever hope to make any real progress in dealing with our drug problems, we are going to have to rise above moral outrage that addicts have "done it to themselves" and develop strategies that are as sophisticated and as complex as the problem itself. Whether addicts are "victims" or not, once addicted they must be seen as "brain disease patients."

Moreover, although our national traditions do argue for compassion for those who are sick, no matter how they contracted their illnesses, I recognize that many addicts have disrupted not only their own lives but those of their families and their broader communities, and thus do not easily generate compassion. However, no matter how one may feel about addicts and their behavioral histories, an extensive body of scientific evidence shows that approaching addiction as a treatable illness is extremely cost-effective, both financially and in terms of broader societal impacts such as family violence, crime, and other forms of social upheaval. Thus, it is clearly in everyone's interest to get past the hurt and indignation and slow the drain of drugs on society by enhancing drug use prevention efforts and providing treatment to all who need it.

Sally L. Satel

NO

The Fallacies of No-Fault Addiction

On November 20, 1995, more than one hundred substance-abuse experts gathered in Chantilly, Virginia for a meeting organized by the government's top research agency on drug abuse. One topic for discussion was whether the agency, the National Institute on Drug Abuse (NIDA), which is part of the National Institutes of Health, should declare drug addiction a disease of the brain. Overwhelmingly, the assembled academics, public-health workers, and state officials declared that it should.

At the time, the answer was a controversial one, but, in the three years since, the notion of addiction as a brain disease has become widely accepted, thanks to a full-blown public education campaign by NIDA. Waged in editorial board rooms, town-hall gatherings, Capitol Hill briefings and hearings, the campaign reached its climax last spring [1999] when media personality Bill Moyers catapulted the brain-disease concept into millions of living rooms with a five-part PBS special called "Moyers on Addiction: Close to Home." Using imaging technology, Moyers showed viewers eye-catching pictures of addicts' brains. The cocaine-damaged parts of the brain were "lit up"—an "image of desire" was how one of the researchers on Moyers' special described it.

These dramatic visuals lend scientific credibility to NIDA's position. But politicians—and, in particular, President Clinton's drug czar, General Barry McCaffrey, who has begun reciting the brain-disease rhetoric—should resist this medicalized portrait. First, it reduces a complex human activity to a slice of damaged brain tissue. Second, and more importantly, it vastly underplays the paradoxically voluntary nature of addictive behavior. As a colleague said: "We could examine brains all day and by whatever sophisticated means we want, but we would never label someone a drug addict unless he acted like one."

No-Fault Addiction

The idea of a "no-fault" disease did not originate at NIDA. For the last decade or so it was vigorously promoted by mental-health advocates working to transform the public's understanding of severe mental illness. Diseases like schizophrenia and manic depressive illness, they properly said, were products of a defective brain, not bad parenting. Until the early 1980s, when accumulated neuroscientific discoveries showed, irrefutably, that schizophrenia was marked by measurable abnormalities of brain structure and function, remnants

From *The Public Interest* by Sally L. Satel, Winter 1999, pp. 52–67. Copyright © 1999 by Public Interest.

of the psychiatric profession and much of the public were still inclined to blame parents for their children's mental illness.

NIDA borrowed the brain-disease notion from the modern mental-health movement, understandably hoping to reap similar benefits—greater acceptance of its efforts and of its own constituent sufferers, that is, addicts. By focusing exclusively on the brain, NIDA ironically diminishes the importance of its own research portfolio, which devotes an ample section to behavioral interventions. It may well be that researchers will someday be able to map the changes in brain physiology that accompany behavioral changes during recovery. Nevertheless, it is crucial to recognize that the human substrate upon which behavioral treatments work, first and foremost, is the will.

Some of those experts that met in Chantilly would say that emphasizing the role of will, or choice, is just an excuse to criminalize addiction. Clinical experience in treating addicts, however, suggests that such an orientation provides therapeutic grounds for optimism. It means that the addict is capable of self-control—a much more encouraging conclusion than one could ever draw from a brain-bound, involuntary model of addiction.

What Does Brain Disease Mean?

A recent article in the journal *Science,* "Addiction Is a Brain Disease, and It Matters," authored by NIDA director Alan I. Leshner, summarizes the evidence that long-term exposure to drugs produces addiction: Taking drugs elicits changes in neurons in the central nervous system that compel the individual to take drugs. Because these changes are presumed to be irreversible, the addict is perpetually at risk for relapse.

> Virtually all drugs of abuse have common effects, either directly or indirectly, on a single pathway deep within the brain. . . . Activation of this pathway appears to be a common element in what keeps drug users taking drugs. . . . The addicted brain is distinctly different from the non-addicted brain, as manifested by changes in metabolic activity, receptor availability, gene expression and responsiveness to environmental cues. . . . That addiction is tied to changes in brain structure and function is what makes it, fundamentally, a brain disease.

Others are less dogmatic. Harvard biochemist Bertha Madras acknowledges a virtual library of documented, replicable brain changes with drug exposure, but she also points out that there have been no scientific studies correlating them with behavior. This missing connection, upon which the addiction-as-a-brain-disease argument clearly depends, has prompted some very unsympathetic reactions. John P. Seibyl, a psychiatrist and nuclear radiologist at Yale University School of Medicine, has called the notion of predicting behavior from brain pathology "modern phrenology."

Not even Alcoholics Anonymous, the institution most responsible for popularizing the disease concept of addiction, supports the idea that drug-induced brain changes determine an addict's behavior. AA employs disease as a metaphor for loss of control. And even though AA assumes that inability to stop drinking, once started, is biologically driven, it does not allow this to overshadow AA's central belief that addiction is a symptom of a spiritual defect, and can thus be overcome through the practice of honesty, humility, and acceptance.

The brain-disease advocates, of course, operate by an entirely different frame of reference. To them, "addiction" means taking drugs compulsively because the brain, having already been changed by drugs, orders the user to do so. As Moyers put it on "Meet the Press," drugs "hijack the brain . . . relapse is normal." The brain-disease advocates assume a correlation between drug-taking behavior and brain-scan appearance, though one has yet to be clearly demonstrated, and speculate, based on preliminary evidence, that pathological changes persist for years. A physiological diagnosis, to stretch the meaning of that word, should of course yield a medicinal prescription. So, brain-disease advocates seem confident, despite evidence to the contrary, that a neuroscience of addiction will give rise to pharmaceutical remedies. Meanwhile, the search for a cocaine medication, having begun with such high hopes, has come up empty. And there is good reason to wonder if this enterprise will ever bear fruit. Even the widely used medication for heroin addiction—methadone—is only partly helpful in curtailing drug use. It fails to remedy the underlying anguish for which drugs like heroin and cocaine are the desperate remedy.

Addicted to Politics

The dispute over whether addiction is a brain disease isn't merely a dispute among doctors. It is, for many reasons, political. The efforts of NIDA do not simply aim to medicalize addiction, presumably a medical concern, but to destigmatize the addict, clearly a sociopolitical concern. This is also the agenda of the newly formed group, Physician Leadership on National Drug Policy. "Concerted efforts to eliminate stigma" should result in substance abuse being "accorded parity with other chronic, relapsing conditions insofar as access to care, treatment benefits and clinical outcomes are concerned," a statement from the Leadership group says. These sentiments have been echoed by the Institute of Medicine, a quasi-governmental body that is part of the National Academy of Sciences. "Addiction . . . is not well understood by the public and policymakers. Overcoming problems of stigma and misunderstanding will require educating the public, health educators, policymakers and clinicians, highlighting progress made, and recruiting talented researchers into the field."

Indeed, the politics of drug addiction have begun to strain the logic of drug-addiction experts. In their *Lancet* article, "Myths About the Treatment of Addiction," researchers Charles O'Brien and Thomas McLellan state that relapse to drugs is an inherent aspect of addiction and should not be viewed as a treatment failure. They sensibly point out that in long-term conditions—for example, asthma, diabetes, and hypertension—relapse is often the result of the patient's poor compliance with proper diet, exercise, and medication. But then they jump to the conclusion that since the relapse of some addicts follows from poor compliance too, addiction is like any other disease. This is incorrect. Asthmatics and diabetics who resist doctor's orders share certain characteristics with addicts. But asthmatics and diabetics can also deteriorate spontaneously on the basis of unprovoked, unavoidable primary, physical reasons alone; relapse to addiction, by contrast, invariably represents a voluntary act in conscious defiance of "doctor's orders." The bottom line is that conditions like asthma and diabetes are not developed through voluntary behavior. An asthmatic does not choose to be short of breath. Addicts, however, choose to use drugs.

Analogies aside, calling addiction a chronic and relapsing disease is simply wrong. Treatment-outcome studies do support the claim, but data from the large Epidemiologic Catchment Area (ECA) study, funded by the National Institute of Mental Health, show that in the general population remission from drug dependence (addiction) and drug abuse is the norm. Contra publicist Bill Moyers and researchers O'Brien and McLellan, relapse is not. According to ECA criteria for remission—defined as no symptoms for the year just prior to the interview—59 percent of roughly 1,300 respondents who met lifetime criteria were free of drug problems. The average duration of remission was 2.7 years, and the mean duration of illness was 6.1 years with most cases lasting no more than 8 years.

Yet, if NIDA and other public-health groups can change how the public views addiction, tangible political gains will follow. Such groups aim at securing more treatment and services for addicts, expanded insurance coverage, and increased funding for addiction research. These are not unreasonable aims insofar as substandard quality of care, limited access to care, and understudied research questions remain serious problems. But the knee-jerk reflex to decry stigma has been naively borrowed from the mental-health community. Stigma deters unwanted behaviors, and it enforces societal norms. Destigmatizing addicts (recasting them as chronic illness sufferers) threatens one of the most promising venues for anti-addiction efforts: the criminal justice system. The courts and probation services can impose sanctions that greatly enhance retention and prevent relapse. (More about this later.)

A Medical Cure for Addiction?

One of NIDA's major goals has been the development of a cocaine medication by the turn of the century. . . . [N]o magic bullet is in sight. To date, over 40 pharmaceuticals have been studied in randomized controlled trials in humans for cocaine abuse or dependence. Some of these were intended to block craving, others to substitute for cocaine itself, but none have yet been found even minimally effective. The NIDA director has downgraded predictions about the curative power of medication, promoting it as potentially "complementary" to behavioral therapy.

The basic problem with putative anticraving medications is their lack of specificity. Instead of deploying a surgical strike on the neuronal site of cocaine yearning, these medications end up blunting motivation in general and may also depress mood. Likewise, experiments with cocaine-like substances have proven frustrating. Instead of suppressing the urge to use the drug, they tend to work like an appetizer, producing physical sensations and emotional memories reminiscent of cocaine itself, triggering a hunger for it.

If a selective medication could be developed, it might be especially helpful to cocaine addicts who have abstained for a time but who experience sudden spontaneous bursts of craving for cocaine, a feeling that is often reported as alien, coming "out of nowhere," and uncoupled from a true desire to use cocaine. Such craving may be triggered by environmental cues (e.g., passing through the neighborhood where the addict used to get high). Generally, the addict learns his idiosyncratic cues, avoids them, and arms himself with exercises and strategies (e.g., immediately calling a 12-step sponsor) that help him fight the urge. It is always conceivable that a medication could help in terms of suppressing the jolt of desire and, ultimately, uncoupling the cue from the conditioned response.

Another pharmacological approach to cocaine addiction has been immunization against the drug's effect. In late 1995, scientists reported the promising effects of a cocaine vaccine in rats. The animals were inoculated with an artificial cocaine-like substance that triggered the production of antibodies to cocaine. When actual cocaine was administered, the antibodies attached to the molecules of cocaine, reducing the amount of free drug available in the bloodstream to enter the brain.

The vaccine is still being developed for use in humans, but the principle behind its presumed effect is already being exploited by an available anti-heroin medication called naltrexone. Naltrexone blocks opiate molecules at the site of attachment to receptors on the neuron. This way, an addict who administers heroin feels no effect. Uncoupling the desired response (getting high) from the action intended to produce it (shooting up) is called "extinction," and, according to behaviorist theory, the subject will eventually stop administering a drug if he no longer achieves an effect. Though naltrexone is effective, most heroin addicts reject it in favor of methadone's calming effect.

Optimism surrounding the pharmaceutical approach to drug dependence stems, in fact, from the qualified success of methadone, an opioid painkiller developed by German chemists during World War II. It was first tested in 1964 as a substitute for heroin in the United States, and now about 19 percent of the nation's estimated 600,000 heroin addicts are enrolled in methadone-maintenance clinics. Numerous studies have documented the socioeconomic benefits of methadone: significant reductions in crime, overdoses, unemployment, and, in some regions, HIV.

Unlike heroin, which needs to be administered every four to eight hours to prevent withdrawal symptoms, methadone requires only daily dosing. "Successful methadone users are invisible," the director of the Beth Israel Medical Center in New York City told the *New York Times*. Between 5 percent and 20 percent remain on the medication for over 10 years, and many are indeed invisible. An example mentioned in the *Times* article is Jimmie Maxwell, an 80-year-old jazz trumpet player who has stayed clean for the past 32 years by taking methadone every day. Unfortunately, people like Maxwell, who lead an optimal life and are otherwise drug-free, represent perhaps 5 percent to 7 percent of methadone patients. Moreover, patients in methadone maintenance are frequently not drug-free; as many as 35 percent to 60 percent also use cocaine or other illicit drugs or black-market sedatives. During a six-year follow-up, D. Dwayne Simpson of the Institute of Behavioral Research at Texas Christian University found over half of all patients were readmitted to their agency at some point.

This should come as little surprise. Methadone will only prevent withdrawal symptoms and the related physiological hunger for heroin, but it alone can't medicate the psychic deficits that led to addiction, such as deep-seated inabilities to tolerate boredom, depression, stress, anger, loneliness. The addict who initiated heavy drug use in his teens hasn't even completed the maturational tasks of adolescence, let alone prepared himself psychologically to solve the secondary layer of troubles that accumulated over years of drug use: family problems, educational deficiencies, disease, personal and economic losses. Only a fraction of heroin addicts become fully productive on methadone alone.

The biological view of addiction conceals an established fact of enormous and pressing clinical relevance: The course of addictive behavior can be influenced by the very consequences of the drug taking itself. Indeed, when the addict reacts to aversive sequelae of drug use—economic, health, legal, and personal—by eventually quitting drugs, reducing use, changing his pattern of use or getting help, he does so voluntarily. Rather than being the inevitable, involuntary product of a diseased brain, the course addiction follows may represent the essence of a free will. Consequences can inspire a change in voluntary behavior, irrespective of its predictability or biological underpinnings. Involuntary behavior cannot be changed by its consequences. A review of the clinical features of addiction will help illustrate the mix of voluntary and involuntary behaviors associated with addiction, belying the claim that addiction is a brain disease.

Harnessing the Will to Stay Clean

It is especially common for heroin-dependent individuals to become immune to the euphoric effect of the drug yet still seek the drug to keep from going into withdrawal. Upon cessation of heroin, a predictable pattern of gross physiological symptoms appears. The same is true of cessation of other opioid drugs including Demerol, morphine, Percocet, codeine, as well as alcohol. To picture this one only need recall actor Jack Lemmon in the movie, *Days of Wine and Roses*, his body wracked with tremors, sweating, anxious, desperate for a drink after running out of whisky. Or Frank Sinatra in *Man with the Golden Arm*, the heroin addict suffering painful muscle cramps and powerful cravings for heroin after his last fix wore off.

Unlike heroin and alcohol, cocaine does not produce such serious physical withdrawal symptoms. The heavy cocaine addict typically uses the drug in a driven, repetitive manner for 24 to 72 hours straight. Cocaine wears off very quickly and, as it fades, the yearning for more is overpowering. Each fresh hit quells the intense craving. The process winds down only when the addict becomes exhausted, runs out of money, or becomes paranoid, a potential effect of cocaine and other stimulants, such as methamphetamine. He then "crashes" into a phase of agitated depression and hunger followed by sleep for 12 to 36 hours. Within hours to days after awakening, he experiences powerful urges to use the drug again, and the cycle resumes.

A regular user in the midst of a cocaine binge or experiencing heroin withdrawal cannot readily stop using if drugs are available. He is presumably in the "brain-disease" state, when use is most compulsive, neuronal disruption most intense. True, even purposeful behavior can occur in this state—for example, the attempt, sometimes violent, to get money or drugs is highly goal-directed. But, at the same time, addicts in such an urgent state will ignore their screaming babies, frantically gouge themselves with dirty needles, and ruin families, careers, and reputations.

Nonetheless, most addicts have broken the cycle many times. Either they decide to go "cold turkey" or end up doing so, unintentionally, by running out of drugs or money or landing in jail. Some heroin addicts admit themselves to the hospital to detoxify because they want to quit, others to reduce the cost of their habit, knowing they'll be more sensitive to the effects of heroin afterward. This latter trip to the hospital, while motivated by an effort to pursue drug use more efficiently, is nonetheless a purposeful move that, under other circumstances, might be taken by the addict to re-exert control.

In the days between binges, cocaine addicts make many deliberate choices including (potentially) the choice to stop using. Heroin-dependent individuals, by comparison, use the drug several times a day but can be quite functional in all respects as long as they have stable access to some form of opiate drug in order to prevent withdrawal symptoms. Certainly, some addicts may "nod off" in abandoned buildings, true to stereotype, if they consume more opiate than the amount to which their body has developed tolerance, but others can be "actively engaged in activities and relationships," according to ethnographers Edward Preble and John J. Casey, Jr. "The brief moments of euphoria after each administration constitute a small fraction of their daily lives. The rest of the time they are aggressively pursuing a career . . . hustling."

According to the Office of National Drug Control Policy, as many as 46 percent of drug users not in treatment reported exclusively legal sources of income, and 42 percent reported both legal and illegal. The National Institute of Justice found that between 33 percent and 67 percent of arrested drug users indicate "full and part time work" as their main source of income. It is reasonable to assume that individuals who are most heavily involved in drug use participate least in the legitimate economy. Nonetheless, the fact that many committed drug users do have jobs shows that addiction does not necessarily preclude purposeful activity.

The temporal architecture of an addict's routine reveals periods in which the individual is capable of reflection and deliberate behavior. During the course of a heroin addict's day, for example, he may feel rather calm, and his thoughts might be quite lucid, if he is confident of access to drugs and if he is using it in doses adequate to prevent withdrawal symptoms, but not large enough to sedate. Likewise, there are periods within a cocaine addict's week when he is neither engaged in a binge nor wracked with intense craving for the drug. During such moments, does anyone believe the addict is the victim of a brain disease?

Society's Expectations

Thus, when properly "fixed," the heroin addict might rationally decide to enter a detoxification program or enter a methadone-maintenance program. And between binges the cocaine addict could decide to enter a treatment program or move across town away from the visual cues and the personal associations that provoke craving. Yes, the addict can do such things. But if asked to do so at any given moment, will he?

Probably not. Even those who wish most passionately for a better life may fear coping without drugs. It gets worse: The addict may believe a better life is just not possible. Yet, chances are that some would say "yes" to the possibility of overcoming their addiction. And this can be encouraged behaviorally through rewards and punishments. For example, society could decide to make some necessities—welfare payments, employment, public housing, or child custody—contingent on abstinence. A systematic plan that closes absolutely all avenues of support to those who can't or won't stop using drugs—allowing them only elective treatment or, once arrested for nonviolent drug-related crime, court-ordered treatment—would be too radical, unfair even.

For one thing, the treatment system—especially residential treatment for both voluntary and criminally coerced addicts—would need to be greatly expanded to accommodate those who did not curtail use under pressure alone. Moral objections to refusing addicts access to many public goods and services—or, better, administering small punishments or rewards contingent on performance—would need to be overcome. According to a behavioral model of addiction, it is not unethical. Society can and should legitimately place expectations and demands on addicts because their "brain disease" is not a persistent state. Furthermore, experimental evidence shows that addicts can control drug taking.

In his book, *Heavy Drinking: The Myth of Alcoholism as a Disease*, philosopher Herbert Fingarette cites numerous independent investigations conducted under controlled conditions showing the degree to which alcoholics are capable of regulating themselves. Researchers found, for example, that the amount of alcohol consumed was related to its cost and the effort required to obtain it. Once offered small payments, subjects were able to refuse freely available alcohol. And, after drinking an initial "priming" dose, the amount of alcohol subsequently consumed was inversely proportionate to size of the payment. Other experiments showed that the drinkers' beliefs and attitudes about alcohol influenced how much they consumed. This is potentially very significant to drug addiction; for example, the demand for heroin and cocaine is elastic, responding to price.

The story of the returning Vietnam servicemen is a revealing natural experiment that "changed our views of heroin" according to epidemiologist Lee Robins and colleagues who wrote the now classic paper on the subject, "Vietnam Veterans Three Years After Vietnam." They found that only 14 percent of men who were dependent on heroin in Vietnam—and who failed a publicized urine test at departure because they did not stop using—resumed regular heroin use back home. The rest had access to heroin, and had even used some occasionally, but what made them decide to stop for good, Robins found, was the "sordid" culture surrounding heroin use, the drug's price, and fear of arrest.

Enlightened Coercion

Behavioral therapies are not then the problem; they make the most practical and theoretical sense. The literature consistently shows that an addict who completes a treatment program—any program—either stops or markedly reduces his use of drugs after discharge. The problem is that only a small number of participants finish their programs. Estimates of attendance beyond 52 weeks, the generally accepted minimum duration for treatment, range from 8 percent to 20 percent of patients entering any of the three most common types of programs: outpatient counseling, methadone maintenance, and residential treatment.

How best to instill "motivation" is a perennial topic among clinicians; at least one form of psychotherapy has been developed for that explicit purpose. But routinely neglected by most mainstream addiction experts is the powerful yet counter-intuitive fact that patients who enter treatment involuntarily under court order will fare as well, sometimes even better, than those who enroll voluntarily. Numerous studies support this. Large government-funded studies spanning three decades—the Drug Abuse Reporting Program (1970s), Treatment Outcome Prospective Study (1980s), and the Drug Abuse Treatment Outcome Study (1990s)—all found that the longer a person stays in treatment the better his outcome. Not surprisingly, those under legal supervision stay longer than their voluntary counterparts.

The best-studied population of coerced addicts was part of California's Civil Addict Program (CAP), started in 1962. During its most active years, in the 1970s, the program was impressively successful. It required addicts to be treated in a residential setting for two years and then closely supervised by specially trained parole officers for another five. These officers had small caseloads, performed weekly urine tests, and had the authority to return individuals to forced treatment if they resumed drug use. Most of the addicts were remanded to CAP for nonviolent drug-related crimes, but some were sent because their addictions were so severe they were unable to care for themselves. This latter group was civilly committed in much the same way that the gravely disabled mentally ill are often institutionalized.

The success came after a difficult start. During the first 18 months, many California judges, unfamiliar with the new procedures, released patients on a writ of habeus corpus almost immediately after they had been committed. This judicial blunder, however, allowed M. Douglas Anglin, director of UCLA's Drug Abuse Research Center, and his colleagues to conduct an extensive evaluation of nearly 1,000 addicts, comparing those who received compulsory treatment with those who were mistakenly freed. The two groups were otherwise comparable with respect to drug use and demographics. The researchers found that 22 percent of the addicts who were committed reverted to heroin use and crime, less than half the rate for the prematurely released group. Other large-scale studies, including the 1984 Treatment Outcome Prospective Study and the 1988 Drug Abuse Reporting Program, also show that drug use and criminal behavior decline more among those receiving compulsory treatment than among the voluntary patients.

Though still legally on the books, CAP has become moribund. The practice of court-ordered residential treatment continues, but parole and probation officers today are not nearly as scrupulous in supervising their charges as were their CAP counterparts. Among the exceptions is a program developed by the Brooklyn District Attorney called Drug Treatment Alternative-to-Prison (DTAP). It is the first prosecution-run program in the country to divert prison-bound drug offenders to residential treatment.

The program targets drug-addicted felons with prior nonviolent convictions who have been arrested for sales to undercover agents. Defendants who accept the program have their prosecution deferred if they enter the 15 to 24 month program. Charges are dismissed upon successful completion of the program. The program's one-year retention rate of 57 percent is markedly superior to the 13 percent to 25 percent rate typically seen in standard residential treatment. Recidivism to crime at 6, 12, and 24 months after program completion is consistently half that of DTAP-eligible defendants who were regularly prosecuted and sent to prison.

The Success of Drug Courts

In addition to coercing criminally involved addicts to undergo residential treatment, the criminal justice system is in an excellent position to use sanctions as leverage for compliance with outpatient treatment. Since 1989, it has been doing so through "drug courts." These specialized courts offer nonviolent defendants the possibility of a dismissed charge if they plead guilty and if they agree to be diverted to a heavily monitored drug-treatment program overseen by the drug-court judge. During regularly scheduled status hearings, the judge holds the defendant publicly accountable for his progress by taking into account dirty or missed urine tests and cooperation with the treatment program. Successes are rewarded and violations are sanctioned immediately, though in a graduated fashion, starting with small impositions that become increasingly aversive if further infractions occur. Ideally, the sanctions become incentives to compliance; repeated failure results in incarceration.

Early data on over 80 drug courts show an average retention rate of 71 percent (defined as the sum of all participants who have completed drug-court programs and those who are still in programs). Even the lowest rate of 31 percent exceeds the average retention rate of about 10 percent to 15 percent (at the one-year mark) for noncriminal addicts in public-sector treatment programs. One study conducted by the Urban Institute was specifically designed to examine the influence of sanctions on offenders in the District of Columbia drug court. In the first option—the "sanctions track"—urines were obtained twice weekly, and the defendant was subject to increasingly severe penalties (e.g., a day or more in jail) for missing or dirty urines. The second, or "treatment track," was an intensive treatment program lasting several hours a day, but it didn't impose sanctions frequently or reliably. And finally, the control group had urine tests twice a week, but there were no predictable consequences for missed or dirty urines.

Researchers found that treatment-track participants were twice as likely to be drug free in the month before sentencing as those in the standard track (27 percent versus 12 percent), while sanctions-track participants, subject to frequent urine testing and known consequences for violations, were three times as likely (37 percent versus 12 percent) to be free of drugs. The certainty of consequences was psychologically powerful to the participants. As senior researcher Adele Harrell learned in her focus groups, study participants credited their ability to stay clean to the "swiftness of the penalties—they had to report to court immediately for a test failure—and their fairness."

And the longer participants stayed in drug court, the better they fared. According to information maintained by the Drug Court Clearinghouse at American University, the differences in re-arrest rates were significant. Up to this point, drug courts operational for 18 months or more reported a completion rate of 48 percent. Depending upon the characteristics and degree of social dysfunction of the graduates, re-arrest—for drug crimes, primarily—was 4 percent within one year of graduation. Even among those who never finished the program (about one in three fail to complete) re-arrest one year after enrollment ranged from 5 percent to 28 percent. Contrast this with the 26 percent to 40 percent re-arrest rate among traditionally adjudicated individuals convicted of drug possession who will commit another offense within one year, according to the Bureau of Justice Statistics.

These examples show how law enforcement brings addicts into a treatment system, enhances the probability that they will stay, and imposes sanctions for poor compliance with treatment. (The Urban Institute study even forces one to question whether treatment is invariably necessary, so long as sanctions are in place.) They also highlight the folly of dividing addicts into two camps—"bad people" for the criminal justice system to dispose of and "chronic illness sufferers" for medical professionals to treat. If the brain-disease model transforms every addict into a "sufferer," then we would be hard pressed to justify the use of coercion to change behavior. Thus the brain-disease model fails to accommodate one of the most productive collaborations in the history of antidrug efforts.

Taking Control

Labeling addiction a chronic and relapsing brain disease is mere propaganda. By downplaying the volitional dimension of addiction, the brain-disease model detracts from the great promise of strategies and therapies that rely on sanctions and rewards to shape self-control. And by reinforcing a dichotomy between punitive and clinical approaches to addiction, the brain-disease model devalues the enormous contribution of criminal justice to combating addiction. The fact that many, perhaps most, addicts are in control of their actions and appetites for circumscribed periods of time shows that they are not perpetually helpless victims of chronic disease. They are the instigators of their own addiction, just as they can be the agents of their own recovery.

POSTSCRIPT

Should Addiction to Drugs Be Labeled a Brain Disease?

One of the most valuable aspects of labeling addiction a disease is that it removes alcohol and drugs from the moral realm. It proposed that addiction sufferers should be treated and helped, rather than scorned and punished. Though the moral model of addiction has by no means disappeared in the United States, today more resources are directed toward rehabilitation than punishment. Increasingly, it is being recognized and understood that fines, victim-blaming, and imprisonment do little to curb alcohol and drug addiction in society.

Several recent studies support the hypothesis that addiction to drugs and alcohol is a brain disease and should be treated as such: "Abuse as a Disease, Not a Crime" (*U.S. News & World Report*, March 26, 2007); "Addiction Is a Disease" (*Scholastic Action*, February 7, 2005); "Drug Addiction and Its Underlying Neurobiological Basis" (*Science*, November 9, 2001); "Frontal Cortex" (*American Journal of Psychiatry*, October 2002); "Addiction Is a Disease" (*Psychiatric Times*, October 1, 2002); "Drug Tolerance, Central to Addiction, Responds to Learned Cues" (*Pain & Central Nervous System Week*, August 5, 2002); "Drug Addiction and the Hippocampus" (*Science*, November 9, 2001); "The Unsatisfied Mind: Are Reward Centers in Your Brain Wired for Substance Abuse?" (*Discover*, November, 2001); and "Cocaine Craving Persists after Drug Use Stops" (*Health & Medicine Week*, August 13, 2001). Other studies link genetics to addiction and include the following: "Genetics Could Determine Proclivity for Addiction" (*Alcoholism and Drug Abuse Weekly*, March 7, 2005); "The Search for Candidate Genes of Alcoholism: Evidence from Expression Profiling Studies" (*Addiction Biology*, March 2005); and "The Genetic Roots of Alcoholism" (*The American Legion*, February 2005).

Critics argue, however, that this belief either underemphasizes or ignores the impact of self-control, learned behaviors, and many other factors that lead to alcohol and drug abuse. Furthermore, most treatment programs in the United States are based on the concept of addiction as a brain disease, and most are considered to be generally ineffective when judged by their high relapse rates. See "Combating Addiction" (*CQ Researcher*, February 9, 2007); "Sick or Sinning?" (*CQ Researcher*, February 9, 2007); "Who Is Responsible for Irresponsible Drinking?" (*Addiction*, November 2004); "Self-Deception and Responsibility for Addiction" (*Journal of Applied Philosophy*, October 2003); "Addiction and Responsibility" (*Social Research*, Fall 2001); "Does Motivation to Change Mediate the Effect of DSM-IV Substance Use Disorders on Treatment Utilization and Substance?" (*Addictive Behaviors*, March–April 2002); and "Playing with Fire—Why

People Engage in Risky Behavior: Various Hypotheses Focus on Personality, Age, Parenting, and Biology" (*The Scientist,* January 27, 2003).

It appears that the causes of addiction are complex and that brain, mind, and behavioral specialists are rethinking the whole notion of addiction. With input from neuroscience, biology, pharmacology, psychology, and genetics, they're questioning assumptions and identifying some common characteristics among addicts, which will, it is hoped, improve treatment outcomes and even prevent people from using drugs in the first place.

Do Religion and Prayer Benefit Health?

YES: Gregg Easterbrook, from "Is Religion Good for Your Health?" *The New Republic* (July 19 & 26, 1999)

NO: Michael Shermer, from "Prayer and Healing: The Verdict Is in and the Results Are Null," *Skeptic* (vol. 12, no. 3, 2006)

ISSUE SUMMARY

YES: Writer Gregg Easterbrook believes men and women who practice in any of the mainstream faiths enjoy better health and that lack of religious involvement does have a negative effect on mortality.

NO: Author Michael Shermer contends that intercessory prayer offered by strangers on the health and recovery of patients undergoing coronary bypass surgery is ineffective. He also addresses flaws in studies showing a relationship between prayer and health.

Practitioners of holistic medicine believe that people must take responsibility for their own health by practicing healthy behaviors and maintaining positive attitudes instead of relying on health providers. They also believe that physical disease has behavioral, psychological, and spiritual components. These spiritual components can be explained by the relationship between beliefs, mental attitude, and the immune system. Until recently, few studies existed to prove a relationship between religion and health.

Much of modern medicine has spent the past century ridding itself of mysticism and relying on science. Twenty years ago, no legitimate physician would have dared to study the effects of religion on disease. Recently, however, at the California Pacific Medical Center in San Francisco, California, Elisabeth Targ, clinical director of psychosocial oncology research, has recruited 20 faith healers to determine if prayer can affect the outcome of disease. Targ states that her preliminary results are encouraging. In addition to Targ's study, other research has shown that religion and spirituality can help determine health and well-being. According to a 1995 investigation at Dartmouth College, one of the strongest predictors of success after open-heart surgery was the level of comfort patients derived from religion and spirituality. Other recent studies have linked health with church attendance, religious commitment, and spirituality. There are, however, other studies that have not been as successful; a recent one involving the effects of prayer on alcoholics found no relationship.

Can spirituality or prayer in relation to health and healing be explained scientifically? Prayer or a sense of spirituality may function in a similar manner as stress management or relaxation. Spirituality or prayer may cause the release of hormones that help lower blood pressure or produce other benefits. Although science may never be able to exactly determine the benefits of spirituality, it does appear to help some people.

In the following selections, Gregg Easterbrook states that religion can have a significant influence over the body. Michael Shermer argues that religious prayer does not heal the sick and the studies showing the relationship between religion and healing are flawed.

YES ↵

Gregg Easterbrook

Is Religion Good for Your Health?

T raditionally, religion is viewed as a haven for the sick and afflicted; Jesus, when he walked the ancient Holy Land, often ministered first to the diseased. But what if the traditional view is wrong and belief actually promotes better health? To the exasperation of some academics, that is what a growing body of medical research is beginning to show.

Recent studies indicate that men and women who practice in any of the mainstream faiths have above-average longevity, fewer strokes, less heart disease, less clinical depression, better immune-system function, lower blood pressure, and fewer anxiety attacks, and they are much less likely to commit suicide than the population at large. These findings come from secular medical schools and schools of public health. The results seem to hold even when researchers control for such variables as believers' health histories, the self-selection effect (whether the kind of people who bound out of bed for a Sabbath service tend to be more able-bodied to begin with), and "social support" (the fact that religious groups offer care networks to those who fall ill). In the most striking finding, Dr. Harold Koenig of Duke University Medical Center has calculated that, with regard to any mainstream faith, "[l]ack of religious involvement has an effect on mortality that is equivalent to 40 years of smoking one pack of cigarettes per day."

Koenig and a group of researchers affiliated with such schools as Duke, Harvard, and Yale recently reviewed some 1,100 health-effects studies involving religious practice and found that most, though not all, show statistically significant relationships between worship-service attendance and improved health. (Researchers use service attendance as their proxy because it is an objective data point, as opposed to trying to classify what people privately believe.) In one study, the blood of regular worshipers contained low levels of interleukin-6, a protein associated with immune problems (low is good for interleukin-6). Even subjects with the AIDS virus who regularly practiced a faith had reduced levels of this protein. Another study found that, in Jerusalem, secular Israeli adults "had a significantly higher risk" of heart disease than practicing religious adults.

A 28-year cohort study of approximately 5,000 Californians, conducted by the researcher William Strawbridge and published two years ago in the *American Journal of Public Health,* found that women who attended one worship service per week significantly extended their life spans, though benefits

From *The New Republic,* July 19 & 26, 1999, pp. 20–23. Copyright © 1999 by New Republic. Reprinted by permission.

were not as clear for men. Strawbridge found that believers as a group were not initially healthier than average (that is, self-selecting and leaving the bedridden behind) but instead tended to start off in worse-than-average health and then gradually improve to superior outcomes. Another new study, conducted mainly by researchers at the University of Texas, found that those who regularly attended worship services lived an average of seven years longer than those who never attended.

Duke's Koenig says the association between religious participation and good health holds for almost all Christianity and Judaism, and he assumes it would hold for Islam as well, though studies have not included enough Muslim subjects to be sure. "The main distinction seems to be whether you are a regular practitioner," Koenig says. "Within Christianity there is very little difference in outcomes among the various denominations, except for nonmainstream denominations. Between Judaism and Christianity there is very little difference." Positive results can pass between generations, too. When parents regularly attend worship services, they increase the odds that their children will live longer, healthier lives.

For nonmainstream denominations, the story is different. Christian Scientists suffer some of the nation's worst longevity statistics, despite their denomination's claim to exalt health. The Faith Assembly, a Christian offshoot whose members may shun medical care, has horrible mortality figures. And when people join cults their health indicators fall off the bottom of the curve—most catastrophically in Jonestown and Waco.

Some in the medical community are unhappy about the proliferation of studies suggesting a faith-health link or about the fact that 60 of the nation's 126 medical schools now have religion courses on their curricula, a much higher figure than a few years ago. Dr. Richard Sloan of Columbia University's medical school says, "The majority of these studies focus on Christians, suggesting a Christian political agenda behind the work." Even Dr. David Larson, the president of the National Institute for Healthcare Research and a leading exponent of faith-and-medicine—his letterhead proclaims, "Bridging the gap between spirituality and health"—notes, "There is a fair concern this research will be misused by the Christian right." But any U.S. research would have to focus on Christians, since they compose the country's predominant religious group. If there really is a faith-health link, patients deserve to know.

⁕⟨◉⟩⁕

John Billings, the Civil War-era surgeon general of the Army and, later, the first librarian of the New York Public Library, wrote that religion appeared to reduce mortality in the groups he studied. But correlation never proves causation; the fact that people practice a faith and also improve their well-being doesn't establish that religion was the reason.

Medical research is replete with "confounders," complications that can never really be controlled out of studies, no matter how hard researchers try. To cite a mundane example, for decades studies of caffeine have landed all over the map—some find it dangerous, some beneficial, some neutral. Caffeine studies are confounded by the huge range of other influences to which every person is exposed: different diets, lifestyle habits, home and work circumstances, heredity. Researchers try to get confounders to "wash out" of studies by examining large cohorts and also by following subjects for long periods, on the theory that whatever persists is statistically strong. But, even so, it is not unusual for two equally well-done studies to reach widely differing conclusions. If medicine still can't be sure whether a cup of Starbucks helps or hurts, it can't be sure about church, mosque, or synagogue, either.

Why would practicing a faith improve your longevity and well-being? When studies first began to show a faith-health relationship, many assumed social support would be the explanation. It's clearly an important factor: people who regularly attend religious services are seen by concerned friends who will notice if something appears wrong, call to check up if a person suddenly stops attending, visit, and provide care and encouragement during illness. All these influences improve health and longevity. Merely having a support group that expresses concern if something seems wrong and encourages treatment can be a big plus, as early therapy is almost always most effective.

But studies tend to find a faith-health link even when social support is factored out. Some researchers thought the faith-health relationship might emanate from denominational bans against alcohol, caffeine, and smoking or from dietary standards such as the kosher laws. But confound those confounders—it now looks as if small amounts of alcohol might be good for you, while studies don't show much health-benefit distinction between self-denying Seventh Day Adventists and anything-goes Episcopalians.

Current thinking tends toward the assumption that spiritual practice confers its main health benefit by promoting a sensible lifestyle. Specifics differ, but every mainstream Western denomination encourages the flock to drink in moderation, shun drugs, stop smoking, live circumspectly, practice monogamy, get married, and stay married. (Bickering and skillet-throwing notwithstanding, as a group married adults have better health indicators than singles of comparable ages, in part because spouses serve as each other's "social support.") The lifestyle choices encouraged by faith for reasons of theology aren't terribly different from the choices physicians encourage for reasons of playing the percentages. Of course, secular systems of life philosophy also encourage people to practice moderation and fidelity. But, encompassing millions of members and calling on an ultimate authority, religions may simply be doing a better job of advocating the circumspect life, thus conferring comparative health advantages on practitioners.

❧⟨◉⟩❧

The believer's lifestyle might even have a historical foundation in the relationship between spiritual practice and longevity. Historians, for instance, are reasonably confident that the Jewish-Muslim prohibition against pork consumption had its origin in protecting believers from trichinosis. Perhaps self-preservation effects such as this extend across many aspects of religion. Those faiths that taught adherents to live circumspectly and care for one another were more likely to prosper, passing down their assumptions, and their health benefits, to the present day.

Jumping off from that, Dr. Herbert Benson of Harvard Medical School has proposed that one reason faith may be linked to better health—indeed, a reason faith and society are historically linked—is that natural selection favors religion. In Benson's theory, during prehistory those clans or groups that possessed the stirrings of religious belief would have developed better health habits and recognized a responsibility to care for family and neighbors. This would have increased "kin fitness," or the likelihood that the group overall would pass along its members' genes. Descendants were then raised with a disposition toward belief; the descendants increased their own survival fitness through faith-motivated health habits and altruistic care of others; they created new descendants and so on. In this way, Benson thinks, human beings became "wired for God," genetically predisposed to have faith. Obviously, religion did not confer a selection advantage in every case: sometimes it caused communities to become targets of war or to engage in internal repression. But, on the macroscale of evolution, those who believed were likelier to live long, healthy lives than those who did not believe. The same, Benson thinks, remains true today.

None of the respectable faith-and-health researchers proposes that religion extends longevity through supernatural agency. Some do, however, take seriously the utility of prayer. Studies of "intercessionary" prayer—Person A prays for the health of Person B—haven't turned up much. But studies do suggest that prayer favorably influences health outcomes for the person who does the praying.

The nonsectarian form of prayer that is akin to meditation has long been recognized by clinicians to improve composure and the sense of well-being; anyone can benefit from a period of meditative prayer each day. Studies at Duke University and elsewhere have recently found that traditional religious "petitionary" prayer, or silently addressing God, also favors health. In one study, subjects who both attended worship services and regularly prayed had lower blood pressure than the control group. Researchers assume that traditional prayer can confer health benefits through the psychological effects of equanimity. Benson's studies, for instance, suggest that a calm state of mind improves the body's self-healing abilities.

Camps in the medical community were displeased when the American Cancer Society recently declared, "Sometimes answers come from prayer when medical science has none." On one level the statement is inarguable; reverence for higher purpose might comfort the victim of illness in ways that no drug or technology ever could. But conventional medicine is comfortable only with the sociological notion that the sick may console themselves by addressing a Maker, real or speculative. The idea that there is an actual reply, that "answers come from prayer," is one that makes much of the medical establishment uneasy, even if the source of the "answer" is no more than the person's own contemplative understanding.

Yet one of the modern era's little secrets is that it is hardly only the Bible-thumpers who pray. John Houghton, among the world's foremost atmospheric physicists and a leading proponent of global-warming theory, regularly prays and has written articles on the value of prayer. The Nobel Prize-winning physicist Charles Townes, principal inventor of the laser beam, says that he prays daily. Pundits might snicker, but, if regular prayer composes the mind and confers health benefits, the person who prays is following the intelligent course, regardless of the verity of any religion.

•◦◉◦•

Another possibility for the link between longevity and faith turns on mental health. Koenig suspects that many physical benefits of religious practice originate with the sense of well-being or purposefulness that believers report: he finds it revealing that the faithful experience fewer bouts of clinical depression than the population at large and that, when depression does strike, they recover faster. In this view, faith doesn't merely have an agreeable placebo effect on the mind but helps believers acquire coping mechanisms that ward off stress and anxiety, lower stress in turn being favorable for physical health. Dr. Esther Sternberg, a researcher at the National Institute of Mental Health, devotes a fine new book, *A Delicate Balance,* to the evidence that health and quality of life are improved by possessing an affirmative emotional sense, including the belief that existence is worthwhile and has purpose.

The mental health point isn't just a detached observation. Sternberg's premise, after all, is not much different from saying that postmodernism is bad for your health. Many in the academic establishment are uncomfortable with evidence that belief promotes mental health, as this implies that faith ought to be the normative condition, compared to unbelief.

Here faith-and-health treads some of the same ground as the emerging "good life" movement in psychology. Postwar psychology and social science have emphasized dysfunction, studying what causes people to become alienated or anti-social. The good-life movement seeks instead to emphasize what causes people to become high-minded and altruistic. "Good life" in this sense means the admirable path, not wine and roses; Eleanor Roosevelt is a favorite topic of good-life proponents. Martin Seligman of the University of Pennsylvania, recently president of the American Psychological Association, is a leader in this evolving discipline, having said that scholars ought to "turn their eyes to the best in life."

The regnant intellectual view is that the awful truth about society is revealed when people are driven to madness; the good-life movement asserts, instead, that the shining truth is revealed when people become selfless. But academia is today much more comfortable with lamenting ugliness than endorsing virtue. To hold up Eleanor Roosevelt—or anyone else—as a psychological archetype goes against the current vogue for radical nonjudgmentalism.

There's an obvious corollary here between good-life psychology and the faith-and-health question. If psychology ought to be focusing on what causes morality, and mainstream religions promote morality and mental health, we have a new argument for taking faith seriously. The cynical view of religion was so deeply ingrained in postwar intellectual thought that, until 1994, the American Psychiatric Association classified strong spiritual belief as a "disorder." Now faith is looking like a health boon. Quite a switcheroo.

And, speaking of fun twists, it's established that physicians have an obligation to advise patients to take steps that research shows to be associated with longevity, such as not smoking. It's also established that doctors may counsel patients on highly personal subjects, such as sexual behavior. So, if faith increases your odds of good health, does this mean your physician has an obligation to advise you to become religious?

Sloan, of Columbia, says he fears doctors may soon be pressured to dispense such advice and counters that, although research has shown that being married correlates with better health, this does not cause physicians to advise patients to rush to the chapel. The trouble with this reasoning is that counseling patients to wed is not utilitarian: there's no guarantee you'll find a compatible partner. Recommending religion, on the other hand, is quite pragmatic advice. Anyone can join a faith; attending services is a lot easier than quitting smoking.

Nevertheless, "Even if the research shows that religion is good for health, that doesn't mean doctors should prescribe it like antibiotics," says Larson, the faith-and-health advocate. Koenig thinks the research only demonstrates that physicians should "ask the patient if he or she practices a religion and, if so, what the physician can do to offer support. At this point, we have enough research to say that is good clinical medicine."

Spiritual awareness may indeed be good for you, but it's just as well that your doctor not double as clergy. If faith ever became a formal adjunct of medicine, HMOs could end up publishing lists of preferred-provider churches, mosques, and synagogues, requiring a precertification number before the priest can perform last rites, and—well, you can guess the rest.

Michael Shermer

NO

Prayer and Healing: The Verdict Is in and the Results Are Null

In a long-awaited comprehensive scientific study on the effects of intercessory prayer on the health and recovery of 1,802 patients undergoing coronary bypass surgery in six different hospitals, prayers offered by strangers
had no effect. In fact, contrary to common belief, patients who knew they
were being prayed for had a higher rate of post-operative complications such
as abnormal heart rhythms, possibly the result of anxiety caused by learning
that they were being prayed for and thus their condition was more serious
than anticipated.

The study, which cost $2.4 million (mast of which came from the John
Templeton Foundation), was begun almost a decade ago and was directed
by Harvard University Medical School cardiologist Dr. Herbert Benson and
published in *The American Heart Journal*. It was by far the most rigorous and
comprehensive study on the effects of intercessory prayer on the health and
recovery of patients ever conducted. In addition to the numerous methodological flaws in the previous research corrected for in the Benson study. Dr.
Richard Sloan, a professor of behavioral medicine at Columbia and author of
the forthcoming book, *Blind Faith: The Unholy Alliance of Religion and Medicine,*
explained: "The problem with studying religion scientifically is that you do
violence to the phenomenon by reducing it to basic elements that can be
quantified, and that makes for bad science and bad religion."

The 1,802 patients were divided into three groups, two of which were
prayed for by members of three congregations: St. Paul's Monastery in St. Paul,
MN; the Community of Teresian Carmelites in Worcester, MA; and Silent Unity,
a Missouri prayer ministry near Kansas City, MO. The prayers were allowed to
pray in their own manner, but they were instructed to include the following
phrase in their prayers: "for a successful surgery with a quick, healthy recovery
and no complications." Prayers began the night before the surgery and continued daily for two weeks after. Half the prayer-recipient patients were told that
they were being prayed for while the other half were told that they might or
might not receive prayers. The researchers monitored the patients for 30 days
after the operations.

Results showed no statistically significant differences between the prayed-
for and non-prayed-for groups. Although the following findings were not
statistically significant, 59% of patients who knew that they were being prayed

From *Skeptic,* vol. 12, no. 3, 2006, pp. 20–21. Copyright © 2006 by Skeptics Society. Reprinted
by permission.

for suffered complications, compared with 51% of those who were uncertain whether they were being prayed for or not; and 18% in the uninformed prayer group suffered major complications such as heart attack or stroke, compared with 13% in the group that received no prayers.

This study is particularly significant because Herbert Benson has long been sympathetic to the possibility that intercessory prayer can positively influence the health of patients. His team's rigorous methodologies overcame the numerous flaws that called into question previously published studies. The most commonly cited study in support of the connection between prayer and healing is Randolph C. Byrd's "Positive Therapeutic Effects of Intercessory Prayer in a Coronory Care Unit Population," *Southern Medical Journal* 81 (1998): 826–829. The two best studies on the methodological problems with prayer and healing are the following: Richard Sloan, E. Bagiella, and T. Powell, 1999. "Religion, Spirituality, and Medicine," *The Lancet,* Feb. 20, Vol. 353: 664–667; and: John T. Chibnall, Joseph M. Jeral, Michael Cerullo, 2001. "Experiments on Distant Intercessory Prayer," *Archives of Internal Medicine,* Nov. 26, Vol. 161: 2529–2536. . . . .

The Most Significant Flaws in All Such Studies Include the Following:

1. *Fraud.* In 2001, the *Journal of Reproductive Medicine* published a study by three Columbia University researchers claiming that prayer for women undergoing in-vitro fertilization resulted in a pregnancy rate of 50%, double that of women who did not receive prayer. Media coverage was extensive. ABC News medical correspondent Dr. Timothy Johnson, for example, reported, "A new study on the power of prayer over pregnancy reports surprising results; but many physicians remain skeptical." One of those skeptics was University of California Clinical Professor of Gynecology and Obstetrics Bruce Flamm, who not only found numerous methodological errors in the experiment, but also discovered that one of the study's authors, Daniel Wirth (AKA "John Wayne Truelove"), is not an M.D., but an M.S. in parapsychology who has since been indicted on felony charges for mail fraud and theft, for which he pleaded guilty. The other two authors have refused comment, and after three years of inquiries from Flamm the journal removed the study from its website and Columbia University has launched an investigation.

2. *Lack of Controls.* Many of these studies failed to control for such intervening variables as age, sex, education, ethnicity, socioeconomic status, marital standing, degree of religiosity, and the fact that most religions have sanctions against such behaviors as sexual promiscuity, alcohol and drug abuse, and smoking. When such variables are controlled for, the formerly significant results disappear. One study on recovery from hip surgery in elderly women failed to control for age; another study on church attendance and illness recovery did not consider that people in poorer health are less likely to attend church; a related study failed to control for levels of exercise.

3. *Outcome differences.* In one of the most highly publicized studies of cardiac patients prayed for by born-again Christians, 29 outcome variables were measured but on only six did the prayed-for group show improvement. In related studies, different outcome measures were significant. To be meaningful, the same measures need to be significant across studies, because if enough outcomes are measured some will show significant correlations by chance.

4. *Selective Reporting.* In several studies on the relationship between religiosity and mortality (religious people allegedly live longer), a number of religious variables were used, but only those with significant correlations were reported. Meanwhile, other studies using the same religiosity variables found different correlations and, of course, only reported those. The rest were filed away in the drawer of nonsignificant findings. When all variables are factored in together, religiosity and mortality show no relationship.

5. *Operational definitions.* When experimenting on the effects of prayer, what, precisely, is being studied? For example, what type of prayer is being employed? (Are Christian, Jewish, Muslim, Buddhist, Wiccan, and Shaman prayers equal?) Who or what is being prayed to? (Are God, Jesus, and a universal life force equivalent?) What is the length and frequency of the prayer? (Are two 10-minute prayers equal to one 20-minute prayer?) How many people are praying and does their status in the religion matter? (Is one priestly prayer identical to ten parishioner prayers?) Most prayer studies either lack such operational definitions, or there is no consistency across studies in such definitions.

6. *Theological implications.* The ultimate flaw in all such studies is theological. If God is omniscient and omnipotent why should he need to be reminded or inveigled that someone needs healing? Scientific prayer makes God a celestial lab rat, leading to bad science and worse religion.

POSTSCRIPT

Do Religion and Prayer Benefit Health?

Can we influence the course of our own illnesses? Can emotions, stress management, and prayer prevent or cure disease? In a telephone poll of 1,004 Americans conducted by TIME/CNN in June 1996, 82 percent indicated that they believed in the healing power of personal prayer. Three-fourths felt that praying for someone else could help cure their illness. Interestingly, fewer than two-thirds of doctors say they believe in God. Benson, who developed the "relaxation response," thinks there is a strong link between religious commitment and good health. He contends that people do not have to have a professed belief in God to reap the psychological and physical rewards of the "faith factor." Benson defined the faith factor as the combined force of the relaxation response and the placebo effect.

In "God at the Bedside" (*New England Journal of Medicine,* March 18, 2004), physician Jerome Groopman is asked by a patient to pray for her after receiving a diagnosis of cancer. Dr. Groopman, although religious, considers prayer and religion a private matter. He debated over whether or not he should sidestep the patient's request or whether he should cross a boundary from the purely professional to the personal and join her in prayer. The article addresses his solution to dealing with this difficult issue.

Dr. Bernard Siegel, writing in his bestseller *Love, Medicine and Miracles* (Harper & Row, 1986), argues that there are no "incurable diseases, only incurable people" and that illness is a personality flaw. In "Welcome to the Mind/ Body Revolution" (*Psychology Today,* July/August 1993), author Marc Barash further discusses how the mind and immune system influence each other. The journal *Social Science and Medicine* published a literature review in July 2006 entitled "Do Religious/Spiritual Coping Strategies Affect Illness Adjustment in Patients with Cancer?: A Systematic Review of the Literature." The study found mixed results. Some researchers determined that religion influenced the outcome of disease, while others did not. The authors also found that many of the studies showed methodological flaws, echoed by Michael Shermer.

In *You Don't Have to Die: Unraveling the AIDS Myth* (Burton Goldberg Group, 1994), a chapter entitled "Mind-Body Medicine" discusses the body's innate healing capabilities and the role of self-responsibility in the healing process. A long-term AIDS survivor who traveled the country interviewing other long-term survivors found that the one thing they all shared was the belief that AIDS was survivable. They all also accepted the reality of their diagnosis but refused to see their condition as a death sentence.

Readings that address these issues include "Prayer and Religion Forum" (*Skeptic*, vol. 13, 2007); "Healing the Sick" (*Sojourners Magazine*, April 2007); "Religion and Healing in America" (*Journal of Church & State*, Winter 2007); "Healing at the Borderline of Medicine and Religion" (*Library Journal*, September 1, 2006); "Spirituality in Care Giving and Care Receiving" (*Holistic Nursing Practice*, January–February 2003); "Spiritual Healing" (*Internal Medicine News*, December 15, 2002); "Hypnosis, Relaxation, Imagery, Prayer, and Faith in Healing" (*Subconsciously Speaking*, July–August 2002); "Seeing Is Believing? The Form and Substance of French Medical Debates over Lourdes" (*Bulletin of the History of Medicine*, Summer 2002); "The Power of Words: Healing Narratives among Lubavitcher Hasidim" (*Medical Anthropology Quarterly*, March 2002); "The Doctor as God's Mechanic?: Beliefs in the Southeastern United States" (*Social Science & Medicine*, February 2002); "Spiritual Matters, Earthly Benefits" (*Tufts University Health & Nutrition Letter*, August 2001); and "Prayer Makes a Difference: I'd Bet My Life on It" (*Commonweal*, April 21, 2000).

Internet References . . .

National Right to Life

Comprehensive information on the pro-life movement. Right to life issues including abortion, euthanasia, and infanticide. Tracking pro-life legislation is included.

http://www.nrlc.org/

Pharmacists for Life International

Information on the association of pro-life professional pharmacists dedicated to restoring respect for the sanctity of human life. Includes a discussion of the issue of conscience clauses.

http://www.pfli.org/

National Institute on Alcohol Abuse and Alcoholism

Resources, publications, research information, FAQs, and updates on alcohol-related issues in the news. It includes a link to the Interagency Coordinating Committee on Fetal Alcohol Syndrome

http://www.niaaa.nih.gov/publications/AlcoholResarch/

Pregnancy, Babies, Prematurity—March of Dimes Foundation

Information and answers about pregnancy, folic acid, prematurity, genetic disorders, birth defects and prevention.

http://www.marchofdimes.com

National Eating Disorders Association

Information about the National Eating Disorders Association (NEDA), a nonprofit organization dedicated to supporting individuals and families affected by eating disorders. There is information on prevention, improved access to quality treatment, and increased research funding.

http://www.nationaleatingdisorders.org/

Cleveland Clinic Fact Sheet—Circumcision

Information about the procedure and the health risks and benefits.

http://my.clevelandclinic.org/services/circumcision/hic_circumcision.aspx

Sexuality and Gender Issues

*F*ew issues could be of greater controversy than those concerning gender and sexuality. Recent generations of Americans have rejected "traditional" sexual roles and values, which has resulted in a significant increase in babies born out of wedlock, the spread of sexually transmitted diseases, and a rise in legal abortions. This unit debates whether or not pharmacists and other health providers should be permitted to deny legal prescriptions or health care based on their conscience and whether or not it is okay for pregnant women to drink moderately. Other issues in this unit include whether or not the vaccine to prevent cervical cancer should be required for all girls, ultrathin models and actresses as role models, the validity of the post-abortion syndrome, and is there a valid reason to routinely circumcise infant males?

- Is It Necessary for Pregnant Women to Completely Abstain from All Alcoholic Beverage?
- Should Pro-Life Health Providers Be Allowed to Deny Prescriptions on the Basis of Conscience?
- Should the Cervical Cancer Vaccine for Girls Be Compulsory?
- Is There a Post-Abortion Syndrome?
- Do Ultrathin Models and Actresses Influence the Onset of Eating Disorders?
- Is There a Valid Reason for Routine Infant Male Circumcision?

ISSUE 10

Is It Necessary for Pregnant Women to Completely Abstain from All Alcoholic Beverages?

YES: **Phyllida Brown,** from "Drinking for Two?" *New Scientist* (July 1, 2006)

NO: **Julia Moskin,** from "The Weighty Responsibility of Drinking for Two," *The New York Times* (November 29, 2006)

ISSUE SUMMARY

YES: Science writer Phyllida Brown maintains that even a small amount of alcohol can damage a developing fetus and cites new research indicating that even small amounts of alcohol consumed during pregnancy may be harmful.

NO: Journalist Julia Moskin argues that there are almost no studies on the effects of moderate drinking during pregnancy and that small amounts of alcohol are unlikely to have much effect.

In 1973, *The Lancet* published a paper describing a pattern of birth defects among children born of alcoholic women called "fetal alcohol syndrome" (FAS) ("Recognition of the Fetal Alcohol Syndrome in Early Infancy," vol. 2, 1973). Since that time, thousands of studies have supported the relationship between heavy alcohol consumption during pregnancy and resulting birth defects. One controversial point related to FAS, however, is the amount of alcohol that must be consumed to cause danger to the developing baby. It seems that some threshold must exist, though it's unclear what that is.

In their 1973 study, Jones and Smith correlated FAS only among children born to alcohol abusing women. Although the researchers were successful in bringing the syndrome to international attention, it also created apprehension that any amount of alcohol consumption during pregnancy could cause danger to the child. Many doctors and researchers believe that even minute levels of alcohol intake during pregnancy can cause FAS, causing a panic that may have exaggerated the dangers of *any* consumption.

Fortunately, FAS is relatively uncommon, though the United States has one of the highest rates in the developed world. This may be related to the pattern of alcohol consumption in this country. In many European countries, alcohol is often consumed daily, whereas in the United States, alcohol intake is more confined to weekends. This results in higher blood alcohol levels on those days. In addition, other variables increase the risk of FAS that cannot be linked solely to the amount of alcohol consumed. For example, women who binge drink are much more likely to bear children with the pattern of birth defects linked to FAS than women who consume the same total amount of alcohol over a period of time. Also, women who bear children with FAS often have liver disease and nutritional deficiencies including anemia, infections, and other conditions that exacerbate alcohol's effects on the fetus. Older mothers and those who have given birth to several children are also at greater risk to have children with FAS. However, the two most significant conditions along with alcohol consumption are low income and cigarette smoking (because it contains toxins that reduce blood flow and level of oxygen available to the fetus). Low income is related to poor diet, smoking and other drug use, and exposure to pollutants such as lead.

While it appears that heavy alcohol consumption, particularly binge drinking, combined with smoking, poor diet, low income, and concomitant health problems increase the risk of FAS, is there an absolutely safe level of alcohol consumption during pregnancy? Two recent studies suggest that alcohol use during pregnancy may be more dangerous for the child than previously thought. In one study, researchers found symptoms of FAS in children whose mothers drank two drinks per day at certain stages of pregnancy. The children born of these women were found to be unusually small and/or had learning or behavioral problems. The researchers also found other defects associated with FAS at a higher rate than expected ("Epidemiology of FASD in a Province in Italy: Prevalence and Characteristics of Children in a Random Sample of Schools," *Alcoholism: Clinical and Experimental Research*, September 2006). A second study confirmed that FAS is not the only concern associated with alcohol consumption during pregnancy. It's also a risk factor for alcohol abuse among the children born of these women ("In Utero Alcohol Exposure and Prediction of Alcohol Disorders in Early Adulthood: A Birth Cohort Study," *Archives of General Psychiatry*, September 2006).

It's apparent that heavy use of alcohol during pregnancy increases the risk of FAS. What is unclear is the risk associated with any amount of alcohol. A 25-year study of babies born to mother who were social drinkers found that even low intakes of alcohol had measurable effects on their babies. The study concluded that no minimum level of drinking was absolutely safe. See "When Two Drinks Are Too Many" (*Psychology Today*, May/June 2004).

The following two selections address whether it is safe for pregnant women to drink during pregnancy. Phyllida Brown argues that even a small amount of alcohol can damage a developing fetus and cites new research indicating that moderate consumption of alcoholic beverages during pregnancy may be harmful and that it's safer to avoid drinking. Journalist Julia Moskin counters that there are almost no studies on the effects of moderate drinking during pregnancy and that small amounts of alcohol consumed during pregnancy are unlikely to have much harmful effect.

YES ⤶

Phyllida Brown

Drinking for Two?

At first, Susie's teachers thought she was a bright child. Her adoptive mother knew different. Give Susie a set of instructions and only a few seconds later she would have forgotten them. She was talkative, with a large vocabulary, but could not seem to form lasting friendships. Then, one day, Susie's adoptive mother heard a lecture that described fetal alcohol syndrome—a condition which affects some children born to heavy drinkers. "Bells went off in my head," she says. "The lecturer described eight traits, and my daughter had seven of them."

Children like Susie could well be just the tip of the iceberg. Fetal alcohol syndrome was once thought to affect only the children of heavy drinkers, such as Susie's biological mother, but a mounting body of research suggests that even a small amount of alcohol can damage a developing fetus—a single binge during pregnancy or a moderate seven small glasses of wine per week.

The new research has already prompted some governments to tighten up their advice on drinking during pregnancy. Others, however, say there is no convincing evidence that modest alcohol intake is dangerous for the fetus. With advice varying wildly from one country to another, the message for pregnant women has never been so confusing.

Last year the US Surgeon General revised official advice warning pregnant women to limit their alcohol intake. Now they are told "simply not to drink" alcohol—not only in pregnancy, but as soon as they plan to try for a baby. France also advises abstinence, as does Canada. The UK's Department of Health says that pregnant women should avoid more than "one to two units, once or twice a week," but is finalising a review of the latest evidence, which it will publish within weeks. In Australia, women are advised to "consider" abstinence, but if choosing to drink should limit their intake to less than seven standard Australian drinks a week, with no more than two standard drinks on any one day. . . .

Whichever guidelines women choose to follow, some level of drinking during pregnancy is common in many countries. The last time pregnant women in the UK were asked, in 2002, 61 per cent admitted to drinking some alcohol. Even in the US, where abstinence is expected, and where pregnant women in some states have been arrested for drinking, 13 per cent still admit to doing it.

Children with fetal alcohol syndrome (FAS) are generally smaller than average and have a range of developmental and behavioural problems such as an inability to relate to others and a tendency to be impulsive. They also have distinctive facial features such as a thin upper lip, an extra fold of skin in the inner corners of the eyes and a flattening of the groove between the nose and upper lip.

In recent years researchers investigating the effects of alcohol in pregnancy have begun to widen their definition of antenatal alcohol damage beyond the diagnosis of FAS. They now talk of fetal alcohol spectrum disorders, or FASD, an umbrella term that covers a range of physical, mental and behavioural effects which can occur without the facial features of FAS. Like children with FAS, those with FASD may have problems with arithmetic, paying attention, working memory and the planning of tasks. They may be impulsive, find it difficult to judge social situations correctly and relate badly to others, or be labelled as aggressive or defiant. In adulthood they may find it difficult to lead independent lives, be diagnosed with mental illnesses, or get into trouble with the law. Some have damage to the heart, ears or eyes.

While some children with FASD have been exposed to as much alcohol before birth as those with FAS, others may be damaged by lower levels, says Helen Barr, a statistician at the University of Washington, Seattle. Barr has spent 30 years tracking children exposed to alcohol before birth and comparing them with non-exposed children. The less alcohol, in general, says Barr, the milder the effects, such as more subtle attention problems or memory difficulties. Other factors that can affect the type of damage include the fetus's stage of development when exposed to alcohol and the mother's genetic make-up.

Although FASD is not yet an official medical diagnosis, some researchers estimate that it could be very common indeed. While FAS is thought to account for 1 in 500 live births, Ann Streissguth and her colleagues at the University of Washington believe that as many as 1 in every 100 babies born in the US are affected by FASD. Others put the figure at about 1 in 300. Whichever figure is more accurate, it would still make the condition far more common than, say, Downs syndrome, which affects 1 in 800 babies born in the US.

Streissguth was among the first to study the long-term effects of moderate drinking in pregnancy. In 1993 she reported that a group of 7-year-olds whose mothers had drunk 7 to 14 standard drinks per week in pregnancy tended to have specific problems with arithmetic and attention. Compared with children of similar IQ whose mothers had abstained during pregnancy, they struggled to remember strings of digits or the details of stories read to them, and were unable to discriminate between two rhythmic sound patterns.

When Streissguth's team followed the alcohol-exposed children through adolescence and into their early twenties they found them significantly more likely than other individuals of similar IQ and social background to be labelled as aggressive by their teachers. According to their parents, these children were unable to consider the effects of their actions on others, and unable to take hints or understand social cues. As young adults, they were more likely to drink heavily and use drugs than their peers.

These findings were borne out by similar studies later in the 1990s by Sandra Jacobson and Joseph Jacobson, both psychologists at Wayne State University in Detroit, Michigan. To try and work out what dose of alcohol might be harmful, the Jacobsons ran a study of children born to 480 women in Detroit. In it, they compared the children born to women who, at their first antenatal appointment, said they drank seven or more standard US drinks a week with the babies of women who drank less than seven, and with those whose mothers abstained altogether. The psychologists then tested the children's mental function in infancy and again at 7 years old. In the children whose mothers had seven drinks or more, the pair found significant deficits in their children's mental function in infancy, and again at age 7, mainly in arithmetic, working memory and attention (*Alcoholism: Clinical and Experimental Research,* vol. 28, p. 1732). Where the mother drank less than that they found no effect.

Spread It Out

Seven drinks a week may be more than many pregnant women manage, but according to the Jacobsons, what's important is when you are drinking them, whether you have eaten, and how quickly your body metabolises alcohol. In their study, only one woman of the 480 drank daily; most of the others restricted their drinking to a couple of weekend evenings. If a woman is drinking seven standard drinks on average across the week, but having them all on two nights, she must be reaching four drinks on one night. That constitutes a binge. "Women don't realise that if they save up their alcohol 'allowance' to the end of the week, they are concentrating their drinking in a way that is potentially harmful," she says. This means that even women who have fewer than seven glasses per week could potentially be putting their babies at risk if they drink them all on one night.

There is also some evidence that fewer than seven drinks a week could have measurable effects on an unborn baby. Peter Hepper at Queen's University, Belfast, UK, examined the movements of fetuses scanned on ultrasound in response to a noise stimulus. Having asked women about their drinking habits, they compared the responses of fetuses exposed to low levels of alcohol—between 1 and 6 British units per week, each containing 10 millilitres of alcohol—and those exposed to none. When tested between 20 and 35 weeks, the fetuses exposed to alcohol tended to show a "startle response" usually found only in the earlier stages of pregnancy, when the nervous system is less developed. Five months after birth, the same babies showed different responses to visual stimuli from the babies whose mothers had abstained. Hepper interprets these findings as evidence that a low dose of alcohol has some as yet unexplained effect on the developing nervous system. Whether or not these differences will translate into behaviour problems in later life is as yet unknown.

When Ed Riley and colleagues at San Diego State University in California looked at children's brains using magnetic resonance imaging, they found obvious changes in the brain structure of children whose mothers drank very heavily, but also some changes in children born to moderate drinkers. For example, there were abnormalities in the corpus callosum, the tract of fibres connecting the right and left hemispheres of the brain. The greater the abnormality, the worse the children performed on a verbal learning task.

Despite these recent studies, the link between alcohol and fetal development is far from clear. Not all babies born to alcoholic women have FAS, yet other babies appear to be damaged by their mothers indulging in just a single binge. And if 61 percent of British women drink while pregnant, how come there are not hundreds of thousands of British children with FASD? Wouldn't we notice if 1 in 100 children being born were affected?

Hepper argues that few teachers would raise an eyebrow if they had two or three children in a class of 30 with marked behaviour difficulties, and several more with milder, manageable problems. He therefore thinks it is plausible to suggest that 1 in 100 children could have alcohol-related problems of some sort.

Hepper's research is widely quoted by anti-drinking campaigners such as FAS Aware, an international organisation which advertises in the women's bathrooms of bars to encourage pregnant women not to drink. The posters warn that "drinking in pregnancy could leave you with a hangover for life" and that "everything you drink goes to your baby's head."

Critics of these tactics point out that trying to scare women into abstinence is not helpful. There are reports in North America of women rushing off for an abortion because they had one drink before they knew they were pregnant or being racked with guilt about past drinking if they have a child with a mild disability.

Researchers like the Jacobsons acknowledge that it is hard to be certain about how alcohol affects a developing fetus on the basis of epidemiological studies, especially when they measure the notoriously messy subject of human behaviour. Any effect on the developing brain would vary depending on exactly when the fetus was exposed, and since some behavioural effects may not become apparent until several years after birth, it is difficult to pin down specific disabilities to specific antenatal exposure to alcohol.

To try and get around the epidemiological problem, John Olney, a neuroscientist at Washington University in St Louis, Missouri, has examined the impact of alcohol on developing rodent brains as a model for what happens in humans. Six years ago Olney and others showed that alcohol causes neurons in the developing rat brain to undergo programmed cell death, or apoptosis (*Science*, vol. 287, p. 1056).

Olney found that alcohol does the most serious damage if exposure happens during synaptogenesis, a critical time in development when neurons are rapidly forming connections. In rats, this happens just after birth, but in humans it begins in the second half of pregnancy and continues for two or more years. In the *Science* study, the team found that exposure to alcohol for baby rats during this developmental stage, at levels equivalent to a binge lasting several hours, could trigger the suicide of millions of neurons, damaging the structure of the animals' forebrains. The alcohol seems to interfere with the action of receptors for two chemical signals or neurotransmitters, glutamate and GABA (gamma amino butyric acid), that must function normally for connections to form.

Lost Neurons

The changes to brain development in rodents, Olney believes, could explain some of the behavioural problems seen in children with FASD, including attention deficit, learning and memory problems. For example, in the rat study, large numbers of neurons were lost in the brain regions that comprise the extended hippocampal circuit, which is disrupted in other disorders of learning and memory (*Addiction Biology*, vol. 9, p. 137). Loss of cells in the thalamus, which is thought to play a role in "filtering" irrelevant stimuli, may partly explain why FASD children are easily distracted.

The timing of alcohol exposure during pregnancy dictates what type of damage will occur, Olney says: if it is early on, when facial structures are forming, the facial characteristics of FAS may be obvious. Later, when synapses are forming, mental function may be affected. This runs counter to the popular view that the fetus is only vulnerable in the first trimester; in fact, different stages may be vulnerable in different ways.

Olney has recently tried to find out exactly how much alcohol is enough to trigger apoptosis. This year he reported that, in infant mice whose brains are at the equivalent stage of development to a third-trimester fetus, some 20,000 neurons are deleted when they are exposed to only mildly raised blood alcohol levels, for periods as short as 45 minutes. In humans, he says, this is equivalent to deleting 20 million neurons with a 45-minute exposure to blood alcohol levels of just 50 milligrams per 100 millilitres of blood—which is well below the legal limit for driving, and easily achieved in "normal social" drinking (*Neurobiology of Disease*, DOI: 10.1016/j.nbd.2005.12.015). At blood alcohol levels below this, the team found no apoptosis.

Olney is quick to stress that, alarming as 20 million neurons sounds, it is "a very small amount of brain damage" in the context of the human brain, which is estimated to have trillions of neurons. He has no evidence that such small-scale damage would translate into any detectable effects on a child's cognitive abilities. "But if a mother is advised that one or two glasses of wine with dinner is OK, and if she then has two glasses with dinner three times a week, this is exposing the fetus to a little bit of damage three times a week," he says.

The bottom line is that, as yet, it's impossible to translate these findings into blanket advice for women about how many drinks they can or can't have when pregnant. A drink before food will raise blood alcohol concentrations faster than a drink with a meal; two drinks downed quickly will raise it more sharply than two drinks spread over 3 hours. Because of this uncertainty, some researchers—and some authorities—would rather take no chances. "The best possible advice I can give mothers is to totally abstain from alcohol the moment they know they are pregnant," Olney says.

Julia Moskin

➡ **NO**

The Weighty Responsibility of Drinking for Two

It happens at coffee bars. It happens at cheese counters. But most of all, it happens at bars and restaurants. Pregnant women are slow-moving targets for strangers who judge what we eat—and, especially, drink.

"Nothing makes people more uncomfortable than a pregnant woman sitting at the bar," said Brianna Walker, a bartender in Los Angeles. "The other customers can't take their eyes off her."

Drinking during pregnancy quickly became taboo in the United States after 1981, when the Surgeon General began warning women about the dangers of alcohol. The warnings came after researchers at the *University of Washington* identified Fetal Alcohol Syndrome, a group of physical and mental birth defects caused by alcohol consumption, in 1973. In its recommendations, the government does not distinguish between heavy drinking and the occasional beer: all alcohol poses an unacceptable risk, it says.

So those of us who drink, even occasionally, during pregnancy face unanswerable questions, like why would anyone risk the health of a child for a passing pleasure like a beer?

"It comes down to this: I just don't buy it," said Holly Masur, a mother of two in Deerfield, Ill., who often had half a glass of wine with dinner during her pregnancies, based on advice from both her mother and her obstetrician. "How can a few sips of wine be dangerous when women used to drink martinis and smoke all through their pregnancies?"

Many American obstetricians, skeptical about the need for total abstinence, quietly tell their patients that an occasional beer or glass of wine—no hard liquor—is fine.

"If a patient tells me that she's drinking two or three glasses of wine a week, I am personally comfortable with that after the first trimester," said Dr. Austin Chen, an obstetrician in TriBeCa. "But technically I am sticking my neck out by saying so."

Americans' complicated relationship with food and drink—in which everything desirable is also potentially dangerous—only becomes magnified in pregnancy.

When I was pregnant with my first child in 2001 there was so much conflicting information that doubt became a reflexive response. Why was tea allowed but not coffee? How could all "soft cheeses" be forbidden if cream cheese was recommended? What were the real risks of having a glass of wine on my birthday?

Pregnant women are told that danger lurks everywhere: listeria in soft cheese, mercury in canned tuna, *salmonella* in fresh-squeezed orange juice. Our responsibility for minimizing risk through perfect behavior feels vast.

Eventually, instead of automatically following every rule, I began looking for proof.

Proof, it turns out, is hard to come by when it comes to "moderate" or "occasional" drinking during pregnancy. Standard definitions, clinical trials and long-range studies simply do not exist.

"Clinically speaking, there is no such thing as moderate drinking in pregnancy," said Dr. Ernest L. Abel, a professor at Wayne State University Medical School in Detroit, who has led many studies on pregnancy and alcohol. "The studies address only heavy drinking"—defined by the *National Institutes of Health* as five drinks or more per day—"or no drinking."

Most pregnant women in America say in surveys that they do not drink at all—although they may not be reporting with total accuracy. But others make a conscious choice not to rule out drinking altogether.

For me, the desire to drink turned out to be all tied up with the ritual of the table—sitting down in a restaurant, reading the menu, taking that first bite of bread and butter. That was the only time, I found, that sparkling water or nonalcoholic beer didn't quite do it. And so, after examining my conscience and the research available, I concluded that one drink with dinner was an acceptable risk.

My husband, frankly, is uncomfortable with it. But he recognizes that there is no way for him to put himself in my position, or to know what he would do under the same circumstances.

While occasional drinking is not a decision I take lightly, it is also a decision in which I am not (quite) alone. Lisa Felter McKenney, a teacher in Chicago whose first child is due in January, said she feels comfortable at her current level of three drinks a week, having been grudgingly cleared by her obstetrician. "Being able to look forward to a beer with my husband at the end of the day really helps me deal with the horrible parts of being pregnant," she said. "It makes me feel like myself: not the alcohol, but the ritual. Usually I just take a few sips and that's enough."

Ana Sortun, a chef in Cambridge, Mass., who gave birth last year, said that she (and the nurse practitioner who delivered her baby) both drank wine during their pregnancies. "I didn't do it every day, but I did it often," she said. "Ultimately I trusted my own instincts, and my doctor's, more than anything else. Plus, I really believe all that stuff about the European tradition."

Many women who choose to drink have pointed to the habits of European women who legendarily drink wine, eat raw-milk cheese and quaff Guinness to improve breast milk production, as justification for their own choices in pregnancy.

Of course, those countries have their own taboos. "Just try to buy unpasteurized cheese in England, or to eat salad in France when you're pregnant," wrote a friend living in York, England. (Many French obstetricians warn patients that raw vegetables are risky.) However, she said, a drink a day is taken for granted. In those cultures, wine and beer are considered akin to food, part of daily life; in ours, they are treated more like drugs.

But more European countries are adopting the American stance of abstinence. Last month, France passed legislation mandating American-style warning labels on alcohol bottles, beginning in October 2007.

If pregnant Frenchwomen are giving up wine completely (although whether that will happen is debatable—the effects of warning labels are far from proven), where does that leave the rest of us?

"I never thought it would happen," said Jancis Robinson, a prominent wine critic in Britain, one of the few countries with government guidelines that still allow pregnant women any alcohol—one to two drinks per week. Ms. Robinson, who spent three days tasting wine for her Masters of Wine qualification in 1990 while pregnant with her second child, said that she studied the research then available and while she was inclined to be cautious, she didn't see proof that total abstinence was the only safe course.

One thing is certain: drinking is a confusing and controversial choice for pregnant women, and among the hardest areas in which to interpret the research.

Numerous long-term studies, including the original one at the University of Washington at Seattle, have established beyond doubt that heavy drinkers are taking tremendous risks with their children's health.

But for women who want to apply that research to the question of whether they must refuse a single glass of Champagne on New Year's Eve or a serving of rum-soaked Christmas pudding, there is almost no information at all.

My own decision came down to a stubborn conviction that feels like common sense: a single drink—sipped slowly, with food to slow the absorption—is unlikely to have much effect.

Some clinicians agree with that instinct. Others claim that the threat at any level is real.

"Blood alcohol level is the key," said Dr. Abel, whose view, after 30 years of research, is that brain damage and other alcohol-related problems most likely result from the spikes in blood alcohol concentration that come from binge drinking—another difficult definition, since according to Dr. Abel a binge can be as few as two drinks, drunk in rapid succession, or as many as 14, depending on a woman's physiology.

Because of ethical considerations, virtually no clinical trials can be performed on pregnant women.

"Part of the research problem is that we have mostly animal studies to work with," Dr. Abel said. "And who knows what is two drinks, for a mouse?"

Little attention has been paid to pregnant women at the low end of the consumption spectrum because there isn't a clear threat to public health there, according to Janet Golden, a history professor at Rutgers who has written about Americans' changing attitudes toward drinking in pregnancy.

The research—and the public health concern—is focused on getting pregnant women who don't regulate their intake to stop completely.

And the public seems to seriously doubt whether pregnant women can be trusted to make responsible decisions on their own.

"Strangers, and courts, will intervene with a pregnant woman when they would never dream of touching anyone else," Ms. Golden said.

Ms. Walker, the bartender, agreed. "I've had customers ask me to tell them what the pregnant woman is drinking," she said. "But I don't tell them. Like with all customers, unless someone is drunk and difficult it's no one else's business—or mine."

POSTSCRIPT

Is It Necessary for Pregnant Women to Completely Abstain from All Alcoholic Beverages?

Since its medical recognition in 1973, fetal alcohol syndrome (FAS) has progressed from a little known condition to a major public health issue. The condition has been characterized by exaggerated and unproved claims, particularly the cause and impact of the condition. For further reading on FAS, see "Fetal Alcohol Syndrome: A Cautionary Note" (*Current Pharmaceutical Design,* vol. 12, 2006). The author discusses the fact that there is likely a safe threshold for alcohol consumption during pregnancy and that FAS typically occurs among women who consume the highest amount of alcohol and/or who binge drink. Binge drinking among women of childbearing age is common in the United States, which has one of the world's highest rates of FAS. In a recent study, researchers determined that one in six women in the United States continues to drink during pregnancy and one in seven consumes more than seven drinks per week; 3 percent of the women drink more than 14 drinks per week. Thirteen percent of U.S. women aged 18 to 44 binge drink. The estimated number of childbearing-age women who engaged in binge drinking rose from 6.2 million in 2001 to 7.1 million in 2003, an increase of .9 million. See "Tracking Binge Drinking among U.S. Childbearing-Age Women" (*Preventive Medicine,* April 2007).

Fortunately, most women who use alcohol reduce their intake dramatically once they realize they are pregnant. But doctors still don't know what risk or harm, if any, results from light to moderate alcohol intake during pregnancy, which is why they caution pregnant women to abstain. For ethical reasons, there have been few, if any, studies conducted on pregnant women to determine if small to moderate intakes of alcohol is harmful. And to confuse the issue, some effects of alcohol consumption during pregnancy may not be apparent until a child starts school or even later in life. See "What Alcohol Does to a Child" (*Time,* June 5, 2006) for a discussion of the adverse effects of alcohol consumption on fetal development. It presents a study that links even small amounts of alcohol by pregnant women to a reduced IQ in their children. In a report published in the *Harvard Mental Health Letter* (January 2007), two studies suggest that drinking during pregnancy may be even riskier for the child than previously determined ("Alcohol Before Birth: New Studies").

Although individual differences in reaction to alcohol prevents determining a "safe level" of drinking for all pregnant women, encouraging total abstinence from alcohol during pregnancy is prudent though not necessarily based on research. The changes in fetal activity associated with one or two drinks clearly indicate that the fetus reacts to low levels of alcohol. But these changes don't necessarily mean that the fetus is damaged. Until relationships are considerably stronger than the evidence now indicates, the research does not support the consensus that low levels of alcohol intake pose a danger to the developing baby. Even though scientists can't prove small amounts of alcohol are harmful, they can't prove they aren't. On the other hand, setting a realistic threshold may be more effective than encouraging women to completely forgo alcohol. Setting a definite limit, two or less drinks per day for example, may be more realistic to those women who continue to drink during pregnancy. Prevention efforts have not been particularly effective among women who drink at levels that pose the greatest risk to their fetus ("Motivational Interventions in Prenatal Clinics," *Alcohol Research & Health*, vol. 25, 2001). They may be able to reduce rather than eliminate all alcohol, which could result in a reduced risk for FAS.

ISSUE 11

Should Pro-Life Health Providers Be Allowed to Deny Prescriptions on the Basis of Conscience?

YES: John A. Menges, from "Public Hearing on HB4346 Before the House State Government Administration Committee," *Illinois House State Government Administration Committee* (February 15, 2006)

NO: R. Alta Charo, from "The Celestial Fire of Conscience—Refusing to Deliver Medical Care," *New England Journal of Medicine* (June 16, 2005)

ISSUE SUMMARY

YES: Pharmacist John Menges believes that it is his right to refuse to dispense any medication designed to end a human life.

NO: Attorney R. Alta Charo argues that health care professionals who protect themselves from the moral consequences of their actions may do so at their patients' risk.

A trend has been making news recently. The Pharmacists' Refusal Clause, also known as the Conscience Clause, allows pharmacists to refuse to fill certain prescriptions because of their own moral objections to the medication. These medications are mostly birth control pills and the "morning-after pill," which can be used as emergency contraception. Though nearly all states offer some type of legal protection for health care providers who refuse to provide certain women's health care services, only three states—Arkansas, Mississippi, and South Dakota—specifically protect pharmacists who refuse to dispense birth control and emergency contraceptive pills. Only a limited number of states have passed refusal clause legislation specific to pharmacists, but more and more states are considering adding it.

In the past several years there have been reports of pharmacists who refused to fill prescriptions for birth control and emergency contraceptive pills. In some of these instances, the pharmacists who refused service were fired, but in others, no legal action was taken. As a result, some women have left their drug stores without getting their pills and not sure where to go to have their prescriptions filled.

Although doctors may refuse to perform abortions or other procedures they morally object to, should pharmacists have the same right? They are members of the health care team and should be treated as medical professionals. Society does not demand that professionals abandon their morals as a condition of their employment. On the other hand, there are a number of reasons against a pharmacist's right to object. First and foremost is the right of a patient to receive timely medical treatment. Pharmacists may refuse to fill prescriptions for emergency contraception because they believe that the drug ends a life. Although the patient may disapprove of abortion, she may not share the pharmacist's beliefs about birth control. If she becomes pregnant, she may then consider abortion, an issue she could have avoided if allowed to fill the morning-after pill. Other concerns include the time-sensitive nature of the morning-after pill, which must be taken within 72 hours of intercourse to effectively prevent pregnancy. Women who are refused the medication by one pharmacist may not be able to get the drug from another. This is especially true if she lives in an area with only one pharmacy. Also, low-income women may not have the time or resources to locate a pharmacy that would fill the prescription.

Other potential abuses could also arise. For instance, some pharmacists may object to filling drugs to treat AIDS if they believe HIV-positive individuals have engaged in behaviors they consider immoral such as IV drug use or homosexual relations. A pharmacist who does not believe in extramarital sex might refuse to fill a prescription for Viagra for an unmarried man. Could a pharmacist's objections here be considered invasive? Further, because a pharmacist does not have access to a patient's medical records or history, refusing to fill a prescription could be medically harmful.

Although arguments could be made for both sides, it appears that there needs to be a compromise between the needs of a patient and the moral beliefs of a pharmacist. In the following selections, physician John Menges argues that health providers' consciences must be respected. R. Alta Charo counters that a provider's conscience can be in conflict with legitimate medical needs of a patient.

YES ↵

Public Hearing on HB4346 Before the House State Government Administration Committee

[**I** am] one of the 4 fired Walgreens pharmacists. I was fired for not signing a policy saying that I would indeed fill a prescription if presented with it. I did not see a prescription! Walgreens does not respect a pharmacist's right to choose. I was one of Walgreens' best pharmacists prior to this issue. I had no problem with telling someone when a pharmacist would be available to fill a prescription. I can not fill the prescriptions myself but I try to the best of my ability to not take a side because I want to be able to tell people that this drug can end a life if a woman does have questions. By taking the position I take I find women asking questions. I believe many women wouldn't use this drug if they knew how it can work. If a woman is going to make a real choice as the other side says then the woman needs to have access to both "pro-choice" pharmacist and pro-life pharmacist like myself, so her choice is an informed choice. I pray that by trying to take a neutral position on this issue that some women will listen and some children will live.

The one thing I could not be neutral on is the issue of dispensing. When my three supervisors fired me, I told them "It feels very good knowing that my Faith and Religion is more important to me than a paycheck."

The following is a testimony I gave on a house bill earlier this year [2006].

Testimony

I would like to thank Rep. Granberg for introducing this bill and all members of this committee for giving me the opportunity to speak to you today.

My name is JOHN A. MENGES and I am a licensed pharmacist in the state of Illinois. I am one of the four pharmacists who lost my job with Walgreens for failing to sign an Emergency Contraceptive Policy that violated my religious beliefs. To make things clear to all members of this committee during the 8 months I worked following the Governor's mandate I was not presented with a prescription to fill. During the 3 years I worked at Walgreens I can only recall being presented with prescriptions for this medication 3 times and during that time I estimate that I filled over 71,000 prescriptions.

I am here today because I can not dispense any drug designed to end a human life. Before I enter any discussion of these drugs I would like to try to

Illinois House State Government Administration Committee, February 15, 2006.

clarify some terminology. For me human life begins when fertilization occurs. Fertilization is the point at which the sperm penetrates the egg. Life for me is the issue. The redefining of the terms "pregnancy" and "conception" in 1965 by the American College of Obstetricians and Gynecologists only confuse this life issue more. Prior to 1965 "pregnancy" and "conception" began at fertilization when life begins. Now "pregnancy" and "conception" begins at implantation of the embryo in the uterus. This still doesn't negate the fact that embryologists world-wide agree unanimously that human life begins at fertilization. This does explain why the morning after pill is classified as a contraceptive by the FDA and not as an abortafacient and I hope this clarifies why many say this drug doesn't end a pregnancy. Understanding the terminology enables one to realize how confusing the words fertilization, pregnancy, and conception have become. With this very simple explanation of the terminology I want to remind you that the beginning of human life at the point of fertilization is the issue for me. I hold human life at this stage in development with the same respect I hold for any human life.

The drugs I was referring to as I tried to explain some definitions are classified as "emergency contraceptives" by the FDA. Presently "Plan B" also known as the "morning after pill" is the only drug approved to be used for emergency contraception but most oral contraceptives can be dosed to work as emergency contraception. Emergency contraceptive doses are doses that are higher than doses of regular birth control. To simplify my discussion of emergency contraceptives I will limit my discussion to "Plan B." Plan B consists of two Progestin tablets containing 0.75 mg of levonorgestrel. The first tablet is to be taken within 72 hours of intercourse and the second tablet 12 hours after the first dose. Without getting into too much detail here the problem I have is the significant post-fertilization mechanism of action by which these drugs work. The mechanisms of action stated in the manufacturers prescribing information include preventing ovulation, altering tubal transport of sperm and/or ova, or inhibiting implantation by altering the endometrium. The time during a woman's menstrual cycle plays an important role in what mechanism of action is at work. The menstrual cycle can last anywhere from 21 to 40 days. Ovulation usually occurs 14 to 15 days before the end of the cycle. If emergency contraception is given early in the cycle it is more likely to prevent ovulation. But during this time ovulation and pregnancy are less likely to occur anyway. As the time for ovulation nears the chance for emergency contraception to prevent ovulation will lessen to the effect that ovulation can occur in some instances after emergency contraception has been taken. Once ovulation has occurred and fertilization has taken place any mechanism that prevents this implantation is the ending of human life.

So what am I doing as a pharmacist if I can't dispense a drug approved by the FDA? Believe me I asked myself this question when the first emergency contraceptive was approved by the FDA in 1998. I was a pharmacy manager in a supermarket pharmacy at the time. My number one priority as pharmacy manager is the same as it is today and that is customer service to my patients. I have always made it known to my employees, supervisors, and patients that I work first for the patient. My employer was a direct beneficiary of this as

I always made them look good. The day the first emergency contraceptive was approved I talked with the staff pharmacist who worked with me about his thoughts. Neither of us could dispense emergency contraceptives as it went against everything we believed in. The question I and many pharmacists had to answer was which patient do we serve? Do we serve the women requesting emergency contraceptive or the human life she could be carrying? I could not make a decision to participate in ending any human life so my decision was to refer women and answer any questions they might have if and when the situation arose.

So here I am almost 8 years after the first emergency contraceptives were approved and I can only recall 5 times that I have been faced with prescriptions. Three of those prescriptions I saw while employed with Walgreens. Not that a person can derive any statistical conclusions from 5 prescriptions but I didn't have incident with any of those encounters. In fact I have been thanked for my willingness to talk about emergency contraceptives as many pharmacists avoid the issue. This leads me to the moral issue I read about in different editorials. My choice to step aside and not fill these prescriptions in no way is a reflection of me trying to push my morals on others. It is my upholding my moral beliefs for myself. Our government allows women to make this choice and my actions have never prevented any women from exercising her choice. I have a choice too and my choice is not to dispense any medication that will end a human life. Those are morals that I have to live up to. The people who think I try to push my morals on others need to ask themselves why I dispense medication to patients who have just had an abortion for pain and bleeding. I give these patients the same respect I give every patient. The answers are simple as I went into pharmacy to help people not hurt people. I don't ask questions as to why people need my help because morals don't play a role in my helping people. I went into pharmacy to care for people and help them improve their lives. I love the profession of pharmacy because of all the good I am able to do as a pharmacist. Pharmacy goes beyond the counseling, recommendations and referrals I give. It is much more than my filling prescriptions fast and accurately. It is the respect I give every patient. I listen to my patients and help them when I can. I will never intentionally do any harm to any patient.

On November 28th of last year I lost my job because of my conscience objective to filling a medication that ends human life. My employer fired me for not signing policy asking me to violate my conscience. During the 8 months following the Governor's mandate I was not presented with a prescription to fill. Even though I believe I am currently covered under The Health Care Right of Conscience Act, I would like to ask every member of the house to vote YES on HB 4346. I am one of a small minority of pharmacists in this state who can't fill these medications. By voting YES on HB 4346 you will protect other pharmacists from having to endure what I, my wife, and my 2 children have had to endure these past months. It is difficult to explain my feelings. It hurts.

Without saying anymore I would like to answer any questions members might have. Thank You.

R. Alta Charo

→ **NO**

The Celestial Fire of Conscience— Refusing to Deliver Medical Care

Apparently heeding George Washington's call to "labor to keep alive in your breast that little spark of celestial fire called conscience," physicians, nurses, and pharmacists are increasingly claiming a right to the autonomy not only to refuse to provide services they find objectionable, but even to refuse to refer patients to another provider and, more recently, to inform them of the existence of legal options for care.

Largely as artifacts of the abortion wars, at least 45 states have "conscience clauses" on their books—laws that balance a physician's conscientious objection to performing an abortion with the profession's obligation to afford all patients nondiscriminatory access to services. In most cases, the provision of a referral satisfies one's professional obligations. But in recent years, with the abortion debate increasingly at the center of wider discussions about euthanasia, assisted suicide, reproductive technology, and embryonic stem-cell research, nurses and pharmacists have begun demanding not only the same right of refusal, but also—because even a referral, in their view, makes one complicit in the objectionable act—a much broader freedom to avoid facilitating a patient's choices.

A bill recently introduced in the Wisconsin legislature, for example, would permit health care professionals to abstain from "participating" in any number of activities, with "participating" defined broadly enough to include counseling patients about their choices. The privilege of abstaining from counseling or referring would extend to such situations as emergency contraception for rape victims, in vitro fertilization for infertile couples, patients' requests that painful and futile treatments be withheld or withdrawn, and therapies developed with the use of fetal tissue or embryonic stem cells. This last provision could mean, for example, that pediatricians—without professional penalty or threat of malpractice claims—could refuse to tell parents about the availability of varicella vaccine for their children, because it was developed with the use of tissue from aborted fetuses.

This expanded notion of complicity comports well with other public policy precedents, such as bans on federal funding for embryo research or abortion services, in which taxpayers claim a right to avoid supporting objectionable practices. In the debate on conscience clauses, some professionals are

From *The New England Journal of Medicine,* vol. 352, no. 24, June 16, 2005, pp. 2471–2473. Copyright © 2005 by Massachusetts Medical Society. All rights reserved. Reprinted by permission.

now arguing that the right to practice their religion requires that they not be made complicit in any practice to which they object on religious grounds.

Although it may be that, as Mahatma Gandhi said, "in matters of conscience, the law of majority has no place," acts of conscience are usually accompanied by a willingness to pay some price. Martin Luther King, Jr., argued, "An individual who breaks a law that conscience tells him is unjust, and who willingly accepts the penalty of imprisonment in order to arouse the conscience of the community over its injustice, is in reality expressing the highest respect for law."

What differentiates the latest round of battles about conscience clauses from those fought by Gandhi and King is the claim of entitlement to what newspaper columnist Ellen Goodman has called "conscience without consequence."

And of course, the professionals involved seek to protect only themselves from the consequences of their actions—not their patients. In Wisconsin, a pharmacist refused to fill an emergency-contraception prescription for a rape victim; as a result, she became pregnant and subsequently had to seek an abortion. In another Wisconsin case, a pharmacist who views hormonal contraception as a form of abortion refused not only to fill a prescription for birth-control pills but also to return the prescription or transfer it to another pharmacy. The patient, unable to take her pills on time, spent the next month dependent on less effective contraception. Under Wisconsin's proposed law, such behavior by a pharmacist would be entirely legal and acceptable. And this trend is not limited to pharmacists and physicians; in Illinois, an emergency medical technician refused to take a woman to an abortion clinic, claiming that her own Christian beliefs prevented her from transporting the patient for an elective abortion.

At the heart of this growing trend are several intersecting forces. One is the emerging norm of patient autonomy, which has contributed to the erosion of the professional stature of medicine. Insofar as they are reduced to mere purveyors of medical technology, doctors no longer have extraordinary privileges, and so their notions of extraordinary duty—house calls, midnight duties, and charity care—deteriorate as well. In addition, an emphasis on mutual responsibilities has been gradually supplanted by an emphasis on individual rights. With autonomy and rights as the preeminent social values comes a devaluing of relationships and a diminution of the difference between our personal lives and our professional duties.

Finally, there is the awesome scale and scope of the abortion wars. In the absence of legislative options for outright prohibition, abortion opponents search for proxy wars, using debates on research involving human embryos, the donation of organs from anencephalic neonates, and the right of persons in a persistent vegetative state to die as opportunities to rehearse arguments on the value of biologic but nonsentient human existence. Conscience clauses represent but another battle in these so-called culture wars.

Most profoundly, however, the surge in legislative activity surrounding conscience clauses represents the latest struggle with regard to religion in America. Should the public square be a place for the unfettered expression of religious beliefs, even when such expression creates an oppressive atmosphere for minority groups? Or should it be a place for religious expression only if and when that does not in any way impinge on minority beliefs and practices? This debate has been played out with respect to blue laws, school prayer, Christmas crèche scenes, and workplace dress codes.

Until recently, it was accepted that the public square in this country would be dominated by Christianity. This long-standing religious presence has made atheists, agnostics, and members of minority religions view themselves as oppressed, but recent efforts to purge the public square of religion have left conservative Christians also feeling subjugated and suppressed. In this culture war, both sides claim the mantle of victimhood—which is why health care professionals can claim the right of conscience as necessary to the nondiscriminatory practice of their religion, even as frustrated patients view conscience clauses as legalizing discrimination against them when they practice their own religion.

For health care professionals, the question becomes: What does it mean to be a professional in the United States? Does professionalism include the rather old-fashioned notion of putting others before oneself? Should professionals avoid exploiting their positions to pursue an agenda separate from that of their profession? And perhaps most crucial, to what extent do professionals have a collective duty to ensure that their profession provides nondiscriminatory access to all professional services?

Some health care providers would counter that they distinguish between medical care and nonmedical care that uses medical services. In this way, they justify their willingness to bind the wounds of the criminal before sending him back to the street or to set the bones of a battering husband that were broken when he struck his wife. Birth control, abortion, and in vitro fertilization, they say, are lifestyle choices, not treatments for diseases.

And it is here that licensing systems complicate the equation: such a claim would be easier to make if the states did not give these professionals the exclusive right to offer such services. By granting a monopoly, they turn the profession into a kind of public utility, obligated to provide service to all who seek it. Claiming an unfettered right to personal autonomy while holding monopolistic control over a public good constitutes an abuse of the public trust—all the worse if it is not in fact a personal act of conscience but, rather, an attempt at cultural conquest.

Accepting a collective obligation does not mean that all members of the profession are forced to violate their own consciences. It does, however, necessitate ensuring that a genuine system for counseling and referring patients is in place, so that every patient can act according to his or her own conscience just as readily as the professional can. This goal is not simple to achieve, but it does represent the best effort to accommodate everyone and is the approach taken by virtually all the major medical, nursing, and pharmacy societies. It is also the approach taken by the governor of Illinois, who is imposing an obligation on pharmacies, rather than on individual pharmacists, to ensure access to services for all patients.

Conscience is a tricky business. Some interpret its personal beacon as the guide to universal truth. But the assumption that one's own conscience is the conscience of the world is fraught with dangers. As C.S. Lewis wrote, "Of all tyrannies, a tyranny sincerely exercised for the good of its victims may be the most oppressive. It would be better to live under robber barons than under omnipotent moral busybodies. The robber baron's cruelty may sometimes sleep, his cupidity may at some point be satiated; but those who torment us for our own good will torment us without end for they do so with the approval of their own conscience."

POSTSCRIPT

Should Pro-Life Health Providers Be Allowed to Deny Prescriptions on the Basis of Conscience?

In the years since *Roe v. Wade*, state and federal legislatures have seen a growth in conscience clauses. Many pro-choice advocates perceive these clauses as another way to limit a woman's right to choose. Within weeks of the *Roe* decision in the early 1970s, Congress adopted legislation that permitted individual health care providers receiving federal funding or working for organizations receiving such funding to refuse to perform or assist in performing abortions or sterilizations if these procedures violated their moral or religious beliefs. The provision also prohibited discrimination against these providers because of the refusal to perform abortions or sterilizations. Currently, 45 states allow health care providers to refuse to be involved in abortions. Also, 12 states allow health care providers to refuse to provide sterilization, while 13 states allow providers to refuse to provide contraceptive services or information related to contraception. See "Refusing to Participate in Health Care: A Continuing Debate" (*The Guttmacher Report*, February 2000).

Pharmacists who refuse to fill prescriptions for birth control pills or emergency contraception largely believe that these medications are actually a method of abortion. In a paper published in the *Archives of Family Medicine* (2000), physicians Walter Larimore and Joseph B. Stanford stated that birth control pills have the potential of interrupting development of the fertilized egg after fertilization. Emergency contraception or the morning-after pill also has been seen as a means of abortion. It prevents pregnancy by either preventing fertilization or preventing implantation of a fertilized egg in the uterus. The morning-after pill is often confused with RU-486, which is clearly a method of abortion. Unlike RU-486, emergency contraception cannot disrupt an established pregnancy and cannot cause an abortion. Clearly, better education about the action of these drugs would be valuable.

Solutions have been proposed to enable patients to receive the drugs prescribed by their physicians. As a rule, it would make sense for pharmacists who will not dispense a drug to have an obligation to meet their customers' needs by referring them to other pharmacies. Pharmacists who object to filling prescriptions for birth control pills or emergency contraception might ensure that there is a pharmacist on duty who will fill the prescription or refer their customers elsewhere.

For further reading on this subject, see: "Morning-After Pill Does Not Reduce Abortion" (*Touchstone: A Journal of Mere Christianity*, March 2007); "The Unconscionability of Conscience Clauses: Pharmacists' Consciences and

Women's Access to Contraception" (*Journal of Law Medicine*, Winter 2006); "Some Anti-Abortion Pharmacists Refuse Women Contraceptives" (*Contemporary Sexuality*, January 2005); "Thou Shalt Dispense Death" (*The Report*, April 24, 2000); "The Limits of Conscientious Objection—May Pharmacists Refuse to Fill Prescriptions for Emergency Contraception?" (*The New England Journal of Medicine*, November 4, 2004); "Pharmacist Refuses Pill for Victim" (*Chicago Tribune*, February 11, 2004); "Pharmacists New Players in Abortion Debate" (*Los Angeles Times*, March 20, 2004); and "The Politics of Emergency Contraception" (*The New York Times*, August 24, 2004).

This issue raises important questions about public health and individual rights. Should pharmacists have a right to reject prescriptions for birth control pills, emergency contraception, Viagra, or any other drug that may be morally objectionable to them?

ISSUE 12

Should the Cervical Cancer Vaccine for Girls Be Compulsory?

YES: Cynthia Dailard, from "Achieving Universal Vaccination Against Cervical Cancer in the United States: The Need and the Means," *Guttmacher Policy Review* (Fall 2006)

NO: Gail Javitt, Deena Berkowitz, and Lawrence O. Gostin, from "Assessing Mandatory HPV Vaccination: Who Should Call the Shots?" *Journal of Law, Medicine & Ethics* (Summer 2008)

ISSUE SUMMARY

YES: The late Cynthia Dailard, a senior public policy associate at the Guttmacher Institute, argued that universal vaccination was needed because virtually all cases of cervical cancer are linked to the human papillomavirus. Most infected people are unaware of their infection, which is linked to nearly 10,000 cases of cervical cancer.

NO: Professors Gail Javitt, Deena Bertowitz, and Lawrence Gostin believe that mandating the cervical cancer vaccine raises significant legal, ethical, and social concerns. They are also concerned about the long-term safety and effectiveness of the vaccine.

$\mathbf{A}$ number of infectious diseases are almost completely preventable through childhood immunization. These include diphtheria, meningitis, pertussis (whooping cough), tetanus, polio, measles, mumps, and rubella (German measles). Largely as a result of widespread vaccination, these once-common diseases have become relatively rare. Before the introduction of the polio vaccine in 1955, polio epidemics occurred each year. In 1952, a record 20,000 cases were diagnosed, as compared to the last outbreak in 1979, when only 10 cases were identified.

While vaccination is a life saver, it may also be controversial. In June of 2006, the Food and Drug Administration approved a new immunization called Gardisil, used to prevent diseases caused by the sexually transmitted human papillomavirus (HPV). The virus causes genital warts and cervical cancer. The Centers for Disease Control and Prevention has determined that up to 50 percent of all sexually active men and women in the U.S. will be infected with HPV at some time in their life. The infection is especially common among women aged 20–24. About 20 states are considering making the vaccination a requirement, while Texas has already done so. Many parents and lawmakers are opposed to the mandatory vaccination for a variety of reasons: the vaccine doesn't target all types of HPV, it doesn't prevent diseases caused by these other types, and while HPV affects both sexes, it's recommended only for girls and women. Other reasons for the opposition include the relatively high cost of the vaccine, the fact that many people don't understand that HPV causes cervical cancer, and questions about its long-term safety.

The Centers for Disease Control and Prevention supports getting as many girls vaccinated as early and as fast as possible. They believe this vaccination will reduce the incidence and prevalence of cervical cancer among older women and lessen the spread of this highly infectious disease. The American Cancer Society also supports early and widespread vaccination of young girls.

In the U.S. it is believed that a valid way to lower the expense of the HPV vaccine and to educate the public on the advantages of vaccination is to make it compulsory for girls entering school. Mumps, measles, rubella, and hepatitis B (which is also sexually transmitted) are currently required. While there is value in preventing cervical cancer, which is estimated to be the most common sexually transmitted infection in the United States, many parents have concerns over mandatory vaccination to prevent a sexually transmitted disease. Some parents believe that young girls should be encouraged to abstain from sexual relations rather than being forced to receive the vaccination.

In the following selections, the late Cynthia Dailard, a senior public policy associate at the Guttmacher Institute, argued that universal vaccination was needed because virtually all cases of cervical cancer are linked to the human papillomavirus. Most infected people are unaware of their infection, which is linked to nearly 10,000 cases of cervical cancer. Professors Gail Javitt, Deena Bertowitz, and Lawrence Gostin believe that mandating the cervical cancer vaccine raises significant legal, ethical, and social concerns. They are also concerned over the long-term safety and effectiveness of the relatively new vaccine.

YES ↵

Cynthia Dailard

Achieving Universal Vaccination Against Cervical Cancer in the United States: The Need and the Means

The advent of a vaccine against the types of human papillomavirus (HPV) linked to most cases of cervical cancer is widely considered one of the greatest health care advances for women in recent years. Experts believe that vaccination against HPV has the potential to dramatically reduce cervical cancer incidence and mortality particularly in resource-poor developing countries where cervical cancer is most common and deadly. In the United States, the vaccine's potential is likely to be felt most acutely within low-income communities and communities of color, which disproportionately bear the burden of cervical cancer.

Because HPV is easily transmitted through sexual contact, the vaccine's full promise may only be realized through near-universal vaccination of girls and young women prior to sexual activity—a notion reflected in recently proposed federal guidelines. And history, as supported by a large body of scientific evidence, suggests that the most effective way to achieve universal vaccination is by requiring children to be inoculated prior to attending school. Yet the link between HPV and sexual activity—and the notion that HPV is different than other infectious diseases targeted by vaccine school entry requirements—tests the prevailing justification for such efforts. Meanwhile, any serious effort to achieve universal vaccination among young people with this relatively expensive vaccine will expose holes in the public health safety net that, if left unaddressed, have the potential to exacerbate longstanding disparities in cervical cancer rates among American women.

The Case for Universal Vaccination

Virtually all cases of cervical cancer are linked to HPV, an extremely common sexually transmitted infection (STI) that is typically asymptomatic and harmless; most people never know they are infected, and most cases resolve on their own. It is estimated that approximately three in four Americans contract HPV at some point in their lives, with most cases acquired relatively soon

From *Guttmacher Policy Review*, vol. 9, no. 4, Fall 2006, pp. 12–16. Copyright © 2006 by Alan Guttmacher Institute. Reprinted by permission.

after individuals have sex for the first time. Of the approximately 30 known types of HPV that are sexually transmitted, more than 13 are associated with cervical cancer. Yet despite the prevalence of HPV, cervical cancer is relatively rare in the United States; it generally occurs only in the small proportion of cases where a persistent HPV infection goes undetected over many years. This is largely due to the widespread availability of Pap tests, which can detect pre-cancerous changes of the cervix that can be treated before cancer sets in, as well as cervical cancer in its earliest stage, when it is easily treatable.

Still, the American Cancer Society estimates that in 2006, almost 10,000 cases of invasive cervical cancer will occur to American women, resulting in 3,700 deaths. Significantly, more than half of all U.S. women diagnosed with cervical cancer have not had a Pap test in the last three years. These women are disproportionately low income and women of color who lack access to afford-able and culturally competent health services. As a result, the incidence of cer-vical cancer is approximately 1.5 times higher among African American and Latina women than among white women; women of color are considerably more likely than whites to die of the disease as well. Two new HPV vaccines—Gardasil, manufactured by Merck & Company, and Cervarix, manufactured by GlaxoSmithKline—promise to transform this landscape. Both are virtually 100% effective in preventing the two types of HPV responsible for 70% of all cases of cervical cancer; Gardasil also protects against two other HPV types associated with 90% of all cases of genital warts. Gardasil was approved by the federal Food and Drug Administration (FDA) in June; GlaxoSmithKline is expected to apply for FDA approval of Cervarix by year's end.

Following FDA approval, Gardasil was endorsed by the Centers for Disease Control and Prevention's Advisory Committee on Immunization Prac-tices (ACIP), which is responsible for maintaining the nation's schedule of recommended vaccines. ACIP recommended that the vaccine be routinely administered to all girls ages 11–12, and as early as age nine at a doctor's discre-tion. Also, it recommended vaccination of all adolescents and young women ages 13–26 as part of a national "catch-up" campaign for those who have not already been vaccinated.

The ACIP recommendations, which are closely followed by health care professionals, reflect the notion that to eradicate cervical cancer, it will be necessary to achieve near-universal vaccination of girls and young women prior to sexual activity, when the vaccine is most effective. Experts believe that such an approach has the potential to significantly reduce cervical can-cer deaths in this country and around the world. Also, high vaccination rates will significantly reduce the approximately 3.5 million abnormal Pap results experienced by American women each year, many of which are caused by transient or persistent HPV infections. These abnormal Pap results require millions of women to seek follow-up care, ranging from additional Pap tests to more invasive procedures such as colposcopies and biopsies. This addi-tional care exacts a substantial emotional and even physical toll on women, and costs an estimated $6 billion in annual health care expenditures. Finally, widespread vaccination fosters "herd immunity," which is achieved when a sufficiently high proportion of individuals within a population are vaccinated that those who go unvaccinated—because the vaccine is contraindicated for them or because they are medically underserved, for example—are essentially protected.

The Role of School Entry Requirements

Achieving high vaccination levels among adolescents, however, can be a difficult proposition. Unlike infants and toddlers, who have frequent contact with health care providers in the context of well-child visits, adolescents often go for long stretches without contact with a health care professional. In addition, the HPV vaccine is likely to pose particular challenges, given that it must be administered three times over a six-month period to achieve maximum effectiveness.

A large body of evidence suggests that the most effective means to ensure rapid and widespread use of childhood or adolescent vaccines is through state laws or policies that require children to be vaccinated prior to enrollment in day care or school. These school-based immunization requirements, which exist in some form in all 50 states, are widely credited for the success of immunization programs in the United States. They have also played a key role in helping to close racial, ethnic and socioeconomic gaps in immunization rates, and have proven to be far more effective than guidelines recommending the vaccine for certain age-groups or high-risk populations. Although each state decides for itself whether a particular vaccine will be required for children to enroll in school, they typically rely on ACIP recommendations in making their decision.

In recent months, some commentators have noted that as a sexually transmitted infection, HPV is "different" from other infectious diseases such as measles, mumps or whooping cough, which are easily transmitted in a school setting or threaten school attendance when an outbreak occurs. Some socially conservative advocacy groups accordingly argue that the HPV vaccine does not meet the historical criteria necessary for it to be required for children attending school; many of them also contend that abstinence outside of marriage is the real answer to HPV. They welcome the advent of the vaccine, they say, but will oppose strenuously any effort to require it for school enrollment.

This position reflects only a limited understanding of school-based vaccination requirements. These requirements do not exist solely to prevent the transmission of disease in school or during childhood. Instead, they further society's strong interest in ensuring that people are protected from disease throughout their lives and are a highly efficient means of eradicating disease in the larger community. For example, states routinely require school-age children to be vaccinated against rubella (commonly known as German measles), a typically mild illness in children, to protect pregnant women in the community from the devastating effects the disease can have on a developing fetus. Similarly, states currently require vaccination against certain diseases, such as tetanus, that are not "contagious" at all, but have very serious consequences for those affected. And almost all states require vaccination against Hepatitis B, a blood borne disease which can be sexually transmitted.

Moreover, according to the National Conference of State Legislatures (NCSL), all 50 states allow parents to refuse to vaccinate their children on medical grounds, such as when a vaccine is contraindicated for a particular child due to allergy, compromised immunity or significant illness. All states except Mississippi and West Virginia allow parents to refuse to vaccinate their children on religious grounds. Additionally, 20 states go so far as to allow parents to refuse to vaccinate their children because of a personal, moral or other belief. Unlike a medical exemption, which requires a parent to provide documentation from a physician, the process for obtaining nonmedical exemptions can vary widely by state.

NCSL notes that, in recent years, almost a dozen states considered expanding their exemption policy. Even absent any significant policy change, the rate of parents seeking exemptions for nonmedical reasons is on the rise. This concerns public health experts. Research shows that in states where exemptions are easier to obtain, a higher proportion of parents refuse to vaccinate their children; research further shows that these states, in turn, are more likely to experience outbreaks of vaccine-preventable diseases, such as measles and whooping cough. Some vaccine program administrators fear that because of the social sensitivities surrounding the HPV vaccine, any effort to require the vaccine for school entry may prompt legislators to amend their laws to create nonmedical exemptions where they do not currently exist or to make existing exemptions easier to obtain. This has the potential not only to thwart the effort to stem the tide of cervical cancer, but to foster the spread of other vaccine-preventable diseases as well.

Financing Challenges Laid Bare

Another barrier to achieving universal vaccination of girls and young women will be the high price of the vaccine. Gardasil is expensive by vaccine standards, costing approximately $360 for the three-part series of injections. Despite this high cost, ACIP's endorsement means that Gardasil will be covered by most private insurers; in fact, a number of large insurers have already announced they will cover the vaccine for girls and young women within the ACIP-recommended age range. Still, the Institute of Medicine estimates that approximately 11% of all American children have private insurance that does not cover immunization, and even those with insurance coverage may have to pay deductibles and copayments that create a barrier to care.

Those who do not have private insurance or who cannot afford the out-of-pocket costs associated with Gardasil will need to rely on a patchwork system of programs that exist to support the delivery of subsidized vaccines to low-income and uninsured individuals. In June, ACIP voted to include Gardasil in the federal Vaccines for Children program (VFC), which provides free vaccines largely to children and teenagers through age 18 who are uninsured or receive Medicaid. The program's reach is significant: In 2003, 43% of all childhood vaccine doses were distributed by the VFC program.

THE POTENTIAL ROLE OF FAMILY PLANNING CLINICS IN AN HPV VACCINE 'CATCH-UP' CAMPAIGN

Family planning clinics, including those funded under Title X of the Public Health Service Act, have an important role to play in a national "catch-up" campaign to vaccinate young women against HPV. This is particularly true for women ages 19–26, who are too old to receive free vaccines through the federal Vaccines for Children program but still fall within the ACIP-recommended age range for the HPV vaccine.

Almost 4,600 Title X—funded family planning clinics provide subsidized family planning and related preventive health care to just over five million women nationwide. In theory, Title X clinics are well poised to offer the HPV vaccine, because they already are a major provider of STI services and cervical cancer screening, providing approximately six million STI (including HIV) tests and 2.7 million Pap tests in 2004 alone. Because Title X clients are disproportionately low income and women of color, they are at particular risk of developing cervical cancer later in life. Moreover, most Title X clients fall within the ACIP age recommendations of 26 and under for the HPV vaccine (59% are age 24 or younger, and 18% are ages 25–29); many of these women are uninsured and may not have an alternative source of health care.

Title X funds may be used to pay for vaccines linked to improved reproductive health outcomes, and some Title X clinics offer the Hepatitis B vaccine (which can be sexually transmitted). Although many family planning providers are expressing interest in incorporating the HPV vaccine into their package of services, its high cost—even at a discounted government purchase price—is likely to stand in the way. Clinics that receive Title X funds are required by law to charge women based on their ability to pay, with women under 100% of the federal poverty level (representing 68% of Title X clients) receiving services completely free of charge and those with incomes between 100–250% of poverty charged on a sliding scale. While Merck has expressed an interest in extending its patient assistance program to publicly funded family planning clinics, it makes no promises. In fact, a statement on the company's Web site says that "Due to the complexities associated with vaccine funding and distribution in the public sector, as well as the resource constraints that typically exist in public health settings, Merck is currently evaluating whether and how a vaccine assistance program could be implemented in the public sector."

The HPV vaccine, however, is not just recommended for children and teenagers; it is also recommended for young adult women up through age 26. Vaccines are considered an "optional" benefit for adults under Medicaid, meaning that it is up to each individual state to decide whether or not to cover a given vaccine. Also, states can use their own funds and federal grants to support the delivery of subsidized vaccines to low-income or uninsured adults.

Many states, however, have opted instead to channel these funds toward childhood-vaccination efforts, particularly as vaccine prices have grown in recent years. As a result, adult vaccination rates remain low and disparities exist across racial, ethnic and socioeconomic groups—mirroring the disparities that exist for cervical cancer.

In response to all this, Merck in May announced it would create a new "patient assistance program," designed to provide all its vaccines free to adults who are uninsured, unable to afford the vaccines and have an annual household income below 200% of the federal poverty level ($19,600 for individuals and $26,400 for couples). To receive free vaccines, patients will need to complete and fax forms from participating doctors' offices for processing by Merck during the patients' visits. Many young uninsured women, however, do not seek their care in private doctors' offices, but instead rely on publicly funded family planning clinics for their care, suggesting the impact of this program may be limited (see box).

Thinking Ahead

Solutions to the various challenges presented by the HPV vaccine are likely to have relevance far beyond cervical cancer. In the coming years, scientific breakthroughs in the areas of immunology, molecular biology and genetics will eventually permit vaccination against a broader range of acute illnesses as well as chronic diseases. Currently, vaccines for other STIs such as chlamydia, herpes and HIV are in various stages of development. Also under study are vaccines for Alzheimer's disease, diabetes and a range of cancers. Vaccines for use among adolescents will also be increasingly common. A key question is, in the future, will individuals across the economic spectrum have access to these breakthrough medical advances or will disadvantaged individuals be left behind?

When viewed in this broader context, the debate over whether the HPV vaccine should be required for school enrollment may prove to be a healthy one. If the HPV vaccine is indeed "the first of its kind," as some have characterized it, it has the potential to prompt communities across the nation to reconsider and perhaps reconceive the philosophical justification for school entry requirements. Because the U.S. health care system is fragmented, people have no guarantee of health insurance coverage or access to affordable care. School entry requirements might therefore provide an important opportunity to deliver public health interventions that, like the HPV vaccine, offer protections to individuals who have the potential to become disconnected from health care services later in life. Similar to the HPV vaccine's promise of cervical cancer prevention, these benefits may not be felt for many years, but nonetheless may be compelling from a societal standpoint. And bearing in mind that school dropout rates begin to climb as early as age 13, middle school might be appropriately viewed as the last public health gate that an entire age-group of individuals pass through together—regardless of race, ethnicity or socioeconomic status.

Meanwhile, the cost and affordability issues raised by the HPV vaccine may help draw attention to the need to reform the vaccine-financing system in this country. In 2003, the Institute of Medicine proposed a series of reforms designed to improve the way vaccines are financed and distributed. They included a national insurance benefit mandate that would apply to all public and private health care plans and vouchers for uninsured children and adults to receive immunizations through the provider of their choice. Legislation introduced by Rep. Henry Waxman (D-CA) and Sen. Edward Kennedy (D-MA), called the Vaccine Access and Supply Act, adopts a different approach. The bill would expand the Vaccines for Children program, create a comparable Vaccines for Adults program, strengthen the vaccine grant program to the states and prohibit Medicaid cost-sharing requirements for ACIP-recommended vaccines for adults.

Whether the HPV vaccine will in fact hasten reforms of any kind remains to be seen. But one thing is clear: If the benefits of this groundbreaking vaccine cannot be enjoyed by girls and women who are disadvantaged by poverty or insurance status, then it will only serve to perpetuate the disparities in cervical cancer rates that have persisted in this country for far too long.

Gail Javitt, Deena Berkowitz, and Lawrence O. Gostin

 **NO**

Assessing Mandatory HPV Vaccination: Who Should Call the Shots?

I. Introduction

The human papillomavirus (HPV) is the most common sexually transmitted infection worldwide. In the United States, more than six million people are infected each year. Although most HPV infections are benign, two strains of HPV cause 70 percent of cervical cancer cases.[1] Two other strains of HPV are associated with 90 percent of genital warts cases.[2]

In June 2006, the Food and Drug Administration (FDA) approved the first vaccine against HPV. Sold as Gardasil, the quadrivalent vaccine is intended to prevent four strains of HPV associated with cervical cancer, precancerous genital lesions, and genital warts.[3] Following FDA approval, the national Advisory Committee on Immunization Practices (ACIP) recommended routine vaccination for girls ages 11–12 with three doses of quadrivalent HPV vaccine.[4] Thereafter, state legislatures around the country engaged in an intense effort to pass laws mandating vaccination of young girls against HPV. This activity was spurred in part by an intense lobbying campaign by Merck, the manufacturer of the vaccine.[5]

The United States has a robust state-based infrastructure for mandatory vaccination that has its roots in the 19th century. Mandating vaccination as a condition for school entry began in the early 1800s and is currently required by all 50 states for several common childhood infectious diseases.[6] Some suggest that mandatory HPV vaccination for minor females fits squarely within this tradition.

Nonetheless, state efforts to mandate HPV vaccination in minors have raised a variety of concerns on legal, ethical, and social grounds. Unlike other diseases for which state legislatures have mandated vaccination for children, HPV is neither transmissible through casual contact nor potentially fatal during childhood. It also would be the first vaccine to be mandated for use exclusively in one gender. As such, HPV vaccine presents a new context for considering vaccine mandates.

In this paper, we review the scientific evidence supporting Gardasil's approval and the legislative actions in the states that followed. We then argue

From *Journal of Law, Medicine and Ethics*, vol. 36, issue 2, Summer 2008, pp. 384–395. Copyright © 2008 by American Society of Law, Medicine & Ethics. Reprinted by permission.

that mandatory HPV vaccination at this time is both unwarranted and unwise. While the emergence of an HPV vaccine refects a potentially significant public health advance, the vaccine raises several concerns. First, the long-term safety and effectiveness of the vaccine are unclear, and serious adverse events reported shortly after the vaccine's approval raise questions about its short-term safety as well. In light of unanswered safety questions, the vaccine should be rolled out slowly, with risks carefully balanced against benefits in individual cases. Second, the legal and ethical justifications that have historically supported state-mandated vaccination do not support mandating HPV vaccine. Specifically, HPV does not threaten an imminent and significant risk to the health of others. Mandating HPV would therefore constitute an expansion of the state's authority to interfere with individual and parental autonomy. Engaging in such expansion in the absence of robust public discussion runs the risk of creating a public backlash that may undermine the goal of widespread HPV vaccine coverage and lead to public distrust of established childhood vaccine programs for other diseases. Third, the current sex-based HPV vaccination mandates present constitutional concerns because they require only girls to be vaccinated. Such concerns could lead to costly and protracted legal challenges. Finally, vaccination mandates will place economic burdens on federal and state governments and individual practitioners that may have a negative impact on the provision of other health services. In light of these potentially adverse public health, economic, and societal consequences, we believe that it is premature for states to add HPV to the list of state-mandated vaccines.

II. Background

Before discussing in detail the basis for our opposition to mandated HPV vaccination, it is necessary to review the public health impact of HPV and the data based on which the FDA approved the vaccine. Additionally, to understand the potentially widespread uptake of HPV vaccine mandates, we review the state legislative activities that have occurred since the vaccine's approval.

A. HPV Epidemiology

In the United States, an estimated 20 million people, or 15 percent of the population, are currently infected with HPV.[7] Modeling studies suggest that up to 80 percent of sexually active women will have become infected with the virus at some point in their lives by the time they reach age 50.[8] Prevalence of HPV is highest among sexually active females ages 14–19.[9]

Human papillomavirus comprises more than 100 different strains of virus, of which more than 30 infect the genital area.[10] The majority of HPV infections are transient, asymptomatic, and cause no clinical problems. However, persistent infection with high risk types of HPV is the most important risk factor for cervical cancer precursors and invasive cervical cancer. Two strains in particular, 16 and 18, have been classified as carcinogenic to humans by the World Health Organization's international agency for research on cancer.[11] These strains account for 70 percent of cervical cancer cases[12] and are responsible for a large proportion of anal, vulvar, vaginal, penile, and urethral cancers.[13]

More than 200,000 women die of cervical cancer each year.[14] The majority of these deaths take place in developing countries, which lack the screening programs and infrastructure for diagnosis, treatment, and prevention that exist in the United States. In the U.S., it is estimated that there were about 9,700 cases of invasive cervical cancer and about 3,700 deaths from cervical cancer in 2006, as compared with 500,000 cases and 288,000 deaths worldwide.[15]

Two other HPV types, 6 and 11, are associated with approximately 90 percent of anogenital warts. They are also associated with low grade cervical disease and recurrent respiratory papillomatosis (RRP), a disease consisting of recurrent warty growths in the larynx and respiratory tract. Juvenile onset RRP (JORRP), a rare disorder caused by exposure to HPV during the peripartum period, can cause significant airway obstruction or lead to squamous cell carcinoma with poor prognosis.[16]

Although HPV types 6, 11, 16, and 18 are associated with significant morbidity and mortality, they have a fairly low prevalence in the U.S. population. One study of sexually active women ages 18 to 25 found HPV 16 and 18 prevalence to be 7.8 percent.[17] Another study found overall prevalence of types 6, 11, 16, and 18 to be 1.3 percent, 0.1 percent, 1.5 percent, and 0.8 percent, respectively.[18]

B. Gardasil Safety and Effectiveness

Gardasil was approved based on four randomized, double blind, placebo-controlled studies in 21,000 women ages 16 to 26. Girls as young as nine were included in the safety and immunogenicity studies but not the efficacy studies. The results demonstrated that in women without prior HPV infection, Gardasil was nearly 100 percent effective in preventing precancerous cervical lesions, precancerous vaginal and vulvar lesions, and genital warts caused by vaccine-type HPV. Although the study period was not long enough for cervical cancer to develop, the prevention of these cervical precancerous lesions was considered a valid surrogate marker for cancer prevention. The studies also show that the vaccine is only effective when given prior to infection with high-risk strains.[19]

Gardasil is the second virus-like particle (VLP) vaccine to be approved by the FDA; the first was the Hepatitis B vaccine. VLPs consist of viral protein particles derived from the structural proteins of a virus. These particles are nearly identical to the virus from which they were derived but lack the virus's genetic material required for replication, so they are noninfectious and nononcogenic. VLPs offer advantages over more traditional peptide vaccines as the human body is more highly attuned to particulate antigens, which leads to a stronger immune response since VLP vaccines cannot revert to an infectious form, such as attenuated particles or incompletely killed particles.

No serious Gardasil-related adverse events were observed during clinical trials. The most common adverse events reported were injection site reactions, including pain, redness, and swelling.[20] The most common systemic adverse reactions experienced at the same rate by both vaccine and placebo recipients were headache, fever, and nausea. Five vaccine recipients reported adverse vaccine-related experiences: bronchospasm, gastroenteritis, headache with hypertension, joint movement impairment near injection site, and vaginal hemorrhage. Women with positive pregnancy tests were excluded from the studies, as were some women who became pregnant following receipt of either vaccine or placebo. The incidence of spontaneous pregnancy loss and congenital anomalies were similar in both groups.[21] Gardasil was assigned pregnancy risk category B by the FDA on the basis that animal reproduction studies failed to demonstrate a risk to the fetus.[22]

As of June 2007, the most recent date for which CDC has made data available, there were 1,763 reports of potential side effects following HPV vaccination made to the CDC's Vaccine Adverse Event Reporting System (VAERS). Ninety-four of these were defined as serious, including 13 unconfirmed reports of Guillain-Barre syndrome (GBS), a neurological illness resulting in muscle weakness and sometimes in paralysis. The CDC is investigating these cases. Seven deaths were also reported among females who received the vaccine, but the CDC stated that none of these deaths appeared to be caused by vaccination.[23]

Although the FDA approved the vaccine for females ages 9–26, based on the data collected in those age groups, the ACIP recommendation for vaccination is limited to females ages 11–12. This recommendation was based on several considerations, including age of sexual debut in the United States and the high probability of HPV acquisition within several years of sexual debut, cost-effectiveness evaluations, and the established young adolescent health care visit at ages 11–12 when other vaccines are also recommended.

C. State Legislative Activities

Since the approval of Gardasil, legislators in 41 states and the District of Columbia have introduced legislation addressing the HPV vaccine.[24] Legislative responses to Gardasil have focused on the following recommendations: (1) mandating HPV vaccination of minor girls as a condition for school entrance; (2) mandating insurance coverage for HPV vaccination or providing state funding to defray or eliminate cost of vaccination; (3) educating the public about the HPV vaccine; and/or (4) establishing committees to make recommendations about the vaccine.

In 2007, 24 states and the District of Columbia introduced legislation specifically to mandate the HPV vaccine as a condition for school entry.[25] Of these, only Virginia and Washington, D.C. passed laws requiring HPV vaccination. The Virginia law requires females to receive three properly spaced doses of HPV vaccine, with the first dose to be administered before the child enters sixth grade. A parent or guardian may refuse vaccination for his child after reviewing "materials describing the link between the human papillomavirus and cervical cancer approved for such use by the Board of Health."[26] The law will take effect October 1, 2008.

Additionally, the D.C. City Council passed the HPV Vaccination and Reporting Act of 2007, which directs the mayor to establish an HPV vaccination program "consistent with the standards set forth by the Centers for

Disease Control for all females under the age of 13 who are residents of the District of Columbia."[27] The program includes a "requirement that the parent or legal guardian of a female child enrolling in grade 6 for the first time submit certification that the child has received the HPV vaccine" and a provision that "allows a parent or guardian to opt out of the HPV vaccination requirement." It also directs the mayor to develop reporting requirements "for the collection and analyzation [sic] of HPV vaccination data within the District of Columbia Department of Health," including "annual reporting to the Department of Health as to the immunization status of each female child entering grade 6." The law requires Congressional approval in order to take effect.

In contrast, an Executive Order issued by the Texas governor was thwarted by that state's legislature. Executive Order 4, signed by Governor Rick Perry on February 4, 2007, would have directed the state's health department to adopt rules mandating the "age appropriate vaccination of all female children for HPV prior to admission to the sixth grade."[28] It would have allowed parents to "submit a request for a conscientious objection affidavit form via the Internet." However, H.B. 1098, enacted by the Texas state legislature on April 26, 2007, states that HPV immunization is "not required for a person's admission to any elementary or secondary school," and "preempts any contrary order issued by the governor."[29] The bill was filed without the governor's signature and became effective on May 8, 2007.

Of the 22 other states in which legislation mandating HPV vaccination was introduced in 2007, all would have required girls to be vaccinated somewhere between ages 11 and 13 or before entry into sixth grade. Most would have provided for some sort of parental or guardian exemption, whether for religious, moral, medical, cost, or other reasons. However, vaccine mandate bills in California and Maryland were withdrawn.

Bills requiring insurance companies to cover HPV vaccination or allocating state funds for this purpose were enacted in eight states.[30] Eight states also enacted laws aimed at promoting awareness of the HPV vaccine using various mechanisms, such as school-based distribution of educational materials to parents of early adolescent children.[31] Finally, three states established expert bodies to engage in further study of HPV vaccination either instead of or as an adjunct to other educational efforts.[32]

In total, 41 states and D.C. introduced legislation addressing HPV vaccination in some manner during the 2007 legislative session, and 17 of these states enacted laws relating to HPV vaccination.

III. Why Mandating HPV Is Premature

The approval of a vaccine against cancer-causing HPV strains is a significant public health advance. Particularly in developing countries, which lack the health care resources for routine cervical cancer screening, preventing HPV infection has the potential to save millions of lives. In the face of such a dramatic advance, opposing government-mandated HPV vaccination may seem foolhardy, if not heretical. Yet strong legal, ethical, and policy arguments underlie our position that state-mandated HPV vaccination of minor females is premature.

A. Long-Term Safety and Effectiveness of the Vaccine Is Unknown

Although the aim of clinical trials is to generate safety and effectiveness data that can be extrapolated to the general population, it is widely understood that such trials cannot reveal all possible adverse events related to a product. For this reason, post-market adverse event reporting is required for all manufacturers of FDA-approved products, and post-market surveillance (also called "phase IV studies") may be required in certain circumstances. There have been numerous examples in recent years in which unforeseen adverse reactions following product approval led manufacturers to withdraw their product from the market. For example, in August 1998, the FDA approved Rotashield, the first vaccine for the prevention of rotavirus gastroenteritis in infants. About 7,000 children received the vaccine before the FDA granted the manufacturer a license to market the vaccine. Though a few cases of intussusception, or bowel obstruction, were noted during clinical trials, there was no statistical difference between the overall occurrence of intussusception in vaccine compared with placebo recipients. After administration of approximately 1.5 million doses of vaccine, however, 15 cases of intussusception were reported, and were found to be causally related to the vaccine. The manufacturer subsequently withdrew the vaccine from the market in October 1999.[33]

In the case of HPV vaccine, short-term clinical trials in thousands of young women did not reveal serious adverse effects. However, the adverse events reported since the vaccine's approval are, at the very least, a sobering reminder that rare adverse events may surface as the vaccine is administered to millions of girls and young women. Concerns have also been raised that other carcinogenic HPV types not contained in the vaccines will replace HPV types 16 and 18 in the pathological niche.

The duration of HPV vaccine-induced immunity is unclear. The average follow-up period for Gardasil during clinical trials was 15 months after the third dose of the vaccine. Determining long-term efficacy is complicated by the fact that even during naturally occurring HPV infection, HPV antibodies are not detected in many women. Thus, long-term, follow-up post-licensure studies cannot rely solely upon serologic measurement of HPV-induced antibody titers. One study indicates that protection against persistent HPV 16 infection remained at 94 percent 3.5 years after vaccination with HPV 16.[34] A second study showed similar protection for types 16 and 18 after 4.5 years.[35]

The current ACIP recommendation is based on assumptions about duration of immunity and age of sexual debut, among other factors. As the vaccine is used for a longer time period, it may turn out that a different vaccine schedule is more effective. In addition, the effect on co-administration of other vaccines with regard to safety is unknown, as is the vaccines' efficacy with varying dose intervals. Some have also raised concerns about a negative impact of vaccination on cervical cancer screening programs, which are highly effective at reducing cervical cancer mortality. These unknowns must be studied as the vaccine is introduced in the broader population.

At present, therefore, questions remain about the vaccine's safety and the duration of its immunity, which call into question the wisdom of mandated vaccination. Girls receiving the vaccine face some risk of potential adverse events as well as risk that the vaccine will not be completely protective. These risks must be weighed against the state's interest in protecting the public from the harms associated with HPV. As discussed in the next section, the state's interest in protecting the public health does not support mandating HPV vaccination.

B. Historical Justifications for Mandated Vaccination Are Not Met

HPV is different in several respects from the vaccines that first led to state-mandated vaccination. Compulsory vaccination laws originated in the early 1800s and were driven by fears of the centuries-old scourge of smallpox and the advent of the vaccine developed by Edward Jenner in 1796. By the 1900s, the vast majority of states had enacted compulsory smallpox vaccination laws.[36] While such laws were not initially tied to school attendance, the coincidental rise of smallpox outbreaks, growth in the number of public schools, and compulsory school attendance laws provided a rationale for compulsory vaccination to prevent the spread of smallpox among school children as well as a means to enforce the requirement by barring unvaccinated children from school.[37] In 1827, Boston became the first city to require all children entering public school to provide evidence of vaccination.[38] Similar laws were enacted by several states during the latter half of the 19th century.[39]

The theory of herd immunity, in which the protective effect of vaccines extends beyond the vaccinated individual to others in the population, is the driving force behind mass immunization programs. Herd immunity theory proposes that, in diseases passed from person to person, it is difficult to maintain a chain of infection when large numbers of a population are immune. With the increase in number of immune individuals present in a population, the lower the likelihood that a susceptible person will come into contact with an infected individual. There is no threshold value above which herd immunity exists, but as vaccination rates increase, indirect protection also increases until the infection is eliminated.

Courts were soon called on to adjudicate the constitutionality of mandatory vaccination programs. In 1905, the Supreme Court decided the seminal case, *Jacobson v. Massachusetts*,[40] in which it upheld a population-wide smallpox vaccination ordinance challenged by an adult male who refused the vaccine and was fined five dollars. He argued that a compulsory vaccination law was "hostile to the inherent right of every freeman to care for his own body and health in such way as to him seems best." The Court disagreed, adopting a narrower view of individual liberty and emphasizing the duties that citizens have towards each other and to society as a whole. According to the Court, the "liberty secured by the Constitution of the United States . . . does not import an absolute right in each person to be, at all times and in all circumstances, wholly freed from restraint. There are manifold restraints to which every person is necessarily subject for the common good." With respect to compulsory vaccination, the Court stated that "[u]pon the principle of self-defense, of paramount necessity, a community has the right to protect itself against an epidemic of disease which threatens the safety of its members." In the Court's opinion, compulsory vaccination was consistent with a state's traditional police powers, i.e., its power to regulate matters affecting the health, safety, and general welfare of the public.

In reaching its decision, the Court was influenced both by the significant harm posed by smallpox—using the words "epidemic" and "danger" repeatedly—as well as the available scientific evidence demonstrating the efficacy of the vaccine. However, the Court also emphasized that its ruling was applicable only to the case before it, and articulated principles that must be adhered to for such an exercise of police powers to be constitutional. First, there must be a public health necessity. Second, there must be a reasonable relationship between the intervention and public health objective. Third, the intervention may not be arbitrary or oppressive. Finally, the intervention should not pose a health risk to its subject. Thus, while *Jacobson* "stands firmly for the proposition that police powers authorize states to compel vaccination for the public good," it also indicates that "government power must be exercised reasonably to pass constitutional scrutiny."[41] In the 1922 case *Zucht v. King*,[42] the Court reaffirmed its ruling in *Jacobson* in the context of a school-based smallpox vaccination mandate.

The smallpox laws of the 19th century, which were almost without exception upheld by the courts, helped lay the foundation for modern immunization statutes. Many modern-era laws were enacted in response to the transmission of measles in schools in the 1960s and 1970s. In 1977, the federal government launched the Childhood Immunization Initiative, which stressed the importance of strict enforcement of school immunization laws.[43] Currently, all states mandate vaccination as a condition for school entry, and in deciding whether to mandate vaccines, are guided by ACIP recommendations. At present, ACIP recommends vaccination for diphtheria, tetanus, and acellular pertussis (DTaP), Hepatitis B, polio, measles, mumps, and rubella (MMR), varicella (chicken pox), influenza, rotavirus, haemophilus Influenza B (HiB), pneumococcus, Hepatitis A, meningococcus, and, most recently HPV. State mandates differ; for example, whereas all states require DTaP, polio, and measles in order to enter kindergarten, most do not require Hepatitis A.[44]

HPV is different from the vaccines that have previously been mandated by the states. With the exception of tetanus, all of these vaccines fit comfortably within the "public health necessity" principle articulated in *Jacobson* in that the diseases they prevent are highly contagious and are associated with significant morbidity and mortality occurring shortly after exposure. And, while tetanus is not contagious, exposure to *Clostridium tetani* is both virtually unavoidable (particularly by children, given their propensity to both play in the dirt and get scratches), life threatening, and fully preventable only through vaccination. Thus, the public health necessity argument plausibly extends to tetanus, albeit for different reasons.

Jacobson's "reasonable relationship" principle is also clearly met by vaccine mandates for the other ACIP recommended vaccines. School-aged children are most at risk while in school because they are more likely to be in close proximity to each other in that setting. All children who attend school are equally at risk of both transmitting and contracting the diseases. Thus, a clear relationship exists between conditioning school attendance on vaccination and the avoidance of the spread of infectious disease within the school environment. Tetanus, a non-contagious disease, is somewhat different, but school-based vaccination can nevertheless be justified in that children will foreseeably be exposed within the school environment (e.g., on the playground) and, if exposed, face a high risk of mortality.

HPV vaccination, in contrast, does not satisfy these two principles. HPV infection presents no public health necessity, as that term was used in the context of *Jacobson*. While non-sexual transmission routes are theoretically possible, they have not been demonstrated. Like other sexually transmitted diseases which primarily affect adults, it is not immediately life threatening; as such, cervical cancer, if developed, will not manifest for years if not decades. Many women will never be exposed to the cancer-causing strains of HPV; indeed the prevalence of these strains in the U.S. is quite low. Furthermore, many who are exposed will not go on to develop cervical cancer. Thus, conditioning school attendance on HPV vaccination serves only to coerce compliance in the absence of a public health emergency.[45]

The relationship between the government's objective of preventing cervical cancer in women and the means used to achieve it—that is, vaccination of all girls as a condition of school attendance—lacks sufficient rationality. First, given that HPV is transmitted through sexual activity, exposure to HPV is not directly related to school attendance.[46] Second, not all children who attend school are at equal risk of exposure to or transmission of the virus. Those who abstain from sexual conduct are not at risk for transmitting or contracting HPV. Moreover, because HPV screening tests are available, the risk to those who choose to engage in sexual activity is significantly minimized. Because it is questionable how many school-aged children are actually at risk—and for those who are at risk, the risk is not linked to school attendance—there is not a sufficiently rational reason to tie mandatory vaccination to school attendance.

To be sure, the public health objective that proponents of mandatory HPV vaccination seek to achieve is compelling. Vaccinating girls before sexual debut provides an opportunity to provide protection against an adult onset disease. This opportunity is lost once sexual activity begins and exposure to HPV occurs. However, that HPV vaccination may be both medically justified and a prudent public health measure is an insufficient basis for the state to compel children to receive the vaccine as a condition of school attendance.

C. In the Absence of Historical Justification, the Government Risks Public Backlash by Mandating HPV Vaccination

Childhood vaccination rates in the United States are very high; more than half of the states report meeting the Department of Health and Human Services (HHS) Healthy People 2010 initiative's goal of 95 percent vaccination coverage for childhood vaccination.[47] However, from its inception, state mandated vaccination has been accompanied by a small but vocal anti-vaccination movement. Opposition has historically been "fueled by general distrust of government, a rugged sense of individualism, and concerns about the efficacy and safety of vaccines."[48] In recent years, vaccination programs also have been a "victim of their tremendous success,"[49] as dreaded diseases such as measles and polio have largely disappeared in the United States, taking with them the fear that motivated past generations. Some have noted with alarm the rise in the number of parents opting out of vaccination and of resurgence in anti-vaccination rhetoric making scientifically unsupported allegations that vaccination causes adverse events such as autism.[50]

The rash of state legislation to mandate HPV has led to significant public concern that the government is overreaching its police powers authority. As one conservative columnist has written, "[F]or the government to mandate the expensive vaccine for children would be for Big Brother to reach past the parents and into the home."[51] While some dismiss sentiments such as this one as simply motivated by right wing moral politics, trivializing these concerns is both inappropriate and unwise as a policy matter. Because sexual behavior is involved in transmission, not all children are equally at risk. Thus, it is a reasonable exercise of a parent's judgment to consider his or her child's specific risk and weigh that against the risk of vaccination.

To remove parental autonomy in this case is not warranted and also risks parental rejection of the vaccine because it is perceived as coercive. In contrast, educating the public about the value of the vaccine may be highly effective without risking public backlash. According to one poll, 61 percent of parents with daughters under 18 prefer vaccination, 72 percent would support the inclusion of information about the vaccine in school health classes, and just 45 percent agreed that the vaccine should be included as part of the vaccination routine for all children and adolescents.[52]

Additionally, Merck's aggressive role in lobbying for the passage of state laws mandating HPV has led to some skepticism about whether profit rather than public health has driven the push for state mandates.[53] Even one proponent of state-mandated HPV vaccination acknowledges that Merck "overplayed its hand" by pushing hard for legislation mandating the vaccine.[54] In the face of such criticisms, the company thus ceased its lobbying efforts but indicated it would continue to educate health officials and legislators about the vaccine.[55]

Some argue that liberal opt-out provisions will take care of the coercion and distrust issues. Whether this is true will depend in part on the reasons for which a parent may opt out and the ease of opting out. For example, a parent may not have a religious objection to vaccination in general, but nevertheless may not feel her 11-year-old daughter is at sufficient risk for HPV to warrant vaccination. This sentiment may or may not be captured in a "religious or philosophical" opt-out provision.

Even if opt-out provisions do reduce public distrust issues for HPV, however, liberal opt outs for one vaccine may have a negative impact on other vaccine programs. Currently, with the exception of those who opt out of all vaccines on religious or philosophical grounds, parents must accept all mandated vaccines because no vaccine-by-vaccine selection process exists, which leads to a high rate of vaccine coverage. Switching to an "a la carte" approach, in which parents can consider the risks and benefits of vaccines on a vaccine-by-vaccine basis, would set a dangerous precedent and may lead them to opt out of other vaccines, causing a rise in the transmission of these diseases. In contrast, an "opt in" approach to HPV vaccine would not require a change in the existing paradigm and would still likely lead to a high coverage rate.

D. Mandating HPV for Girls and Not Boys May Violate Constitutional Principles of Equality and Due Process

1. VACCINATION OF MALES MAY PROTECT THEM FROM HPV-RELATED MORBIDITY

The HPV vaccine is the first to be mandated for only one gender. This is likely because the vaccine was approved for girls and not boys. Data demonstrating the safety and immunogenicity of the vaccine are available for males aged 9–15 years. Three phase 1 studies demonstrated that safety, tolerance, and immunogenicity of the HPV vaccine were similar to men and women. The first two studies focused on HPV 16 and 11, respectively, while the third study demonstrated high levels of immunogenicity to prophylactic HPV 6/11/16/18 vaccine in 10–15-year-old males.[56] Phase III clinical trials examining the vaccine's efficacy in men and adolescent boys are currently underway, with results available in the next couple of years.[57]

HPV infection is common among men.[58] One percent of the male population aged 15–49 years has genital warts, with peak incidence in the 20–24-year-old age group.[59] A recent cohort study found the 24-month cumulative incidence of HPV infection among 240 men aged 18–20 years to be 62.4 percent, nearly double the incidence of their female counter-parts.[60] This result may have been due to the increased sensitivity of the new HPV-PCR-based testing procedure used in the study. Nonetheless, the results reaffirm that HPV is common and multifocal in males. Males with genital warts have also been shown to carry the genital type specific HPV virus on their fingertips.[61] While HPV on fingertips may be due to autoinoculation, it may also represent another means of transmission.[62] Men are also at risk for HPV-related anogenital cancers. Up to 76 percent of penile cancers are HPV DNA positive.[63] Fifty-eight percent of anal cancers in heterosexual men and 100 percent among homosexual men are positive for HPV DNA.[64] Therefore, assuming vaccine efficacy is confirmed in males, they also could be protected through HPV vaccination.

2. INCLUDING MALES IN HPV VACCINATION MAY BETTER PROTECT THE PUBLIC THAN FEMALE VACCINATION ALONE

As no clinical trial data on vaccine efficacy in men has been published to date, mathematical models have been used to explore the potential benefits and cost effectiveness of vaccinating boys in addition to girls under various clinical scenarios. Even under the most generous assumption about vaccine efficacy in males and females, cost-effective analyses have found contradictory results. Several studies suggest that if vaccine coverage of women reaches 70–90 percent of the population, then vaccinating males would be of limited value and high cost.[65] Ruanne Barnabas and Geoffrey Garnett found that a multivalent HPV vaccine with 100 percent efficacy targeting males and females 15 years of age with vaccine coverage of at least 66 percent was needed to decrease cervical cancer by 80 percent. They concluded that vaccinating men in addition to women had little incremental benefit in reducing cervical cancer,[66] that vaccine acceptability in males is unknown, and that in a setting with limited resources, the first priority in reducing cervical cancer mortality should be to vaccinate females.

Yet several models argue in favor of vaccinating males. Vaccination not only directly protects through vaccine-derived immunity, but also indirectly through herd immunity, meaning a level of population immunity that is sufficient to protect unvaccinated individuals. If naturally acquired immunity is low and coverage of women is low, then vaccinating men will be of significant benefit. James Hughes et al. found that a female-only monovalent vaccine would be only 60–75 percent as efficient as a strategy that targets both genders.[67] Elamin Elbasha and Erik Dasbach found that while vaccinating 70 percent of females before the age of 12 would reduce genital warts by 83 percent and cervical cancer by 78 percent due to HPV 6/11/16/18, including men and boys in the program would further reduce the incidence of genital warts, CIN, and cervical cancer by 97 percent, 91 percent, and 91 percent, respectively.[68] In all mathematical models, lower female coverage made vaccination of men and adolescent boys more cost effective, as did a shortened duration of natural immunity.

All the models include parameters that are highly inferential and lacking in evidence, such as duration of vaccine protection, reactivation of infections, transmission of infection, and health utilities. The scope of the models is limited to cervical cancer, cancer-in-situ, and genital warts. None of the models accounts for HPV-related anal, head, and neck cancers, or recurrent respiratory papillomatosis. As more data become available, the scope of the models will be broadened and might strengthen the argument in favor of vaccinating males. Given that male vaccination may better protect the public than female vaccination alone, female-specific mandates may be constitutionally suspect, as discussed below.

3. THE GOVERNMENT MUST ADEQUATELY JUSTIFY ITS DECISION TO MANDATE VACCINATION IN FEMALES ONLY

While courts have generally been deferential to state mandate laws, this deference has its limits. In 1900, a federal court struck a San Francisco Board of Health resolution requiring all Chinese residents to be vaccinated with a serum against bubonic plague about which there was little evidence of efficacy. Chinese residents were prohibited from leaving the area unless they were vaccinated. The court struck down the resolution as an unconstitutional violation of the Equal Protection and Due Process clauses. The court found that there was not a defensible scientific rationale for the board's approach and that it was discriminatory in targeting "the Asiatic or Mongolian race as a class." Thus, it was "not within the legitimate police power" of the government.[69]

A sex-based mandate for HPV vaccination could be challenged on two grounds: first, under the Equal Protection Clause because it distinguishes based on gender and second, under the Due Process Clause, because it violates a protected interest in refusing medical treatment. In regard to the Equal Protection concerns, courts review laws that make sex-based distinctions with heightened scrutiny: the government must show that the challenged classification serves an important state interest and that the classification is at least substantially related to serving that interest. To be sure, courts would likely view the goal of preventing cervical cancer as an important public health objective. However, courts would also likely demand that the state justify its decision to burden females with the risks of vaccination, and not males, even though males also contribute to HPV transmission, will benefit from an aggressive vaccination program of females, and also may reduce their own risk of disease through vaccination.

With respect to the Due Process Clause, the Supreme Court has, in the context of right-to-die cases, recognized that individuals have a constitutionally protected liberty interest in refusing unwanted medical treatment.[70] This liberty interest must, however, be balanced against several state interests, including its interest in preserving life. Mandated HPV laws interfere with the right of girls to refuse medical treatment, and therefore could be challenged under the Due Process Clause. Whether the government could demonstrate interests strong enough to outweigh a girl's liberty interest in refusing vaccination would depend on the strength of the government's argument that such vaccination is life-saving and the extent to which opt outs are available and easily exercised in practice.

Even if courts upheld government mandates as consistent with the Due Process and Equal Protection clauses, such mandates remain troubling in light of inequalities imposed by sex-based mandates and the liberty interests that would be compromised by HPV mandates, therefore placing deeply cherished national values at risk.

E. Unresolved Economic Concerns

Mandated HPV vaccination may have negative unintended economic consequences for both state health departments and private physicians, and these consequences should be thoroughly considered before HPV vaccination is mandated. In recent years, state health departments have found themselves increasingly strapped by the rising number of mandated vaccines. Some states that once provided free vaccines to all children have abandoned the practice due to rising costs. Adding HPV could drive more states to abandon funding for other vaccinations and could divert funding from other important public health measures. At the federal level, spending by the federal Vaccines for Children program, which pays for immunizations for Medicaid children and some others, has grown to $2.5 billion, up from $500 million in 2000.[71] Such rapid increases in budgetary expenses affect the program's ability to assist future patients. Thus, before HPV vaccination is mandated, a thorough consideration of its economic consequences for existing vaccine programs and other non-vaccine programs should be undertaken.

The increasing number of vaccines has also has placed a burden on physicians in private practice. Currently, about 85 percent of the nation's children get all or at least some of their inoculations from private physicians' offices.[72] These offices must purchase vaccines and then wait for reimbursement from either government or private insurers. Some physicians have argued that the rising costs of vaccines and the rising number of new mandatory vaccines make it increasingly difficult for them to purchase vaccinations initially and that they net a loss due to insufficient reimbursement from insurers. Adding HPV to the list of mandated vaccines would place further stress on these practices, and could lead them to reduce the amount of vaccines they purchase or require up-front payment for these vaccines. Either of these steps could reduce access not only to HPV but to all childhood vaccines.

Access to HPV is one reason that some proponents favor state mandates. They argue that in the absence of a state mandate, parents will not know to request the vaccine, or will not be able to afford it because it will not be covered by insurance companies or by federal or state programs that pay for vaccines for the uninsured and underinsured. However, mandates are not the only way to increase parental awareness or achieve insurance coverage. In light of the potentially significant economic consequences of state mandates, policymakers should consider other methods of increasing parental awareness and insurance coverage that do not also threaten to reduce access to those who want vaccination.

IV. Conclusion

Based on the current scientific evidence, vaccinating girls against HPV before they are sexually active appears to provide significant protection against cervical cancer. The vaccine thus represents a significant public health advance. Nevertheless, mandating HPV vaccination at the present time would be premature and ill-advised. The vaccine is relatively new, and long-term safety and effectiveness in the general population is unknown. Vaccination outcomes of those voluntarily vaccinated should be followed for several years before mandates are imposed. Additionally, the HPV vaccine does not represent a public health necessity of the type that has justified previous vaccine mandates. State mandates could therefore lead to a public backlash that will undermine both HPV vaccination efforts and existing vaccination programs. Finally, the economic consequences of mandating HPV are significant and could have a negative impact on financial support for other vaccines as well as other public health programs. These consequences should be considered before HPV is mandated.

The success of childhood vaccination programs makes them a tempting target for the addition of new vaccines that, while beneficial to public health, exceed the original justifications for the development of such programs and impose new financial burdens on both the government, private physicians, and, ultimately, the public. HPV will not be the last disease that state legislatures will attempt to prevent through mandatory vaccination. Thus, legislatures and public health advocates should consider carefully the consequences of altering the current paradigm for mandatory childhood vaccination and should not mandate HPV vaccination in the absence of a new paradigm to justify such an expansion.

Note

The views expressed in this article are those of the author and do not reflect those of the Genetics and Public Policy Center or its staff.

References

1. D. Saslow et al., "American Cancer Society Guideline for Human Papillomavirus (HPV) Vaccine Use to Prevent Cervical Cancer and Its Precursors," *CA: A Cancer Journal for Clinicians* 57, no. 1 (2007): 7–28.

2. Editorial, "Should HPV Vaccination Be Mandatory for All Adolescents?" *The Lancet* 368, no. 9543 (2006): 1212.

3. U.S. Food and Drug Administration, *FDA Licenses New Vaccine for Prevention of Cervical Cancer and Other Diseases in Females Caused by Human Papillomavirus: Rapid Approval Marks Major Advancement in Public Health, Press Release,* June 8, 2006, *available at* . . . (last visited March 5, 2008).

4. Centers for Disease Control and Prevention, *CDC's Advisory Committee Recommends Human Papillomavirus Virus Vaccination,* Press Release, June 29, 2006, *available at* . . . (last visited March 5, 2008).

5. A. Pollack and S. Saul, "Lobbying for Vaccine to Be Halted," *New York Times,* February 21, 2007, *availiable at* . . . (last visited March 14, 2008).

6. Centers for Disease Control and Prevention, *Childcare and School Immunization Requirements, 2005–2006, August 2006, available at* . . . (last visited March 5, 2008).

7. Centers for Disease Control and Prevention, "A Closer Look at Human Papillomavirus (HPV)," 2000, *available at* . . . (last visited March 5, 2008); Centers for Disease Control and Prevention, "Genital HPV Infection—CDC Fact Sheet," May 2004, *available at* . . . (last visited March 5, 2008).

8. See Saslow et al., *supra* note 1.

9. S. D. Datta et al., "Sentinel Surveillance for Human Papillomavirus among Women in the United States, 2003–2004," in Program and Abstracts of the 16th Biennial Meeting of the International Society for Sexually Transmitted Diseases Research, Amsterdam, The Netherlands, July 10–13, 2005.

10. Centers for Disease Control and Prevention, "Human Papillomavirus (HPV) Infection," July 2, 2007, *available at* . . . (last visited March 5, 2008).

11. J. R. Nichols, "Human Papillomavirus Infection: The Role of Vaccination in Pediatric Patients," *Clinical Pharmacology and Therapeutics* 81, no. 4 (2007) 607–610.

12. See Saslow et al., *supra* note 1.

13. J. M. Walboomers et al., "Human Papillomavirus Is a Necessary Cause of Invasive Cervical Cancer Worldwide," *Journal of Pathology* 189, no. 1 (1999) 12–19.

14. J. K. Chan and J. S. Berek, "Impact of the Human Papilloma Vaccine on Cervical Cancer," *Journal of Clinical Oncology* 25, no. 20 (2007): 2975–2982.

15. See Saslow et al., *supra* note 1.

16. B. Simma et al., "Squamous-Cell Carcinoma Arising in a Non-Irradiated Child with Recurrent Respiratory Papillomatosis," *European Journal of Pediatrics* 152, no. 9 (1993): 776–778.

17. E. F. Dunne et al., "Prevalence of HPV Infection among Females in the United States," *JAMA* 297, no. 8 (2007): 813–819.

18. L. E. Markowitz et al., "Quadrivalent Human Papillomavirus Vaccine: Recommendations of the Advisory Committee on Immunization Practices (ACIP)," *Morbidity and Mortality Weekly Report* 55, no. RR-2 (2007): 1–24.

19. L. A. Koutsky et al., "A Controlled Trial of a Human Papillomavirus Type 16 Vaccine," *New England Journal of Medicine* 347, no. 21 (2002): 1645–1651; D. R. Brown et al., "Early Assessment of the Efficacy of a Human Papillomavirus Type 16L1 Virus-Like Particle Vaccine," *Vaccine* 22, nos. 21–22 (2004): 2936-2942; C. M. Wheeler, "Advances in Primary and Secondary Interventions for Cervical Cancer: Human Papillomavirus Prophylactic Vaccines and Testing," *Nature Clinical Practice Oncology* 4, no. 4 (2007): 224–235; L. L. Villa et al., "Prophylactic Quadrivalent Human Papillomavirus (Types 6, 11, 16, and 18) L1 Virus-Like Particle Vaccine in Young Women: A Randomized Double-Blind Placebo-Controlled Multicentre Phase II Efficacy Trial," *The Lancet Oncology* 6, no. 5 (2005): 271–278; see Saslow, *supra* note 1.

20. *Id.* (Villa).

21. See Wheeler, *supra* note 19.

22. N. B. Miller, *Clinical Review of Biologics License Application for Human Papillomavirus 6, 11, 16, 18 L1 Virus Like Particle Vaccine (S. cerevisiae) (STN 125126 GARDASIL), manufactured by Merck, Inc.,"* Food and Drug Administration, June 8, 2006, *available at* . . . (last visited March 5, 2008).

23. Centers for Disease Control and Prevention, *HPV Vaccine—Questions and Answers for the Public,* June 28, 2007, *available at* . . . (last visited April 2, 2008).

24. National Conference of State Legislatures, "HPV Vaccine," July 11, 2007, *available at* . . . (last visited March 5, 2008).

25. *Id.*

26. S.B. 1230, 2006 Session, Virginia (2007); H.B. 2035, 2006 Session, Virginia (2007).

27. *HPV Vaccination and Reporting Act of 2007,* B.17–0030, 18th Council, District of Columbia (2007).

28. Governor of the State of Texas, Executive Order RP65, February 2, 2007, *available at* . . . (last visited March 5, 2008).

29. S.B. 438, 80th Legislature, Texas (2007); H.B. 1098, 80th Legislature, Texas (2007).

30. The states are Colorado, Maine, Nevada, New Mexico, New York, North Dakota, Rhode Island, and South Carolina. See National Conference of State Legislatures, *supra* note 24.

31. The states are Colorado, Indiana, Iowa, North Carolina, North Dakota, Texas, Utah, and Washington. *Id.* (National Conference of State Legislatures).

32. The states are Maryland, Minnesota, and New Mexico. *Id.* (National Conference of State Legislatures).

33. Centers for Disease Control and Prevention, *RotaShield (Rotavirus) Vaccine and Intussusception,* 2004, *available at . . .* (last visited March 14, 2008); M. B. Rennels, "The Rotavirus Vaccine Story: A Clinical Investigator's View," *Pediatrics* 106, no. 1 (2000): 123–125.

34. C. Mao et al., "Efficacy of Human Papillomavirus-16 Vaccine to Prevent Cervical Intraepithelial Neoplasia: A Randomized Controlled Trial," *Obstetrics and Gynecology* 107, no. 1 (2006): 18–27.

35. L. L. Villa et al., "Immunologic Responses Following Administration of a Vaccine Targeting Human Papillomavirus Types 6, 11, 16 and 18," *Vaccine* 24, no. 27–28 (2006): 5571–5583; D. M. Harper et al., "Sustained Efficacy Up to 4.5 Years of a Bivalent L1 Virus-Like Particle Vaccine against Human Papillomavirus Types 16 and 18: Follow Up from a Randomized Controlled Trial," *The Lancet* 367, no. 9518 (2006): 1247–1255.

36. J. G. Hodge and L. O. Gostin, "School Vaccination Requirements: Historical, Social, and Legal Perspectives," *Kentucky Law Journal* 90, no. 4 (2001-2002): 831–890.

37. J. Duffy, "School Vaccination: The Precursor to School Medical Inspection," *Journal of the History of Medicine and Allied Sciences* 33, no. 3 (1978): 344–355.

38. See Hodge and Gostin, *supra* note 36.

39. *Id.*

40. *Jacobson v. Commonwealth of Massachusetts,* 197 U.S. 11 (1905).

41. L. O. Gostin and J. G. Hodge, "The Public Health Improvement Process in Alaska: Toward a Model Public Health Law," *Alaska Law Review* 17, no. 1 (2000): 77–125.

42. *Zucht v. King,* 260 U.S. 174 (1922).

43. A. R. Hinman et al., "Childhood Immunization: Laws that Work," *Journal of Law, Medicine & Ethics* 30, no. 3 (2002): 122–127; K. M. Malone and A. R. Hinman, "Vaccination Mandates: The Public Health Imperative and Individual Rights," in R. A. Goodman et al., *Law in Public Health Practice* (New York: Oxford University Press, 2006).

44. See Centers for Disease Control and Prevention, *supra* note 6.

45. B. Lo, "HPV Vaccine and Adolescents' Sexual Activity: It Would Be a Shame if Unresolved Ethical Dilemmas Hampered This Breakthrough," *BMJ* 332, no. 7550 (2006): 1106–1107.

46. R. K. Zimmerman, "Ethical Analysis of HPV Vaccine Policy Options," *Vaccine* 24, no. 22 (2006): 4812–4820.

47. C. Stanwyck et al., "Vaccination Coverage Among Children Entering School—United States, 2005–06 School Year," *JAMA* 296, no. 21 (2006): 2544–2547.

48. See Hodge and Gostin, *supra* note 36.

49. S. P. Calandrillo, "Vanishing Vaccinations: Why Are So Many Americans Opting Out of Vaccinating Their Children?" *University of Michigan Journal of Legal Reform* 37 (2004): 353–440.

50. *Id.*

51. B. Hart, "My Daughter Won't Get HPV Vaccine," *Chicago Sun Times, February* 25, 2007, at B6.

52. J. Cummings, "Seventy Percent of U.S. Adults Support Use of the Human Papillomavirus (HPV) Vaccine: Majority of Parents of Girls under 18 Would Want Daughters to Receive It," *Wall Street Journal Online* 5, no. 13 (2006), *available at* . . . (last visited March 5, 2008).

53. J. Marbella, "Sense of Rush Infects Plan to Require HPV Shots," *Baltimore Sun,* January 30, 2007, *available at* . . . (last visited March 14, 2008).

54. S. Reimer, "Readers Worry about HPV Vaccine: Doctors Say It's Safe," *Baltimore Sun,* April 3, 2007.

55. A. Pollack and S. Saul, "Lobbying for Vaccine to Be Halted," *New York Times,* February 21, 2007, available at . . . (last visited March 14, 2008).

56. J. Partridge and L. Koutsky, "Genital Human Papillomavirus in Men," *The Lancet Infectious Diseases* 6, no. 1 (2006): 21–31.

57. See Markowitz et al., *supra* note 18.

58. *Id.*

59. See Partridge and Koutsky, *supra* note 56.

60. J. Partridge, "Genital Human Papillomavirus Infection in Men: Incidence and Risk Factors in a Cohort of University Students," *Journal of Infectious Diseases* 196, no. 15 (2007): 1128–1136. It should be noted that the higher incidence might be due to the increased sensitivity of the HPV-PCR-based testing procedure used in this recent study.

61. *Id.*

62. J. Kim, "Vaccine Policy Analysis Can Benefit from Natural History Studies of Human Papillomavirus in Men," *Journal of Infectious Diseases* 196, no. 8 (2007): 1117–1119.

63. See Partridge and Koutsky, *supra* note 56.

64. *Id.*

65. R. V. Barnabas, P. Laukkanen, and P. Koskela, "Epidemiology of HPV 16 and Cervical Cancer in Finland and the Potential Impact of Vaccination: Mathematical Modeling Analysis," *PLoS Medicine* 3, no. 5 (2006): 624–632.

66. *Id.*

67. J. P. Hughess, G. P. Garnett, and L. Koutsky, "The Theoretical Population Level Impace of a Prophylactic Human Papillomavirus Vaccine," *Epidemiology* 13, no. 6 (2002): 631–639.

68. D. Elbasha, "Model for Assessing Human Papillomavirus Vaccination Strategies," *Emerging Infectious Diseases* 13, no. 1 (January 2007): 28–41. Please note that these researchers are employed by Merck, the producer of Gardasil vaccine.

69. *Wong Wai v. Williamson,* 103 F. 1 (N.D. Cal. 1900).

70. *Vacco v. Quill,* 521 U.S. 793 (1997); *Washington v. Glucksberg,* 521 U.S. 702 (1997).

71. A. Pollack, "Rising Costs Make Doctors Balk at Giving Vaccines," *New York Times,* March 24, 2007.

72. *Id.*

POSTSCRIPT

Should the Cervical Cancer Vaccine for Girls Be Compulsory?

Currently, all 50 states require children to be vaccinated for a variety of illnesses before enrolling in school. Exemptions apply for children whose parents' religious beliefs prohibit vaccinations. Some children are exempt for medical reasons, which must be certified by their doctors. However, almost all children are vaccinated by the time they enter school. The recent development of Gardasil could add another shot to the many children receive by age 5. Should all states make it mandatory for school attendance?

There is considerable opposition to the HPV vaccination due partly to the increasing trend among some parents to refuse to have their children vaccinated. These parents believe, erroneously, that many vaccines are more dangerous than the diseases they prevent. The HPV vaccine adds the additional element of parents' beliefs that their children will remain abstinent until marriage. Abstinence provides effective and absolute protection against this sexually transmitted infection. Unfortunately, by age 19, nearly 70 percent of American girls are sexually active. Another concern among parents is that the vaccine will actually increase sexual activity among teens by removing the threat of HPV infection.

Some additional arguments against the HPV vaccine maintain that cervical cancer is different from measles or polio, diseases that are spread through casual contact. While cervical cancer kills approximately 3,700 women each year in the United States, and nearly 10,000 cases are diagnosed, the disease has a high survival rate though treatment can leave women infertile. In addition, cervical cancer deaths have dropped 75 percent from 1955 to 1992, and the numbers continue to decrease due to the widespread use of the Pap smear. Most women diagnosed with cervical cancer today either have never had a Pap smear or did not have one on a regular basis. Would it make more sense to use public funds to ensure all women have access to Pap smears? Also, not all viral strains are prevented through use of the vaccine, and women would still need to have routine Pap smears.

The American Cancer Society continues to endorse mandatory vaccination for HPV for all girls before entering school. They contend that because not all women get regular Pap smears, the vaccine would be a way to effectively prevent cervical cancer among American women. Attorney R. Alta Charo supports mandatory vaccination with Gardasil and is concerned that "cancer prevention has fallen victim to the culture wars." See "Politics, Parents, and Prophylaxis—Mandating HPV Vaccination in the United States" (*New England*

Journal of Medicine, May 10, 2007). *See also* "Prevalence of HPV Infection among Females in the United States" (*Journal of the American Medical Association*, February 28, 2007) and "A New Vaccine for Girls, but Should It Be Mandatory?" (*New York Times*, July 18, 2006).

ISSUE 13

Is There a Post-Abortion Syndrome?

YES: Ian Gentles, from "Poor God-Crazed Rhonda: Daring to Challenge the 'Scientific' Consensus," *The Human Life Review* (Spring 2007)

NO: Emily Bazelon, from "Is There a Post-Abortion Syndrome?" *The New York Times Magazine* (January 21, 2007)

ISSUE SUMMARY

YES: Ian Gentles, vice president of the deVeber institute for Bioethics and Social Research in Ontario, maintains that there is a causal connection between abortion and increased risk of suicide.

NO: Senior editor and author Emily Bazelon counters that the psychological risks posed by abortion are no greater than the risk of carrying an unwanted pregnancy to term.

$\mathbf{F}$ew issues have created as much controversy and resulted in as much opposition as abortion. Not only is the issue controversial, but studies have linked abortion with a variety of physical and mental health concerns. Several scientific studies have shown a correlation between abortion and depression labeled "post-abortion syndrome." Pro-life groups claim that this information about the relationship between abortion and depression should be available to all women contemplating an abortion, whereas pro-choice organizations believe that the data linking the two are weak.

Those involved in both sides of the abortion debate not only have firm beliefs, but each side has a self-designated label—pro-life and pro-choice—that clearly reflects what they believe to be the basic issues. The supporters of a woman's right to choose an abortion view individual choice as central to the debate. They maintain that if a woman cannot choose to end an unwanted pregnancy, she has lost one of her most basic human rights. The pro-choice supporters assert that although the fetus is a potential human being, its life cannot be placed on the same level with that of a woman. On the other side, the supporters of the pro-life movement argue that the fetus *is* a human being from the moment of conception and that it has the same right to life as the mother. They contend that abortion is not only immoral; it is murder.

Although abortion appears to be a modern issue, it has a very long history. In the past, women in both urbanized and tribal societies used a variety of dangerous methods to end unwanted pregnancies. Women consumed toxic chemicals, or various objects were inserted into the uterus in hopes of expelling its contents. Modern technology has simplified and sanitized the abortion procedure and has made it considerably safer. Before abortion was legalized in the United States, approximately 20 percent of all deaths from childbirth or pregnancy were caused by botched illegal abortions.

In 1973 the U.S. Supreme Court's decision of *Roe v. Wade* determined that an abortion in the first three months of pregnancy (first trimester) is a decision between a woman and her physician and is protected by a right to privacy. The Court ruled that during the second trimester an abortion can be performed on the basis of health risks. During the final trimester an abortion can be performed only to preserve the mother's life.

Since 1973 abortion has become one of the most controversial issues in America. The National Right to Life Committee, one of the major abortion foes, currently has over 11 million members, who have become increasingly militant. Demonstrators have also become more aggressive and violent. In 1993 Dr. David Gunn, a physician who performed abortions in Pensacola, Florida, was gunned down by a pro-life fanatic. Gunn's replacement, Dr. John Britton, was killed along with his bodyguard in August 1994 by a regular protester at an abortion clinic. In Massachusetts later that year, several people were gunned down in two women's health clinics that performed abortions. More recently, in 1997, Dr. Barnard Slepian, a Buffalo, New York gynecologist who performed abortions, was shot to death in his home.

In addition to escalating violence which has limited the number of abortion providers, the Right to Life Movement has recently focused on several studies that link abortion with depression or post-abortion syndrome. They feel that if the public were more aware of this connection, fewer women would choose abortion, fearing that it would increase their odds of serious mental health issues following the procedure. The pro-choice movement disagrees with the findings of these studies, claiming the research is flawed and that abortion either does not increase the risk of post-procedure mental health issues, or increases them very slightly. In the following articles, Ian Gentles argues that there is a strong connection between abortion and post-abortion syndrome. Senior editor and author Emily Bazelon counters that the psychological risks posed by abortion are no greater than the risk of carrying an unwanted pregnancy to term.

YES

Ian Gentles

Poor God-Crazed Rhonda: Daring to Challenge the "Scientific" Consensus

We are not far into Emily Bazelon's *New York Times* article on the post-abortion syndrome before she hands us some not-too-subtle clues as to how much faith we should put in the credibility of anti-abortion crusader Rhonda Arias. First of all, Arias wears silver earrings and low black boots. She talks a lot about God, even claiming to have had a revelation from Him. She is interested in Messianic Judaism. She prays out loud. She also has a history of "depression, drinking, and freebasing cocaine" as well as attempted suicide. As a child she suffered sexual abuse. The typical university-educated, left-leaning NYT reader will thus know how much stock to place in the evidence and arguments presented by this caricature of a pro-life zealot. Just in case there is any doubt about the matter, Bazelon, in an aside, coolly informs us that "the scientific evidence strongly shows that abortion does not increase the risk of depression, drug abuse, or any other psychological problem any more than having an unwanted pregnancy or giving birth." Those few researchers who dispute the "scientific" consensus—people like David Reardon and his "ally" Vincent Rue—are dismissed as hardline anti-abortionists and consigned to the waste-basket. After all, we are reminded, not even Ronald Reagan's anti-abortion surgeon general could find any psychological harm attributable to abortion. The dismissal of any factual basis to Arias's moral crusade is completed by references to a number of proabortion "authorities" who categorically (but perhaps too emphatically) deny any link between abortion and psychological distress.

With the scientific question authoritatively disposed of, the progressive-minded reader is then free to enjoy the amusing tale of a wacky moral crusade being conducted by a 53-year-old exemplar of southern trailer-park trash.

But is there a possibility that Arias, in spite of Bazelon's strong hints that she is intellectually challenged, and hysterical to boot, might have a point?

Let's begin with Bazelon's statement that "no causal connection has been found" linking abortion with an increased risk of suicide. Of course a *causal* connection has not been found. No epidemiologist worth his or her salt talks about causes, only about correlations. Between induced abortion and suicide the correlation has been shown to be massive and powerful, in numerous international studies published in the most prestigious journals. These studies

From *The Human Life Review,* Spring 2007, pp. 58–63. Copyright © 2007 by Ian Gentles. Reprinted by permission of the author and The Human Life Foundation, Inc.

are based on the experiences of hundreds of thousands of women, who have been tracked through record linkage. Record linkage in this context means using official hospital and mortality records to trace a given population to find how many have abortions, psychiatric-hospital admissions, or die after their abortion. Research based on record linkage is far more authoritative than research based on interviews. Record-linkage studies typically involve large populations; they are not contaminated by interviewer bias; and they do not suffer from the problem of the refusal of some subjects to participate, or the attrition of those who do agree to participate.

Ironically, it is David Reardon, the anti-abortion researcher, who, in his study of 173,279 low-income California women, found the *weakest* correlation between induced abortion and suicide. In the four years following their abortion, women who had abortions experienced a suicide rate 160 percent higher than women who delivered their babies.[1] A much larger study of 408,000 British women in the 1990s established that women who had induced abortions were 225 per cent more likely to commit suicide than women admitted for delivery of their babies.[2] The largest study, based on the records of more than 1.1 million births, induced and spontaneous abortions, and ectopic pregnancies experienced by Scandinavian women between 1987 and 2000 uncovered a suicide rate among women who underwent abortions *over six times* (518 percent) higher than among pregnant women who had their babies.[3] The Scandinavian researchers also made the astonishing discovery that mortality from all external causes—suicide, homicide, external injuries—was more than twice as high among women who had induced abortions as among non-pregnant women, and over six times as high as among women whose pregnancy ended in birth. In light of this they cautiously suggest that not having an abortion may be better for a woman's mental health than having one. Remember that for decades we were glibly told that "abortion is safer than childbirth." That myth has now been buried, by the research published in the last decade.

And yet, we continue to be assured—by the American Psychological Association, no less—that "well-designed studies of psychological responses following abortion have consistently shown that risk of psychological harm is low . . . the percentage of women who experience clinically relevant distress is small and appears to be no greater than in general samples of women of reproductive age."[4] It is dogmatic statements like these that fill Bazelon with enormous confidence in her own rightness. But as a New Zealand research team with impeccable credentials has recently pointed out, the APA statement is "based on a relatively small number of studies which had one or more of the following limitations: a) absence of comprehensive assessment of mental disorders; b) lack of comparison groups; and c) limited statistical controls. Furthermore, the statement appears to disregard the findings of a number of studies that had claimed to show negative effects for abortion."[5] Perhaps that explains why the APA will no longer let you read the paper on their website.

Apart from the overwhelming evidence about the link between abortion and suicide, what else do we know at present about the impact of induced abortion on women's mental health? In fact, a great deal. But the subject is a minefield of political correctness and evasiveness. Some abortion researchers deny in the conclusions to their papers the very information that they have uncovered in their research.[6] Thus Zoe Bradshaw and Pauline Slade conclude that women who have abortions do "no worse psychologically than women who give birth to wanted or unwanted children." Yet in the abstract they tell us that prior to undergoing an abortion 40 to 45 percent of women experience significant levels of anxiety, and around 20 percent experience significant levels of depressive symptoms. Following the abortion, "around 30 percent of women are still experiencing emotional problems after a month." In the discussion part of the paper they also concede that the studies on which they base their conclusion are plagued by high rates of nonparticipation and attrition. Common sense suggests that women who refuse to participate in an abortion study, or who drop out in the middle of it are more likely to be psychologically distressed than those who sign on and participate to the end. They also reveal that negative effects on sexual functioning were reported by 10 to 20 percent of women in the year following their abortion. Negative effects were also reported on couple relationships.[7]

Nevertheless, Bradshaw and Slade assure us that in the long run abortion has little adverse effect on women's psychological health, citing two studies whose authors' bias in favor of abortion is glaringly obvious. They completely ignore Cougle and Reardon's analysis of the U.S. National Survey of Youth, which revealed that women who aborted had significantly higher depression scores *ten* years after their abortion than those who bore their children. After controlling for a wide range of variables, Cougle and Reardon ascertained that post-abortive women were 41 percent more likely to score in the "high-risk" range for clinical depression. Aborting women were 73 percent more likely to complain of "depression, excessive worry, or nervous trouble of any kind," on average *seventeen* years later.[8] This finding is buttressed by a Canadian study of 50 post-abortive women in psychotherapy. The researchers found that "although none had entered therapy because of adverse emotional reactions to abortion, they expressed deep feelings of pain and bereavement about the procedure as treatment continued. Typically, the bereavement response emerged during the period when the patient was recovering from the presenting problem."[9]

However much pro-abortion researchers may like to assure us that abortion causes little psychological distress among women, or even, perversely, that abortion is actually *good* for women, they cannot refute record-linkage studies showing a much higher incidence of hospitalization for women who have induced abortions. Such a study was completed just a few years ago by researchers for the College of Physicians and Surgeons of Ontario—hardly an institution known for its anti-abortion bias. Comparing 41,039 women who had induced abortions and a similar number who did not undergo induced abortions, the study revealed that in a mere three months the women who had abortions suffered a nearly five times higher rate of hospitalization for psychiatric problems than the control group (5.2 vs. 1.1 per thousand). In this short period the hospital (as opposed to clinic) patients also experienced a more than four times higher rate of hospitalization for infections, and a five times higher rate of "surgical events."[10]

⋯⊙⋯

Fortunately, the study of abortion's aftermath is less politically charged outside North America. Illuminating in this regard is the recent study by Fergusson, Horwood, and Ridder. They gathered data on a birth cohort of 520 females in Christchurch, New Zealand, and tracked them for a 25-year longitudinal study. After eliminating a host of "confounding" factors that have been the bane of most studies of this nature—such as mother's education, childhood sexual or physical abuse, prior personality problems, smoking, alcohol and cannabis consumption, prior history of suicidal ideation, etc.—they judiciously conclude that "mental health problems [are] highest amongst those having abortions and lowest amongst those who had not become pregnant."

The presentation of the evidence in their tables show how understated this conclusion actually is. By almost every measure—major depression, anxiety disorder, suicidal ideation, alcohol dependence, illicit-drug dependence, mean number of mental-health problems—those who terminated their pregnancy by abortion suffered much higher rates of disorder than those who were never pregnant, and those who were pregnant but did not abort. After "covariate adjustment"—in other words, taking account of the various "confounding" factors noted above—they found that those in the "not pregnant" and "pregnant no abortion" categories ran far lower risks of suffering various disorders.

Isn't it interesting that women who didn't have abortions were 80 to 85 percent less likely to have an illicit-drug dependence than those who did?

Table

Percentage Lower Risks Experienced by Not Pregnant and Pregnant No Abortion, Compared to Pregnant Abortion[11]

| | Percentage Lower Risk Than Pregnant Abortion Subjects | |
Measure	Not Pregnant	Pregnant No Abortion
Major depression	52	65
Anxiety disorder	48	56
Suicidal ideation	58	76
Illicit drug dependence	80	85
Number of mental-health problems	34	42

Striking support for Rhonda Arias's hunch that a good part of America's big drug problem is "because of abortion."

Another recent, non-North-American study shines a spotlight on the various pressures brought on women to terminate their pregnancies, and the devastating impact this can have on their emotional well-being. The authors of this study of 80 Norwegian women admit up front that their sample represents only 46 percent of those who were asked to participate, and concede that because of this "our study may well be an underestimation of the negative emotional responses" to abortion. Fully one-quarter of the women reported pressure from their male partner as a reason for having the abortion. This is only the eleventh most frequently cited reason. However, the fourth most cited reason, given by over a third of the women, was that their partner "does not favor having a child at the moment." Small but significant numbers of women also listed pressure from friends, mother, father, siblings, and others as reasons for their abortion. If all these various sources of coercive pressure are combined, pressure to have the abortion emerges as by far the leading factor leading these Norwegian women to undergo the operation.[12] A sobering finding, that cries out for similar studies to be carried out in other countries.

To conclude, the whole subject of induced abortion and women's mental health is, in North America, fiercely contested political turf. The establishment media and such heavily politicized professional bodies as the American Psychological Association would have us believe that induced abortion has next to no adverse effects on women's mental health. Indeed, some social scientists go so far as to argue that abortion is often good for women: It relieves them of a terrible burden, and enables them to turn over a new page in their lives. If only certain groups would stop trying to make them feel guilty for what they have done. On the other hand there are three large-scale record-linkage studies from the U.S., Britain, and Scandinavia that establish irrefutably a strong correlation between abortion and subsequent death from suicide and other causes. Other studies have established that women who undergo an induced abortion have a much higher rate of hospital admission for psychiatric problems. Studies have shown that these problems do not clear up quickly; on the contrary, they often haunt women for decades afterwards. Finally, a methodologically impeccable study from New Zealand has recently shown a clear correlation between induced abortion and a variety of mental-health problems including major depression, anxiety disorder, suicidal ideation, and illicit-drug dependence. So much for Emily Bazelon's glib assurance that abortion does not increase the risk of psychological problems "any more than giving birth."

Notes

1. Reardon, DC, Ney PG, Scheurer FJ, Cougle JR, Coleman PK. Suicide deaths associated with pregnancy outcome: A record linkage study of 173,279 low income American women. *Archives of Women's Mental Health* 2001; 3(4) Suppl.2:104.

2. Morgan CL, Evans M, Peter JR. Suicides after pregnancy. Mental health may deteriorate as a direct effect of induced abortion. *British Medical Journal* 1997 March 22; 314(7084): 902.

3. Gissler M, Berg C, Bouvier-Colle M-H, Buekens P. Injury deaths, suicides and homicides associated with pregnancy, Finland 1987–2000. *European Journal of Public Health* 2005; 25(5): 460; Gissler M, Hemminki E, Lonnqvist J. Suicide after pregnancy in Finland, 1987–1994: Register linkage study. *British Medical Journal* 1996 December 7; 313(7070): 1431–1434.

4. American Psychological Association. *APA Briefing Paper on the Impact of Abortion on Women* (2005), cited in Fergusson DM, Horwood LI, Ridder EM. Abortion in young women and subsequent mental health. *Journal of Child Psychology & Psychiatry* 2006; 47(1): 16–24. At the time of writing, the APA has withdrawn the paper from its website with the explanation that it is "currently being updated."

5. Fergusson et al. Abortion in young women. See note 4.

6. For a general discussion of this problem see Elizabeth Ring-Cassidy and Ian Gentles. *Women's Health after Abortion: The Medical and Psychological Evidence.* Toronto: deVeber Institute for Bioethics and Social Research, 2003, ch. 17.

7. Bradshaw Z, Slade P. The effects of induced abortion on emotional experiences and relationships: A critical review of the literature. *Clinical Psychology Review* 2003; 23, pp. 929, 943–4, 948.

8. Cougle JR, Reardon DC, Coleman P K. Depression associated with abortion and childbirth: A long-term analysis of the NLSY cohort. *Archives of Women's Mental Health* 2001; 3(4) Supp. 2: 105.

9. Kent I, Greenwood RC, Loeken J, Nicholls W. Emotional sequelae of elective abortion. *BC Medical Journal* 1978 April; 20(4): 118–119.

10. Ostbye T, Wenghofer EF, Woodward CA, Gold G, Craighead J. Health services utilization after induced abortions in Ontario: A comparison between community clinics and hospitals. *American Journal of Medical Quality* 2001 May; 6(3): 99–106.

11. The figures in this table are derived from Table 3 in Fergusson et al.'s study.

12. Broen AN, Torbjorn M, Bodtker AS, Akeberg O. Reasons for induced abortion and their relation to women's emotional distress: A prospective two-year follow-up study. *General Hospital Psychiatry* 2005; 27: 36–43.

Emily Bazelon → **NO**

Is There a Post-Abortion Syndrome?

Early on a windy Saturday morning in November, Rhonda Arias drove her Dodge Caravan past a Wal-Mart at the end of her block and onto the Interstate. She was beginning the 50-mile drive from her house in southwest Houston to Plane State Jail, where she is, as she puts it, an "abortion-recovery counselor." To Arias, that means helping women at the prison who have had abortions to understand how that procedure has stained them, and how it explains what has gone wrong in their lives. The prisoners' abortions, she told me, "have a great deal to do with their pain."

Arias, who is 53, often wears silver hoop earrings and low black boots, and she has a weakness for edgy zingers. She started doing post-abortion counseling 15 years ago. After what she describes as a revelation from God, she decided that her own pain and unhappiness were rooted in the abortion she had in 1973, when she was 19. "It was the year Roe v. Wade was decided, and I remember saying, 'No guy in Washington is going to tell me what to do with my body!'" Arias said with a sharp laugh as we were driving. But after the procedure, she says, strange feelings washed over her. "I remember having evil thoughts, about hurting children," she said. "It was like I'd done the worst thing I could possibly do. A piece of evil had entered me."

In 1983, Arias became pregnant again and planned to keep the baby. But in the fourth month, she says, she became scared about raising a child alone. She called her obstetrician. He scheduled her for a second-trimester saline abortion the following morning. Arias said she woke up from the anesthesia to the certain knowledge that she had killed her child.

Because of this knowledge, she is now equally certain, she slipped into years of depression, drinking and freebasing cocaine. One night when she was in her early 30s, she got as high as she could, lay down in the dark in a bathtub filled with water and slit her wrists. In her mind, all of her troubles—the drugs, the suicide attempt, the third and fourth abortions she went on to have, the wrestling match of a marriage she eventually entered—are the aftermath of her own original sin, the 1973 abortion. It's a pattern she sees reflected everywhere: "In America we have a big drug problem, and we don't realize it's because of abortion."

From *The New York Times Magazine,* January 21, 2007, pp. 42–44, 46–47, 62, 66, 70. Copyright © 2007 by Emily Bazelon. Reprinted by permission of PARS International.

In the '90s, Arias volunteered and then was on staff at the Women's Pregnancy Center, a Houston group that tries to persuade women to keep their pregnancies. In 2001, after being ordained as an evangelical preacher, she founded her own abortion-recovery ministry, Oil of Joy for Mourning, named after a verse from the Book of Isaiah. She now operates 10-week counseling programs at seven penitentiaries in the state, including Plane State Jail.

When Arias talks about the effects of abortion, she's so fervent that it's hard to maintain her gaze. But the idea that abortion is at the root of women's psychological ills is not supported by the bulk of the research. Instead, the scientific evidence strongly shows that abortion does not increase the risk of depression, drug abuse or any other psychological problem any more than having an unwanted pregnancy or giving birth. For Arias, however, abortion is an act she can atone for. And this makes it different from the many other sources of anguish in her past. As a child, she was sexually abused by her stepbrother, she told me. An older boy forced her to have sex when she was 14; seven months later, she says, she woke in the middle of the night to wrenching cramps and gave birth to a baby girl who was placed for adoption. A year later, Arias's father, a bricklayer to whom she was close, plummeted from several stories of scaffolding to his death. She left home and fell out of touch with her mother and two brothers.

By concentrating on the babies she feels she has lost (she has named the first two Adam and Jason), Arias has drained other aching memories of some of their power. "I think about the baby girl I gave up for adoption, and I think I made a good parenting choice. I know she had a good life," she said. "I think about my sons, Adam and Jason, my sons who I never held in my arms, and I know I'm forgiven. But"—her voice cracked. "I didn't give them life. And I am so very sorry."

Thirty-four years ago this week, the Supreme Court decided Roe v. Wade, and since then the American abortion wars have pitted the rights of "unborn babies" against those of living women. Rhonda Arias and a growing number of abortion-recovery activists want to dismantle that framework and replace it with this: Abortion doesn't help women. It hurts them. With that conviction, these activists hope to accomplish what the anti-abortion movement has failed to do for more than three decades: persuade the "mushy middle" of the American electorate—the perhaps 40 to 50 percent who are uncomfortable with abortion but unwilling to ban it—to see that, for women's sake, abortion should not be legal. Spread across the country are anti-abortion groups that offer post-abortion counseling. The Catholic Church runs abortion-recovery ministries in at least 165 dioceses in the United States. The federal government finances at least 50 nonsectarian "crisis pregnancy centers," like the one where Arias worked in Houston. Many of the centers affiliate with two national groups, Heartbeat International and Care Net, which train abortion-recovery counselors. Then there are small, private counseling and Bible-study groups, both Catholic and evangelical, which raise their own money. Some abortion-recovery counselors just minister to other women. But many also feel called to join the fight to end abortion.

If the activists have a Moses, it is David Reardon, whose 1996 book, "Making Abortion Rare," laid out the argument that abortion harms women and that this should be a weapon in the anti-abortion arsenal. "We must change the abortion debate so that we are arguing with our opponents on their own turf, on the issue of defending the interests of women," he wrote. The anti-abortion movement will never win over a majority, he argued, by asserting the sanctity of fetal life. Those in the ambivalent middle "have hardened their hearts to the unborn 'fetus'" and are "focused totally on the woman." And so the anti-abortion movement must do the same.

For anti-abortion activists, this strategy offers distinct advantages. It challenges the connection between access to abortion and women's rights—if women are suffering because of their abortions, then how could making the procedure readily available leave women better off? It replaces mute pictures of dead fetuses with the voices of women who narrate their stories in raw detail and who claim they can move legislators to tears. And it trades condemnation for pity and forgiveness. "Pro-lifers who say, 'I don't understand how anyone could have an abortion,' are blind to how hurtful this statement can be," Reardon writes on his Web site. "A more humble pro-life attitude would be to say, 'Who am I to throw stones at others?'"

This way of thinking was first articulated in the early 1980s. Vincent Rue, a family therapist and ally of Reardon's, testified before Congress in 1981 about a variant of post-traumatic stress disorder that he claimed was afflicting women— "post-abortion syndrome." Six years later, Ronald Reagan asked his surgeon general, C. Everett Koop, to issue a report on the health effects of abortion. Koop was against abortion, but he refused to issue the report and called the psychological harm caused by abortion "minuscule from a public-health perspective." Nor did Koop believe that the anti-abortion cause would be served by shifting its focus to the suffering of women. "As soon as you contaminate the morality of your stand by getting worried about the health effects of abortion on women, you have weakened the whole thing," he said at the time in an interview with the Rutherford Institute, a conservative law center.

Mainstream anti-abortion groups didn't shout Koop down, and the issue seemed dead. But the Catholic Church, which began financing abortion-recovery counseling in the early 1980s, continued to do so, and in 1986, Theresa Burke began developing a model of weekly support groups and later weekend retreats for women suffering from what she called post-abortion trauma. In 1993, Burke founded Rachel's Vineyard, an independent religious group, to broaden her reach. The gatherings multiplied across the country—more than 500 retreats are planned internationally in 2007—as well as an annual training conference. "It just grew and grew," Burke says.

Meanwhile, the anti-abortion movement was in need of fresh ideas. Bill Clinton, in 1993, came into office as the first president to favor abortion rights in more than a decade; the Supreme Court had recently reaffirmed the right to abortion in Planned Parenthood v. Casey. Reardon's book, published during this time of dimmed hopes for the anti-abortion movement, imagined a future in which millions of women and men with experience of abortion would express outrage, demand reform and file lawsuits that would bankrupt abortion clinics.

These millions have not materialized. The number of women who seek out groups like Rachel's Vineyard is a small fraction of the number of American women who have abortions. Almost 3 million of the 6 million pregnancies that occur each year in the United States are unplanned; about 1.3 million end in abortion. At the current rate, about one-third of women nationally will undergo the procedure by age 45. The number of women who go to abortion-recovery counseling is probably in the tens of thousands, and the number who become dedicated activists is at most a few hundred. And yet they and their cause are emerging as a political force. "These women were minority voices for a long time, and now they are gaining traction within the anti-abortion movement," says Reva Siegel, a Yale law professor who favors abortion rights and has been tracing this grass-roots movement from its origins.

Abortion-recovery counselors like Arias could focus on why women don't have the material or social support they need to continue pregnancies they might not want to end. They could call for improving the circumstances of women's lives in order to reduce the number of abortions. Instead they are working to change laws to restrict and ban abortion. In 2000, a conservative law center in Texas, the Justice Foundation, began representing Norma McCorvey—Jane Roe of Roe v. Wade. McCorvey had come to regret her role in legalizing abortion, and the Justice Foundation filed suit to reopen her case. Her lawyers argued that when the Supreme Court initially ruled in Roe, it could not have known that legalizing abortion would cause harm to women. To prove such harm exists, the Justice Foundation began collecting affidavits from women about their abortion experiences, a project it called Operation Outcry, which now has chapters in 22 states. Arias heads up Operation Outcry in Texas.

Arias raises her own money for the prison counseling and to speak at rallies and to legislatures in her state and around the country, telling her story and urging women to send in affidavits. The Justice Foundation has also collected affidavits through counseling programs like Rachel's Vineyard, along with a hot line for post-abortive women and a television program, "Faces of Abortion," which features interviews with women who regret their abortions and which appears on satellite networks that reach 10 million homes. To date, 1,940 women have submitted Operation Outcry affidavits.

Last year, the Supreme Court refused to hear McCorvey's case. But the affidavits continue to be used as evidence in other litigation, including the so-called partial-birth-abortion case that is currently before the Supreme Court. Similar testimony has also been submitted in two cases that involve efforts to raise the standard for informed consent, which abortion providers must obtain from their patients. "There will be a great deal of litigation in this area," says Roger Evans, Planned Parenthood's senior director for public policy, law and litigation. "This is where they are headed."

Abortion-recovery activists may well have the greatest impact in state-houses. When the South Dakota Legislature banned abortion in 2005, it relied on a state task-force report, which said that women cannot end their pregnancies without "suffering significant psychological trauma and distress," because "to do so is beyond the normal, natural and healthy capability of a woman whose natural instincts are to protect and nurture her child." This "woman-protective anti-abortion argument," Siegel points out in a coming article in The University of Illinois Law Review, "mixes new ideas about women's rights with some very old ideas about women's roles."

In 1985, Reardon started a social-science fight over the effects of abortion. He surveyed members of a group called Women Exploited by Abortion (since disbanded), which defined itself as a "refuge" for "post-abortive women." Reardon distributed a survey to about 250 WEBA members and found high rates of nervous breakdowns, substance abuse and suicide attempts. He presented this as proof of a national link between abortion and these conditions.

Soon after Koop's refusal in 1987 to report on the health effects of abortion, the American Psychological Association appointed a panel to review the relevant medical literature. It dismissed research like Reardon's, instead concluding that "well-designed studies" showed 76 percent of women reporting feelings of relief after abortion and 17 percent reporting guilt. "The weight of the evidence," the panel wrote in a 1990 article in Science, indicates that a first-trimester abortion of an unwanted pregnancy "does not pose a psychological hazard for most women." Two years later, Nada Stotland, a psychiatry professor at Rush Medical College in Chicago and now vice-president of the American Psychiatric Association, was even more emphatic. "There is no evidence of an abortion-trauma syndrome," she concluded in an article for The Journal of the American Medical Association.

Academic experts continue to stress that the psychological risks posed by abortion are no greater than the risks of carrying an unwanted pregnancy to term. A study of 13,000 women, conducted in Britain over 11 years, compared those who chose to end an unwanted pregnancy with those who chose to give birth, controlling for psychological history, age, marital status and education level. In 1995, the researchers reported their results: equivalent rates of psychological disorders among the two groups.

Brenda Major, a psychology professor at the University of California, Santa Barbara, followed 440 women for two years in the 1990s from the day each had her abortion. One percent of them met the criteria for post-traumatic stress and attributed that stress to their abortions. The rate of clinical depression among post-abortive women was 20 percent, the same as the national rate for all women ages 15 to 35, Major says. Another researcher, Nancy Adler, found that up to 10 percent of women have symptoms of depression or other psychological distress after an abortion—the same rates experienced by women after childbirth.

Researchers say that when women who have abortions experience lasting grief, or more rarely, depression, it is often because they were emotionally fragile beforehand, or were responding to the circumstances surrounding the abortion—a disappointing relationship, precarious finances, the stress of an unwanted pregnancy.

But David Reardon continues to research the psychological effects of abortion, and he no longer makes beginner's mistakes. He is said to have a doctorate in biomedical ethics from Pacific Western University, an unaccredited correspondence school, according to Chris Mooney, the author of "The Republican War on Science." (Reardon did not respond to several requests to be interviewed.) According to his Web site, in 1988, Reardon founded the Elliot Institute, a research center in Springfield, Ill., which in 2005 had a $120,000 budget. He has recently teamed up with Priscilla Coleman, a professor of family and consumer studies at Bowling Green State University in Ohio, and published more than a dozen papers in peer-reviewed journals. Reardon and Coleman cull data from national surveys and state records in which unplanned pregnancy is not the focus of the data collection. Using the National Longitudinal Survey of Youth, Reardon found a higher risk of clinical depression in a group of married women who had abortions, and published the results in a 2002 article in The British Medical Journal; using California Medicaid records, he and Coleman found a higher risk of psychiatric hospital and clinic admissions among poor post-abortive women, which they reported in 2003 in The Canadian Medical Association Journal; two years later, using the National Survey of Family Growth, they found a higher risk of generalized anxiety disorder post-abortion and published their results in The Journal of Anxiety Disorders.

Nancy Russo, a psychology professor at Arizona State University and a veteran abortion researcher, spends much of her professional time refuting Reardon and Coleman's results by retracing their steps through the vast data sets. Russo examined the analysis in the 2002 and 2005 articles and turned up methodological flaws in both. When she corrected for the errors, the higher rates of mental illness among women who had abortions disappeared. Russo published her findings on depression in The British Medical Journal last year; her article on anxiety disorders is under review. "Science eventually corrects itself, but it takes a while," she says. "And you can feel people's eyes glaze over when you talk about coding errors and omitted data sets." Priscilla Coleman, for her part, says that research that concludes that abortion has negative effects is more scrutinized because it's "so politically incorrect." When researchers attack his findings, Reardon writes to the journals' letters pages. "Even if pro-abortionists got five paragraphs explaining that abortion is safe and we got only one line saying it's dangerous, the seed of doubt is planted," he wrote in his book.

The A.P.A. has convened a new task force to review the more recent scientific literature about the effects of abortion; the panel will issue findings in 2008. Assuming the A.P.A. affirms the prevailing social-science research, the belief that abortion harms women may be hard to dislodge. Even if no solid evidence provides a causal link to increased rates of depression or other emotional problems, abortion is often a grim event. And for a minority of women, it is linked to lasting pain. You don't have to be an anti-abortion advocate to feel sorrow over an abortion, or to be haunted about whether you did the right thing.

Rhonda Arias, however, heeds a simpler call: repent, and save other women from doing what you did. That is the gospel she preaches in the Texas prisons. On the drive to Plane State Jail, Arias talked about her daughters. Jessica, 20, is an art student in Florida. Jacqui, 17, and Joanna, 13, live at home. Arias was married to the girls' father for 18 years before the two divorced last year.

Arias told Jessica and Jacqui about her abortions when they were 9 and 6. She wanted to ask for their forgiveness. A few years ago, Jacqui taped a segment of the TV program "Faces of Abortion," in which she said that as a child, she tried to behave so her mother wouldn't wish she'd aborted her, too. That made Arias wonder whether she'd been unwise to talk to the girls when they were so young. "I wished I'd asked myself if they were developmentally ready," she told me.

Last March, Arias took Jessica on a monthlong ministry to Israel. They are both interested in Messianic Judaism—a mezuza is nailed to the doorpost of the family's home. For Arias, the trip was glorious. She ministered on Ben Yehuda Street in Jerusalem. (On a previous trip she threw her wedding ring into a valley, pledging to live as a new virgin.) She returned home to the news that Jacqui was pregnant. "I was the last person they told," she said of Jacqui and her boyfriend, whom Jacqui met in church. Arias taught her daughters about saving themselves for marriage but not about contraception. "Abstinence works better than birth control, really," she said. "It's just that people don't do it." Jacqui's father pressured her to have an abortion; Jacqui warded him off. And then she and Arias started planning for the baby, who was born in December.

In the parking lot of Plane State, Arias paused to finish a cup of coffee and to pray. "Oh, Lord, I go from prison to prison, hundreds of women and thousands of babies, and sometimes I feel like I'm carrying a lot of grief," she said in a whisper. Outside, the wind blew through a row of spindly trees. Arias closed her eyes and gripped the steering wheel. "Lord Jesus, carry this grief. It's too heavy for me. I ask you to take it from me and from these women. I implore you. Lift it from their shoulders. Deliver us, Lord."

At the entrance to the jail, Arias met three Oil of Joy volunteers: Nikki Heitzeberg and Debbie Harper, whom she knows through abortion-recovery counseling, and Shawna Kimbrough, who joined the group after fleeing New Orleans for Houston during Hurricane Katrina. Unlike the other volunteers, Kimbrough is black, and Arias says she values the connection Kimbrough makes to African-American prisoners.

Over 10 weeks in Oil of Joy, participants talk about their views of God and of the men in their lives. They fill out an "emotion time line" to chart their lives. They explore the circumstances of their abortions. They're encouraged to think about whether they were pressured into ending their pregnancies and to connect this with other experiences of feeling powerless. Often, Arias says, they are victims of physical or sexual abuse. They fill "bitterness bags" with rocks, one for each offense they want to forgive, often including those they committed themselves. They pick out a pair of baby shoes—choices include satin christening slippers, work boots, sneakers and Dora the Explorer flip-flops—attach a card with the name they have chosen for the baby they didn't have and give them to Arias for a traveling memorial that she has taken to Washington, D.C. During the ninth session, which was taking place the day I was there, Arias held a memorial service for the prisoners' aborted and miscarried babies.

Inside the Tom Baker Chapel of Hope at the jail, Harper and Kimbrough arranged long pieces of gauzy white cloth over the altar and onto the floor, so that the material lined a short aisle. Into the cloth they tucked white teddy bears with red hearts around their necks that read "Happy Mother's Day" and "No. 1 Mommy." Kimbrough sprinkled silk rose petals over the altar and floor. On a side table, Arias placed baskets of cloth "heritage dolls." Their heads and hands were tied with thin ribbons. Their faces were blank. Heitzeberg erected a curved metal frame over the altar and draped it with more white cloth. Kimbrough climbed on a chair to hang a string of Christmas lights over the top. Arias surveyed the altar. "It looks like a bassinet," she said approvingly. The volunteers arranged a semicircle of 25 chairs up front, with sheets of pink Kleenex on each seat.

A guard came in. "Last time, I was in here crying myself," the guard said, and then dimmed the lights and cued soft gospel music over a sound system. About two dozen inmates filed into the chapel, wearing white V-neck prison uniforms, canvas sneakers and orange plastic wrist bands. They'd been instructed to enter quietly. Some oohed at the lights over the altar. Others walked in sniffling. The volunteers greeted them with hugs.

The group sat, and Arias took the microphone. "Today we mourn for your children," she said. The sniffling grew louder. "Many of you never got a chance to mourn the loss of your sons and daughters. Today you have permission to cry, to feel the feelings you've pressed down for so long." Kimbrough passed out more Kleenex.

Arias wove a sermon from Biblical stories: Jesus meeting the woman at the well in Samaria, Hannah praying to God to give her a child, Eve celebrating the birth of her sons. It was time, Arias told the inmates, to release their babies to the Lord. Kimbrough and Harper passed around the baskets of heritage dolls, telling the women to take one for each baby they'd aborted or miscarried. The women rocked the blank-faced dolls, many holding three or four. Their faces dampened with tears. The music reached a crescendo as a singer crooned: "Holy child from God's great hands/is a holy word from God to man/How long will we push our children away?/Is there room in our world for a new word today?" One prisoner took her Bible from under her chair. Inside was a photograph of two elementary-school-age girls with ponytails—her daughters. She kissed their images.

For a few minutes, Arias let the women cry. Then she put out a hand to quiet the sobbing around her. "Is my Jason a 25-year-old-man now, or is he still a little baby?" she asked, her voice high and trembling. "We are very limited in our understanding. But Corinthians tells us that what has died will be resurrected. You might think about your D and C"—the abortion method dilation and curettage—"and wonder how does your baby's body look, since it went through that little tube. The Bible tells us, 'The body is sown into corruption.' I can't think of anything more corrupt than going through a tube or being ripped apart by an abortionist. But surely in heaven the body is made whole."

Arias moved forward, closer to the women. "And in heaven, our children will know us when they see us. They will call, 'Mommy!' and they will reach out their arms"—she extended hers—"and they will embrace us! They're not going to ask, 'What did you do that for?' They already know. They know more than you do. I have a 17-year-old who thinks she knows more than me. She is wrong." A few wry laughs broke through the crying. "But I have four children in heaven who really do know more than I do. To get to heaven, you have to be forgiven, and you must forgive others."

She instructed the women to stand up, speak in memory of their lost babies and take their heritage dolls to the altar. The women stood one by one. They clutched their dolls and said they were sorry. They imagined a baby with his father's dimple or curly hair or green eyes. One woman mentioned a child who had been born and taken into state custody, and the woman who kissed the pictures of her daughters sent them her love. For the most part, though, the messy mothering of living children—and the reality of their lives outside the prison—did not intrude on the ceremony. The women focused on mourning the elusive, innocent loss represented by the dolls. They gave them fairy-tale names: Sarah Jewell, Angel Pillow, Xavier Dante. At a side table, Kimbrough and Harper wrote the names on certificates for children "expected to be born." The documents promised, "By virtue of being conceived, the spirit of this child lives eternally with Jesus and in the heart and the mind of the mother, now and forevermore."

After the certificates were filled out and the women returned to their seats, Kimbrough gave a closing prayer. "I thank you for Sister Rhonda, who has laid down years of her life that we may have healing and closure," she said. Women shouted, "Yes, Lord!" and beamed at Arias. She smiled back, and then her face got stern. "I want to ask you a question," she said. "If you found yourself in the situation of another crisis pregnancy, would you consider abortion?"

"No!" a chorus shouted.

"Can you see yourself living a life of chastity when you leave this place?"

This time, the response was muted. Arias talked about her vow of chastity and then nodded to the guard working the sound system. The music changed to an upbeat song. The women danced, crying and hugging. An older inmate with long hair began calling to Jesus, her screams shrill and shaky. She lapsed into loud sobbing. Heitzeberg patted her on the back. "Hallelujah!" Arias cried. "I don't know what God did here, but I know it's good."

It was nearly 2:30 p.m. The women had been in the chapel for three hours. Arias called them back to their seats. One prisoner raised her hand to ask how she could help in the fight against abortion. "I'm so glad you brought that up," Arias said, and described Operation Outcry. She asked the women their release dates and told them how to send in an affidavit and sign up on her Web site once they'd left the jail. "Ladies, thank you for your courage," Arias concluded. The women went up shyly to say goodbye. Then they shuffled out of the chapel.

While it seems that some anti-abortion advocates exaggerate the mental-health risks of abortion, some abortion advocates play down the emotional aftereffects. Materials distributed at abortion clinics and on abortion-rights Web sites stress that most women feel relief after an abortion, and that the minority who don't tend to have pre-existing problems. Both claims are supported by research. But the idea that "abortion is a distraction from underlying dynamics," as Nancy Russo put it to me, can discourage the airing of sadness and grief. "The last thing pro-choice people, myself included, want to do is to give people who want to make abortions harder to get or illegal one iota of help," says Ava Torre-Bueno, a social worker who was the head of counseling for 10 years at Planned Parenthood in San Diego. "But then what you hear in the movement is 'Let's not make noise about this' and 'Most women are fine, I'm sure you will be too.' And that is unfair."

Initially, Torre-Bueno's encounters with grieving patients surprised her, because sadness wasn't an issue in the first years after Roe. "In 1975, I'd say, 'I wonder how you're feeling,' and women would answer, 'Thank God it's legal!'" she says. But by the early 1980s, Torre-Bueno and a handful of other counselors who favor abortion rights say, the emotional tide began to turn along with the political one. Congress cut off Medicaid money for abortion. The Supreme Court retrenched. Protesters picketed clinics and made bomb threats. Some clinic directors decided it was not enough to treat abortion as a straightforward medical procedure. Charlotte Taft, who founded an abortion clinic in Dallas in 1978, later began practicing what she calls "emotional triage" to identify women at risk of adverse reactions. She would ask prospective patients: Are you against abortion but feel you have no choice? Do you believe that abortion is murder? Do you think God will never forgive you? Is someone pressuring you? Do you have a history of depression? "Some women are clearly fine," Taft told me. "Others are torn apart, and they need more process." When women answered Taft's questions by saying things like "I'm going to hell, but I have to do this," Taft sent them home with exercises to help them work through their emotions.

In 1989, two dozen like-minded abortion providers started a group they called the November Gang. In hopes of improving pre-abortion counseling, Peg Johnston, founder of Southern Tier Women's Services in Binghamton, N.Y., wrote a 90-page pregnancy-options workbook, which she says she gives to women who are ambivalent and to those who are grieving after their abortions, about 10 percent of her clients; it asks them if they feel fear and shame and tries to help them with these feelings. While abortion-rights advocates frame abortion as a woman's legal right, the November Gang providers tend to think in terms of a woman's responsibility to decide when and whether to bring life into the world. And instead of telling women who grieve over their abortions to look elsewhere for the source of their distress, they try to use the moment as a catalyst. Sometimes an abortion "pops open the box where old anxieties have been kept," Torre-Bueno says. "It's an opportunity to revisit past traumas like child abuse, or to face them for the first time." This doesn't mean that the abortion was a mistake, or that other circumstances—the unresolved past, a loutish boyfriend, money problems—aren't the real trouble, Torre-Bueno reasons. But women sometimes need help sorting this out.

In her 1994 book, "Peace After Abortion," Torre-Bueno talks about the pain some women feel on the anniversary dates of their abortions, the spiritual conflict to which abortion can give rise and the hurt caused by keeping it secret—all topics in abortion-recovery counseling. She describes grieving rituals: writing a letter to whomever the woman feels she has harmed (the baby, herself, God, her partner), lighting a candle, filling and then burning a "letting go" box. Adapting the Jewish ritual of placing stones on the tombstones of departed loved ones, Peg Johnston offers a "worry stone" to patients at her clinic, to "give them strength through the procedure."

These counselors don't suggest that women should *need* to heal from an abortion, or that most women do need to. And they are avowedly in favor of abortion rights. Still, the position of these providers within their own movement is tenuous. Torre-Bueno says that when she self-published her book and asked if she could hold a book party at Planned Parenthood in San Diego, the director said no. "He called me a 'dupe of the antis,'" she remembers. (The director, who has since retired, says he doesn't remember the conversation.) In 1995, after 17 years directing the Dallas clinic, Charlotte Taft says she resigned because the owner wanted to run a more traditional practice. By then, she says, Planned Parenthood had stopped sending her referrals.

The country's largest abortion provider, with more than 77 clinics around the country, Planned Parenthood has standards for informed consent, and these acknowledge that some women experience sadness or guilt, adding that "these feelings usually go away quickly" and that "serious psychiatric disturbances" occur rarely. The National Abortion Federation, an umbrella group for abortion clinics, has similar guidelines. In practice, pre-abortion counseling varies. Many clinics say that women are encouraged to talk about their feelings but aren't asked the pointed questions that Taft posed. "That sets people up as having to defend themselves and tell us personal things," says Leslie Rottenberg, director of Planned Parenthood's Manhattan center. "You should be able to make an appointment regardless of your beliefs or feelings. It's a question of access."

Rottenberg's clinic provides post-abortion counseling—one or two sessions with a social worker—to any patient who asks for it. Other clinics can't afford to offer that service and refer women who need help to local clergy members or therapists. Few clinics run support groups. Those who do say they're often undersubscribed. It may be that women who experience grief after an abortion are more comfortable receiving counseling outside a clinic. Many providers have lately referred patients to a hot line called Exhale, founded seven years ago by Aspen Baker, shortly after she had an abortion when she was 23 and a recent graduate of U.C. Berkeley. Baker assumed counseling would be offered after the procedure. It wasn't. She volunteered at California Naral and tried to talk about the sadness she was feeling. No one seemed receptive. So Baker raised $1,000 from friends and in 2002 set up Exhale as a volunteer-staffed hot line based in Oakland, Calif. She favors abortion rights, but her aim is to counsel women without taking sides in the debate. Since Exhale's services became nationally available in June 2005, the hot line has received an average of 300 calls a month. A similar service, Backline, started in Portland, Ore., two years ago.

The abortion providers I talked to were unanimous in their praise for Exhale. Yet so far, this hasn't translated into much financial support. Exhale has an annual budget of $315,000, most of which comes from foundations that don't advocate for or against abortion. Backline's budget is a tiny $36,000.

Its founder, Grayson Dempsey, maintains that there is a demand for pro-choice post-abortion support groups and retreats. But she can't afford to fill it.

There is considerably more money for post-abortion counseling on the anti-abortion side. In addition to the diocese-based services paid for by the Catholic Church, the Bush administration, in its first four years, spent more than $30 million on the 50-some crisis pregnancy centers, according to a report by Representative Henry A. Waxman, a Democrat from California.

Last summer, Waxman's office investigated some of the crisis pregnancy centers and found that when women there asked about abortion's health effects, 20 of 23 centers gave out false information. At 13 centers, this included characterizing the psychological effects of abortion as "severe, long-lasting and common." "One center said that the suicide rate in the year after an abortion 'goes up by seven times,'" Waxman's report states.

Religious abortion-recovery programs don't qualify for government money. Rachel's Vineyard relies on financing from Priests for Life, a $7 million anti-abortion group that is independent of the Catholic Church. Oil of Joy's finances are tighter. Last year, Arias raised $34,000. She is straining to pay her mortgage; meanwhile, as the Texas leader of Operation Outcry, she is expected to make donations to the Justice Foundation, which has a $1 million annual budget and paid its lead lawyer, Allan Parker, $123,000 in 2005.

While national groups like Focus on the Family, the National Right to Life Committee and Concerned Women for America warn about the dire effects of abortion on their Web sites and link to counseling ministries like Rachel's Vineyard, they don't finance abortion-recovery counseling. In part, that may be because the government and the Catholic Church do. But the lack of money may also reflect the strain of skepticism that Koop voiced. Francis Beckwith, a professor of church-state studies at Baylor University who is anti-abortion, has criticized abortion-recovery activists for their "questionable interpretation of social-science data" and for potentially undermining the absolutist moral argument against abortion. "For every woman who has suffered trauma as a result of an abortion, I bet you could find half a dozen who would say it was the best decision they ever made," he told me. "And in any case, suffering isn't the same as immorality." Beckwith speaks at churches and colleges, and he says that most anti-abortion leaders don't want the woman-protective argument to supersede the traditional fetus-centered focus, "because that's where the real moral force is."

These tensions surfaced in the campaign to retain South Dakota's abortion ban. The state leader for the anti-abortion side, Leslee Unruh, who had an abortion in her 20s, called on post-abortive women to campaign and started a state tour for them called Fleet for Little Feet. Unruh says, "My strategy was to put the women on TV and have them tell their stories." But the national pro-life groups refused to send her money to run those TV ads early in the election cycle, she says. "They won't acknowledge women as the first victim. We're always second to the baby." Polls show that voters rejected the ban (by a 55 percent to 45 percent margin) because it did not include an exception for rape and incest survivors. But Unruh blames internal division. "I can tell you that the support I needed from the national groups I did not get," she says. "I just got talk."

One theme in the Justice Foundation's 1,940 affidavits is the story of the woman who says that she was told at an abortion clinic she was carrying "a blob of tissue" and that she went through with the procedure only because of this lie. This narrative is being used in two pending lawsuits over what constitutes informed consent. In one suit in Middlesex County, N.J., Rosa Acuna claims that in April 1996, when she asked her doctor in the sixth or seventh week of her pregnancy whether "the baby was already there," he answered, "Don't be stupid, it's only blood." She is suing for emotional distress. The doctor denies the allegation. But the case is at a preliminary stage in which the question is whether Acuna can try to prove her allegations at a trial. Last April, the appellate division of the New Jersey courts said she could. The question at trial, the court said, would be what medical information a doctor must disclose "when the patient asks if the 'baby' is already 'there.'"

If what Acuna says is true, then her doctor may have breached his duty by lying to her about the basic facts of pregnancy. But Acuna's lawyer, Harold Cassidy, argues in court documents not that her doctor should have told her she was carrying an embryo but that he had a duty to tell her that the embryo "was a complete, separate, unique and irreplaceable human being." Later this year, the Supreme Court of New Jersey will review Acuna's case. A key issue is whether her trial will include evidence about the human status of the fetus. Cassidy argues that this is a medical fact. The doctor's lawyers say it is a religious and philosophical question.

Cassidy is also involved in defending a 2005 South Dakota informed-consent law, which Planned Parenthood has challenged. In its 1992 ruling in Casey, which affirmed (with some caveats) the right to legal abortion enshrined in Roe, the Supreme Court said that states can require doctors to give patients "truthful and not misleading" information about abortion. Eighteen states include in their materials a description of abortion's psychological effects. According to a 2006 analysis by the Guttmacher Institute, seven of these states describe only harmful effects. South Dakota's informed-consent law requires physicians to give patients written state-approved information that supplies a link between abortion and an increased risk of suicide, though no causal connection has been found. Both the patient and the doctor must certify that the patient has read and understood the materials; failure to do so is a misdemeanor offense.

Does such a law violate a doctor's constitutional right to free speech? Robert Post, a Yale law professor, argues that the state should not be able to force doctors to convey inaccurate or misleading information. South Dakota's law "endangers the integrity of physician-patient communications, because it threatens to transform physicians into mouthpieces for political majorities," he writes in a coming law-review article.

South Dakota's law also requires abortion providers to tell their patients what Cassidy argues Acuna's doctor should have told her in the New Jersey case—"that the abortion will terminate the life of a whole, separate, unique, living human being." A federal district judge agreed with Planned Parenthood that the law would force doctors to articulate the state's viewpoint on "an unsettled medical, philosophical, theological and scientific issue, that is, whether a fetus is a human being." The judge granted a preliminary injunction that prevented the informed-consent provisions from taking effect. In October, a three-judge panel of the United States Court of Appeals for the Eighth Circuit affirmed that ruling. But the panel's decision was vacated this month when the Eighth Circuit as a whole voted to rehear the case in April. The question of whether the state can require doctors to say that a fetus is a full human being and that abortion increases the risk of suicide is in legal limbo.

On a rainy morning in November, a dozen women gathered a block from the Supreme Court, at a row house owned by the Gospel of Life Ministries, an anti-abortion group. The women planned to spend the day rallying on the steps of the court while the justices heard a challenge to the federal partial-birth-abortion ban. They came from a constellation of groups: Operation Outcry; Rachel's Vineyard; Project Rachel, the abortion-recovery ministry of the Catholic Church; and the Silent No More awareness campaign. Like Rachel's Vineyard, Silent No More gets money from Priests for Life; it also has the backing of Anglicans for Life, another independent group. Once inside, the women closed their umbrellas and handed out mugs of coffee. Georgette Forney and Janet Morana, co-founders of Silent No More, checked on late arrivals from their cellphones. Theresa Burke was on her way from Pennsylvania. Alveda King, the niece of Martin Luther King Jr., would arrive later from Atlanta.

At the courthouse, the women unfurled banners and signs that read, "I Regret My Abortion" and lined up to hold them. A giant picture of a bloody fetus floated above the crowd. Behind Forney's group, two dozen people in NOW and Naral T-shirts chanted: "Right to life, that's a lie. You don't care if women die," and "You get pregnant, let me know. Anti-choicers got to go." Forney eyed them. "All these years and they still haven't figured out it would be wise to find common ground with women like us," she said.

I asked her what she had in mind. She talked about making abortion "unthinkable" by making sure that women have better choices. At first this sounded like Bill Clinton's "safe, legal and rare" formulation, or Hillary Clinton's characterization of abortion as a "tragedy." But along with promoting adoption, the reforms Forney and Morana described were Baby Moses laws, which make it easier not for women to avoid pregnancy in the first place or to take care of children to whom they give birth but to abandon newborns at places like fire stations and hospitals.

Forney and Morana compare abortion to smoking. "The suppression of truth about the harms of abortion is the same as the suppression of truth about the harms of cigarettes," Morana said. Once the public understands the trauma of abortion, as they now do the health problems associated with cigarettes, then "changing the law will be an afterthought," Forney predicted.

Rhonda Arias says she does not think that abortion will quietly disappear. She wants states to ban abortion outright, Roe or no Roe, "to end this covenant of death." We were talking on the Sunday morning after the visit to Plane State Jail. Arias was stretched out on the couch in her living room; without makeup, her face looked lived-in and also alight. She opened her Bible to the first Book of Kings, Chapter 11. "Solomon builds a temple for Moab and

Moloch—the false god who demanded child sacrifice," she recounted. "And then 'the Lord therefore said to Solomon: Because you have done this, and have not kept my covenant, and my statutes, which I have commanded you, I will surely tear the kingdom, and give it to your servant.' So you see, when we allow the killing of children, we defy the will of God. There is so much blood defiling the land."

Arias hugged a pillow to her and unwrapped a favorite memory. A few years ago, after she preached at a pro-life rally on the steps of the state capitol in Austin, a man jumped out of his pickup truck and grabbed her. "He said, 'You made me want to worship God!' That is the highest compliment anyone ever paid me."

At the prison the day before, I watched the inmates drink in Arias's preaching, too. Abortion-rights leaders would accuse her of manipulation, of instilling guilt in women to serve the anti-abortion movement's political ends. But Rhonda Arias ministers from the heart; the lack of scientific support for her ideas merely underscores that she is a true believer.

Her ardor and influence is better explained, perhaps, by the theory of social contagion, which psychologists use to explain phenomena like the Salem witch trials or the wave of unfounded reports of repressed memories of sexual abuse. Reva Siegel of Yale compares South Dakota's use of criminal law to enforce a vision of pregnant women as weak and confused to the 19th-century diagnosis of female hysteria. These ideas can make and change laws. The claim that women lacked reliable judgment was used to deny women the vote and the right to own property. Repressed-memory stories led states to extend their statutes of limitations. Women who devote themselves to abortion recovery make up for the wrong they feel they've done by trying to stop other women from doing it too—by preventing them from having the same choices.

And then there is the relief in seizing on a single clear explanation for a host of unwanted and overwhelming feelings, a cause for everything gone wrong. When Arias surveyed 104 of the prisoners she had counseled in 2004, two-thirds reported depression related to abortion, 32 percent reported suicide attempts related to abortion and 84 percent linked substance abuse to their abortions. They had a new key for unlocking themselves. And a way to make things right. "You have well-meaning therapists or political crusaders, paired with women who are troubled and experiencing a variety of vague symptoms," Brenda Major, the U.C. Santa Barbara psychology professor, explained to me. "The therapists and crusaders offer a diagnosis that gives meaning to the symptoms, and that gives the women a way to repent. You can't repent depressive symptoms. But you can repent an action." You can repent an abortion. You can reach for a narrative of sin and atonement, of perfect imagined babies waiting in heaven.

POSTSCRIPT

Is There a Post-Abortion Syndrome?

The abortion issue continues to be complex and polarizing. With pressure and support from pro-life groups throughout the country, *Roe v. Wade* may continue to come before the Supreme Court for reconsideration. Pro-life groups have been successful in keeping the abortion issue in the media and in the political arena by linking it to psychological issues such as post abortion syndrome.

Does having an abortion lead to post-abortion syndrome? Previous studies have found that for most women the answer is no, but research by pro-life supporters claim otherwise. Researchers from the Springfield, Ill.-based Elliot Institute, which does not support abortion, concluded that post-abortion depression in a group of married women was related to aborting an unplanned pregnancy years earlier. The association between abortion and depression was not seen for unmarried women, however. The researchers found that an average of eight years after having an abortion, married women were 138% more likely to be at high risk of clinical depression than were married women who carried unintended first pregnancies to term. Among all women surveyed, however, depression scores correlated with other variables such as income.

The impact of an abortion on a woman's mental health has been debated for years. While some studies have suggested that many women suffer depression, regret, and even a form of post-traumatic stress disorder, a recent study finds that 80% of women were not depressed after having an abortion. In fact, the rate of depression in the post-abortion group was equal to the rate of depression in the general population. As for post-traumatic stress symptoms, the rate was 1% in the post-abortion group compared with an estimated 11% in women of the same age in the general population. The study's authors say the results agree with previous studies—including one by former Surgeon General C. Everett Koop, MD—showing that severe mental distress following an abortion is rare. "Most women were satisfied with their decision, believed they had benefited more than had been harmed by their abortion, and would have the abortion again," writes study author Brenda Major, Ph.D., a professor of psychology at the University of California in Santa Barbara. "These findings refute claims that women typically regret an abortion." For the study, published in the *Archives of General Psychiatry,* Major and colleagues interviewed 882 women undergoing abortion. The interviews were conducted prior to abortion, immediately after the procedure, and, for 442 women, again two years later. Nearly 70% of women reported being satisfied with the decision, and 72% reported more benefit than harm. Of those who reported depression

238

or regret after the abortion, most were depressed or had emotional problems prior to becoming pregnant. Experts express little surprise at the findings and say this study is more proof that for the majority of women, abortion has few aftereffects. For a male perspective see: "Mourning After: Men with Post Abortion Syndrome Are the New Poster Children for the Right to Life Movement," (*The Nation*, February 4, 2008).

Research by Brockington (*Archives of Women's Mental Health*, May 2005), however, indicates that there is a genuine condition. The author discusses several types of post-abortion psychosis. An article by Lopez (*Human Life Review*, Spring 1999) takes a look into the thoughts of some mothers who have not forgotten the children they aborted. Rue focuses on the Bazelton article and expresses strong opposition in her conclusion that post-abortion syndrome is not real (*Human Life Review*, Spring, 2007).

Do Ultrathin Models and Actresses Influence the Onset of Eating Disorders?

YES: Janet L. Treasure, Elizabeth R. Wack, and Marion E. Roberts, from "Models as a High-Risk Group: The Health Implications of a Size Zero Culture," *The British Journal of Psychiatry* (2008)

NO: Fred Schwarz, from "Not Our Stars but Ourselves," *National Review* (February 23, 2009)

ISSUE SUMMARY

YES: Physician Janet L. Treasure and psychologists Elizabeth R. Wack and Marion E. Roberts maintain that the promotion of an ultrathin ideal produces an environment that favors eating disorders.

NO: Journalist Fred Schwarz disagrees and contends that skinny models and actresses do not make girls and women anorexic since the disease predates the era of an ultrathin beauty standard.

Eating disorders are conditions characterized by abnormal eating habits that may involve either too little or excessive food intake, which can harm an individual's mental and physical health. Anorexia nervosa and bulimia are the most common types of eating disorders in the United States. Anorexia is characterized by refusal to maintain a healthy body weight and an obsessive fear of gaining weight. Anorexia can cause menstruation to stop, often leads to bone loss, and stresses the heart, increasing the risk of heart attacks and related heart problems. The risk of dying is significantly increased in individuals with this condition. Bulimia nervosa is typified by regular binge eating followed by purging, which includes self-induced vomiting and/or excessive use of laxatives and/or diuretics.

An estimated, 5–10 million girls and women are affected in the United States, although eating disorders affect males as well. Currently, approximately 1 million men and boys have an eating disorder. Although the prevalence of eating disorders is rising globally among both men and women, there is evidence to suggest that it is women in the developed world who are at the highest risk of an eating disorder diagnosis. The exact cause of these conditions is not completely known or understood, although there is evidence that it may be linked to other physical and mental health conditions. For instance, there are data that indicate girls with attention deficit hyperactive disorder (ADHD) have a greater chance of getting an eating disorder than those not affected by ADHD. Some researchers also think that peer pressure and idealized ultrathin body types seen in the media are also important risk factors. However, research shows that for some people there may be genetic reasons why they are prone to developing an eating disorder. Overall, however, the disease is believed to be due to a combination of biological, psychological, and/or environmental abnormalities. This may indicate that some people might be born with a predisposition to developing an eating disorder, triggered by the environment and reactions to it. Many men and women with eating disorders may also suffer from body dysmorphic disorder, which alters the way a person sees himself or herself. In general, although there are many theories, the exact causes of eating disorders are unclear and not well understood.

Although genetics may play a role, in various studies, peer pressure was shown to be a major contributor to body image concerns and attitudes toward eating, especially among girls and young women in their teens and early 20s. Researchers from the University of Miami studied 236 teen girls from public high schools in southeast Florida. They found that teenage girls who were focused on their weight, how they appear to others, and their perceptions that their peers want them to be thin are more likely to have eating issues. According to one study, 40 percent of 9- and 10-year-old girls are already on diets. This dieting is linked to influence from peers, and many individuals on a diet report that their friends also were trying to lose weight. The number of friends dieting and the number of friends who pressured them to diet also played a significant role in their own choices.

There is also a cultural focus on ultrathinness, which is especially persistent in Western culture. There is an unrealistic stereotype of what comprises beauty and the ideal body type as depicted by the media, fashion, and entertainment industries. The societal pressure on men and women to meet this unrealistic ideal may be an important predisposing factor for the rise in eating disorders. In the following selections, physician Janet L. Treasure and psychologists Elizabeth R. Wack and Marion E. Roberts claim that the promotion of an ultrathin ideal produces an environment that favors eating disorders. Journalist Fred Schwartz disagrees and contends that skinny models and actresses do not make girls and women anorexic since the disease predates the era of an ultrathin beauty standard.

YES

Janet L. Treasure et al.

Models as a High-Risk Group: The Health Implications of a Size Zero Culture

There has been widespread concern that the fashion industry, by promulgating ever-diminishing extremes of thinness, is creating a 'toxic' environment in which eating disorders flourish. The Academy of Eating Disorders has written a position statement for the attention of the fashion industry outlining several recommendations to improve both the health of the public and that of models (www.aedweb.org/media/fashion.cfm).

The aim of this editorial is to consider the implications of the fashion industry's expectation of extreme leanness on the models' own health and also to set this into the context of public health. The direct risks for the models are twofold. First, starvation has a general effect upon all organs in the body, including the brain, and the impact may be profound if the deprivation occurs during development. Second, the demand for, and overvaluation of, extreme thinness within a culture of scrutiny and judgement about weight, shape and eating, increases the risk of developing an eating disorder.

The Health Consequences of Low Weight

There are many health consequences of being underweight. We briefly consider the impact on reproduction, bones and the brain.

Leptin decreases as body weight falls. Without adequate levels of leptin the cascade of hormonal events that controls ovulation and implantation becomes disrupted. Menstruation becomes irregular or absent and fertility is diminished. The Dutch famine in 1944 and the Chinese famine of 1959–1961 were associated with a fall in fertility. In addition, children *in utero* and beyond had an increased risk of metabolic and reproductive problems and mental illness later in life.[1] Poor nutrition stunts bone development (in the growth phase) and reduces bone turnover and repair, leading to osteoporosis (the impact on bones in eating disorders is a clear exemplar of these effects). Even minor disturbance in eating behaviour during adolescence is associated with adverse health outcomes later in life.[2]

In humans, the brain accounts for 20% of an individual's energy expenditure and plays a key role in nutritional homoeostasis. The brain itself shrinks in

From *The British Journal of Psychiatry*, 2008. Copyright © 2008 by Royal College of Psychiatrists. Reprinted by permission.

anorexia nervosa and there is uncertainty as to whether this is fully reversible. The response to starvation includes adjustment of metabolic and physiological processes and changes in drive, thoughts, feelings and behaviour. Starved individuals become preoccupied with food. Keys *et al* described in great detail subjective and objective reactions to a short period of experimental starvation in men.[3]

Binge Priming

Animal models explain how environmental changes might produce eating disorders. For example, if after a period of food restriction animals are intermittently exposed to highly palatable food, they will significantly overeat. This pattern continues when their weight is restored.[4] This tendency to overconsume, or 'binge', when exposed to palatable foods remains several months after the period of 'binge priming.' Not only do these animals overeat palatable food but they are also more prone to show addictive behaviours to the more typical substances of misuse, such as alcohol and cocaine. Underpinning these behavioural changes is an imbalance in chemical transmitters in the reward network, for example, dopamine, acetylcholine, endogenous opiates and cannabinoids. The persistent priming of reward circuits by palatable foods resembles the phenomenon of reward sensitisation produced by drug misuse.

Translating into the human situation, we would predict that binge priming caused by irregular dieting and/or extreme food restriction, interspersed with intermittent consumption of snacks and other highly palatable food, might lead to permanent changes in the reward system. Several hypotheses follow from this:

(a) if binge priming occurs in adolescence, when the developing brain is more susceptible to reward, persistent eating problems may follow;
(b) people exposed to binge priming will be more prone to develop substance misuse.

Some empirical evidence supports the first hypothesis in that there are developmental continuities between eating patterns in early life and the later development of eating disorders. For example, people with eating disorders report a higher consumption of high-palatability foods (fast foods and snack foods) and less regular meal times in childhood. Binge eating is persistent, with binge eating disorder present on average for 14 years, and bulimia nervosa for 5.8 years.[5] Abnormal eating behaviours in early adolescence precede substance misuse[6] and alcohol use disorders commonly supersede clinical bulimic disorders,[7] confirming the second hypothesis.

Models and the Risk of Eating Disorders

Eating patterns that an individual may have found to be integral in the maintenance of a particular shape during her modelling career may lead to deleterious health consequences and maladaptive eating behaviours that affect her far beyond the typically rather short years of such a career. Furthermore, binge priming might also explain why models have such a high rate of substance misuse.[8]

In addition to the biological factors described above, social factors contribute to the unhealthy lifestyle common among those pursuing a modelling career. Constant exposure to media images depicting thin women reduces body-related self-esteem. A meta-analysis of data from 25 studies found that this effect was most pronounced in adolescents and in participants who valued thinness.[9] Body-related self-esteem is particularly pertinent in young models as it relates to their career success. Criticism, teasing and bullying focused on food, weight and shape issues increáse the risk of developing an eating disorder. Fashion models are frequently judged and evaluated on these domains and critical and hostile comments, under the guise of professional development, will increase the risk of developing eating disorders.

Successful Intervention in Other Domains

Prevention and regulation of toxic environments is not impossible. Progress has been made in sport and dance. High-performance athletes are also at risk of eating disorders especially in those areas in which excess weight is a handicap or where aesthetic factors are judged. Concerted efforts have been made in the UK to set forth guidelines for high-performance athletes and their coaches in an attempt to reduce the prevalence of eating disorders, unhealthy weight loss and maintenance practices. The UK Sport guidelines[10] are based on practical strategies that consider the demands of the sport and the long-term health consequences often resulting from those demands.

Following this template, similar approaches to standardisation of care and health for fashion models could be introduced. Unfortunately, such initiatives are yet to be embraced by the fashion industry, as evidenced by the recent inconclusive outcomes from the UK Model Health Inquiry.[11] As models are embedded within the fashion industry, which holds responsibility for the idealisation of emaciation, it is hoped that the drive for ever more extreme thinness could be stemmed at the source, resulting in benefits for all of society.

The Future

The current fashion for extreme thinness among models unnecessarily puts their physical and psychological health in jeopardy. Starvation disrupts growth and reproductive function and can have profound and persistent effects on brain development. These risks are particularly profound in young women who, in a binge-priming environment, may be more prone to develop other addictive behaviours. Along with an increased risk of substance and alcohol use and misuse, the risk of developing an eating disorder will also be increased. The longer-term health implications on models' bone and reproductive health are unknown but evidence suggests the outcomes are not promising. The recent guidelines from the British Fashion Council, proposing not to include children under 16 years of age as models, is a welcome first step. Might this be taken further (e.g. legislation on age limit for competitive gymnastics)?

Beyond the catwalk, there are wider public health implications. The promotion of the thin ideal, in conjunction with the ready access of highly palatable foods, produces a binge-priming environment. This might explain the exponential increase in eating disorders seen in women born in the last half of the 20th century and in part also contributes to the increase in obesity.

Public health initiatives can be integrated to tackle both of these problems. The fashion and beauty industry can play a key role in preventing the development of unhealthy lifestyles in young people. Indeed, Body Talk, a prevention programme focused on self-esteem developed by Dove in partnership with the UK eating disorder charity beat (http://www.b-eat.co.uk) takes steps to modify the unrealistic 'ideal form' both as displayed in the flesh by fashion models and through the use of digitally enhanced photography. More focus on these issues will decrease unhealthy forms of dieting, dysregulated eating behaviours and body dissatisfaction among young people. Although it may take time to change such an ideal we should not be faint hearted but remember what has similarly been achieved in relationship to cigarette smoking. People are now starting to listen to the abundance of scientific evidence concerning the harm that such images hold not only for those paid to portray it, but for those who pay to emulate it.

References

1. Altschuler EL. Schizophrenia and the Chinese famine of 1959–1961. *JAMA* 2005; **294**: 2968.

2. Johnson JG, Cohen P, Kasen S, Brook JS. Eating disorders during adolescence and the risk for physical and mental disorders during early adulthood. *Arch Gen Psychiatry* 2002; **59**: 545–52.

3. Keys A, Brozek J, Henschel A. *The Biology of Human Starvation*. University of Minnesota Press, 1950.

4. Corwin RL. Bingeing rats: a model of intermittent excessive behavior? *Appetite* 2006; **46**: 11–15.

5. Pope HG Jr, Lalonde JK, Pindyck LJ, Walsh T, Bulik CM, Crow SJ, McElroy SL, Rosenthal N, Hudson JI. Binge eating disorder: a stable syndrome. *Am J Psychiatry* 2006; **163**: 2181–3.

6. Measelle JR, Stice E, Hogansen JM. Developmental trajectories of cooccurring depressive, eating, antisocial, and substance abuse problems in female adolescents. *J Abnorm Psychol* 2006; **115**: 524–38.

7. Bulik CM, Klump KL, Thornton L, Kaplan AS, Devlin B, Fichter MM, Halmi KA, Strober M, Woodside DB, Crow S, Mitchell JE, Rotondo A, Mauri M, Cassano GB, Keel PK, Berrettini WH, Kaye WH. Alcohol use disorder comorbidity in eating disorders: a multicenter study. *J Clin Psychiatry* 2004; **65**: 1000–6.

8. Santonastaso P, Mondini S, Favaro A. Are fashion models a group at risk for eating disorders and substance abuse? *Psychother Psychosom* 2002; **71**: 168–72.

9. Groesz LM, Levine MP, Murnen SK. The effect of experimental presentation of thin media images on body satisfaction: a meta-analytic review. *Int J Eat Disord* 2002; **31**: 1–16.

10. UK Sport. *Eating Disorders in Sport: A Guideline Framework for Practitioners Working with High Performance Athletes*. UK Sport, 2007 (http://www.uksport.gov.uk/pages/uk_sport_publications/).

11. Model Health Inquiry. *Fashioning a Healthy Future: the Report of the Model Health Inquiry, September 2007*. Model Health Inquiry, 2007 (http://www.modelhealthinquiry.com/docs/The%20Report%20of%20the%20Model%20Health%20Inquiry,%20September%202007.pdf).

Fred Schwarz

NO

Not Our Stars but Ourselves: Skinny Actresses and Models Do Not Make Girls Anorexic

What causes anorexia nervosa, the terrible mental illness whose victims (mostly young women) starve themselves, sometimes to death? To many observers, the answer is clear: Hollywood, Madison Avenue, and Seventh Avenue. Film and television actresses are impossibly thin; advertisers hawk an endless profusion of diet products and banish average-looking people from their commercials; the fashion industry recruits tall, scrawny teenagers as its models and tosses them aside if they become too womanly. When girls and young women are constantly bombarded with thin-is-beautiful messages, is it any wonder that some of them overreact?

Christy Greenleaf, assistant professor of kinesiology, health promotion, and recreation at the University of North Texas, doesn't think so. She has written: "Girls and women, in our society, are socialized to value physical appearance and an ultra-thin beauty that rarely occurs naturally and to pursue that ultra-thin physique at any cost. Research demonstrates that poor body image and disordered eating attitudes are associated with internalizing the mediated (i.e., commodified, airbrushed) bodies that dominate the fashion industry." The narrative is a plausible one, and it fits a familiar template: Big business uses mass media to destroy consumers' health by creating harmful desires. Yet there are large parts of it that don't hold up.

In the first place, anorexia is not in any way an artifact of our modern, weight-obsessed society. Thomas Hobbes wrote about it in the 1680s. A 1987 study showed that anorexia in the United States increased throughout the 19th century and peaked around 1900, when chorus girls were voluptuous and the boyish flapper look was still two decades away. A similar historical pattern has been found for eating disorders in France. Some interplay of genetic and environmental factors may be at work in these cases, or they may have resulted from the common pattern in medicine of certain diagnoses' rising and falling in popularity. But it's clear that none of these outbreaks can be attributed to the late-20th- and early-21st-century emphasis on skinniness.

There are plenty of other examples. The medical historian I. S. L. Loudon has identified chlorosis, the 19th-century "virgin's disease," with anorexia and shown that diagnoses of it reached "epidemic proportions" in Victorian

England before disappearing completely between 1900 and 1920. A pair of Dutch historians have traced the practice of severe self-starvation all the way back to the early Christians and described the various explanations that were offered for it over the centuries (holiness, witchcraft, demonic possession, miracles, various nervous or emotional disturbances) before a newly scientific medical profession defined it as an illness in the mid-19th century.

All these statistics must be taken as rough indications only. Eating-disorder rates, like those for most psychiatric illnesses, are notoriously slippery, since the conditions are so hard to pin down. Journalists sometimes say that anorexia rates have been increasing for decades, as Americans' lives have become more media-saturated; one source reports that anorexia in young adult females has tripled over the past 40 years. This is a case of the common phenomenon in which growing awareness of a condition leads to increased diagnosis of it, even when there is no real increase in its prevalence. Researchers who have carefully studied the data conclude that there has been no significant change in the rate of anorexia in America since at least the mid-20th century.

Moreover, while it's tempting to blame America's appearance-obsessed culture for the plight of its self-starving daughters, anorexia is a global phenomenon. A 2001 article reviewed the extensive literature on eating disorders among residents of Europe, Asia, Africa, the Middle East, and Australia. In some regions, the reported rates of anorexia were several times that of the United States (though, as above, such figures must be taken with caution). In a case of political correctness attacking itself, one researcher says those who attribute anorexia to media sexism are being ethnocentric: "The biomedical definition of anorexia nervosa emphasizes fat-phobia. . . . However, evidence exists that suggests anorexia nervosa can exist without the Western fear of fatness and that this culturally biased view of anorexia nervosa may obscure health care professionals' understanding of a patient's own cultural reasons for self-starvation."

If it isn't skinny models, what's the cause? In the last dozen years or so, scientists have linked anorexia to many different physiological conditions: high levels of estrogen in the womb; low levels of serotonin in the brain; a genetic mutation; overactivity by dopamine receptors; a general tendency toward anxiety and obsessionality; high age at menarche; elevated amounts of a mysterious peptide called CART; autism (which is underdiagnosed in girls, perhaps because it sometimes manifests itself in the form of eating disorders); premature birth or other birth complications; irregular activity in the insular cortex of the brain; post-traumatic stress disorder; an autoimmune disorder affecting the hypothalamus and pituitary gland; variations in the structure of the anterior ventral striatum (the brain region responsible for emotional responses); and even being born in June (seriously—one theory is that a winter-type disease in the mother at a certain vulnerable point during the pregnancy is responsible). Some of these causes may overlap with one another, but biomedical researchers are virtually unanimous that anorexia has physical roots, though the mechanism remains poorly understood.

Might these physiological factors be what makes one *susceptible* to anorexia, but cultural images are what sets it off? Walter Kaye, a psychiatry professor at UC–San Diego, has suggested such a mechanism: "Less than half of

1 percent of all women develop anorexia nervosa, which indicates to us that societal pressure alone isn't enough to cause someone to develop this disease. Our research has found that genes seem to play a substantial role in determining who is vulnerable to developing an eating disorder. However, the societal pressure isn't irrelevant; it may be the environmental trigger that releases a person's genetic risk."

Maybe, but probably not. As noted above, anorexia has flourished in many times and places with no mass media and no ideal of thinness. Anorexia could be just another manifestation of self-destructiveness, like slashing one's wrists. It could stem from some cause unrelated to body image, such as disgust with the processes of digestion and elimination (as well as menstruation, which often ceases in long-term anorexics). Psychiatrists believe that many anorexic women want to reverse the effects of puberty, such as breasts and hips, and while most of today's film and television sex symbols are indeed slender, they rarely lack for breasts and hips.

Despite the uncertain connection, some observers still think the media need to change their act. Professor Greenleaf has suggested: "A potentially healthier approach is to include [in advertising] a variety of body shapes and sizes (as opposed to idealizing only one physique). Healthy bodies come in all shapes and sizes—and health is what should be valued, which may not fit with the fashion industry's emphasis on ultra-thin beauty."

The suggestion is not outlandish. Many advertisers and fashion magazines have, in fact, tried using "a variety of body shapes and sizes" among their models—once. It makes a decent publicity gimmick, but there's a reason they always go back to slender models: Clothes look better on them. (Also, it usually isn't practical to custom-sew garments for individual models, so clothing samples are made for a standard size 6.) And for some reason, viewers of films and television, male and female, tend to like beautiful actresses rather than healthy ones—not to mention the common observation that "the camera adds ten pounds."

If increasing the labor pool for models and actresses by including heftier ones yielded equally good results, the industries in question would have done it long ago. Why deal with a bunch of stuck-up teenagers if you don't have to? If media and fashion conglomerates really do dictate our image of the ideal female, why don't they manipulate us into going crazy for plumpish housewives instead? And even if it's true that media images make some people weight-conscious, the benefits must easily exceed the costs, since obesity is a much greater problem in America than anorexia.

Nonetheless, some lawmakers are calling for bans on skinny models. Madrid and Milan have prohibited those with a body-mass index lower than 18 from their fashion shows. (Body-mass index is the weight in kilograms divided by the square of the height in meters. A BMI of 18 is considered the low end of the normal range, but you wouldn't expect models as a group to have "normal" physiques, any more than you would expect it from football players.) Similar bans have been proposed in Quebec, London, New York City, New York State, and France's national assembly. The main goal of these bills, which began to be introduced after several models starved themselves to death, is supposedly to reduce anorexia within the industry, though proponents always invoke the baleful effects that waif-like models have on society as a whole. Yet this assumes that self-starvation is a willful choice that anorexics will abandon if given the proper incentive, when in fact it is a mental illness that for centuries has proven stubbornly impervious to rational arguments.

Anorexia is a dreadful disease, and still poorly understood. If the growing scientific knowledge about it can be pieced together, we may eventually learn to identify, prevent, treat, and possibly cure it. But political activists do not help its sufferers when they oversimplify a complicated condition and blame it on their stock assortment of evil forces in American society.

POSTSCRIPT

Do Ultrathin Models and Actresses Influence the Onset of Eating Disorders?

It is estimated that of the several million people in the United States who are suffering from an eating disorder, approximately 10 percent are men and boys. Researchers believe that the number of males with the condition is actually much higher, but because of the incorrect belief that this illness affects only females, few men present for treatment. When males do seek help, there is evidence that clinicians may be less likely to diagnose either bulimia or anorexia. Men are more likely to be diagnosed as suffering from depression with associated eating changes than receive a primary diagnosis of an eating disorder.

Males who are involved in weight-oriented sports such as wrestling, gymnastics, and track are at an increased risk of developing an eating disorder such as anorexia or bulimia nervosa. The pressure to win, excel, and be competitive combined with any nonathletic pressures in their lives can contribute to the development of eating disorders. Men who suffer from an eating disorder may also experience problems with alcohol and/or substance abuse concurrently. In addition, as with women, there may also be a correlation between ADHD in male sufferers of anorexia and bulimia nervosa. More research is needed in this area.

For both males and females who suffer from an eating disorder, there are many possible concurrent psychological illnesses including anxiety, depression, substance abuse, and obsessive-compulsive disorder that can be present. Most of the underlying psychological factors that lead to an eating disorder are similar for both males and females and include low self-esteem, a need to be accepted, depression and anxiety, and other existing psychological conditions. All of the physical risks and complications associated with eating disorders are the same for both males and females. The primary difference is the greater number of female sufferers. For further reading on males with eating disorders, see "More Than Just Anorexia and Steroid Abuse: Effects of Media Exposure on Attitudes Toward Body Image and Self-Efficacy," *Atlantic Journal of Communication* (January–March 2010); "Preliminary Development of the Weight Pressures in Sport Scale for Male Athletes," *Journal of Sport Behavior* (March 2011); and "Body Dissatisfaction and Perceived Socio-Cultural Pressures: Gender and Age Differences," *Mental Health* (January 2010). For further reading on the relationship between media influences and the development of eating disorders, see "Eating Disorders in the Media," *European Eating Disorders Review* (November/December 2010); "Influence of Mass Media on Body Image and Eating Disordered Attitudes and Behaviors in Females," *Media Psychology* (October–December 2010); and "Media Images and Female Body Dissatisfaction," *Eating Behaviors* (December 2010).

ISSUE 15

Is There a Valid Reason for Routine Infant Male Circumcision?

YES: **Hanna Rosin,** from "The Case Against the Case Against Circumcision; Why One Mother Heard All of the Opposing Arguments, Then Circumcised Her Sons Anyway," *New York Magazine* (October 26, 2009)

NO: **Michael Idov,** from "Would You Circumcise This Baby?" *New York Magazine*, (October 26, 2009)

ISSUE SUMMARY

YES: Writer Hanna Rosin argues that male circumcision decreases the risk of disease transmission and that people who oppose the operation are filled with anger that transcends the actual outcome.

NO: Michael Idov, author and contributing editor of *New York Magazine*, counters that newborns feel pain and that there is no valid medical reason to perform the surgery.

Male circumcision is the removal of the foreskin (prepuce) from the penis, and in the United States it is typically performed shortly after birth. In the Jewish religion, male circumcision is considered a commandment from God. It is also a common practice among Muslims. Worldwide, about 30 percent of males are circumcised and of those, about two-thirds are Muslim. About 55–65 percent of all newborn boys are circumcised in the United States each year, although this rate varies by region (western states have the lowest rates and the north central region has the highest). Up to 20 percent of men who are not circumcised during the newborn periods will be circumcised sometime later in life. Circumcision is much more common in the United States, Canada, and the Middle East than in other parts of the world. Currently, the United States is the only country in the developed world where the majority of male infants are circumcised for nonreligious reasons.

Circumcision is an elective procedure that has both pros and cons. As a benefit, circumcised infants are less likely to develop urinary tract infections (UTI) especially in the first year of life. Urinary tract infections are about 10 times more common in uncircumcised infants compared with circumcised ones. However, even with this increased risk of UTIs, only 1 percent or less of uncircumcised baby boys are typically affected. Circumcised men may also be at lower risk for penile cancer, although the disease is uncommon in both circumcised and uncircumcised males. Some studies indicate that circumcision might also help protect against sexually transmitted diseases including AIDS/HIV. Irritation, inflammation, infection, and other problems of the penis occur more frequently among uncircumcised males since it is easier to keep a circumcised penis clean. There are also claims that circumcision affects the sensitivity of the tip of the penis, decreasing or increasing sexual pleasure later in life.

Although circumcision appears to offer some medical benefits, it also carries potential risks since it is a surgical procedure. Complications of newborn circumcision are rare, occurring in between 0.2 and 3 percent of cases. Of these, the most frequent are treatable minor bleeding and local infection. Anesthesia is used more frequently than in the past to prevent the newborn from feeling pain.

There are also negative outcomes of a psychological nature that have been anecdotally reported. These include sexual dysfunction of various forms and degrees, including impotence; awareness of a loss of normal protective, sensory, and mechanical functioning; anger; resentment; feelings of parental betrayal; feeling (awareness) of being mutilated; feelings of one's right to a normal intact body having been violated and removed; feelings of not being whole and natural; addictions or dependencies; sense of anatomical and sexual inferiority to genitally intact (noncircumcised) men; foreskin (or intact penis) envy. The quality and quantity of long-term psychologically negative effects of infant circumcision on men, however, have never been scientifically investigated.

Medical practice has long respected an adult's right to self-determination in health care decision making through the practice of informed consent. This process requires the physician to explain any procedure or treatment and to address the risks, benefits, and alternatives for the patient to make an informed choice. Since infants or small children lack the ability to decide for themselves, parents must make these choices. However, it is often uncertain as to what is in the best interest of any individual patient. In cases such as the decision to perform a circumcision shortly after birth when there are potential benefits and risks and the procedure is not essential to the child's current well-being, it is the parents who determine what is in the best interest of the child. In the United States, it is valid for the parents to take into account cultural, religious, and ethnic traditions, in addition to medical factors, when making this choice.

Overall, infant male circumcision is neither essential nor harmful to a boy's health. The American Academy of Pediatrics (AAP) and the American Academy of Family Physicians (AAFP) do not endorse the procedure as a way to prevent any of the medical conditions mentioned previously. The AAP also does not find sufficient evidence to medically recommend circumcision or argue against it.

In the following selections, Hanna Rosin argues that male circumcision decreases the risk of disease transmission and that people who oppose the operation are filled with anger that transcends the actual outcome. Author and contributing editor of *New York Magazine* Michael Idov counters that newborns feel pain and that there is no valid medical reason to perform the surgery.

YES ↵

The Case Against the Case Against Circumcision; Why One Mother Heard All of the Opposing Arguments, Then Circumcised Her Sons Anyway

Anyone with a heart would agree that the Jewish bris is a barbaric event. Grown-ups sit chatting politely, wiping the cream cheese off their lips, while some religious guy with minimal medical training prepares to slice up a newborn's penis. The helpless thing wakes up from a womb-slumber howling with pain. I felt near hysterical at both of my sons' brisses. Pumped up with new-mother hormones, I dug my nails into my palms to keep from clawing the rabbi. For a few days afterward, I cursed my God and everyone else for creating the bloody mess in the diaper. But then the penis healed and assumed its familiar heart shape and I promptly forgot about the whole trauma. Apparently some people never do.

I am Jewish enough that I never considered not circumcising my sons. I did not search the web or call a panel of doctors to fact-check the health benefits, as a growing number of wary Americans now do. Despite my momentary panic, the words "genital mutilation" did not enter my head. But now that I have done my homework, I'm sure I would do it again—even if I were not Jewish, didn't believe in ritual, and judged only by cold, secular science.

Every year, it seems, a new study confirms that the foreskin is pretty much like the appendix or the wisdom tooth—it is an evolutionary footnote that serves no purpose other than to incubate infections. There's no single overwhelming health reason to remove it, but there are a lot of smaller health reasons that add up. It's not critical that any individual boy get circumcised. For the growing number of people who feel hysterical at the thought, just don't do it. But don't ruin it for the rest of us. It's perfectly clear that on a grand public-health level, the more boys who get circumcised, the better it is for everyone.

Twenty years ago, this would have been a boring, obvious thing to say, like feed your baby rice cereal before bananas, or don't smoke while pregnant. These days, in certain newly enlightened circles on the East and West Coasts,

From *New York Magazine*, October 26, 2009. Copyright © 2009 by New York Magazine. Reprinted by permission.

it puts you in league with Josef Mengele. Late this summer, when *The New York Times* reported that the U.S. Centers for Disease Control might consider promoting routine circumcision as a tool in the fight against AIDS, the vicious comments that ensued included references to mass genocide.

There's no use arguing with the anti-circ activists, who only got through the headline of this story before hunting down my e-mail and offering to pay for me to be genitally mutilated. But for those in the nervous middle, here is my best case for why you should do it. Biologists think the foreskin plays a critical role in the womb, protecting the penis as it is growing during the third month of gestation. Outside the womb, the best guess is that it once kept the penis safe from, say, low-hanging thorny branches. Nowadays, we have pants for that.

Circumcision dates back some 6,000 years and was mostly associated with religious rituals, especially for Jews and Muslims. In the nineteenth century, moralists concocted some unfortunate theories about the connection between the foreskin and masturbation and other such degenerate impulses. The genuinely useful medical rationales came later. During the World War II campaign in North Africa, tens of thousands of American GIs fell short on their hygiene routines. Many of them came down with a host of painful and annoying infections, such as phimosis, where the foreskin gets too tight to retract over the glans. Doctors already knew about the connection to sexually transmitted diseases and began recommending routine circumcision.

In the late eighties, researchers began to suspect a relationship between circumcision and transmission of HIV, the virus that causes AIDS. One researcher wondered why certain Kenyan men who see prostitutes get infected and others don't. The answer, it turned out, was that the ones who don't were circumcised. Three separate trials in Uganda, Kenya, and South Africa involving over 10,000 men turned up the same finding again and again. Circumcision, it turns out, could reduce the risk of HIV transmission by at least 60 percent, which, in Africa, adds up to 3 million lives saved over the next twenty years. The governments of Uganda and Kenya recently started mass-circumcision campaigns.

These studies are not entirely relevant to the U.S. They apply only to female-to-male transmission, which is relatively rare here. But the results are so dramatic that people who work in AIDS prevention can't ignore them. Daniel Halperin, an AIDS expert at the Harvard School of Public Health, has compared various countries, and the patterns are obvious. In a study of 28 nations, he found that low circumcision rates (fewer than 20 percent) match up with high HIV rates, and vice versa. Similar patterns are turning up in the U.S. as well. A team of researchers from the CDC and Johns Hopkins analyzed records of over 26,000 heterosexual African-American men who showed up at a Baltimore clinic for HIV testing and denied any drug use or homosexual contact. Among those with known HIV exposure, the ones who did turn out to be HIV-positive were twice as likely to be uncircumcised. There's no causal relationship here; foreskin does not cause HIV transmission. But researchers guess that foreskins are more susceptible to sores, and also have a high concentration of certain immune cells that are the main portals for HIV infection.

Then there are a host of other diseases that range from rare and deadly to ruin your life to annoying. Australian physicians give a decent summary: "STIs such as carcinogenic types of human papillomavirus (HPV), genital herpes, HIV, syphilis and chancroid, thrush, cancer of the penis, and most likely cancer of the prostate, phimosis, paraphimosis, inflammatory skin conditions such as balanoposthitis, inferior hygiene, sexual problems, especially with age and diabetes, and, in the female partners, HPV, cervical cancer, HSV-2, and chlamydia, which is an important cause of infertility." The percentages vary in each case, but it's clear that the foreskin is a public-health menace.

Edgar Schoen, now a professor emeritus of pediatrics at the University of California San Francisco, has been pushing the pro-circumcision case since 1989, when he chaired an American Academy of Pediatrics Task Force on the practice. The committee later found insufficient evidence to recommend routine circumcision, but to Schoen, this is the "narrow thinking of neonatologists" who sit on the panels. All they see is a screaming baby, not a lifetime of complications. In the meantime, sixteen states have eliminated Medicaid coverage for circumcision, causing the rates among Hispanics, for one, to plummet. For Schoen and Halperin and others, this issue has become primarily a question of "health-care parity for the poor." The people whom circumcision could help the most are now the least likely to get it.

This mundane march of health statistics has a hard time competing with the opposite side, which is fighting for something they see as fundamental: a right not to be messed with, a freedom from control, and a general sense of wholeness. For many circumcision opponents, preventive surgery is a bizarre, dystopian disruption. I can only say that in public health, preventive surgery is pretty common—appendix and wisdom teeth, for example. "If we could remove the appendix in a three- or four-minute operation without cutting into the abdomen, we would," says Schoen. Anesthesia is routine now, so the infants don't suffer the way they used to. My babies didn't seem to howl more than they did in their early vaccines, particularly the one where they "milk" the heel for blood.

Sexual pleasure comes up a lot. Opponents of circumcision often mention studies of "penile sensitivity regions," showing the foreskin to be the most sensitive. But erotic experience is a rich and complicated affair, and surely can't be summed up by nerve endings or friction or "sensitivity regions." More-nuanced studies have shown that men who were circumcised as adults report a decrease in sexual satisfaction when they were forced into it, because of an illness, and an increase when they did it of their own will. In a study of Kenyan men who volunteered for circumcision, 64 percent reported their penis to be "much more sensitive" and their ease of reaching orgasm much greater two years after the operation. In a similar study, Ugandan women reported a 40 percent increase in sexual satisfaction after their partners were circumcised. Go figure. Surely this is more psychology than science.

People who oppose circumcision are animated by a kind of rage and longing that seems larger than the thing itself. Websites are filled with testimonies from men who believe their lives were ruined by the operation they had as an infant. I can only conclude that it wasn't the cutting alone that did the ruining.

An East Bay doctor who came out for circumcision recently wrote about having visions of tiny foreskins rising up in revenge at him, clogging the freeways. I see what he means. The foreskin is the new fetus—the object that has been imbued with magical powers to halt a merciless, violent world—a world that is particularly callous to children. The notion resonates in a moment when parents are especially overprotective, and fantasy death panels loom. It's all very visual and compelling—like the sight of your own newborn son with the scalpel looming over him. But it isn't the whole truth.

Michael Idov ➡ **NO**

Would You Circumcise This Baby? Why a Growing Number of Parents, Especially in New York and Other Cities, Are Saying No to the Procedure

To cut or not to cut. The choice loomed the moment New Yorkers Rob and Deanna Morea found out, three months into Deanna's pregnancy, that their first child was going to be a boy. Both had grown up with the view of circumcision as something automatic, like severing the umbilical cord. To Rob—white, Catholic, and circumcised—an intact foreskin seemed vaguely un-American. Deanna, African-American and also Catholic, dismissed the parents who don't circumcise their children as a "granola-eating, Birkenstock-wearing type of crowd." But that was before they knew they were having a son.

Circumcision is still, as it has been for decades, one of the most routinely performed surgical procedures in the United States—a million of the operations are performed every year. Yet more Americans are beginning to ask themselves the same question the Moreas did: Why, exactly, are we doing this? Having peaked at a staggering 85 percent in the sixties and seventies, the U.S. newborn-circumcision rate dropped to 65 percent in 1999 and to 56 percent in 2006. Give or take a hiccup here and there, the trend is remarkably clear: Over the past 30 years, the circumcision rate has fallen 30 percent. All evidence suggests that we are nearing the moment (2014?) when the year's crop of circumcised newborns will be in the minority.

Opposition to circumcision isn't new, of course. What is new are the opponents. What was once mostly a fringe movement has been flowing steadily into the mainstream. Today's anti-circumcision crowd are people like the Moreas—people whose religious and ideological passions don't run high either way and who arrive at their decision through a kind of personal cost-benefit analysis involving health concerns, pain, and other factors. At the same time, new evidence that circumcision can help prevent the spread of AIDS, coupled with centuries-old sentiments supporting the practice, are touching off a backlash to the backlash. Lately, arguments pro and con have grown fierce, flaring with the contentious intensity of our time.

The idea of separating the prepuce from the penis is older than the Old Testament. The first depiction of the procedure exists on the walls of an Egyptian tomb built in 2400 B.C.—a relief complete with hieroglyphics that read, "Hold him and do not allow him to faint." The notion appears to have occurred to several disparate cultures, for reasons unknown. "It is far easier to imagine the impulse behind Neolithic cave painting than to guess what inspired the ancients to cut their genitals," writes David L. Gollaher in his definitive tome *Circumcision: A History of the World's Most Controversial Surgery*. One theory suggests that the ritual's original goal was to simply draw blood from the sexual organ—to serve as the male equivalent of menstruation, in other words, and thus a rite of passage into adulthood. The Jews took their enslavers' practice and turned it into a sign of their own covenant with God; 2,000 years later, Muslims followed suit.

Medical concerns didn't enter the picture until the late-nineteenth century, when science began competing with religious belief. America took its first step toward universal secular circumcision, writes Gollaher, on "the rainy morning of February 9, 1870." Lewis Sayre, a leading Manhattan surgeon, was treating an anemic 5-year-old boy with partially paralyzed leg muscles when he noticed that the boy's penis was encased in an unusually tight foreskin, causing chronic pain. Going on intuition, Sayre drove the boy to Bellevue and circumcised him, improvising on the spot with scissors and his fingernails. The boy felt better almost immediately and fully recovered the use of his legs within weeks. Sayre began to perform circumcisions to treat paralysis—and, in at least five cases, his strange inspiration worked. When Sayre published the results in the *Transactions of the American Medical Association,* the floodgates swung open. Before long, surgeons were using circumcision to treat all manner of ailments.

There was another, half-hidden appeal to the procedure. Ever since the twelfth-century Jewish scholar and physician Maimonides, doctors realized that circumcision dulls the sensation in the glans, supposedly discouraging promiscuity. The idea was especially attractive to the Victorians, famously obsessed with the perils of masturbation. From therapeutic circumcision as a cure for insomnia there was only a short step toward circumcision as a way to dull the "out of control" libido.

In the thirties, another argument for routine circumcision presented itself. Research suggested a link between circumcision and reduced risk of penile and cervical cancer. In addition to the obvious health implications, the finding strengthened the idea of the foreskin as unclean. On par with deodorant and a daily shower, circumcision became a means of assimilating the immigrant and urbanizing the country bumpkin—a civilizing cut. And so at the century's midpoint, just as the rest of the English-speaking world began souring on the practice (the British National Health Service stopped covering it in 1949), the U.S. settled into its status as the planet's one bastion of routine neonatal circumcision—second only to Israel.

That belief held sway for decades. Men had it done to their sons because it was done to them. Generations of women came to think of the uncircumcised penis as odd. To leave your son uncircumcised was to expose him to ostracism in the locker room and the bedroom. No amount of debunking seemed to alter that. As far back as 1971, the American Academy of Pediatrics declared that there were "no valid medical indications for circumcision in the neonatal period." The following year, some 80 percent of Americans circumcised their newborns.

What changed? The shift away from circumcision is driven by a mass of converging trends. For one, we live in an age of child-centric parenting. New research suggests that the babies feel and process more than previously thought, including physical pain (see "How Much Does It Hurt?"). In a survey conducted for this story, every respondent who decided against circumcision cited "unwillingness to inflict pain on the baby" as the main reason. The movement toward healthier living is another factor. Just as people have grown increasingly wary of the impact of artificial foods in their diets and chemical products in the environment, so too have they become more suspicious of the routine use of preventive medical procedures. We've already rejected tonsillectomy and appendectomy as bad ideas. The new holistically minded consensus seems to be that if something is there, it's there for a reason: Leave it alone. Globalization plays a part too. As more U.S. women have sex with foreign-born men, the American perception of the uncut penis as exotic has begun to fade. The decline in the number of practicing Jews contributes as well. Perhaps as a reflection of all of these typically urban-minded ideas, circumcision rates are dropping in big coastal cities at a faster rate than in the heartland. In 2006, for example, a minority of male New York City newborns were circumcised—43.4 percent. In Minnesota, the rate was 70 percent. Circumcision, you could say, is becoming a blue-state-red-state issue.

The Moreas considered all of this and more, having imbibed more information about both the pros and cons of circumcision during the last four months of Deanna's pregnancy than they care to recall. They still hadn't decided what to do until the day after their son, Anderson, was born. Then, when a nurse came to take the boy to be circumcised, the decision came clear to them. "We didn't want to put him through that—we didn't want to cut him," says Deanna. "It's mutilation. They do it to girls in Africa. No matter how accepted it is, it's mutilation."

And yet, the pendulum is already swinging back. Earlier this year, *The New York Times* published a front-page story noting that the Centers for Disease Control was considering recommending routine circumcision to help stop the spread of AIDS. The idea was based largely on studies done in Africa indicating that circumcised heterosexual men were at least 60 percent less susceptible to HIV than uncircumcised ones. The story promptly touched off a firestorm, with pro- and anti-circumcision commenters exchanging angry barbs. The CDC will now say only that it's in the process of determining a recommendation.

Caught at the crossroads of religion and science, circumcision has proved to be a free-floating symbol, attaching itself to whatever orthodoxy captures a society's imagination. Its history is driven by wildly shifting rationales: from tribal rite of passage to covenant with God to chastity guarantor to paralysis cure to cancer guard to unnecessary, painful surgery to a Hail Mary pass in the struggle with the AIDS pandemic. There's no reason to think a new rationale won't come down the pike when we least expect it. Our millennia-long quest to justify one of civilization's most curious habits continues.

POSTSCRIPT

Is There a Valid Reason for Routine Infant Male Circumcision?

In southern Africa, the small country of Swaziland is experiencing one of the highest rates of HIV in the world. Slightly less than 20 percent of Swaziland's 1 million people are HIV positive, an epidemic linked to poverty, a lack of medical resources, and a culture in which having multiple sex partners is common. Nearly half of women ages 25–29 and men 35–39 are infected. During recent times, the average life expectancy has dropped from about 61 years to 47 years due to the AIDS epidemic. To help fight the disease and prevent new cases, Swaziland has been preparing its male citizens for mass circumcision since 2006. This is in response to a 2005 study conducted in South Africa that determined that circumcised men are as much as 60 percent less likely to contract HIV through heterosexual sex. Researchers do not fully understand why, but the study was so convincing that it was halted after 18 months, because preventing the uncircumcised control group from getting the procedure would not have been ethical. According to a recent article in *The Atlantic Monthly* ("The Kindest Cut," January/February 2011), there is currently a nationwide campaign in Swaziland to circumcise 160,000 HIV-negative males by the end of 2011. Although Swaziland is in the process of circumcising thousands of men, not all researchers are convinced of the benefits of the procedure as a means to combat AIDS. In "Circumcision" (*Journal of Pediatrics & Child Health*, January/February 2011), author David Isaacs argues that there is insufficient proof of the health benefits of the procedure. However, the article "Role of the Foreskin in Male Circumcision: An Evidence-Based Review" (*Journal of Reproductive Immunology*, March 2011) presents evidence that shows HIV transmission is reduced when a man is circumcised. Similar results were found in the study published in *Preventive Medicine* in March 2011 ("Male Circumcision as an HIV Prevention Intervention in the US: Influence of Health Care Providers and Potential for Risk Compensation"), which also found male circumcision was an HIV prevention intervention and reduced the potential for disease transmission. Although it is clear that researchers do not always agree, a general overview of the procedure discusses circumcision in "Circumcision" (*American Journal of Perinatology*, February 2011). Although many studies argue that circumcision may help prevent diseases among males, the article "Prevention: Male Circumcision May Help Protect Sexual Partners Against Cervical Cancer" (*The New York Times*, January 18, 2011) shows that the procedure also appears to help protect his sexual partners against cervical cancer. Overall, the procedure remains controversial, and many experts disagree on the risks and benefits.

Internet References . . .

Global Vaccine Awareness League

This site is dedicated to the education of parents and concerned citizens regarding vaccination. It includes a live, interactive message board and a list of related links and articles that reflect both pro-vaccine and pro-choice opinions.

http://www.gval.com

National Clearinghouse for Alcohol and Drug Information

Affiliated with the U.S. Department of Health and Human Services, this site offers information aimed at preventing alcohol and drug abuse. It includes "Prevention Primer," a reference for prevention practitioners and a variety of studies about drug use and prevention.

http://www.health.org

La Leche League International

Their mission is to help mothers worldwide to breastfeed through mother-to-mother support, encouragement, information, and education, and to promote a better understanding of breastfeeding as an important element in the healthy development of the baby and mother.

http://www.llli.org/

American Cancer Society—Cell Phones and Cancer

Extensive references and information about a possible cell phone and cancer connection.

http://www.cancer.org/Cancer/CancerCauses/OtherCarcinogens/AtHome/ cellular-phones

Environmental Protection Agency

This site includes educational resources, information about global warming and other environmental concerns, FAQs, environmental laws, news releases, air quality by state, and links to additional resources.

http://www.epa.gov

Autism Society

The site provides information on treatment, diagnosis, causes, and symptoms of autism. It also has a national directory of autism services.

http://www.autism-society.org/

Public Health Issues

*T*here are many health issues that concern the public. This unit addresses a number of these issues, including the issue of a possible link between vaccination and autism. Many are concerned with the potential risks of childhood immunization. Is there any valid connection between the two? Does parental refusal to immunize their children risk potential disease outbreaks? Or does immunization depress the immune system, thereby increasing one's risk of disease? With the rise in cell phone usage, questions arise relative to their safety. Do they cause cancer? Two other issues in this unit address the relationship between global warming and health issues plus the overall health benefits of breastfeeding.

- Is There a Link Between Vaccination and Autism?
- Do Cell Phones Cause Cancer?
- Will Global Warming Negatively Impact Human Health?
- Is Breastfeeding the Best Way to Feed Babies?

ISSUE 16

Is There a Link Between Vaccination and Autism?

YES: Robert F. Kennedy Jr., from "Deadly Immunity," *Rolling Stone* (June 30–July 14, 2005)

NO: Matthew Normand and Jesse Dallery, from "Mercury Rising: Exposing the Vaccine-Autism Myth," *Skeptic* (vol. 13, no. 3, 2007)

ISSUE SUMMARY

YES: Environmentalist and attorney Robert F. Kennedy Jr. argues that childhood vaccines containing thimerosal are linked to autism and that the government has colluded with pharmaceutical companies to cover up this information.

NO: Psychology professors Matthew Normand and Jesse Dallery contend that studies have failed to uncover any specific link between autism and mercury-containing thimerosal vaccines.

The brain development disorder known as autism is characterized by impaired communication and interpersonal interactions and restricted and repetitive behavior. These symptoms tend to begin before a child is three years old. The autism spectrum disorders (ASD) also include related conditions such as Asperger syndrome that have milder signs and symptoms.

Overall, males are affected more often than females by about 4:1. It appears that between 4–10 individuals per 10,000 children are affected, though recent surveys have shown a much higher prevalence of 40–60 cases/10,000 people. While there has been much publicity over the increased numbers of autism cases identified over the past 20–30 years, there is limited evidence that the actual number of new cases has risen over this time frame. Changes in the way autism is diagnosed have been suggested as a reason for the increased rates. Researchers studied population groups in California and documented a rise in the number of children diagnosed with autism and a decrease in the number diagnosed with mental retardation. This may suggest that a change in diagnosis from mental retardation to autism may be responsible for the increase in the incidence of autism. It is clear that further research is needed to determine if the actual numbers of cases of autism is truly increasing.

Scientists aren't clear about what causes autism, but it's likely that both genetics and environment play a role. Researchers have identified a number of genes associated with the disorder. Research involving individuals with autism has found abnormalities in multiple regions of the brain. Other studies indicate that people with autism have unusual levels of serotonin or other neurotransmitters in the brain. These irregularities imply that autism may develop from the disruption of normal brain growth early in fetal development. These irregularities are caused by defects in genes that control brain growth and that regulate how neurons communicate with each other. While these findings are interesting, they are preliminary and require additional research.

Vaccination against infectious diseases such as measles, polio, and mumps has been a very successful preventive agent. However, because of this success, many people have forgotten how dreadful these diseases were and can be. Most of the concerns about the role of vaccines in autism have focused on the measles, mumps, and rubella (MMR) vaccine and on thimerosal, the mercury-based preservative used in some vaccines before 2001. In 1998, researcher Andrew Wakefield published a paper in the British medical journal, *Lancet*. It reported on 12 children who had autism spectrum disorder as well as bowel symptoms. In eight of these children, the parents or the child's doctor linked the MMR vaccination with the onset of the behavioral symptoms. The paper was seized upon by the media and parents groups, creating a furor that led to a significant drop in the number of British children who were vaccinated, leading to a return of mumps and measles cases in England. Interestingly, in February 2009 a special federal court ruled that there was no proven link between certain early childhood vaccines such as MMR and autism that developed in 3 children.

Though a special federal court ruled that there was no proven link between the MMR vaccine and autism, many parents and their doctors believe otherwise. In the following selections, attorney and environmentalist Robert F. Kennedy Jr. argues that the mercury-based thiomersal used as a preservative is linked to autism and that the government is in collusion with pharmaceutical companies. Psychology professors Matthew Normand and Jesse Dallery disagree and contend that studies have failed to uncover any specific link between autism and mercury-containing thimerosal vaccines.

YES ↵   Robert F. Kennedy Jr.

Deadly Immunity

In June 2000, a group of top government scientists and health officials gathered for a meeting at the isolated Simpsonwood conference center in Norcross, Georgia. Convened by the Centers for Disease Control and Prevention, the meeting was held at this Methodist retreat center, nestled in wooded farmland next to the Chattahoochee River, to ensure complete secrecy. The agency had issued no public announcement of the session—only private invitations to fifty-two attendees. There were high-level officials from the CDC and the Food and Drug Administration, the top vaccine specialist from the World Health Organization in Geneva and representatives of every major vaccine manufacturer, including GlaxoSmithKline, Merck, Wyeth and Aventis Pasteur. All of the scientific data under discussion, CDC officials repeatedly reminded the participants, was strictly "embargoed." There would be no making photocopies of documents, no taking papers with them when they left.

The federal officials and industry representatives had assembled to discuss a disturbing new study that raised alarming questions about the safety of a host of common childhood vaccines administered to infants and young children. According to a CDC epidemiologist named Tom Verstraeten, who had analyzed the agency's massive database containing the medical records of 100,000 children, a mercury-based preservative in the vaccines—thimerosal—appeared to be responsible for a dramatic increase in autism and a host of other neurological disorders among children. "I was actually stunned by what I saw," Verstraeten told those assembled at Simpsonwood, citing the staggering number of earlier studies that indicate a link between thimerosal and speech delays, attention-deficit disorder, hyperactivity and autism. Since 1991, when the CDC and the FDA had recommended that three additional vaccines laced with the preservative be given to extremely young infants—in one case, within hours of birth—the estimated number of cases of autism had increased fifteen-fold, from one in every 2,500 children to one in 166 children.

Even for scientists and doctors accustomed to confronting issues of life and death, the findings were frightening. "You can play with this all you want," Dr. Bill Weil, a consultant for the American Academy of Pediatrics, told the group. The results "are statistically significant." Dr. Richard Johnston, an immunologist and pediatrician from the University of Colorado whose grandson had been born early on the morning of the meeting's first day, was even more alarmed. "My gut feeling?" he said. "Forgive this personal comment—I

From *Rolling Stone*, June 30–July 14, 2005, pp. 57–58, 60, 64, 66. Copyright © 2005 by Rolling Stone LLC. Reprinted by permission of Wenner Media.

do not want my grandson to get a thimerosal-containing vaccine until we know better what is going on."

But instead of taking immediate steps to alert the public and rid the vaccine supply of thimerosal, the officials and executives at Simpsonwood spent most of the next two days discussing how to cover up the damaging data. According to transcripts obtained under the Freedom of Information Act, many at the meeting were concerned about how the damaging revelations about thimerosal would affect the vaccine industry's bottom line. "We are in a bad position from the standpoint of defending any lawsuits," said Dr. Robert Brent, a pediatrician at the Alfred I. duPont Hospital for Children in Delaware. "This will be a resource to our very busy plaintiff attorneys in this country." Dr. Bob Chen, head of vaccine safety for the CDC, expressed relief that "given the sensitivity of the information, we have been able to keep it out of the hands of, let's say, less responsible hands." Dr. John Clements, vaccines adviser at the World Health Organization, declared flatly that the study "should not have been done at all" and warned that the results "will be taken by others and will be used in ways beyond the control of this group. The research results have to be *handled*."

In fact, the government has proved to be far more adept at handling the damage than at protecting children's health. The CDC paid the Institute of Medicine to conduct a new study to whitewash the risks of thimerosal, ordering researchers to "rule out" the chemical's link to autism. It withheld Verstraeten's findings, even though they had been slated for immediate publication, and told other scientists that his original data had been "lost" and could not be replicated. And to thwart the Freedom of Information Act, it handed its giant database of vaccine records over to a private company, declaring it off-limits to researchers. By the time Verstraeten finally published his study in 2003, he had gone to work for GlaxoSmithKline and reworked his data to bury the link between thimerosal and autism.

Vaccine manufacturers had already begun to phase thimerosal out of injections given to American infants—but they continued to sell off their mercury-based supplies of vaccines until last year. The CDC and FDA gave them a hand, buying up the tainted vaccines for export to developing countries and allowing drug companies to continue using the preservative in some American vaccines—including several pediatric flu shots as well as tetanus boosters routinely given to eleven-year-olds.

The drug companies are also getting help from powerful lawmakers in Washington. Senate Majority Leader Bill Frist, who has received $873,000 in contributions from the pharmaceutical industry, has been working to immunize vaccine makers from liability in 4,200 lawsuits that have been filed by the parents of injured children. On five separate occasions, Frist has tried to seal all of the government's vaccine-related documents—including the Simpsonwood transcripts—and shield Eli Lilly, the developer of thimerosal, from subpoenas. In 2002, the day after Frist quietly slipped a rider known as the "Eli Lilly Protection Act" into a homeland security bill, the company contributed $10,000 to his campaign and bought 5,000 copies of his book on bioterrorism. The measure was repealed by Congress in 2003—but earlier this year, Frist slipped another provision into an anti-terrorism bill that would deny

Figure 1

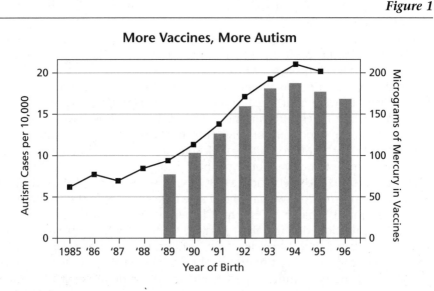

More Vaccines, More Autism

After the CDC began recommending additional vaccinations in 1989, the number of autism cases nationwide spiked sharply. Figures for California show the link to the increasing "mercury load" in vaccines, as surveyed two years after birth.

compensation to children suffering from vaccine-related brain disorders. "The lawsuits are of such magnitude that they could put vaccine producers out of business and limit our capacity to deal with a biological attack by terrorists," says Andy Olsen, a legislative assistant to Frist.

Even many conservatives are shocked by the government's effort to cover up the dangers of thimerosal. Rep. Dan Burton, a Republican from Indiana, oversaw a three-year investigation of thimerosal after his grandson was diagnosed with autism. "Thimerosal used as a preservative in vaccines is directly related to the autism epidemic," his House Government Reform Committee concluded in its final report. "This epidemic in all probability may have been prevented or curtailed had the FDA not been asleep at the switch regarding a lack of safety data regarding injected thimerosal, a known neurotoxin." The FDA and other public-health agencies failed to act, the committee added, out of "institutional malfeasance for self protection" and "misplaced protectionism of the pharmaceutical industry."

❧◈❧

The story of how government health agencies colluded with Big Pharma to hide the risks of thimerosal from the public is a chilling case study of institutional arrogance, power and greed. I was drawn into the controversy only reluctantly. As an attorney and environmentalist who has spent years working on issues of mercury toxicity, I frequently met mothers of autistic children who were absolutely convinced that their kids had been injured by vaccines. Privately, I was skeptical. I doubted that autism could be blamed on a single source, and

I certainly understood the government's need to reassure parents that vaccinations are safe; the eradication of deadly childhood diseases depends on it. I tended to agree with skeptics like Rep. Henry Waxman, a Democrat from California, who criticized his colleagues on the House Government Reform Committee for leaping to conclusions about autism and vaccinations. "Why should we scare people about immunization," Waxman pointed out at one hearing, "until we know the facts?"

It was only after reading the Simpsonwood transcripts, studying the leading scientific research and talking with many of the nation's preeminent authorities on mercury that I became convinced that the link between thimerosal and the epidemic of childhood neurological disorders is real. Five of my own children are members of the Thimerosal Generation—those born between 1989 and 2003—who received heavy doses of mercury from vaccines. "The elementary grades are overwhelmed with children who have symptoms of neurological or immune-system damage," Patti White, a school nurse, told the House Government Reform Committee in 1999. "Vaccines are supposed to be making us healthier; however, in twenty-five years of nursing I have never seen so many damaged, sick kids. Something very, very wrong is happening to our children."

More than 500,000 kids currently suffer from autism, and pediatricians diagnose more than 40,000 new cases every year. The disease was unknown until 1943, when it was identified and diagnosed among eleven children born in the months after thimerosal was first added to baby vaccines in 1931.

Some skeptics dispute that the rise in autism is caused by thimerosal-tainted vaccinations. They argue that the increase is a result of better diagnosis—a theory that seems questionable at best, given that most of the new cases of autism are clustered within a single generation of children. "If the epidemic is truly an artifact of poor diagnosis," scoffs Dr. Boyd Haley, one of the world's authorities on mercury toxicity, "then where are all the twenty-year-old autistics?" Other researchers point out that Americans are exposed to a greater cumulative "load" of mercury than ever before, from contaminated fish to dental fillings, and suggest that thimerosal in vaccines may be only part of a much larger problem. It's a concern that certainly deserves far more attention than it has received—but it overlooks the fact that the mercury concentrations in vaccines dwarf other sources of exposure to our children.

What is most striking is the lengths to which many of the leading detectives have gone to ignore—and cover up—the evidence against thimerosal. From the very beginning, the scientific case against the mercury additive has been overwhelming. The preservative, which is used to stem fungi and bacterial growth in vaccines, contains ethylmercury, a potent neurotoxin. Truckloads of studies have shown that mercury tends to accumulate in the brains of primates and other animals after they are injected with vaccines—and that the developing brains of infants are particularly susceptible. In 1977, a Russian study found that adults exposed to much lower concentrations of ethylmercury than those given to American children still suffered brain damage years later. Russia banned thimerosal from children's vaccines twenty years ago, and Denmark, Austria, Japan, Great Britain and all the Scandinavian countries have since followed suit.

"You couldn't even construct a study that shows thimerosal is safe," says Haley, who heads the chemistry department at the University of Kentucky. "It's just too darn toxic. If you inject thimerosal into an animal, its brain will sicken. If you apply it to living tissue, the cells die. If you put it in a petri dish, the culture dies. Knowing these things, it would be shocking if one could inject it into an infant without causing damage."

Internal documents reveal that Eli Lilly, which first developed thimerosal, knew from the start that its product could cause damage—and even death—in both animals and humans. In 1930, the company tested thimerosal by administering it to twenty-two patients with terminal meningitis, all of whom died within weeks of being injected—a fact Lilly didn't bother to report in its study declaring thimerosal safe. In 1935, researchers at another vaccine manufacturer, Pittman-Moore, warned Lilly that its claims about thimerosal's safety "did not check with ours." Half the dogs Pittman injected with thimerosal-based vaccines became sick, leading researchers there to declare the preservative "unsatisfactory as a serum intended for use on dogs."

In the decades that followed, the evidence against thimerosal continued to mount. During the Second World War, when the Department of Defense used the preservative in vaccines on soldiers, it required Lilly to label it "poison." In 1967, a study in *Applied Microbiology* found that thimerosal killed mice when added to injected vaccines. Four years later, Lilly's own studies discerned that thimerosal was "toxic to tissue cells" in concentrations as low as one part

Figure 2

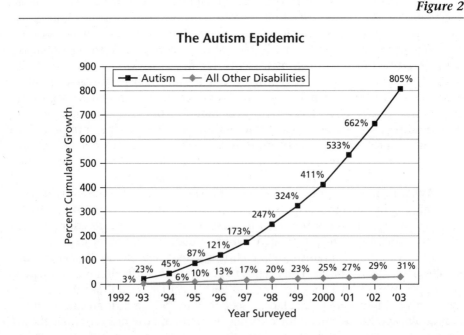

The Autism Epidemic

Skeptics insist that the nationwide rise in autism is the result of better diagnosis. But as Department of Education figures show, the disease increased much more rapidly between 1992 and 2003 than other disabilities among six- to twenty-two-year-olds.

per million—100 times weaker than the concentration in a typical vaccine. Even so, the company continued to promote thimerosal as "nontoxic" and also incorporated it into topical disinfectants. In 1977, ten babies at a Toronto hospital died when an antiseptic preserved with thimerosal was dabbed onto their umbilical cords.

In 1982, the FDA proposed a ban on over-the-counter products that contained thimerosal, and in 1991 the agency considered banning it from animal vaccines. But tragically, that same year, the CDC recommended that infants be injected with a series of mercury-laced vaccines. Newborns would be vaccinated for hepatitis B within twenty-four hours of birth, and two-month-old infants would be immunized for haemophilus influenzae B and diphtheria-tetanus-pertussis.

The drug industry knew the additional vaccines posed a danger. The same year that the CDC approved the new vaccines, Dr. Maurice Hilleman, one of the fathers of Merck's vaccine programs, warned the company that six-month-olds who were administered the shots would suffer dangerous exposure to mercury. He recommended that thimerosal be discontinued, "especially when used on infants and children," noting that the industry knew of nontoxic alternatives. "The best way to go," he added, "is to switch to dispensing the actual vaccines without adding preservatives."

For Merck and other drug companies, however, the obstacle was money. Thimerosal enables the pharmaceutical industry to package vaccines in vials that contain multiple doses, which require additional protection because they are more easily contaminated by multiple needle entries. The larger vials cost half as much to produce as smaller, single-dose vials, making it cheaper for international agencies to distribute them to impoverished regions at risk of epidemics. Faced with this "cost consideration," Merck ignored Hilleman's warnings, and government officials continued to push more and more thimerosal-based vaccines for children. Before 1989, American preschoolers received only three vaccinations—for polio, diphtheria-tetanus-pertussis and measles-mumps-rubella. A decade later, thanks to federal recommendations, children were receiving a total of twenty-two immunizations by the time they reached first grade.

•••

As the number of vaccines increased, the rate of autism among children exploded. During the 1990s, 40 million children were injected with thimerosal-based vaccines, receiving unprecedented levels of mercury during a period critical for brain development. Despite the well-documented dangers of thimerosal, it appears that no one bothered to add up the cumulative dose of mercury that children would receive from the mandated vaccines. "What took the FDA so long to do the calculations?" Peter Patriarca, director of viral products for the agency, asked in an e-mail to the CDC in 1999. "Why didn't CDC and the advisory bodies do these calculations when they rapidly expanded the childhood immunization schedule?"

But by that time, the damage was done. Infants who received all their vaccines, plus boosters, by the age of six months were being injected with levels of ethylmercury 187 times greater than the EPA's limit for daily exposure to methylmercury, a related neurotoxin. Although the vaccine industry insists that ethylmercury poses little danger because it breaks down rapidly and is removed by the body, several studies—including one published in April by the National Institutes of Health—suggest that ethylmercury is actually *more* toxic to developing brains and stays in the brain *longer* than methylmercury.

Officials responsible for childhood immunizations insist that the additional vaccines were necessary to protect infants from disease and that thimerosal is still essential in developing nations, which, they often claim, cannot afford the single-dose vials that don't require a preservative. Dr. Paul Offit, one of CDC's top vaccine advisers, told me, "I think if we really have an influenza pandemic—and certainly we will in the next twenty years, because we always do—there's no way on God's earth that we immunize 280 million people with single-dose vials. There has to be multidose vials."

But while public-health officials may have been well-intentioned, many of those on the CDC advisory committee who backed the additional vaccines had close ties to the industry. Dr. Sam Katz, the committee's chair, was a paid consultant for most of the major vaccine makers and shares a patent on a measles vaccine with Merck, which also manufactures the hepatitis B vaccine. Dr. Neal Halsey, another committee member, worked as a researcher for the vaccine companies and received honoraria from Abbott Labs for his research on the hepatitis B vaccine.

Indeed, in the tight circle of scientists who work on vaccines, such conflicts of interest are common. Rep. Burton says that the CDC "routinely allows scientists with blatant conflicts of interest to serve on intellectual advisory committees that make recommendations on new vaccines," even though they have "interests in the products and companies for which they are supposed to be providing unbiased oversight." The House Government Reform Committee discovered that four of the eight CDC advisers who approved guidelines for a rotavirus vaccine laced with thimerosal "had financial ties to the pharmaceutical companies that were developing different versions of the vaccine."

Offit, who shares a patent on the vaccine, acknowledged to me that he "would make money" if his vote to approve it eventually leads to a marketable product. But he dismissed my suggestion that a scientist's direct financial stake in CDC approval might bias his judgment. "It provides no conflict for me," he insists. "I have simply been informed by the process, not corrupted by it. When I sat around that table, my sole intent was trying to make recommendations that best benefited the children in this country. It's offensive to say that physicians and public-health people are in the pocket of industry and thus are making decisions that they know are unsafe for children. It's just not the way it works."

Other vaccine scientists and regulators gave me similar assurances. Like Offit, they view themselves as enlightened guardians of children's health, proud of their "partnerships" with pharmaceutical companies, immune to the seductions of personal profit, besieged by irrational activists whose anti-vaccine campaigns are endangering children's health. They are often resentful of questioning. "Science," says Offit, "is best left to scientists."

Still, some government officials were alarmed by the apparent conflicts of interest. In his e-mail to CDC administrators in 1999, Paul Patriarca of the FDA blasted federal regulators for failing to adequately scrutinize the danger posed by the added baby vaccines. "I'm not sure there will be an easy way out of the potential perception that the FDA, CDC and immunization-policy bodies may have been asleep at the switch re: thimerosal until now," Patriarca wrote. The close ties between regulatory officials and the pharmaceutical industry, he added, "will also raise questions about various advisory bodies regarding aggressive recommendations for use" of thimerosal in child vaccines.

꜀ᐧ⟨◉⟩ᐧ꜀

If federal regulators and government scientists failed to grasp the potential risks of thimerosal over the years, no one could claim ignorance after the secret meeting at Simpsonwood. But rather than conduct more studies to test the link to autism and other forms of brain damage, the CDC placed politics over science. The agency turned its database on childhood vaccines—which had been developed largely at taxpayer expense—over to a private agency, America's Health Insurance Plans, ensuring that it could not be used for additional research. It also instructed the Institute of Medicine, an advisory organization that is part of the National Academy of Sciences, to produce a study debunking the link between thimerosal and brain disorders. The CDC "wants us to declare, well, that these things are pretty safe," Dr. Marie McCormick, who chaired the IOM's Immunization Safety Review Committee, told her fellow researchers when they first met in January 2001. "We are not ever going to come down that [autism] is a true side effect" of thimerosal exposure. According to transcripts of the meeting, the committee's chief staffer, Kathleen Stratton, predicted that the IOM would conclude that the evidence was "inadequate to accept or reject a causal relation" between thimerosal and autism. That, she added, was the result "Walt wants"—a reference to Dr. Walter Orenstein, director of the National Immunization Program for the CDC.

For those who had devoted their lives to promoting vaccination, the revelations about thimerosal threatened to undermine everything they had worked for. "We've got a dragon by the tail here," said Dr. Michael Kaback, another committee member. "The more negative that [our] presentation is, the less likely people are to use vaccination, immunization—and we know what the results of that will be. We are kind of caught in a trap. How we work our way out of the trap, I think is the charge."

Even in public, federal officials made it clear that their primary goal in studying thimerosal was to dispel doubts about vaccines. "Four current studies are taking place to rule out the proposed link between autism and thimerosal," Dr. Gordon Douglas, then-director of strategic planning for vaccine research at the National Institutes of Health, assured a Princeton University gathering in May 2001. "In order to undo the harmful effects of research claiming to link the [measles] vaccine to an elevated risk of autism, we need to conduct and publicize additional studies to assure parents of safety." Douglas formerly served as president of vaccinations for Merck, where he ignored warnings about thimerosal's risks.

In May of last year, the Institute of Medicine issued its final report. Its conclusion: There is no proven link between autism and thimerosal in vaccines. Rather than reviewing the large body of literature describing the toxicity of thimerosal, the report relied on four disastrously flawed epidemiological studies examining European countries, where children received much smaller doses of thimerosal than American kids. It also cited a new version of the Verstraeten study, published in the journal *Pediatrics,* that had been reworked to reduce the link between thimerosal and autism. The new study included children too young to have been diagnosed with autism and overlooked others who showed signs of the disease. The IOM declared the case closed and—in a startling position for a scientific body—recommended that no further research be conducted.

The report may have satisfied the CDC, but it convinced no one. Rep. David Weldon, a Republican physician from Florida who serves on the House Government Reform Committee, attacked the Institute of Medicine, saying it relied on a handful of studies that were "fatally flawed" by "poor design" and failed to represent "all the available scientific and medical research." CDC officials are not interested in an honest search for the truth, Weldon told me, because "an association between vaccines and autism would force them to admit that their policies irreparably damaged thousands of children. Who would want to make that conclusion about themselves?"

⎯⚜⎯

Under pressure from Congress, parents and a few of its own panel members, the Institute of Medicine reluctantly convened a second panel to review the findings of the first. In February, the new panel, composed of different scientists, criticized the earlier panel for its lack of transparency and urged the CDC to make its vaccine database available to the public.

So far, though, only two scientists have managed to gain access. Dr. Mark Geier, president of the Genetics Center of America, and his son, David, spent a year battling to obtain the medical records from the CDC. Since August 2002, when members of Congress pressured the agency to turn over the data, the Geiers have completed six studies that demonstrate a powerful correlation between thimerosal and neurological damage in children. One study, which compares the cumulative dose of mercury received by children born between 1981 and 1985 with those born between 1990 and 1996, found a "very significant relationship" between autism and vaccines. Another study of educational performance found that kids who received higher doses of thimerosal in vaccines were nearly three times as likely to be diagnosed with autism and more than three times as likely to suffer from speech disorders and mental retardation. Another soon-to-be published study shows that autism rates are in decline following the recent elimination of thimerosal from most vaccines.

As the federal government worked to prevent scientists from studying vaccines, others have stepped in to study the link to autism. In April, reporter Dan Olmsted of UPI undertook one of the more interesting studies himself. Searching for children who had not been exposed to mercury in vaccines—the kind of population that scientists typically use as a "control" in experiments—Olmsted scoured the Amish of Lancaster County, Pennsylvania, who refuse to immunize their infants. Given the national rate of autism, Olmsted calculated that there should be 130 autistics among the Amish. He found only four. One had been exposed to high levels of mercury from a power plant. The other three—including one child adopted from outside the Amish community—had received their vaccines.

At the state level, many officials have also conducted in-depth reviews of thimerosal. While the Institute of Medicine was busy whitewashing the risks, the Iowa legislature was carefully combing through all of the available scientific and biological data. "After three years of review, I became convinced there was sufficient credible research to show a link between mercury and the increased incidences in autism," says state Sen. Ken Veenstra, a Republican who oversaw the investigation. "The fact that Iowa's 700 percent increase in autism began in the 1990s, right after more and more vaccines were added to the children's vaccine schedules, is solid evidence alone." Last year, Iowa became the first state to ban mercury in vaccines, followed by California. Similar bans are now under consideration in thirty-two other states.

But instead of following suit, the FDA continues to allow manufacturers to include thimerosal in scores of over-the-counter medications as well as steroids and injected collagen. Even more alarming, the government continues to ship vaccines preserved with thimerosal to developing countries—some of which are now experiencing a sudden explosion in autism rates. In China, where the disease was virtually unknown prior to the introduction of thimerosal by U.S. drug manufacturers in 1999, news reports indicate that there are now more than 1.8 million autistics. Although reliable numbers are hard to come by, autistic disorders also appear to be soaring in India, Argentina, Nicaragua and other developing countries that are now using thimerosal-laced vaccines. The World Health Organization continues to insist thimerosal is safe, but it promises to keep the possibility that it is linked to neurological disorders "under review."

I devoted time to study this issue because I believe that this is a moral crisis that must be addressed. If, as the evidence suggests, our public-health authorities knowingly allowed the pharmaceutical industry to poison an entire generation of American children, their actions arguably constitute one of the biggest scandals in the annals of American medicine. "The CDC is guilty of incompetence and gross negligence," says Mark Blaxill, vice president of Safe Minds, a nonprofit organization concerned about the role of mercury in medicines. "The damage caused by vaccine exposure is massive. It's bigger than asbestos, bigger than tobacco, bigger than anything you've ever seen."

It's hard to calculate the damage to our country—and to the international efforts to eradicate epidemic diseases—if Third World nations come to believe that America's most heralded foreign-aid initiative is poisoning their children. It's not difficult to predict how this scenario will be interpreted by America's enemies abroad. The scientists and researchers—many of them sincere, even idealistic—who are participating in efforts to hide the science on thimerosal claim that they are trying to advance the lofty goal of protecting children in developing nations from disease pandemics. They are badly misguided. Their failure to come clean on thimerosal will come back horribly to haunt our country and the world's poorest populations.

**Matthew Normand
and Jesse Dallery**

➡ **NO**

Mercury Rising: Exposing the Vaccine-Autism Myth

On June 11, 2007, nearly 5,000 parents of autistic children filed a lawsuit against the federal government, claiming that childhood vaccines (specifically the mercury-containing thimerosal in the vaccines) caused their children's autism. The previous year the *New York Times* ran a column that was skeptical of the alleged link between autism and vaccines. It generated the following comment on an Internet message board, typical of the anecdotal analyses that perpetuate the claim:

> You say, "There is no proven link" between mercury and autism. There also is "no proven link" between going outside in the rain and cold without a hat or coat and getting the sniffles. Look at the data: the epidemic of autism mirrors the administration of vaccines with mercury. Now that they are off the shelves (more or less), the cases are going down.

Here we see how the writer dismisses scientific evidence that fails to support a link between cold and illness and vaccines and autism in favor of her personal experiences. And the vaccine-autism controversy is not constrained to a small fringe group of parents or advocates. Increasingly, people of position and power are leaping into the fray, spurred on by vocal groups demanding action. For example, an article by Robert F. Kennedy, Jr. appeared in a June 2005 issue of *Rolling Stone* magazine[1] that alleged thimerosal-containing vaccines were at the heart of the autism epidemic and, moreover, that the government was aware of this and actively engaged in a cover-up.

This article makes five points concerning the relation between thimerosal-containing vaccines and autism: (1) the dangers of mercury are well established, but this does not lead inexorably to a relationship between vaccines containing thimerosal and autism; (2) a number of well controlled studies have failed to uncover any correlation between the delivery of the vaccines and the onset of autism; (3) even if some correlation existed there are a number of alternative explanations for the correlation that do not assume any causal relationship between the vaccine and autism; (4) much attention has been given to a possible government cover up, which is certainly of concern if true but is otherwise independent of the problems with claims of a link between thimerosal and autism; and (5) the type of public hysteria manifested in the

From *Skeptic,* vol. 13, no. 3, 2007, pp. 32–36. Copyright © 2007 by Skeptic Magazine. Reprinted by permission of Millennium Press.

current controversy is not new and we would be well served to learn from similar controversies of recent times.

Mercury, Thimerosal, and the Potential for Harm

Science has told us unequivocally that mercury is bad for our bodies. In sufficient doses, mercury kills cells that it contacts, causes neurological damage in humans and other animals, and generally wreaks havoc on living things. Yet since the 1930s, thimerosal has been used as a preservative in vaccines.[2] One of the breakdown products of thimerosal is ethylmercury, which is an organic compound of mercury. Public concern about thimerosal is certainly understandable, but does this mean that concern about a link between vaccines and autism is justified as well? In a word, no. Mercury might do a number of nasty things to the human body, and concern about it is therefore justified, but that does not mean it causes autism.

Ethylmercury is not the same thing as its cousin, methylmercury. Cumulative and high doses of methylmercury can produce renal and neurologic damage. It can build up in the brain and stay in the body for a long time. Ethylmercury is more, well, mercurial. It is expelled rapidly from the body and it does not accumulate. Nevertheless, guidelines for the ingestion of ethylmercury were based on those for methylmercury. Around the same time these guidelines were formalized, children were receiving more vaccines that contained thimerosal. For example, in the early 1990s the Haemophilus influenzae b and hepatitis B became staple features of the vaccine schedule for infants, which already included another thimerosal-containing vaccine (diphtheria tetanus and variants). Based on the very conservative guidelines established by the Environmental Protection Agency (EPA), it was concluded that by age two some children might be receiving excessive levels of ethylmercury when considered in the context of known risks of methylmercury exposure.[3]

Against this backdrop enter skyrocketing rates of autism diagnoses. In California, the Department of Developmental Services reported a 273% increase from 1987 to 1998 in the number of individuals served under the category of autism.[4] Surely this increase in rates was caused by an environmental source, right? In 2001, the Institute of Medicine (IOM) Immunization Safety Review Committee held a public meeting to address the link between one environmental source—thimerosal—and autism. At the meeting, Mark Blaxill, a board member of a nonprofit organization dedicated to investigating the risks of mercury exposure, presented a graph showing the *estimated* cumulative dose of thimerosal to the *estimated* prevalence of autism in California.[5] The increasing trend lines during the early 1990s were right on top of each other, about as close as you can get to perfect correlation in ecological data. Such orderly correlations are all that it takes to convince the uncritical eye.

Even before the IOM meeting, thimerosal was removed as a preservative in vaccines in the U.S., based on a request from the Food and Drug Administration (FDA) (it remains in some influenza vaccines and in some vaccines outside of the U.S.). The request was made as a precautionary measure, and not because there was evidence to accept or reject a causal relationship between thimerosal and autism. (Thimerosal is still used during manufacture of some vaccines to ensure sterility, but the trace amounts remaining are 50 times lower than when thimerosal is used as a preservative.) Since the FDA decision, a number of research reports published in some of the most esteemed peer-reviewed journals in the world have failed to find any relation between thimerosal and autism. Despite these negative findings and the removal of thimerosal from vaccines, parents, politicians and health professionals remain alarmed that children are at risk.

Much is at stake in this debate. Based on the assumption that metals such as mercury are causing autism, some parents are avoiding vaccinations altogether. Others have sought treatments like chelation therapy, which uses special chemicals to rid the body of heavy metals following acute poisoning. However, chelation is not a risk-free procedure and should not be undertaken lightly. In August of 2005, a Pittsburgh, PA area newspaper reported that a 5-year old boy with autism died following chelation therapy. Finally, there are ongoing class action lawsuits against the manufacturers of vaccines. These lawsuits could potentially endanger the production and distribution of effective vaccines according to well-established protocols, putting scores of young children at risk.

Evidence of Harm

Let's begin with the hypothesis that thimerosal is one of the causes of autism and that it is the main culprit in the increased incidence of autism during the 1990s. This is a plausible hypothesis, but as Karl Popper taught us, a good scientific hypothesis must be falsifiable. That is, it must be possible to conceive of evidence that would prove it wrong. What evidence might suggest that the thimerosal hypothesis is false? For obvious ethical reasons, we can't perform the kind of gold-standard experiment—a randomized double-blind study—which would most convincingly indicate the lack of a causal relation. We must rely on natural experiments. One such experiment was occasioned by the removal of thimerosal in Denmark in 1992. If the thimerosal hypothesis were false, we would not expect to see changes in the rates of autism following the removal of thimerosal. In fact, the results were more robust: despite the removal of thimerosal, the rates of autism continued to climb. And not only in Denmark but in Sweden, too, where thimerosal was removed at about the same time.[6]

Another way the thimerosal hypothesis could be falsified is if it could be shown that there is no link between the amount of thimerosal exposure and the likelihood of autism. That is, we would ask if there is a dose-response relation between thimerosal exposure and developmental problems. Several studies have confirmed that there is no convincing evidence of a dose-response relation.[7] In fact, one study suggested a beneficial effect of thimerosal! For example, exposure at three months was inversely related to problems of hyperactivity, conduct, and motor development months or years later.[8] Now, these results do not imply causation, nor do they pertain to autism *per se*, but they do question the general validity of the thimerosal hypothesis.

So what of the data favoring the thimerosal hypothesis? Indeed, we must consider all sources of evidence in evaluating the truth of a claim—we must be comprehensive. Recently, some researchers have suggested that the incidence rate of autism has been on the decline since thimerosal was officially removed from vaccines in the US. If true, this would be evidence of a possible causal relationship between thimerosal and autism, and such data has been reported by one team of researchers, Mark and David Geier. Unfortunately, the study that proposed such a relationship used the Vaccine Adverse Event Reporting System (VAERS) database to make the claim.[9] The VAERS is a passive reporting system that is subject to reporting biases and errors. A health-care professional, parent, or even someone trying to prove a point[10] can enter data into the VAERS. There is no way to verify diagnoses, identify mistakes in filing, or substantiate causal hypotheses.

The irreparably flawed studies by the Geiers prompted a strong rebuke from the Centers for Disease Control (CDC) and by the American Academy of Pediatrics.[11] Simply put, the VAERS data may be useful to raise some potential questions about a phenomenon, but it certainly cannot be used to prove a hypothesis. Studies that use methods consistent with well-established scientific standards have failed to find any association between thimerosal and autism. In 2004, the Institute of Medicine concluded, "Given the lack of direct evidence for a biological mechanism and the fact that all well-designed epidemiological studies provide evidence of no association between thimerosal and autism, the committee recommends that cost-benefit assessments regarding the use of thimerosal-containing versus thimerosal-free vaccines and other biological or pharmaceutical products, whether in the United States or other countries, should not include autism as a potential risk."[12]

But what if it were determined that a strong correlation existed between the administration of thimerosal-containing vaccines and the onset of autism? Much would still be left unanswered. Consider that the average age for many vaccinations is between 12 and 18 months. Now consider that many of the "symptoms" of autism—such as social withdrawal and delayed language—aren't readily detectable until this same age or just a bit later. It could very well be that any relationship between vaccination and diagnosis is purely coincidental. If these vaccinations were not commonly given until age four, perhaps no correlation would be observed. Not to mention that the vast majority of children receive these vaccinations without incident.[13]

The bottom line is that *correlation is not causation*.

Autism Epidemic or Statistical Artifact?

Another problem for the purported vaccine-autism link is that there is good reason to be suspicious of claims of an autism epidemic. A number of factors can account for the dramatic increase in numbers, including the expansion of diagnostic criteria in 1994, and changes in criteria for inclusion in child-count data for children with autism. Remember that 273% increase over a decade in autism spectrum disorders in California? Consider, as did the authors of a recent paper published in *Current Directions in Psychological Science*,[14] that this increase could be due to an expanded diagnostic definition of autism. The authors found that a similar expansion in the definition of "tall"—from 74.5 inches to 72 inches—generated a 273% increase if these two criteria were applied a decade apart in one county in Texas.

More important, autism is not even a "thing" that can be clearly correlated with any other thing. Unlike cancer or a broken bone, there are no discrete physical, biological, or genetic markers on which to base a diagnosis. Instead, autism is a diagnostic label based on the presence of a number of behavioral excesses and deficits. The diagnosis is subjective and subject to great variability. When you consider that many resources are made available only to those children with some formal diagnosis, it is easy to see why some diagnoses might be made with scant supporting evidence. The physician or psychologist notices some obvious learning delays and behavior problems in a patient and recognizes the need for intensive services, but the only way the family can obtain those services is if the child fits a certain diagnostic category.

Correlations are tenuous things under the best conditions. Degrade one of the variables, and you are in serious trouble. Such is the case with the autism-vaccine correlation.

A Vast Government Conspiracy?

So what do vaccine opponents make of the evidence against the vaccine-autism hypothesis? Mostly, they assert a vast conspiracy propagated by government and industry. It is proposed that government agencies such as the Centers for Disease Control and Prevention, in conjunction with scientists with varying ties to the pharmaceutical industry, have gone to great lengths to suppress evidence supporting a link between vaccines and autism. Indeed, this was the main point of Robert Kennedy Jr.'s *Rolling Stone* article. He and others claim that a conspiracy does exist and was formally discussed at a top-secret meeting in Simpsonwood, GA in 2000.

One hotly discussed result of this meeting is the purported doctoring of data by Thomas Verstraeten who, according to the vaccine opponents, presented data supporting the autism-vaccine link but later altered the data to support the opposite conclusion because he was, by then, employed by a large pharmaceutical company. Verstraeten has denied such manipulation and the data he reports support the conclusions reached by a number of other independent researchers.[15] The problem is that the only evidence of doctored data sets, dubious activity at the Simpsonwood meeting, and assorted cover-ups seems to come from a small number of zealous vaccine opponents who can offer no corroborating evidence to support the hearsay.

Now let us return to the research team purporting to have data supporting the autism-vaccine hypothesis. In addition to the flawed methods on which their conclusions are based, there are conflicts of interest that should cause one to question their motives. As it turns out, David Geier is the president of MedCon, Inc., a legal firm that seeks compensation for people claiming to have been harmed by vaccines. He also has filed, with his father Mark Geier, two patents related to a treatment for autism involving a combination of drugs and chelation. Chelation therapy is, of course, predicated on the assumption of excessive amounts of heavy metals in the blood stream of children with autism. The Geiers are clearly in a position to benefit if claims concerning a vaccine-autism link are accepted by the public.

History Repeating

A revealing aspect of this controversy is how closely it resembles past controversies, pitting science against vaccine-induced autism claims, spurred on by desperate parents, media support, and various servants of the public interest. Not so long ago, science was up against a similar set of public crusaders pushing a different cause: carcinogenic power lines. In 1979, a small, poorly controlled and poorly conducted sampling of leukemia patients in Denver, CO supposedly revealed a correlation between the patients and the proximity of their homes to high-power lines.[16] The published report of these suspect findings was largely ignored by the scientific community because of the many fatal flaws evident in the methodology. Enter Paul Brodeur, a journalist with a track record of sensationalism (in the 1960s he wrote *The Zapping of America,* a book "exposing the dangers" of microwave ovens), now warned the world of the dangers posed by power lines in his book *Currents of Death.*

No amount of scientific evidence to the contrary could persuade the journalists, advocacy groups, and legal teams demanding accountability. Of course, the million-dollar question was, "Accountability for what?" Ultimately, after numerous well-controlled studies failed to find any correlation between power-lines and cancer, the story grew cold and the public outrage slowly faded away. But not before tens of millions of dollars in research funding, decreased property values, and lawsuits were lost because the matter was pursued long after science had delivered a verdict. Are we doomed to repeat this history with the vaccine controversy?

Clarifying Claims

Claims of a causal link between the administration of thimerosal-containing vaccines and the onset of autism are unfounded. The controversy has been driven more by public fervor than it has by science. This is not to suggest that the advocates and parents fueling the fire are malicious or intentionally misleading the public. The reality is that too many families face the unimaginable hardship of learning that their child has been diagnosed with autism and must encounter the subsequent trials and tribulations of providing the best possible care and education for their child. These parents are in desperate need of both assistance and answers. Compounding the difficulty is that many must navigate the waters of emerging science without having received the necessary training to do so. Clarifying misguided claims of causative factors can help redirect necessary resources to more promising treatments, and perhaps reveal a better understanding of the real factors that cause autism.

References

1. Kennedy, R. F., Jr. 2005. "Deadly Immunity." *Rolling Stone, 977/978,* June–July, 57–61.

2. U.S. Food and Drug Administration. n.d. *Thimerosal in Vaccines.* Accessed on March 23, 2007 from . . .

3. U.S. Food and Drug Administration. n.d.

4. Gernsbacher, M. A., Dawson, M., Goldsmith, H. H. 2005. "Three Reasons Not to Believe in an Autism Epidemic." *Current Directions in Psychological Science, 14,* 55–58.

5. Blaxill, M. 2001. "The Rising Incidence of Autism: Associations with Thimerosal." Accessed on March 23, 2007 from . . .

6. Stehr-Green P., Tull P., Stellfeld M., Mortenson P. B., Simpson D. 2003. Autism and Thimerosal-Containing Vaccines: Lack of Consistent Evidence for an Association. *American Journal of Preventive Medicine, 25,* 101–106.

7. Hvild A., Stellfeld M., Wohlfahrt J., Melbye M., 2003. "Association Between Thimerosal-Containing Vaccines and Autism." *Journal of the American Medical Association, 290,* 1763–1766.

8. Heron J., Golding J.; ALSPAC Study Team. "Thimerosal Exposure in Infants and Developmental Disorders: A Prospective Cohort Study in the United Kingdom Does Not Support a Causal Association." *Pediatrics, 114,* 577–583.

9. Geier, M. R., & Geier, D. A., 2003. "Thimerosal in Childhood Vaccines, Neurodevelopment Disorders and Heart Disease in the United States." *Journal of American Physicians and Surgeons, 8,* 6–11.

10. Such a system cannot be used to prove a hypothesis. Consider that Dr. James Laidler allegedly reported that the influenza virus turned him into the Incredible Hulk, and the VAERS system accepted his report! Dr. Laidler reports that a representative of the CDC did contact him after noticing the report and, ultimately, it was deleted from the VAERS system, but only because Dr. Laidler granted permission. According to Laidler, had his permission not been granted, the report would have remained in the VAERS system. Others have reported submitting spurious reports to the VAERS system—for example that a vaccine turned someone into Wonder Woman—with similar success.

11. American Academy of Pediatrics. n.d. "Study Fails to Show a Connection Between Thimerosal and Autism." Accessed on March 23, 2007 from . . .

12. Institute of Medicine. Accessed on March 28, 2007 from . . .

13. Of course, this does not exclude the possibility that thimerosal might differentially affect an especially sensitive subset of children. Recently, researchers have reported that the neurotoxic effects of thimerosal exposure are related to autoimmune disease-sensitivity in mice. It is unclear whether these results will hold true for humans and whether such neurotoxicity has any relationship to autism, but it is an important area for further research. Unfortunately, because the "differential sensitivity" hypothesis is not yet well researched, there is no way to identify and

protect those that might be at risk if it proves true. However, we know without question the dangers of disease and risks of avoiding vaccination. No matter the suspicions, the most prudent course of action is to go the vaccine route until there is real evidence to do otherwise. Also, we should note that existing evidence already casts doubt on the differential sensitivity hypothesis. If the rates of sensitivity to thimerosal remained constant before and after thimerosal was removed from vaccines, we would still expect a decrease in rates of autism. As reviewed above, this was not the case.

14. Gernsbacher, M. A., Dawson, M., Goldsmith, H. H. 2005. "Three Reasons Not to Believe in an Autism Epidemic." *Current Directions in Psychological Science, 14,* 55–58.

15. Stehr-Green et al., 2003.

16. Park, R. 2000. *Voodoo Science: The Road from Foolishness to Fraud.* Oxford: University Press.

POSTSCRIPT

Is There a Link Between Vaccination and Autism?

Nine-year-old Hannah Poling had an uneventful birth and appeared to be developing normally. And then, right after receiving several routine vaccines, she became ill. Hannah recovered from her acute illness but lost her speech and eye contact and, in a matter of months, began displaying the repetitive behaviors and social withdrawal that indicate autism. Her parents reported that after her vaccinations, "she just deteriorated and never came back."

Parents of children with autism have been blaming vaccines—and, especially, the mercury-based vaccine preservative thimerosal—as a cause of autism for over a decade, but researchers have repeatedly failed to identify a connection.

What is unusual about Hannah's case is that for the first time federal authorities have agreed there is a connection between her autistic symptoms and the vaccines she received, though the relationship is by no means clear. A panel of medical evaluators at the Department of Health and Human Services determined that Hannah had been injured by vaccines and recommended that her family be compensated for the injuries. The panel said that Hannah had an underlying cellular disorder that was aggravated by the vaccines, causing brain damage with features of autism spectrum disorder.

The Poling case is also causing concern among public health officials, who are anxious to reassure parents that immunizations are safe and valuable. In a recent public statement, Dr. Julie Gerberding, director of the Centers for Disease Control and Prevention (CDC), insisted that "the government has made absolutely no statement about indicating that vaccines are the cause of autism, as this would be a complete mischaracterization of any of the science that we have at our disposal today." Dr. Gerberding and other health authorities point out that the benefits of vaccines far exceed their risks. They also note that thimerosal was eliminated from routinely administered childhood vaccines manufactured after 2001, and yet autism rates have not dropped. The current CDC estimate is that 1 of 150 American children has an autism spectrum disorder.

But there are circumstances that take Hannah's case out of the ordinary. For one thing, she received an unusually large number of vaccines in 2000 (when thimerosal was still in use). Because of a series of ear infections, Hannah had lagged behind in the vaccine schedule, so in one day she was given five immunizations to prevent a total of nine diseases: measles, mumps, rubella, polio, varicella, diphtheria, pertussis, tetanus, and Haemophilus influenzae. A second issue in Hannah's situation is that she suffers from a mitochondrial disorder, a dysfunction in basic cell metabolism. In Hannah's case, the vaccine court determined that the underlying dysfunction of her mitochondria put her at an increased risk of injury from vaccines.

Experts on autism spectrum disorders believe that most cases are caused by a combination of genetic vulnerabilities and environmental factors. There may be hundreds of routes to autism, involving multiple combinations of genes and external variables. While it is possible thimerosal or some other aspect of vaccines is one of these factors, it has not been definitively proven, and further research is needed. It's challenging to draw any clear conclusions from the case of Hannah Poling, other than the need for more research. One plausible conclusion is that pediatricians should avoid giving small children a large number of vaccines at once, even if they are thimerosal-free. For further reading, see "Vaccines and Autism Revisited—The Hannah Poling Case" (*New England Journal of Medicine*, May 19, 2008) and "Vaccines and the Changing Epidemiology of Autism (*Child Care and Development*, vol. 32, 2006). For two opposing viewpoints published in the November/December 2007 issue of the journal *Skeptical Inquirer,* see "Vaccine Safety: Vaccines Are One of Public Health's Great Accomplishments" and "The Anti-Vaccination Movement."

ISSUE 17

Do Cell Phones Cause Cancer?

YES: Ronald B. Herberman, from "Tumors and Cell Phone Use: What the Science Says," http://cellphones.procon.org/sourcefiles/ Herberman_Testimony.pdf (September 25, 2008)

NO: Bernard Leikind, from "Do Cell Phones Cause Cancer?" *Skeptic* (2010).

ISSUE SUMMARY

YES: Physician and Director of Pittsburgh Cancer Institute Ronald B. Herberman maintains that radio frequency radiation associated with cell phones is a potential health risk factor for users, especially children.

NO: Physicist Bernard Leikind argues that there is no plausible mechanism by which cell phone radiation can cause cancer.

A cell phone is a device used to make mobile telephone calls across a wide geographic area. It can make and receive telephone calls to and from the public telephone network, which includes other mobile and landline phones throughout the world. Cell phones work by connecting to a mobile network managed by a cellular phone company. In addition to operating as a telephone, mobile phones usually offer additional services including text messaging, e-mail and Internet access along with a variety of business and gaming applications, and photography. They are extremely popular both in the United States and throughout the world. Currently, there are nearly 4.5 billion cell phones used globally.

Although cell phones have many communication advantages and are extensively used, they are also associated with health and safety risks. Cell phone use while driving is widespread, but controversial. Distractions like texting or talking on a cell phone while operating a car or other motor vehicle have been shown to increase the risk of accidents. Because of this, many areas prohibit the use of cell phones while driving and several states ban handheld cell phone use only, while allowing hands-free calling. Texting while driving is also illegal in some states.

In addition to the links between cell phone use and motor vehicle accidents, there may be a relationship between mobile phones and long-term health risks including certain cancers. Some countries, including France, have warned against the use of cell phones, especially by minors, due to health risk uncertainties. Groups of scientists claim that because mobile phone use is employing relatively new technology, long-term conclusive evidence has been impossible to determine and that the use should be restricted, or monitored closely, to be on the safe side.

Cell phones use radiation in the microwave range, which some scientists believe may be harmful to human health. In epidemiological and animal and human research, the majority show no definite causal relationship between cell phone exposure and harmful biological effects in humans. Overall, most evidence shows no harm to humans is caused by cell phones, although a significant number of individual studies do suggest such a relationship, or are inconclusive. Based upon the majority view of scientific and medical communities, the World Health Organization (WHO) has asserted that cancer is unlikely to be caused by cellular phones or their base stations and that studies have found no convincing evidence for other health problems. Some national radiation scientists have recommended measures to minimize exposure only as a precautionary approach.

While most research investigations have found no relationship between cell phones and tumor growth, at least some recent studies have found an association between cell phone use and certain kinds of brain and salivary gland cancers. A major meta-analysis of 11 studies from peer-reviewed journals concluded that cell phone usage for at least 10 years may double the risk of being diagnosed with a brain tumor on the same side of the head that is most often used for cell phone conversations.

Clearly, there is no definitive answer on the potential safety issues associated with cell phone use. In the YES selection, Ronald B. Herberman, a physician and director of Pittsburgh Cancer Institute, maintains that radio frequency radiation associated with cell phones is a potential health risk factor for users, especially children. In the NO selection, physicist Bernard Leikind argues that there is no plausible mechanism by which cell phone radiation can cause cancer.

YES

Ronald B. Herberman

Tumors and Cell Phone Use: What the Science Says

T hank you for inviting me to speak with you today about the important matter of cell phones and our health. I have served as the Founding Director of the University of Pittsburgh Cancer Institute (UPCI) since 1985, and as the Founding Director of University of Pittsburgh Medical Center (UPMC) Cancer Centers since 2001. The organizations that I lead employ more than 660 oncologists, other cancer experts and research faculty and more than 2,000 other staff members. In addition to the cutting edge cancer research performed at UPCI, our cancer centers, located throughout western Pennsylvania and adjacent states, annually treat more than 27,000 new cancer patients each year.

The UPCI is a National Cancer Institute (NCI)-designated comprehensive cancer center, and is one of the top ranked cancer research facilities in the nation. In fact, in 2007, UPCI was ranked 10th nationally in its level of NCI funding for cancer research. During the past two decades, UPCI has recruited some of the world's top scientists.

At UPCI, I am the Hillman Professor of Oncology, Professor of Medicine and Associate Vice Chancellor for Cancer Research at the University of Pittsburgh. I also was the founding Chairman of the Board of Directors, and I currently am the President, of the Pennsylvania Cancer Control Consortium, a state-wide cancer control organization. I am a longstanding member and Chairman of the Research and Clinical Trials Team, of C-Change, a national cancer organization, that has President George H.W. Bush, First Lady Barbara Bush, and Sen. Dianne Feinstein as the honorary co-chairs. For the past few years, C-Change has focused mainly on innovative strategies to reduce smoking and other personal risk factors for cancer, and to facilitate medical interventions to protect people at increased risk for cancer.

I also served from 1999–2001 as the President of the Association of American Cancer Institutes, an organization that includes almost all of the major academic cancer centers in the US. All of the organizations that I am associated with are focused on eliminating cancer as a public health problem, a commitment that I take very seriously.

As a cancer researcher, I have published more than 700 peer-reviewed articles in major biomedical journals, and for two decades my scientific publications placed me as among the 100 most cited biomedical scientists. In addition, I

From Oversight and Government Reform Committee, September 25, 2008.

have served as an associate editor on more than 10 major, peer-reviewed journals, including Cancer Research, the Journal of the National Cancer Institute
(JNCI), and the Journal of Immunology, and I have been a peer reviewer for over
1,000 manuscripts submitted for publication. For nearly two decades before I
was recruited to Pittsburgh to found the UPCI, I led research teams at the NCI
that focused mainly on characterizing the cellular basis for human anti-tumor
immunity and utilizing the insights derived from those studies to develop innovative approaches to use immunotherapy to improve the treatment of cancer.
The work of my research team at NCI resulted in the initial identification and
then extensive characterization of natural killer (NK) cells. Research by my team
at NCI and then at UPCI, along with other leading researchers around the world,
have shown that NK cells are a key component of our natural defense against
the development and metastatic spread of cancer.

In addition to world class studies in cancer immunology and immunotherapy at UPCI, other programs at our institute are developing prognostic indicators of response to treatment. UPCI also includes experts working on strategies
for cancer prevention, early detection, and treatment and approaches for cancer
control. Through our innovative Center for Environmental Oncology, we are
carrying out studies to better define the role of environmental exposures on
cancer risk, coupled with measures to reduce cancer risk by reducing exposure
to environmental carcinogens, or using nutritional and other interventions to
protect people who have been exposed to environmental hazards.

As part of our overall efforts, we are also working to identify important
policy changes that should be developed to reduce the burden of cancer.
After years of protracted delays, our nation has finally made progress against
smoking by getting individuals to stop smoking. But, smoking control policies proved difficult to implement for many years, because of complex strategies to manipulate information on its dangers. Analogous efforts to identify
and then effectively implement actions for other controllable causes of cancer
have been fairly limited.

Now, to turn to the issues of direct interest to this committee, I first want
to point out that, in contrast to several of the other speakers at this important
hearing, who are longstanding experts on some aspects of radiofrequency (RF)
radiation associated with cell phones or on the design and implementation of
population-based studies, I have only recently become involved in the issue
of the possible health risks of cell phones, by issuing a precautionary message
to the faculty and staff of the UPCI and the UPMC Cancer Centers. For you to
understand why a non-expert in the field took this action, I believe it is important to explain the process that led up to the issuance of the advisory to reduce
direct cell phone exposures to the head and body.

Last year, as she was finalizing her well-researched book, The Secret History of the War on Cancer, my colleague, Dr. Devra Davis, Director of the
UPCI's Center for Environmental Oncology and an internationally acclaimed
expert in environmentally-induced health risks, shared with me the growing
scientific literature on the possible association between extensive cell phone
and increased risk of malignant and benign brain tumors. My attention
was directed to a large body of evidence, including expert analyses showing

absorption of RF into the brain and the comprehensive Bioinitiative Report, review of experimental and public health studies pointing to potential adverse biologic effects of RF signals, including brain tumors, associated with long-term and frequent use of cell phones held to the ear. I also learned of a recent series of similar precautionary advisories from international experts and various governments in Europe and Canada. I reacted to this information in the same fashion as I do with other reports of claims of biologically and/or clinically important findings, namely I first carefully reviewed the reports and consulted with a variety of relevant experts.

My evaluation of the scientific and technical information indicating the potential hazards of cell phones was built on the foundation of my extensive experience in cancer research and critical evaluations of reports being submitted for peer-reviewed publications. I recognized that there was sufficient evidence to justify the precautionary advisories that had been issued in other countries, to alert people about the possibility of harm from long-term, frequent cell phone use, especially by young children. Then, Dr. Davis and I consulted with international experts in the biology of radiofrequency (RF) effects and the epidemiology of brain tumors, and with experts in neurology, oncology and neurosurgery at UPCI. Without exception, all of the experts contacted confirmed my impression that there was a sound basis to make the case for precaution, especially since there are simple and practical measures that can be taken, to be able to continue to use cell phones while substantially reducing the potential hazards.

Another factor influencing my decision was my growing conviction that substantially more attention should be devoted to promoting a range of strategies to reduce the future burden of cancer. Of course, I appreciate the tremendous progress that the US has made in treating cancer, some of which was achieved by studies at the University of Pittsburgh, on melanoma, breast, brain, and colorectal cancer. I also recognize that approaches that aim to prevent new cases from occurring are the most likely ways to more effectively and efficiently reduce the overall burden of cancer. Accordingly, I decided to act, consistent with my responsibilities as the leader of a major US cancer institute, by informing my colleagues about my concerns that cell phone use may be a substantial risk to public health. I also wanted to stimulate broader awareness and discussion of the evidence that I came to be familiar with, and to encourage changes in the behavior of some of my colleagues and by extension, also their families and friends.

Summary of Review of the Published Scientific Evidence for an Association Between Cell Phone Use and Brain Tumors

Obviously, scientific research plays a central role in identifying exposures that may affect our health. In public health research, scientists generally rely on two major types of evidence to evaluate potential risks. First, a combination of laboratory-based experimental studies using animals, cell cultures, and computer models can be used to examine mechanisms, identify biological effects and predict the potential impact for humans. Then, population-based human studies can also be used to determine if observed patterns of disease can be correlated with specific exposures, and other more detailed studies of people with a particular disease in comparison with healthy controls, so-called case-control studies, can be carried out to determine if there are different health patterns in those with and without certain exposures.

Although in some cases a clear association between an exposure and health effect can be demonstrated, often methodological differences among studies can introduce subtle differences in the way data are evaluated, and in some cases can lead to very different conclusions. This is especially true for human population-based cancer epidemiology studies where it is some-times very difficult to select non-exposed controls, where the critical timing of exposure is not precisely known, where the mechanism by which an exposure might cause cancer is not well defined or understood, or where the characteristics of the exposure change over time. A critical review of the literature on the biological effects of cell phones exemplifies this point. Despite the lack of consistency in outcomes in all the cell phone publications, there are several well-designed studies that suggest that long-term (10 years or more) use of wireless phone devices is associated with a significant increase in risk for glioblastoma (glioma), a very aggressive and fatal brain tumor, and acoustic neuroma, a benign tumor of the auditory nerve that is responsible for our hearing.

For more than eight years, the World Health Organization has been conducting a combined effort to study cell phones and brain cancer in thirteen countries, called the Interphone study. No results synthesizing this overall effort have been published yet. But, several reports from countries participating in the Interphone study have appeared. Some analyses have found no increased risk of cell phones, while others, from countries where study participants used cell phones for a decade or longer, have found increased risks for brain tumors. But, even in these negative studies, when the subset of long-term users are examined separately, there is evidence of increased risk of brain tumors.

Clearly, not all of the published cell phone studies have reached the same conclusion. What are some of the characteristics of study design that can explain the differences among cell phone use studies generally and between the Interphone-related studies and the independent, non-Interphone-related studies?

To address this question, in 2008, Dr. Lennart Hardell, a distinguished oncologist and senior author on several cell phone studies in Sweden that have shown increases in brain tumor risk with long-term use, published a combined analysis (also called a meta-analysis) of published case-control studies that evaluated the effects of cell phone use on brain tumor risk. For gliomas, a malignant tumor of the supporting tissue of the brain, he and his colleagues found 10 studies; 7 were part of the Interphone Study, one was partly based on Interphone participation and partly independent, and 2 were not part of Interphone (one was a Swedish study from Hardell's team, and the second was a Finnish study). In contrast to the Interphone-related studies which found no increased risk for glioma, both of the independent studies found an increased risk of 40–50%. Since 8 of these 10 studies were Interphone-related, and these studies all showed no effect of cell phone use on glioma risk, the combined data result (meta-analysis) also showed no effect. It should be noted, however, that most of these studies included as cell phone users those who only made a single phone call a week and did so over a limited duration.

In contrast, focusing on those who had used cell phones for a decade provided a different story. Of these 10 studies, 6 evaluated long-term exposure effects, resulting from 10 or more years of cell phone use. Of these 6 studies, all showed an increase risk for developing a glioma on the same side of the head where the phone was used, and this increased risk ranged from a low of 20% increased risk for low grade (less aggressive) glioma to more than 400% increase risk of high grade (very aggressive) glioma. The meta-analysis for the combined data indicated that those who regularly used cell phones had twice the risk of malignant brain tumors overall, and four times the risk if they were high users of phones.

For acoustic neuroma, 9 case-control studies have been published that have compared the reported history of cell phone use of persons with and without this benign tumor on the hearing nerve. Eight of these studies are Interphone study-related and one, by Hardell's group, was independent. Whereas six of the 7 Interphone studies showed that no increased risk with regular cell phone use, Hardell found that regular cell phone users had a 70% greater risk. What struck me as especially relevant, and to possibly account for the divergent reports, is one simple fact: all three studies that looked at cell phone users for at least a decade, found a significantly increased risk. In long term users, acoustic neuromas are twice as frequent in regular, long-term users.

Within the last month, as also noted by Dr. David Carpenter in this hearing, Dr. Hardell reported at a meeting of the Royal Society of London that very frequent and long term users of cell phones by teenagers that started before age 20, resulted in a five times higher rate of brain cancer by the age of 29, when compared with non-cell phone users.

Brain cancer, which is one of the health effects of very serious concern, is believed to develop in adults over a period of at least one decade and in some cases, up to several decades. Among the known causes of brain cancer is ionizing radiation, such as x-rays. RF radiation is not ionizing, but it is absorbed into the brain, according to modeling studies that have been produced by the cell phone industry, in particular by French Telecom. There is no debate that radiation emitted by cell phones is absorbed into the brain—dramatically more so in children than in adults.

In summary, my review of the literature suggests that most studies claiming that there is no link between cell phones and brain tumors are outdated, had methodological concerns, and did not include sufficient numbers of long-term cell phone users to find an effect, since most of these negative studies primarily examined people with only a few years of phone use and did not inquire about cordless phone use. In addition, many studies defined regular cell phone use as "once a week."

One major negative study, published by the Danish Cancer Society and supported by the cell phone industry, started with nearly three quarters of a million cell phone users during the period between 1982 and 1995. This study excluded more than 200,000 business users, who were most likely to be the most frequent users during that time period. Recall bias was a problem with all of these studies as solid data such as cell phone records were not used to document usage and people were simply asked, often the day after surgery, whether or not they had used a cell phone and for how long.

Scientists appreciate that diseases like brain cancer can take decades to develop. This means that even well conducted studies of those who have used phones for only a few years, as most of us have, cannot tell us whether or not there are hazards from long-term use.

In contrast, some recent studies in Nordic countries, where phones have been used longest, find that persons who have used cell phones for at least a decade have 30% to more than 200% more brain tumors than do those without such use, and only on the side of the head where the user holds his or her phone. To put these numbers in context, this is at least as high an increase as the added risk of breast cancer that women face from long-term use of hormone replacement therapy. Based on these findings and the increased absorption into the brains of the young, the French Ministry of Health advised that children should be discouraged from using cell phones, a position also taken by British, German and other authorities.

Precautionary Advisory Based on Review of the Published Reports and Consideration of the Precautionary Advisories from Several Countries in Europe and Elsewhere

While those issues are being debated and resolved, and as we eagerly await the results, my review of the available published evidence suggesting some increased brain tumor risk following long-term cell phone use, combined with the current near ubiquity of exposure to cell phones and cordless phone RF fields (more than 90% of the population in the Western European countries and about 90% of the population in the USA use cellular phones), led me to work with both international experts and experts at UPCI to develop a set of prudent and simple precautions that I felt could reduce potential risk, while awaiting more definitive evidence. Certainly, if it turns out that long-term use of cell phones does increase brain tumor risk, the public health implications of *not* taking action are obvious.

On July 21, 2008, I issued the advisory on the safe use of cell phones to the physicians, researchers and staff at UPCI and UPMC Cancer Centers. Before its issuance, this document was reviewed by UPCI experts in neuro-oncology, epidemiology, environmental oncology, and neurosurgery as well as national and international scientific and engineering experts. A copy can be found at the end of my testimony. My sole goal in issuing the cell phone advisory was to suggest simple precautions that would reduce exposure to cell phone electromagnetic radiation. The advisory clearly indicated that the human evidence on the potential hazard of cell phones is still evolving, but it pointed out that there are some studies using experimental and population-based approaches that suggest an association between long-term cell phone use and development of brain tumors. It also pointed out that modeling studies suggest the possibility that there may be additional differences in susceptibility between young children and adults. Based on my review of the data, I felt that there was sufficient evidence for possible human health risks, to warrant providing precautionary advice on cell phone use, especially by children.

What are the main points of the advisory? Adults can reduce direct exposure of the head and bone marrow to radiofrequency radiation by using ear pieces or the speaker phone mode whenever possible. Cell phone use by children should be restricted. Here we advised, as do a number of governments, that cell phone use by children be limited to emergencies calls and for older children, text messaging. In circulating this warning, I joined with an international expert panel of pathologists, oncologists and public health specialists, who recently declared that RF radiation emitted by cell phones should be considered a potential human health risk.[1] In fact, shortly before I sent my precautionary message to faculty and staff at UPCI and UPMC Cancer Centers, a number of countries including France, Germany and India, and the province of Ontario, Canada, issued similar advice, suggesting that exposure to RF radiation from cell phones be limited. Very soon after the UPCI advisory was issued, Israel's Health Ministry endorsed my recommendations, and Toronto's Department of Public Health advised that teenagers and young children limit their use of cell phones, to avoid potential health risks.

I appreciate the interest of this committee in exploring the current state of the scientific evidence on the potential hazards of cell phones. I have provided appendices that include links and references to reviews and advisories that have been issued within the past few years by other authorities. In addition, the web site for UPCI's Center for Environmental Oncology (www.preventingcancernow.org) includes the actual papers as pdf files for all major studies published over the past two years. In addition, the Bioinitatives Report (www.bioinitiativereport.org) provides comprehensive, critical review, that includes references to the more than 4,000 relevant studies that have been published to date on this subject.

Most people throughout the developed world are using cell phones. Cell phones save lives and have revolutionized our world in many positive ways. Without doubt, the most immediate danger from the use of cell phones is that of traffic crashes. But, the longer term spectre of harm cannot easily be dismissed at this point. The absence of definitive positive studies should not be confused with proof that there is no association. Rather, it reflects the difficulties of assembling definitive proof and the absence of well-conducted, large-scale independent studies on the problem.

Throughout my career I have witnessed the tremendously important discoveries that have improved cancer care. I also recognize that cancer professionals and physicians in general have failed to pay adequate attention to the need to identify and then promptly and effectively control avoidable causes of cancer. Nowhere is our failure more evident than in the protracted and prolonged debate that played out over the hazards of tobacco. By all accounts, we have also missed the boat with respect to our national policies on known workplace cancer causes such as exposure to asbestos, and we waited far too long before acting to reduce dangers associated with hormone replacement therapy.

It is worth noting that in the case of tobacco and lung cancer, debates over whether there was a true increase in lung cancer associated with smoking raged far longer than they should have, fomented by an active disinformation campaign of which this Congress is well aware. The dilemma of public policy when it comes to controlling and identifying the causes of cancer is profound. If we insist we must be certain of human harm and wait for definitive evidence of such damage, we are effectively saying that we can only act to prevent future cancers, once past ones have become evident. Recalling the 70 years that it took to remove lead from paint and gasoline and the 50 years that it took to convincingly establish the link between smoking and lung cancer, I argue that we must learn from our past to do a better job of interpreting evidence of potential risk. In failing to act quickly, we subject ourselves, our children and our grandchildren to the possibility of grave harm and to living with the knowledge that with more rapid action that harm could have been averted.

I do not envy policy makers and regulators as they do not always have adequate solid data on which to base standards. In the present case, the link between cell phones and health effects is suggestive but not solidly established. From my careful review of the evidence, I cannot tell you conclusively that phones cause cancer or other diseases. But, I can tell you that there are published peer reviewed studies that have led me to suspect that long term cell phone use may cause cancer. It should be noted in this regard that worldwide, there are three billion regular cell phone users, including a rapidly growing number of children. If we wait until the human evidence is irrefutable and then act, an extraordinarily large number of people will have been exposed to a technology that has never really been shown to be safe. In my opinion, for public health, when there is some evidence of harm and the exposed group is very large, it makes sense to urge caution. This is why I issued advice to our faculty and staff, especially to take precautions to reduce cell phone RF exposures to children.

Now that the issue of a possible association of long-term cell phone with increased brain tumor risk has reached national and international attention, the central question is where we go from here. Should we simply wait and watch? Or, should we take some actions now? I am not sufficiently expert to comment on possible new regulations to affect cell phone usage. Rather, from my perspective as a scientist and cancer center director, I want to do all that I can to see that the matter of cell phones and our health is resolved. I believe that we should undertake additional, more definitive research that will tell the whole story. Many of my colleagues at UPCI, Rutgers University, University of California, San Francisco and a number of senior faculty at M.D. Anderson Cancer Institute are joining with me in calling for an independent scientific investigation, avoiding as many of the limitations of the prior studies as possible, to determine if long-term, frequent use of cell phones and cordless phones increases brain tumor risk We will urge that these studies engage both university and NIH experts and also the full cooperation of the cell phone industry, which will be asked to provide solid usage data in the form of access to billing records and substantial contribution to the funding of the study but without any direct review or control of the results, in order to clearly settle this issue in the not too distant future.

In the meantime, while we continue to conduct progressively better research on this question, I believe it makes sense to urge caution: it's better to be safe than sorry.

Note

1. *The Case for Precaution in the Use of Cell Phones Advice from University of Pittsburgh Cancer Institute Based on Advice from an International Expert Panel,* available at www.preventingcancernow.org

Bernard Leikind   ➔ **NO**

Do Cell Phones Cause Cancer?

News reports threaten that our cell phones may cause cancer—brain cancer, eye cancer, and others. We are told that fragile children's developing brains are at risk. Concerned epidemiologists collect their data and warn that they cannot rule out the possibility of harm from cell phone radiation and that they must do more research. Medical professionals assert, as a precaution and in the absence of definitive data, that we should place our phones at arm's length. News accounts fill us with alarm. Danger lurks.

Fears that cell phones cause cancer are groundless. There is not a shred of evidence that the electromagnetic radiation from your cell phones causes harm, much less that from the wiring in the walls of your house, your hair dryer, electric blanket, or the power distribution wires nearby.

We know exactly what happens to energy from any of these sources when it meets the atoms and molecules in your body, and that energy cannot cause cancer. There is no known way that this energy can cause any cancer, nor is there any unknown way that this energy can cause any cancer.

There is a link between some forms of electromagnetic radiation and some cancers. These forms of electromagnetic radiation are ultraviolet radiation, X-rays, and gamma rays. They are dangerous because they may break covalent chemical bonds in your body. Breakage of certain covalent bonds in key molecules leads to an increased cancer risk. For example, there is a link between ultraviolet light from the sun and skin cancers.

All other forms of electromagnetic radiation other than these may add to molecules' or atoms' thermal agitation, but can do nothing else. Visible light has sufficient energy to affect chemical bonds. When light strikes the cones and rods in our retinas rhodopsin bends from its resting state to another, but it does not break. When visible light strikes the chlorophyll molecules in plants, electrons shift about but the chlorophyll does not break. Visible light does not cause cancer.

Electromagnetic radiation transfers its energy to atoms and molecules in chunks called *photons*. The energy of single photon is proportional to the photon's frequency. The photons of high frequency radiation, such as ultraviolet light, X-rays, and gamma rays, carry relatively large amounts of energy compared to those of lower frequency radiation. That is why high-energy photons can break covalent chemical bonds while the photon energy of all other forms

From *Skeptic,* vol. 15, no. 4, 2010. Copyright © 2010 by Skeptic Magazine. Reprinted by permission of Millennium Press.

Figure 1

The units of this scale are familiar to chemists. Chemists like to think about test-tube-sized quantities of stuff. A mole is a unit that measures how much stuff you have. It is a count of objects: atoms, molecules, photons, chemical bonds. One mole of any object contains 6.023×10^{23} of those objects. Physicists prefer to state the energy in one bond or in one photon. A physicist would divide all the numbers in this figure by the number of objects in a mole to show the energy in Joules in a single object. An (old) physicist might prefer to express this energy in units of electron volts. Measured in electron volts, the energy in one green light photon is about 2.5 electron volts. The energy in one banana is 150 to 200 Calories, which corresponds to 600 or 800 kJ/banana; that is, one banana, not a mole of bananas.

Biochemistry's Energy World

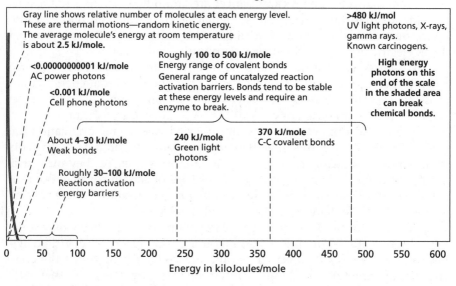

of electromagnetic radiation, including visible light, infrared light, microwave, TV and radio waves, and AC power cannot.

Figure 1 shows a range of energy that is important for life and for the science of biochemistry. The figure displays an energy scale to help you place relevant energy states or processes in context. Horizontal positions indicate the energy range.

Look at the area covered by the long bracket in the middle. It shows the general energy range of the major strong chemical bonds—covalent bonds—which are significant for all of life's molecules. Below to the right you can see where the energy of an important organic covalent bond—that which occurs between two carbon atoms—falls on the scale. Further up the scale, on the upper right, is the energy range of carcinogenic electromagnetic radiation.

Figure 2

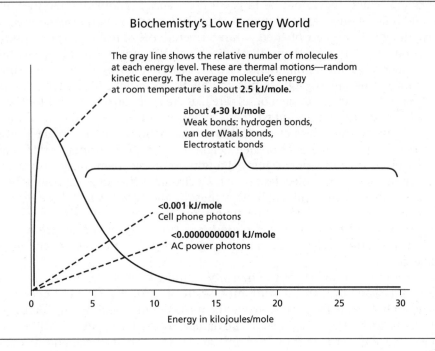

Biochemistry's Low Energy World

The gray line shows the relative number of molecules at each energy level. These are thermal motions—random kinetic energy. The average molecule's energy at room temperature is about **2.5 kJ/mole.**

about **4-30 kJ/mole**
Weak bonds: hydrogen bonds, van der Waals bonds, Electrostatic bonds

<0.001 kJ/mole
Cell phone photons

<0.00000000001 kJ/mole
AC power photons

0   5   10   15   20   25   30

Energy in kilojoules/mole

Notice where the call out for green light falls on this scale. Visible light does not cause cancer.

Notice that the energy of cell phone radiation and AC power radiation in this scale is very low. Cell phone radiation cannot break, damage, or weaken any covalent bond.

Figure 2 shows the lowest energy part of Figure 1's energy scale. Figure 1 ranges from 0 kJ/mole to 600 kJ/mole. Figure 2 ranges from 0 kJ/mole to 30 kJ/mole.

Notice the bracket that shows the range of weak bonds in each figure. These are hydrogen bonds, van der Waals bonds, electrostatic bonds, and various other effects, such as hydrophobic or hydrophilic forces. In the complex molecules of life, these bonds play critical roles holding strands together and creating the three-dimensional shapes of molecules.

Covalent bonds hold together the single strands of DNA. Hydrogen bonds connect one strand to its mate. Enzymes fold and twist to create the forms they require as they perform their role as catalysts. The various weak bonds maintain the shapes of these folds and twists.

Drawn in both figures is a graph that suggests the energy of molecular thermal motions at body temperature. Everything in our bodies partakes in these thermal motions. The molecules jostle one another. They twist and vibrate. The thick grey line on the graph shows how energy distributes itself among these various motions. The motion's average energy is about 2.5 kJ/mole. Some molecules, but not many, have much more energy.

If energy transfers of 2.5 kJ/mole, more or less, were sufficient to damage life's molecules, life would be impossible because random thermal motions would quickly break most of them. Fortunately, covalent bonds require ten to fifty times this amount of energy transfer before they break. Thermal jostling does not interfere with them. Weak biochemical bonds, however, live within the upper range of thermal bonds and shakes. That is why they do not enter into life's structure as single bonds, but always as groups. In the long double helices of DNA, the hydrogen bonds are like the individual teeth of a long zipper. Together they withstand what any single one of them could not.

These collisions are electromagnetic interactions. The molecules' outer electrons sense the presence of their neighbors though electromagnetic forces. These electrons resist oncoming neighbors, pushing them away, and pushing upon their own molecules as well. Electromagnetic forces transmit these pushes. All of the molecules of biology must be able to withstand these electromagnetic forces to maintain their shapes and their functions. The forces that electromagnetic fields from cell phones exert on life's molecules are no different from any of these molecular pushes, except that they are much, much smaller.

Cancer is a disease of the heredity of individual cells. Something must cause a cell to begin transferring mistakes to its progeny. One cell goes haywire, replicating wildly, transmitting the mistaken instructions—the damaged DNA—to each of its daughters. If the damage is too great, the cell will die. If the damage is not sufficient, it is not cancer. The damaged cell and its damaged progeny must continue to function in their crippled, uncontrolled states. Cancer generally requires more than one mutation in a single cell.

It is worth understanding how chemical changes occur, why life's molecules are stable in the cytoplasm, and how life controls its chemical reactions, turning them on or off. Consider Figure 3.

This famous diagram appears in all biochemistry books. It is a schematic representation of a reaction. Consider this reaction $A + B \rightarrow C + D$, where A and B are reactants and C and D are products. In the diagram and the equation, the reaction begins on the left and moves to the right. The vertical scale is energy. Don't worry about the technical details. Begin with the upper solid black line with the label *Reaction Energy Barrier without an Enzyme*. For this reaction, the molecules A and B must assemble sufficient energy to carry them over the hill. This energy may come from the incessant thermal collisions, from some other molecule's internal energy, from an incoming photon of electromagnetic radiation, or other sources. The total energy of the entire system, including the surroundings, is a constant.

Through the continual random exchange of energy between the molecules A and B and their surroundings, if A and B happen to meet when they have sufficient energy to make it over the top of the hill, then they will react, forming C and D. These products appear on the diagram's right.

This diagram is illustrative. The actual diagram of even a simple reaction might have several dimensions in place of the single horizontal axis. The hills would be complicated surfaces with mountains and valleys. The diagram would have to take into account factors such as the orientation of the reactant

Figure 3

The symbol E_a is the activation energy, the amount of energy the reactants must have to react. This energy is available to the products on the right. The reactants collect energy E_a from their surroundings. The products have returned it and a little extra ΔE to the surroundings. The surroundings, in this case, are warmer than before the reaction.

Reaction energy barrier with and without an enzyme

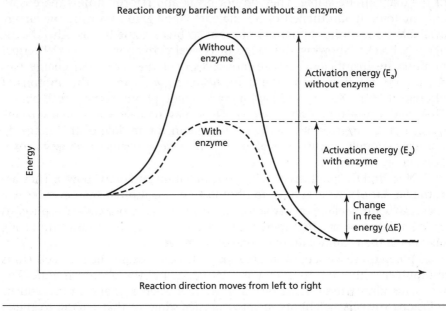

Reaction direction moves from left to right

molecules, and much else. It is the case, however, that all of life's stable molecules live in a well—a valley—similar to the left side of the diagram. They will require an injection of energy from their surroundings to escape. Biological molecules have many possible reactions in which they might take part. Remove an atom and replace it with another. Switch any molecular piece with another molecular piece. Natural selection has designed all of the molecules of life so that they are stable in chemical composition, form, and function. High activation energy barriers in all directions make all possible reactions rare. If this were not the case, then the molecules of life would not be stable.

When life requires a particular reaction to take place, there will be an enzyme to facilitate it. An enzyme is a biological catalyst. Consider the lower dashed line in Figure 3. This line has the label *Reaction Energy Barrier with an Enzyme*. This depicts the same reaction $A + B \rightarrow C + D$, but this time there is an enzyme to facilitate the reaction. Without going into the remarkable details of enzymatic function, we can say that the enzyme has the effect of lowering the activation energy barrier for the reaction. With lower activation energy, the thermal jostling or other sources of reaction energy have a much easier time pushing the reactants over the hill. The reaction rate goes from nearly zero to some reasonable value.

There are no enzymes for unwanted reactions. Enzymes have and maintain the proper constitution and form to work correctly. For a mutation to occur or an enzyme to change, the energy for the chemical reaction must come from some place. An X-ray photon—from a cosmic ray, from the earth's radioactivity, or from an X-ray machine—may provide the required energy. Photons from any other form of electromagnetic radiation cannot.

Glance at Figure 1 again. All of those chemical bonds across the middle of the diagram are stable. They do not break and reform, unless there is an enzyme to do it. On the left of the diagram is the graph showing the energy available from ordinary thermal motions to break these bonds. Also on the left is a bracket showing the range of typical activation energies. Thermal motions are insufficient to take molecules over the activation energy barrier for any reaction. Far to the right, however, you can see the photons of ultraviolet light, X-rays, and gamma rays. These photons may break bonds. They may cause mutations directly. They may damage individual enzyme molecules. Even green visible light photons in the middle of this range do not have enough energy to break bonds and take molecules over any activation energy barrier.

Now find the photons of cell phone radiation and of AC power. They are at the far left of this diagram. No photon from a cell phone can ever break a chemical bond. Making the radiation more intense does not make the photons stronger. It just means that there are more of them. The photons cannot gang up. Lots of them cannot do what one of them cannot.

When those weak photons disappear into a molecule, the molecule shifts and quivers a tiny bit. Its energy is a bit larger and the photon is gone. The molecule adjusts itself to its new slightly higher energy, and in subsequent collisions with its neighbors, it may transfer some of that energy to them. The temperature of the biological soup—the cytoplasm—is then a bit higher. The amount of heating due to cell phone radiation is small compared to your microwave, or standing in the sunshine, or wearing a scarf around your neck. This small increase in temperature does not cause cancer.

If cell phone photons or AC power photons, far to the left of Figure 1, were able to cause cancer by any mechanism, known or unknown, then those thermal vibrations also shown to the left side of the diagram would also cause cancer. So would all the forms of electromagnetic radiation that have more energetic photons than cell phone radiation.

Some of the concern over cellphone radiation may have originated from the normal statistical fluctuations that occur when studies are conducted. In recent years, epidemiologists have found significant environmental hazards, such as smoking and asbestos. They are now searching for hazards among much weaker effects. Some studies of a supposed hazard will show a small risk. Others studies of the same hazard will show no risk. In fact, some studies of the same potential hazard will show a benefit. This is the sign that there is no hazard, only statistical fluctuations. But only the studies that suggest risks, even small risks, will make news.

We can all be confident that any epidemiological study that purports to show that cell phone radiation causes any cancer must have at least one mistake. We can be certain because there is no plausible—or even implausible—mechanism by which cell phone radiation can cause any cancer.

When asked for a physicist's advice about cell phone safety, I explain that the radiation cannot cause cancer by any mechanism, known or unknown. If I am further pressed for comment I respond, "don't text while you drive, and don't eat your cell phone."

Acknowledgment: I thank physicists Dr. Arthur West and Dr. Craig Bohren, and biochemists Dr. Joseph H. Guth and Dr. Jill Ferguson, for their careful review of this paper and for their suggestions.

POSTSCRIPT

Do Cell Phones Cause Cancer?

In May 2010, the largest cell phone cancer study, the Interphone Study, conducted by the WHO proved to be inconclusive (*International Journal of Epidemiology*, May 2010). More than 6,000 people with brain tumors and a similar number of healthy people were asked about their cell phone usage. The hypothesis was that cell phones increase the risk of brain tumors and there would be greater use in the cancer group compared with the healthy population. The study found the opposite to be true initially. However, when the researchers contacted healthy people who declined to take part in the initial investigation, they found that these individuals were less likely to regularly use cell phones than the healthy people who took part in the study. This indicates that the "benefit" that cell phones seemed to offer could be based on an over-representation of individuals who were healthy and regular mobile phone users. It might also mean that any negative effects might have been hidden. The researchers then compared frequent mobile phone users with infrequent ones and found that the level of use seemed to increase the risk of two different types of brain tumors by 40 and 15 percent, respectively.

Although the results of the study are intriguing, they are certainly not conclusive. The study relied on people's memories regarding their cell phone use. It may be that people with brain tumors tend to have different memories of cell usage than those who are healthy. Several other studies are in progress, and the final verdict is not yet out. In "Jury Still Out on Cell Phone–Cancer Connection" (*Cancer*, January 5, 2010), author Michael Thun indicates that further research is needed. Similar results were found in "Cell Phones and Tumor: Still in No Man's Land" (*Indian Journal of Cancer*, January–March 2009) and "The Reality of Mobile Phones and Cancer" (*New Scientist*, December 12, 2009). Other articles addressing the safety of cell phone use include "Commentary: Call Me on My Mobile Phone . . . or Better Not?" (*Epidemiology*, June 2010) and "Do Cell Phones Cause Cancer" (*American Journal of Nursing*, September 2010).

ISSUE 18

Will Global Warming Negatively Impact Human Health?

YES: Carl Bloice and Conn Hallinan, from "Global Warming," *California Nurse* (December 2005)

NO: Indur M. Goklany, from "Stop the Panic on Climate Change," *USA Today Magazine* (May 2008)

ISSUE SUMMARY

YES: Carl Bloice and Conn Hallinan maintain that rising global temperatures will increase mosquito-borne diseases, asthma, and heat stroke.

NO: Indur Goklany argues that rising global temperatures are not responsible for increased illnesses and deaths.

The temperature of the earth's atmosphere is influenced by the balance between the high energy ultraviolet radiation absorbed from the sun and the amount of heat radiated back into the atmosphere. Carbon dioxide, water, methane, and other "greenhouse gases" are the key elements that regulate the earth's temperature. Greenhouse gases are similar to the glass in a greenhouse—they allow light to enter and warm the interior but trap radiation, which heats the inside. Greenhouse gases in the atmosphere cause a buildup of heat that raises the temperature on the earth's surface, a process called the greenhouse effect.

There is now near unanimous scientific consensus that greenhouse gas emissions produced by human activity are rising and changing the earth's climate. Due to the combustion of fossil fuels—coal, oil, and natural gas—the level of carbon dioxide in the atmosphere has increased significantly since the Industrial Revolution. Cutting down forests by burning to create farmland, harvest hardwoods, and grazing lands has also increased carbon dioxide emissions. It has also reduced the number of trees and plants available to absorb carbon dioxide and convert it into oxygen.

The National Research Council in 2006 reported that the earth's average temperature had risen 0.6 degrees Centigrade in the twentieth century. Most researchers agree that global temperatures will continue to rise, though it's not clear how much. If global temperatures continue to escalate, the impact may be catastrophic, particularly for human health. Climate change will affect human health in a variety of ways, mostly negative. Increased heat will impact rainfall and flooding in some areas while drought will occur in others. According to Andrew Goudie, a rise in the number of dust storms may also be a serious problem affecting health because dust storms can be carriers of allergens and disease-carrying organisms ("Dust Storms: Are They Getting Worse?" *Geodate,* August 2006). Areas along the coasts, where approximately 50 percent of the world's people live, would be most affected by global warming. In addition to flooding, dust storms, and drought, there would likely be a rise in deaths from heat stress and urban air pollution. A more serious threat would be from the rise in tropical diseases. According to physician Larry Brilliant in "Spreading Epidemic" (*Forbes,* May 7, 2007), the nonnative tiger mosquito, which spreads diseases that include dengue, yellow fever, and encephalitis, is increasing its range across the North American continent. Malaria-carrying mosquitoes are now able to survive at higher altitudes and are about to spread into the highlands of tropical Africa and northern Europe. See "All Washed Up," *Economist,* April 7, 2007. The article reports that winters will soon no longer be cold enough to kill off mosquitoes, and diseases like malaria and dengue fever will increase. The complex factors that cause cholera epidemics in developing countries are linked to global warming. (See "Cholera Outbreaks and Ocean Climate," *Social Research,* Fall 2006.) These include a rise in sea surface temperature and zooplankton populations. In addition to the spread of diseases that were once confined to hotter climates, global warming may also decrease available food. Higher temperatures may reduce crop yields and livestock available for consumption. Deaths may increase from severe weather events such as tornadoes, hurricanes, droughts, and floods.

Since record-keeping began in the mid-1800s, nine of the ten hottest years have occurred since 1990. The year 2005 is tied with 1988 as the hottest year, but after the data are finalized, 2006 ended up hotter than both those years. Most scientists agree that human activity, particularly the burning of fossil fuels, is responsible for global warming. Despite the evidence, there are skeptics who believe rising temperatures are natural phenomena and that humans are not responsible for the greenhouse effect.

The following two selections address whether global warming is negatively affecting human health. Carl Bloice and Conn Hallinan argue rising temperatures will increase the risk of a variety of diseases. Indur Goklany, assistant director of science and technology at the Department of the Interior, argues that the effect of climate change on human health is minimal and will be overshadowed by factors unrelated to global warming.

YES ⬅

Carl Bloice and Conn Hallinan

Global Warming

On July 21, farm worker Constantino Cruz put in a nine-hour day. It was the third week of 100 degree plus weather in Shafter, a town in California's fertile Central Valley. At the end of his shift, the 24-year-old fieldworker collapsed. He died 10 days later. Record heat killed three other farm workers that same month.

Ninety-degree water temperatures in the Gulf of Mexico transformed Hurricane Katrina from a troublesome storm to a city killer. July is early in the season for a hurricane, but by July 9, Hurricane Dennis, the earliest recorded hurricane in history, already had pummeled Florida.

Public health officials in Colombia are worried because malaria-carrying mosquitoes, normally restricted to the wet lowlands, are appearing well above 5,000 feet. Researchers also have noticed an increase of ticks bearing Lyme disease in coastal areas of Massachusetts and Scandinavia.

Asthma has shown a worrisome jump worldwide, with a disturbing trend toward increased lethality. U.S. asthma death rates have risen from 8.2 per 100,000 in 1979 to 18 per 100,000 in 1995, with the heaviest burden, according to the National Institute of Allergy and Infectious Diseases, falling on "poor, inner-city African Americans."

Heat waves, violent weather, and disease epidemics sound almost Biblical, but a broad consensus of scientists says all this has less to do with the sacred than the profane: Human activity is heating the world at a dramatic pace, and the healthcare issues of a substantially warmer world are profound.

There are a handful of scientists who still resist the idea of global warming, but they constitute, "maybe a half a dozen in the world," Susanne Moser told *Revolution*. "Ninety-nine point nine percent of scientists are convinced global warming is underway."

Moser is with the National Center for Atmospheric Research in Boulder, Colo., and one of the authors of "Rising Heat and Risks to Human Health," a study by the Union of Concerned Scientists on the potential impact of climate change on the state of California.

"Climate change is big," says Moser, "but you can't see global warming in the same sense that you can see a dirty stream."

According to the United Nation's Intergovernmental Panel on Climate Change (IPCC), global warming "is projected to increase threats to human health, particularly among lower-income populations, predominantly within tropical/subtropical countries."

From *California Nurse*, December 2005, pp. 13–16. Copyright © 2005 by Conn Hallinan. Reprinted by permission.

Tracking the health implications of climate change is a little like that old spiritual: "The knee bone's connected to the thigh bone, the thigh bone's connected to the hip bone. . ." It is enormously complex, intrieately inter-related, and embraces a staggeringly-wide number of phenomena. It is also subtle, which makes getting people to take notice difficult.

Experts generally break down the health implications of global warming into three broad categories: heat, disease, and extreme weather events, like floods, droughts, and storms. While all are different, there is a nexus between them that sometimes comes out looking like some enormous environmental Rubik's Cube.

The Heat Is On

Heat is a case in point. The heat that killed four farm workers this past July was hardly the first heat wave to strike California, but if the Union of Concerned Scientists' predictions are accurate, such heat waves will be hotter and far more frequent in the future.

According to a study of the effects of climate change on health by Laurence Kalkstein and Kathleen Valimont of the Environmental Protection Agency's (EPA) Science and Advisory Committee, temperature studies dating back to the early 1960s demonstrate a link between heat and such health problems as heart failure, cerebrovascular complications, peptic ulcers, glaucoma, goiter, and eczema.

The heat wave that enveloped Europe in the summer of 2003 killed more than 35,000 people, 15,000 in France alone, an event that Pulitzer Prize-winning investigative journalist and author Ross Gelbspan says had global warming written all over it. "That heat wave had a very specific signature of human-induced heating," he told *Revolution*.

Gelbspan has worked for *The Washington Post, Philadelphia Bulletin,* and *Boston Globe,* and is author of two books, *The Heat Is On,* and *Boiling Point*.

One of the characteristics of global warming is the buildup of carbon dioxide (CO_2), one of the so-called "greenhouse gases." Increasing CO_2 levels, says Gelbspan, causes "nighttime temperature levels to rise, so that there is no cooling-off period when the sun goes down. It means there is no recuperation time for people caught in it."

CO_2 has risen from 280 parts per million in the 18th century, to 375 parts per million today. The gas is very stable, lasting upwards of 100 years.

The Union of Concerned Scientists study of potential environmental and human health effects of global warming as it would affect California found that the greatest temperature increases would be in the state's Central Valley. However, it is coastal cities like San Francisco that are predicted to have the highest mortality. Residents in San Francisco, says the report, are unaccustomed to hot weather and housing is not designed to moderate its effects.

That mortality will largely fall, according to an EPA study of past U.S. heat waves, on "poor inner-city residents who have little access to cooler environments." Indeed, the overwhelming majority of those who died in the European heat wave were old and poor.

The Union of Concerned Scientists report urges "significant efforts" to provide early warning systems, plus "cooling centers," education and community support systems. Right now, most states do not have any ability to predict heat waves.

Hard Choices

But for cash-strapped public health officials trying to hold the floodgates of HIV and antibiotic-resistant tuberculosis, killer heat waves and disease-bearing mosquitoes are a bit of an abstraction.

"It's a matter of priorities," Contra Costa Public Health Director Dr. Wendell Brunner told *Revolution*. He points to West Nile virus as an example. While he is all for getting rid of mosquitoes, he says the county is spending more on mosquito abatement than on HIV. "We have one case of West Nile, we have thousands infected with HIV, almost all of whom will die."

The city of San Francisco has chosen to focus on long-range solutions rather than short-range programs, according to Dr. Rajiv Bhatia, director of occupational and environmental health for the city's public health department.

"I think it is important to think in terms of the whole world, not just our portion of it. It would be a wrong use of energy and resources to direct our efforts toward dealing with the effects of climate change rather than efforts to prevent it," he told *Revolution*.

Bhatia compares the problem to the proliferation of atomic weapons. "We should not be preparing for a nuclear attack—building bomb shelters—but banning and destroying nuclear weapons."

Kay McVay, RN, California Nurses Association liaison coordinator and former CNA president, strongly believes that "healthcare professionals and healthcare workers should be in the forefront of efforts to educate the public and to support strong measure to head off global warming."

But she worries that "nobody is being taught how to respond—there is no plan."

"Our public health system has been decimated," McVay says. "Hospitals have been closed by the hundreds, and RNs have been moved away from the bedside, and there is a shortage of public health nurses. We just don't have the structure in place to handle [climate change]."

One thing seems clear: Given the inadequate finances of public health, people in the field are wrestling with hard choices of where to bullet their efforts.

Like the knee bone to the thigh bone, higher temperatures have a cascading effect on a number of environmental factors. Severe drought is presently affecting one in six countries and has already created a continent-wide crisis in Africa. "Southern Africa is definitely becoming drier and everyone there agrees the climate is changing," Wulf Killman of the U.N. Food and Agriculture Organization's Climate Change Group, told the British newspaper *The Guardian*.

Some 34 African countries, with upwards of 30 million people, are experiencing drought and consequent food shortages. "Drought affects people's ability to feed themselves. A lack of food means a weakened population, one that is more susceptible to disease," says Moser, "and if you are stressed to the max, you don't need much of an extreme event to push you over the edge."

When people do go over that edge, there is virtually no net to catch them. A 2003 study by the World Health Organization (WHO) found that while developing countries carry 90 percent of the disease burden, they have only 10 percent of the world's health resources. WHO estimates that 23,000 of Africa's best-trained health workers emigrate to Europe and the West each year, leaving only 800,000 doctors and nurses for the entire continent.

While aid can mitigate some of that burden, aid is not enough, according to "Africa—Up in Smoke?" by the Working Group on Climate Change and Development, a coalition of organizations ranging from Oxfam to Greenpeace. "All the aid we pour into Africa will be inconsequential if we don't tackle climate change," Nicola Saltman of the World Wide Fund for Nature and a member of the U.N.'s Climate Change Group told the *Independent*.

Getting Bit

Climate change does not mean that the world gets drier everywhere. "Global warming means some places are going to get wetter, which is perfect for mosquitoes," says Dr. Don Francis of Global Solutions in an interview with *Revolution*. Francis, a former epidemiologist for the Center for Disease Control and an expert on diseases like smallpox, HIV and Ebola, predicts, "Infectious diseases, particularly those with vectors like mosquitoes, will move north. And with warmer temperatures and milder winters, there will be longer transmission periods for diseases like malaria and encephalitis."

That process is already underway. According to Dr. Jonathan Patz of the University of Michigan, malaria has surged since the 1970s, and expanded into areas—like the Colombian highlands—that were formally off limits to its carrier, the Anopheles mosquito.

Malaria kills between one and two million people, and generates some 300 million to 500 million new cases a year. The malaria plasmodium is also increasingly resistant to standard treatment with chloroquine, although a new palette of drugs based on artemisinin extracted from the sweet wormwood bush has been effective.

However, while chloroquine costs 10 cents a dose, the new drug from the pharmacology giant, Novartis, runs $2.50 a pop. Artemisinin should also be taken with fatty meals, not normally a part of the developing world's menu.

While malaria is the most dangerous of these mosquito-borne diseases, there are other unpleasant beasts out there, including dengue, or "break-bone fever," which infects 20 million people a year and kills more than 24,000.

Yellow fever could also spread, as might more exotic diseases like chagus, a trypanosoma that damages the heart and is spread by the nocturnal assassin bug. Chagus, which takes about 50,000 lives a year, is endemic in Latin America, and closely associated with poverty and substandard housing that gives the carrier places to hide during the day.

There is a close link between vector-borne diseases and unstable weather, the latter a major consequence of global warming. According to a 2003 WHO study, "Climate Change and Human Health—Risks and Responses," dengue epidemics are closely associated with El Niño, when the surface of the Pacific Ocean heats up and brings on warm and wet conditions. Malaria epidemics increase fivefold as well.

The same study found similar patterns with malaria in India when monsoon rains are heavy and humidity high. In a 40-year study of Bangladeshi medical records, Mercedes Pascual of the University of Michigan found that climate change increases the incidence of cholera by spreading the disease through either floods or droughts. In the latter case, restricted water supplies are more vulnerable to disease causing organisms.

Recent heavy rains in West Africa have seen cholera rates more than double. More than 31,000 have been stricken since June. Flooding and drought also spread water-borne diarrheal diseases like shigella, dysentery, and typhoid, which kill over 2 million people each year, the majority of them children. Flooding also helps rodents disseminate diseases like hantavirus, tularemia, and bubonic plague.

Storm Surge

Melting continental ice, coupled with the expansion of the oceans through warming, is projected to raise sea levels anywhere from three-and-a-half inches to three feet by 2100. This will not only inundate lowlands where hundreds of millions of people presently live, it will generate more powerful storms.

According to the Massachusetts Institute of Technology study, tropical storms have increased in intensity by 50 percent in both the Atlantic and the Pacific over the past 30 years. "Future warming may lead to an upward trend in tropical cyclones' destructive potential, and, taking into account an increasing coastal population, lead to a substantial increase in hurricane-related losses in the 21st century," MIT's Kerry Emanuel told Seripps Howard News Service on July 15.

Tropical storms all draw their power from warm water. The hotter the water temperature, the stronger the storm. Hurricane Katrina was a case in point.

Hurricanes, heat waves, and vector-borne diseases are the most obvious effects of global warming. Other outcomes, like asthma, are hidden in a web of interconnecting events.

U.S. asthma rates have increased 40 percent in the last 10 years, afflicting 25 million Americans, nine million of those children. It is the No. 1 cause for school absenteeism, and between lost workdays and medical care, costs the country about $11 billion a year. Hospitalization for asthma is at record levels, particularly for African-American children.

This latter figure, however, may have more to do with social policy than asthma rates among certain populations. "African-American kids are hospitalized at four times the rate as Euro-American kids in Contra Costa County," says Brunner, but says that is because they don't have quality care. "Kids in Walnut

Greek and Danville (affluent areas of the County) don't end up in hospitals because they do [have access to care]."

There are, however, asthma "triggers" that global warming is accelerating. A major component of air pollution is ozone, and "ozone is definitely a proven asthma trigger," Brunner says.

Pollen, which can cause allergies and asthma, is likely to increase with climate change. Studies by Dr. Paul Epstein found that ragweed pollen, a major cause of allergies, will soar 64 percent if CO_2 levels double, as predicted by the year 2050. Studies of loblolly pines in North Carolina reached the same conclusion.

That Ounce of Prevention

As daunting as problems like asthma seem, a little effort can make a major difference. A Canadian Public Health Association study of the 1996 Atlanta Olympics found that when the city restricted auto traffic for the 17 days of the games, ozone levels fell 30 percent, and emergencies and hospitalizations for asthma dropped 40 percent.

Because of the Bush administration's refusal to touch the subject of global warming or impose mandatory controls on greenhouse gases, a number of states and cities have begun to take action on their own. Nine northeastern states have signed on to their own version of the Kyoto Treaty, agreeing to reduce CO_2 levels by 10 percent over the next 15 years. Hundreds of cities across the country have signed on.

Seattle has built a monorail, uses streetcars, offers residents free city-owned hybrid gas cars, runs municipal vehicles on bio-diesel fuel, and has restored 2,500 acres of urban forest. As a result, the city cut greenhouse gases by 48 percent from 1990 to 2000.

"There is much that is doable," says San Francisco's Bhatia. "The effects of global warming being projected are not inevitable. We can do much to prevent it."

He cites a California EPA study that 58 percent of CO_2 is produced by transportation, a figure that will increase as the state's population grows. Only five percent of the city's residents use public transportation exclusively. "We can double that number soon."

"Can we do something about global warming?" asks Moser. "Hell, Yes!"

She points to the recommendations of the Union of Concerned Scientists report: increased disease surveillance, temperature warnings, cooling stations, and education. And better healthcare. "Many people don't have healthcare, but that is the system that will have to deal with the consequences of climate change. We haven't had that conversation in this country yet," she says.

Americans, she argues, are willing to tackle the problem. "People want to do something positive, to leave a legacy. You have to appeal to that part of them. People understand you have to go though a little pain for long-term benefits. They put money away for their kids to go to college, they buy insurance."

The Program on International Policy Attitudes found that 56 percent of Americans would be willing to incur significant economic costs to address global warming, and 73 percent said the United States should join the Kyoto Accords.

But Moser says the involvement by the federal government is essential. "You can't give up driving your car if there are no buses, or no bus shelters, or [public transportation] costs too much."

Francis concurs, "Government could have a tremendous impact on this. Remember seat belts? We got the data, passed laws, and people started wearing seat belts."

Gelbspan even sees a certain silver lining in all this. "We live in a deeply fractured world. Here is an opportunity to bring all the nations of the world together. We can move beyond stale nationalism, create jobs, and undermine the economics of poverty and desperation."

Indur M. Goklany   ➔ **NO**

Stop the Panic on Climate Change

The state-of-the-art British-sponsored fast-track assessment (FTA) of the global impacts of climate change, whose authors include leading contributors to the latest report of the Intergovernmental Panel on Climate Change (IPCC), indicates that, through the year 2100, the effect of climate change on human health and environmental threats generally will be overshadowed by factors not related to global warming. Hence, climate change is unlikely to be the world's most important environmental problem of the 21st century.

Analysis using the much-heralded Stern Review on the Economics of Climate Change, which also drew on the FTA, reveals that, notwithstanding global warming, for the foreseeable future, human and environmental well-being will be highest under the "richest-but-warmest" scenario and lowest for the "poorest-but-coolest" scenario. In addition, the developing world's future well-being should exceed present levels by several-fold under each scenario, even exceeding present well-being in today's developed world under all but the poorest scenario. Accordingly, equity-based arguments, which hold that present generations should divert scarce resources from today's urgent problems to solve the potential dilemmas of tomorrow's wealthier generations, are unpersuasive.

Halting global warming would reduce cumulative mortality from various climate-sensitive threats, namely, hunger, malaria, and coastal flooding, by four to 10% in 2085, while increasing populations-at-risk from water stress and possibly worsening matters for biodiversity. Yet, according to cost information from the United Nations Millennium Project and the IPCC, measures focused specifically on reducing present vulnerability to these threats would reduce cumulative mortality from these risks by 50–75% at a fraction of the cost of reducing greenhouse gases (GHGs). Simultaneously, such measures would reduce major hurdles to the developing world's sustainable economic development, a lack of which is why they are most vulnerable to climate change.

The world best can combat global warming and advance well-being, particularly of its most at-risk populations, by reducing present-day vulnerabilities to climate-sensitive problems that could be exacerbated by climate change and broadly advancing their economic and technological development rather than through overly aggressive GHG reductions.

Economic and technological development can, on the one hand, improve human and environmental well-being by making better health care and environmental quality more affordable. On the other hand, it can increase greenhouse gas emissions, which can reduce well-being. Because of this tension, it is appropriate to ask whether, despite any economic growth, future well-being would be lower in richer-but-warmer worlds than in poorer-but-cooler worlds and whether climate change will make future generations worse off than current generations.

Proponents of aggressive greenhouse gas controls would answer both questions in the affirmative. Many world leaders—including former Pres. Bill Clinton and his French counterpart, Jacques Chirac—maintain that climate change is the most important environmental issue of this century, while UN Secretary-General Ban Ki-moon calls it the defining issue of this generation. Yet, do analyses of the future impacts of global warming support these dire claims?

The Stern Review estimated that unmitigated climate change will reduce welfare by an amount equivalent to a reduction in consumption per capita of five to 20% "now and forever" if one accounts for market impacts, nonmarket (*i.e.*, health and environmental) impacts, and the risk of catastrophe. It also suggests that, by the year 2200, the 95th percentile of the equivalent losses could rise to 35.2%. Many economists believe that these losses are overestimated. The IPCC, for instance, suggests that losses could be as high as a mere five percent.

Nevertheless, if one adjusts gross domestic product per capita used in the IPCC's richest-and-warmest scenario downward by 35.2% in 2100 (rather than 2200), which overestimates the equivalent loss of welfare due to climate change per even the Stern Review's upperbound estimate, net welfare per capita is found to be higher in 2100 than it was in 1990. The same result holds for the other (poorer) scenarios, assuming that the welfare losses due to climate change vary with the square of the average global temperature increase from 1990 to 2085 estimated for the scenario in question. Remarkably, despite overestimating the welfare losses due to climate change, net welfare in developing countries per capita should be higher in 2100 than it was for developed countries in 1990 for all but the poorest scenario.

These results call into question the basic premise underlying arguments that present generations morally are bound to take aggressive actions now to mitigate climate change because future generations' well-being otherwise will be worse off. Future generations not only will be better off, they will have at their disposal better and more effective technologies to address not just climate change, but any other sources of adversity.

Equally striking, however, is the fact that, although global temperature would increase by 4°C (7.2°F) between 1990–2085, net well-being in 2100 should be highest for the richest-but-warmest IPCC scenario and lowest for the poorest-but-coolest scenario. These findings were reached despite the tendency of impact analyses to overestimate net adverse impacts of warming, especially for wealthier societies, because they do not account fully for the ability of wealthier and more technologically advanced societies to adapt to climate change. This increase in adaptive capacity can be evidenced, for instance, in the remarkable 20th century declines (99% or greater) in mortality and morbidity rates in the U.S. for various water-related diseases—typhoid, paratyphoid, dysentery, malaria, and various gastrointestinal maladies, and the concurrent many-fold increases in agricultural yields. However, few, if any, impacts analyses allow for increases in adaptive capacity with wealth and the passage of time.

If future well-being is measured by per capita income adjusted for welfare losses due to climate change, the surprising conclusion using the Stern Review's own estimates is that, under all scenarios, future generations will be better off than current ones notwithstanding any climate change, and they will be best off in the richest-but-warmest world. This suggests that, if protecting future well-being is the objective of public policy, governmental intervention to address climate change ought to be aimed at maximizing wealth creation, not minimizing CO_2 emissions.

A review paper in *Nature* claims that global warming may have been responsible for about 170,000 deaths worldwide in 2000. Data from the World Health Organization (WHO) indicates that 55,800,000 people died that year. Thus, climate change contributes less than 0.3% of global mortality. In fact, it does not make the list of top 10 global health risk factors related to food, nutrition, and environmental and occupational exposure. Specifically, WHO attributes 1,120,000 deaths in 2001 to malaria; 3,240,000 to malnutrition; 1,730,000 to unsafe water, inadequate sanitation, and hygiene; 1,620,000 to indoor air pollution from heating and cooking with wood, coal, and dung; 800,000 to urban air pollution; and 230,000 to lead exposure.

Climate change clearly is not the most important environmental, let alone public, health problem facing the world today. Yet, is it possible that, in the foreseeable future, the impact of global warming on public health could outweigh that of other factors? To shed light on that question, let us examine the future contribution of climate change to specific climate-related risk factors such as hunger, malaria, and so forth.

The FTA study on hunger shows that, under every scenario, despite any increase in population, notwithstanding any climate change, fewer people would suffer from hunger in 2085 than in 1990. This mainly is because, at the global scale, any future declines in yield due to poorer climatic conditions would be more than offset by increases in agricultural yields due to a combination of higher atmospheric concentrations of carbon dioxide and greater access to existing yield-enhancing technologies in a wealthier world.

The contribution of climate change to the total population at risk from hunger in 2085 would be largest under the warmest scenario. Although that contribution (at 21%) is substantial, it results from a small (two percent) warming-related drop in future global food production between 1990–2085—meaning unmitigated warming would reduce the annual growth in food productivity from 0.84% per year to 0.82% per annum, that is, an annual reduction of 0.02%. This suggests two things. First, a small decline in the rate of productivity growth—perhaps "forced" by the study's assumption that no new technologies will develop autonomously to adapt to climate change—would lead to disproportionately large effects in terms of the population at risk from hunger. Second, a small boost in annual productivity of the food and agricultural sector could go a long way toward ensuring that hunger does not increase in the future.

The most recent FTA analysis for malaria does not provide estimates for the contribution of climate change to the total future global population at risk of that disease. For that, one has to use the results from an earlier version of the FTA, which utilized a "business-as-usual" scenario developed for the 1995 IPCC Assessment. The UK Meteorological Office's Had-CM2 model projected that, under this scenario, average global temperature would increase by 3.2°C between 1990–2085. That study indicates that, in 2085, the global population at risk of malaria in the absence of climate change would double from 4,410,000 in 1990 to 8,820,000 while climate change would add between 256–323,000,000 people to this population at risk, so, global warming would contribute only a small portion (no greater than 3.5%) of the total population at risk for malaria in 2085.

Note that the current range of malaria is dictated less by climate than by human adaptability. Despite any global warming that might have occurred so far, malaria has been eradicated in richer countries although it once was prevalent there and, in earlier centuries, when it was cooler worldwide, it sometimes extended into Canada and even as far north as the Arctic Circle. This is because wealthier societies have better nutrition and general health as well as greater access to public health measures and technologies targeted at controlling diseases in general and malaria in particular. That the disease is a significant health risk only in the poorest of countries reaffirms the importance of incorporating adaptive capacity into impact assessments.

Let us translate the future populations at risk estimated by the FTA for hunger, coastal flooding, and malaria into mortality projections, assuming that the mortality from each risk factor scales linearly with population at risk between 1990–2085, and there was no change in mortality for these threats between 1990–2001. For each scenario, the contribution of climate change to the total mortality burden in 2085 from malaria, hunger, and coastal flooding is substantially smaller than that due to other factors. The contribution of climate change varies from 3.6% to 10.3%. Thus, if global warming were frozen (forgive that turn of phrase) at its 1990 level, it would reduce the mortality burden from these three factors by, at most, 10.3% (under the richest-but-warmest scenario) in 2085, which corresponds to 237,000 deaths out of a possible 2,304,000.

More Heat Means More Water

The FTA also indicates that, in 2085, climate change would, in fact, reduce the net population at risk of water stress. This occurs because additional warming would increase the average amount of global precipitation and, although some areas may receive less precipitation, other, more populated regions, would receive more.

With respect to ecological impacts, the FTA shows that, in 2100, the amount of habitat diverted to cropland, which currently is the greatest threat to species existence and terrestrial biodiversity, would be least under the IPCC's richest-but-warmest scenario. This is because higher levels of carbon dioxide in the atmosphere and economic development, which translates into greater access to more productive technologies, would increase crop yields, thereby reducing demand for cropland.

The FTA notes that, under all scenarios, the contribution of sea level rise to global wetland loss between 1990–2085 will be substantially outweighed by factors other than climate change (such as development or subsidence due to extraction of water and other natural resources).

These results indicate that the effect of non-climate-change-related factors generally outweighs the effect of climate change with respect to either human or environmental well-being. Therefore, climate change is unlikely to be the most important environmental problem confronting human or environmental well-being, at least through the foreseeable future.

The two most common methods of addressing global warming are mitigation (which entails reducing atmospheric concentrations of greenhouse gases through either emission reductions or carbon sequestration) and adaptation (either by coping with its adverse impacts or taking advantage of any positive effects).

With respect to mitigation, the FTA results show that halting climate change at its 1990 level would reduce the total mortality from hunger, malaria, and coastal flooding in 2085 by, at most, 10.3% (under the richest-but-warmest scenario). By contrast, the less ambitious Kyoto Protocol would reduce climate change in 2085 by less than 10%. Consequently, it would reduce mortality from these risk factors by less than one percent. The cost of halting climate change would, however, be astronomical compared to that of the Protocol, which is estimated to cost $165,000,000,000 annually.

A more effective approach to reducing mortality would be to look beyond mitigation by focusing on reducing not just the portion of the mortality due to climate change alone, but the entire 100%, regardless of its cause.

The UN Millennium Project estimates that malaria could be reduced by 75% at an annual cost of $3,000,000,000. We will assume triple this cost to allow for a more-than-doubling in the future population at risk. The Project also estimates that hunger could be reduced by 50% at an annual cost of $12–$15,000,000,000 by 2015. Moreover, according to estimates in the latest (2007) IPCC report, the annual cost of protecting against a sea level rise of about 0.66 meters in 2100 would vary from $2,600,000,000–$10,000,000,000 during the 21st century. We will assume $10,000,000,000 for our purposes. Notably, the IPCC estimates that sea levels may rise this century from 0.18 to 0.59 meters. Combining the above estimates, it figures that the global death toll from hunger, malaria, and coastal flooding could be reduced by a cumulative 64% at a cost of $34,000,000,000 per year through adaptations focused on reducing current vulnerabilities to these specific risk factors.

With respect to malaria, such "focused adaptation" measures include those targeted specifically at malaria as well as measures that generally would enhance the capacity to respond to public health problems and deliver public health services more effectively and efficiently. Malaria-specific measures include indoor residual (home) spraying with insecticides, insecticide-treated bed nets, improved case management, more comprehensive antenatal care, and development of safe, effective, and inexpensive vaccines and therapies.

As for hunger, specific measures could include investment in agricultural research and development targeted toward solving developing countries' current food and agricultural problems that might be exacerbated by warming. Such investments should raise productivity sufficiently to more than compensate for the estimated 0.02% annual shortfall in productivity caused by climate change.

Current agricultural problems that could be exacerbated by warming—and should be the focus of vulnerability-reduction measures—include growing crops in poor climatic or soil conditions (low-moisture soil in some areas, too much water in others, or soils with high salinity, alkalinity, or acidity). Because of warming, such conditions could become more prevalent and agriculture might have to expand into areas with poorer soils. Thus, actions focused on increasing agricultural productivity under current marginal conditions likewise would alleviate hunger in the future whether or not the climate changes.

Moreover, because CO_2 and temperatures will increase, crop varieties should be developed to take advantage of such conditions. Progress on these approaches does not depend on improving our skill in forecasting location-specific details of climate change impacts. These focused adaptation measures should be complemented by development of higher-yield, lower-impact crop varieties and improved agronomic practices so that more food is produced for every acre of land and drop of water diverted to agriculture. That would help cut back on hunger while reducing pressures on species and biodiversity conservation, and advancing sustainable development.

Focused adaptation measures applicable to coastal flooding include building coastal defenses, developing early warning systems, evacuation plans, and improved building codes. Governments could, moreover, discourage maladaptation by refusing to subsidize insurance or protective measures that allow individuals to offload private risks to the broader public.

Although the FTA indicates that climate change could reduce the total population at risk of water shortage, there are many measures that would help societies cope with present and future water stress regardless of their causes. Among them are institutional reforms to treat water as an economic commodity by allowing market pricing and transferable property rights. Such reforms should stimulate widespread adoption of existing—but underused—conservation technologies and lead to more private-sector investment in R&D, which would reduce the demand for water by all sectors. For example, new or improved crops and techniques for more efficient use of water in agriculture could enhance agricultural productivity. That would provide numerous ancillary benefits, including reductions in the risk of hunger and pressures on freshwater biodiversity while also enhancing the opportunity for other in-stream uses (like recreation). Notably, diversion of water to agricultural uses might be the largest current threat to freshwater biodiversity.

Improvements in water conservation following such reforms are likely to be most pronounced for the agricultural sector, which is responsible for 85% of global water consumption. A reduction of 18% in agricultural water consumption would, on average, double the amount of water available for all other uses.

Remember, though, that developing countries are most at risk of global warming not because they will experience greater climate change, but because they lack the adaptive capacity to cope with its impacts. Hence, another approach to addressing climate change would be to enhance the adaptive capacity of developing countries by promoting broad development—economic development and human capital formation, which, of course, is the point of sustainable economic development. Moreover, since the determinants of adaptive and mitigative capacity largely are the same, enhancing the former also should boost the latter. Perhaps more important, advancing economic development and human capital formation also would advance society's ability to cope with all manner of threats, whether climate related or otherwise.

One approach to estimating the costs and benefits of sustainable economic development is to examine the literature on the UN's Millennium Development Goals (MDGs), which were devised to promote sustainable development in Third World countries. The benefits associated with these goals—halving global poverty, hunger, and the lack of access to safe water and sanitation; reducing child and maternal mortality by 66% or more; providing universal primary education; and reversing growth in malaria, AIDS-HIV, and other major diseases—would exceed the benefits flowing from the deepest mitigation. Yet, according to the UN Millennium Project, the additional annual cost to the richest countries of attaining the MDGs by 2015 is pegged at about 0.5% of their GDP (or $165,000,000,000 annually). That is approximately the same cost as that of the ineffectual—but expensive—Kyoto Protocol.

Sustaining the Economy

Since focused adaptation only would address the climate-sensitive barriers to sustainable economic development (malaria, hunger, water stress, etc.) without necessarily solving other significant problems (poverty, access to safe water and sanitation, illiteracy, child and maternal mortality, etc.), broad pursuit of sustainable economic development would, not surprisingly, deliver greater benefits and probably cost more than focused adaptation.

It sometimes has been argued that it is only fair that present generations expend resources on mitigation now, instead of leaving future generations with a bigger mess and a larger clean-up bill. However, as the data presented clearly demonstrates thus far, well-being tomorrow is best enhanced by adaptation, or sustainable development, or both—not by mitigation. In light of the benefits associated with focused adaptation and sustainable development, the most cost-effective and comprehensive policies to address climate change in the near-to-medium term will eschew direct greenhouse gas emission controls that go beyond "no-regret" policies—that is, policies that would entail no net costs. Instead, policy-makers would be wise to work to enhance adaptation and promote economic development. They should:

- Strengthen or develop the institutions necessary to advance economic growth and reduce barriers to such expansion, human capital, and the propensity for technological change. Doing so would improve adaptive and mitigative capacities, as well as the prospects for sustainable development.
- Implement no-regret mitigation measures now while expanding the range and diversity of future no-regret options. The latter could

be advanced by research and development to improve existing—and develop new—technologies that would reduce atmospheric greenhouse gas concentrations more cost-effectively than currently possible. Should new information indicate that more aggressive mitigation action is necessary, future emission reductions might then be cheaper, even if they have to be deeper to compensate for a delay in a more aggressive response in the short term.

- Allow the market to run its course in implementing no-regret (no-cost) options. Among other things, that implies reducing subsidies that directly or indirectly increase energy use, land clearance, coastal development, and other activities that contribute to greater greenhouse gas emissions or climate change damages. As part of this effort, Organisation for Economic Co-operation and Development (OECD) nations should reduce, if not eliminate, agricultural subsidies and barriers to trade. Not only are such subsidies and barriers expensive for consumers in these nations, they damage the economies and well-being of many developing countries whose economies and employment are dominated by the agricultural sector. Ironically, one of the arguments advanced for rapid reductions in greenhouse gases is that they would help developing countries that are considered to be least able to cope with climate change because they currently lack the necessary economic and human capital to implement adaptive technologies.

- Develop a more robust understanding of the science, impacts, and policies of global warming in order to develop response strategies that would forestall "dangerous" results while at the same time advancing human well-being.

- Monitor climate change to give advance warning of "dangerous" impacts and, if necessary, to rearrange priorities should these adverse impacts occur faster, threaten to be more severe, or are more likely to occur than currently is projected.

Together, these policies constitute an adaptive management approach to addressing climate change that would help solve today's urgent problems while bolstering our ability to address tomorrow's global warming challenge.

POSTSCRIPT

Will Global Warming Negatively Impact Human Health?

Global warming appears to correlate with the rise in disease; increased deaths from heat, flooding, and drought; reduced food supply; and illness and death from severe weather events such as hurricanes and tornados. Rising temperatures may, however, have some advantages for humans. For example, higher winter temperatures would likely mean fewer deaths related to cold in North America and Europe. There would probably be fewer car accidents linked to icy roads. In some areas of the tropics, drier and hotter weather might lower the survival of mosquitoes, which spread disease. Clearly some extremely cold climates may become more hospitable to growing crops and livestock. (See "Climate Change and Human Health: Present and Future Risks," *Lancet,* March 3, 2006.) While there are some potential benefits to global warming, most of its effects would likely be harmful. It appears that all regions of the world would be affected, though the most negative outcomes would likely hit the poorest areas of the tropics and subtropics. Even wealthy countries have experienced health problems likely linked to global warming. A heat wave in Europe during the summer of 2003 killed more than 10,000 in France. Many of those who died were elderly, a group most susceptible to heat-related health concerns.

The summer of 1999 was one of the hottest and driest in the century. During that year, 62 cases of West Nile encephalitis were reported in New York City, causing 7 deaths. The disease appears to spread by mosquitoes that prey on birds. Periods of high heat and drought reduced bird populations, causing the mosquitoes to bite humans instead, triggering the West Nile outbreak. In 2002, West Nile spread across the U.S. and appeared in more than 40 states and 5 Canadian provinces. The disease so far has killed more than 500 Americans and Canadians. In a growing scientific consensus, public health officials are convinced that the next drought will increase the reach of the virus by reducing the population of mosquito predators.

Other diseases that may increase due to global warming include Lyme disease, diarrheal diseases, and hanta virus. Lyme disease, spread by ticks that live on rodents and deer, has migrated to higher latitudes in parts of Europe. During periods of drought, fresh water becomes less available, and outbreaks of diarrhea occur related to poor hygiene. During flooding, diarrheal diseases increase due to the contamination of waterways and drinking water. Higher than average temperatures also are linked to an increase in food poisoning. The hantavirus is also correlated to increased temperatures. The disease, spread by desert mice, has been reported in the U.S. southwest.

The article "Global Warming and Health" discusses the effect of climate change on people's health. Greenhouse gases, according to the article, contribute to global warming, which affects human health in many ways. The most apparent is heat stroke. It adds that climate change may help spread diseases, disrupt sanitation, and limit the supply of fresh water and food production (*Harvard Men's Health Watch*, March 2009). For additional readings on disease and global warming, see the following articles: "Climate Panel Issues Dark Predictions for Effects of Global Warming," *Chronicle of Higher Education*, May 20, 2007; "Too Hot to Handle," *Current Health*, April/May 2007; "Climate Change and Health," *Nursing Ethics*, November 2006; and "Top Scientists Warn of Water Shortages and Disease Linked to Global Warming," *The New York Times*, March 12, 2007.

ISSUE 19

Is Breastfeeding the Best Way to Feed Babies?

YES: **Pat Thomas**, from "Suck on This," *The Ecologist* (May 2006)

NO: **Hanna Rosin**, from "The Case Against Breastfeeding," *The Atlantic* (April 2009)

ISSUE SUMMARY

YES: Author Pat Thomas believes that breastfeeding is the best and healthiest way to feed infants and children and that formula manufacturers are promoting their products at the expense of babies and children.

NO: *The Atlantic* editor Hanna Rosin claims the data on the benefits of breastfeeding are inconclusive and suggests a more relaxed approach to the issue.

Breastfeeding is a means of providing nourishment to a baby or a young child with milk directly from human breasts rather than from a bottle filled with baby formula or artificial milk. Babies have a sucking reflex that allows them to suck and swallow milk.

Most doctors, scientists, and child advocacy groups believe that human milk is the most healthful form of milk for human infants. Breastfeeding promotes health, helps to prevent disease, and reduces health care and feeding costs. In both poor and wealthy nations, bottle-feeding is linked to more deaths from gastroenteritis in infants. Most doctors and scientists concur that breastfeeding is advantageous, but may disagree about the length of breastfeeding that is most valuable and about the safety of using infant formulas.

The World Health Organization (WHO) and the American Academy of Pediatrics (AAP) suggest exclusive breastfeeding for the first 6 months of life and then breastfeeding up to 2 years or more (WHO) or at least 1 year of breastfeeding in total (AAP). There are many benefits to both mother and infant when the child is fed human milk. These benefits include the optimal levels of lipid, carbohydrates, water, and protein that are needed for a baby's growth and development. Breast milk also contains several anti-infective factors to help prevent disease. Although there are obvious physical benefits, two initial studies also suggest some babies average seven IQ points higher if breastfed compared with babies fed cow or soy milk. Breastfeeding also appears to protect against type 1 diabetes, obesity, allergies, and celiac disease and reduce the risk of acquiring urinary tract infections in infants up to 7 months. Breastfeeding appears to decrease symptoms of upper respiratory tract infections in premature infants up to 7 months after release from the hospital. A longer period of breastfeeding is associated with a shorter duration of some middle ear infections in the first 2 years of life.

Although breastfeeding appears to benefit infants, it also positively impacts the health of nursing mothers. A recent study indicates lactation of at least 24 months is correlated with a reduced risk of heart disease, endometrial, breast, and ovarian cancer, and osteoporosis. Women who breastfeed for longer also have less chance of developing rheumatoid arthritis.

Other reasons to breastfeed include the fact that the hormones released during breastfeeding strengthen the bond between mother and infant. Also, the fat stores that build up during pregnancy are used to produce milk, and extended breastfeeding for at least 6 months can help mothers lose weight. However, weight loss is unpredictable among nursing mothers, and diet and exercise are more dependable means of weight loss.

A lactating woman may not ovulate or have regular periods during the entire period she is nursing. The period in which ovulation is absent differs for each woman, although it can be used as an imperfect form of natural contraception, with greater than 98 percent effectiveness during the first 6 months after birth if the mother is regularly breastfeeding. It is likely, however, for some new mothers to ovulate within 2 months after birth while fully breastfeeding.

Although breastfeeding is a natural way of infant feeding, difficulties may occur. There are some situations in which breastfeeding may be harmful to the infant, including infection with the virus that causes AIDS and acute poisoning by environmental contaminants such as DDT and lead. Rarely, a mother may be unable to produce milk because of a deficiency of the hormone prolactin. In developed nations, many mothers do not breastfeed their children due to work pressures. They may need to return to work shortly after giving birth or are not able to regularly feed their babies while on the job. Other factors found to have an effect on breastfeeding are urban/nonurban residence, race, parental education, household income, neighborhood safety, familial support, maternal physical activity, and household smoking status.

Although there are obvious, significant benefits of breastfeeding, many bottle-fed children grow up perfectly healthy. In the YES selection, Pat Thomas argues that the health benefits of breastfeeding are enormous and that formula companies promote their products at the expense of infant health. In the NO selection, *The Atlantic* editor Hanna Rosin discusses inconsistent research data on the benefits of breastfeeding. Rosin, a nursing mother, sees benefits of breastfeeding as far from conclusive and suggests a more relaxed approach to the issue.

YES ↩

Suck on This

The human species has been breastfeeding for nearly half a million years. It's only in the last 60 years that we have begun to give babies the highly processed convenience food called 'formula'. The health consequences—twice the risk of dying in the first six weeks of life, five times the risk of gastroenteritis, twice the risk of developing eczema and diabetes and up to eight times the risk of developing lymphatic cancer—are staggering. With UK formula manufacturers spending around £20 per baby promoting this 'baby junk food', compared to the paltry 14 pence per baby the government spends promoting breastfeeding, can we ever hope to reverse the trend? Pat Thomas uncovers a world where predatory baby milk manufacturers, negligent health professionals and an ignorant, unsympathetic public all conspire to keep babies off the breast and on the bottle.

✌◈✌

All mammals produce milk for their young, and the human species has been nurturing its babies at the breast for at least 400,000 years. For centuries, when a woman could not feed her baby herself, another lactating woman, or 'wet nurse', took over the job. It is only in the last 60 years or so that we have largely abandoned our mammalian instincts and, instead, embraced a bottle-feeding culture that not only encourages mothers to give their babies highly processed infant formulas from birth, but also to believe that these breastmilk substitutes are as good as, if not better than, the real thing.

Infant formulas were never intended to be consumed on the widespread basis that they are today. They were conceived in the late 1800s as a means of providing necessary sustenance for foundlings and orphans who would otherwise have starved. In this narrow context—where no other food was available—formula was a lifesaver.

However, as time went on, and the subject of human nutrition in general—and infant nutrition, in particular—became more 'scientific', manufactured breastmilk substitutes were sold to the general public as a technological improvement on breastmilk.

'If anybody were to ask 'which formula should I use?' or 'which is nearest to mother's milk?', the answer would be 'nobody knows' because there is not one single objective source of that kind of information provided by anybody,' says Mary Smale, a breastfeeding counsellor with the National Childbirth Trust (NCT) for 28 years. 'Only the manufacturers know what's in their stuff, and they aren't telling. They may advertise special 'healthy' ingredients like oligosaccharides, long-chain fatty acids or, a while ago, beta-carotene, but they never actually tell you what the basic product is made from or where the ingredients come from.'

The known constituents of breastmilk were and are used as a general reference for scientists devising infant formulas. But, to this day, there is no actual 'formula' for formula. In fact, the process of producing infant formulas has, since its earliest days, been one of trial and error.

Within reason, manufacturers can put anything they like into formula. In fact, the recipe for one product can vary from batch to batch, according to the price and availability of ingredients. While we assume that formula is heavily regulated, no transparency is required of manufacturers: they do not, for example, have to log the specific constituents of any batch or brand with any authority.

Most commercial formulas are based on cow's milk. But before a baby can drink cow's milk in the form of infant formula, it needs to be severely modified. The protein and mineral content must be reduced and the carbohydrate content increased, usually by adding sugar. Milk fat, which is not easily absorbed by the human body, particularly one with an immature digestive system, is removed and substituted with vegetable, animal or mineral fats.

Vitamins and trace elements are added, but not always in their most easily digestible form. (This means that the claims that formula is 'nutritionally complete' are true, but only in the crudest sense of having had added the full complement of vitamins and mineral to a nutritionally inferior product.)

Many formulas are also highly sweetened. While most infant formulas do not contain sugar in the form of sucrose, they can contain high levels of other types of sugar such as lactose (milk sugar), fructose (fruit sugar), glucose (also known as dextrose, a simple sugar found in plants) and maltodextrose (malt sugar). Because of a loophole in the law, these can still be advertised as 'sucrose free'.

Formula may also contain unintentional contaminants introduced during the manufacturing process. Some may contain traces of genetically engineered soya and corn.

The bacteria *Salmonella* and aflatoxins—potent toxic, carcinogenic, mutagenic, immunosuppressive agents produced by species of the fungus *Aspergillus*—have regularly been detected in commercial formulas, as has *Enterobacter sakazakii*, a devastating foodborne pathogen that can cause sepsis (overwhelming bacterial infection in the bloodstream), meningitis (inflammation of the lining of the brain) and necrotising enterocolitis (severe infection and inflammation of the small intestine and colon) in newborn infants.

The packaging of infant formulas occasionally gives rise to contamination with broken glass and fragments of metal as well as industrial chemicals such as phthalates and bisphenol A (both carcinogens) and, most recently, the packaging constituent isopropyl thioxanthone (ITX; another suspected carcinogen).

Infant formulas may also contain excessive levels of toxic or heavy metals, including aluminum, manganese, cadmium and lead.

Soya formulas are of particular concern due to the very high levels of plant-derived oestrogens (phytoestrogens) they contain. In fact, concentrations of phytoestrogens detected in the blood of infants receiving soya formula can be 13,000 to 22,000 times greater than the concentrations of natural oestrogens. Oestrogen in doses above those normally found in the body can cause cancer.

Killing Babies

For years, it was believed that the risks of illness and death from bottlefeeding were largely confined to children in developing countries, where the clean water necessary to make up formula is sometimes scarce and where poverty-stricken mothers may feel obliged to dilute formula to make it stretch further, thus risking waterborne illnesses such as diarrhoea and cholera as well as malnutrition in their babies. But newer data from the West clearly show that babies in otherwise affluent societies are also falling ill and dying due to an early diet of infant convenience food.

Because it is not nutritionally complete, because it does not contain the immune-boosting properties of breastmilk and because it is being consumed by growing babies with vast, ever-changing nutritional needs—and not meeting those needs—the health effects of sucking down formula day after day early in life can be devastating in both the short and long term.

Bottlefed babies are twice as likely to die from any cause in the first six weeks of life. In particular, bottlefeeding raises the risk of SIDS (sudden infant death syndrome) by two to five times. Bottlefed babies are also at a significantly higher risk of ending up in hospital with a range of infections. They are, for instance, five times more likely to be admitted to hospital suffering from gastroenteritis.

Even in developed countries, bottlefed babies have rates of diarrhoea twice as high as breastfed ones. They are twice as likely (20 per cent vs 10 per cent) to suffer from otitis media (inner-ear infection), twice as likely to develop eczema or a wheeze if there is a family history of atopic disease, and five times more likely to develop urinary tract infections. In the first six months of life, bottlefed babies are six to 10 times more likely to develop necrotising enterocolitis—a serious infection of the intestine, with intestinal tissue death—a figure that increases to 30 times the risk after that time.

Even more serious diseases are also linked with bottlefeeding. Compared with infants who are fully breastfed even for only three to four months, a baby drinking artificial milk is twice as likely to develop juvenile-onset insulin-dependent (type 1) diabetes. There is also a five- to eightfold risk of developing lymphomas in children under 15 who were formulated, or breastfed for less than six months.

In later life, studies have shown that bottlefed babies have a greater tendency towards developing conditions such as childhood inflammatory bowel disease, multiple sclerosis, dental malocclusion, coronary heart disease, diabetes, hyperactivity, autoimmune thyroid disease and coeliac disease.

BREASTMILK VS FORMULA: NO CONTEST

Breastmilk is a 'live' food that contains living cells, hormones, active enzymes, antibodies and at least 400 other unique components. It is a dynamic substance, the composition of which changes from the beginning to the end of the feed and according to the age and needs of the baby. Because it also provides active immunity, every time a baby breastfeeds it also receives protection from disease.

Compared to this miraculous substance, the artificial milk sold as infant formula is little more than junk food. It is also the only manufactured food that humans are encouraged to consume exclusively for a period of months, even though we know that no human body can be expected to stay healthy and thrive on a steady diet of processed food.

Breastmilk	Formula	Comments
Fats		
Rich in brain-building omega-3s, namely, DHA and AA. Automatically adjusts to infant's needs; levels decline as baby gets older. Rich in cholesterol; nearly completely absorbed. Contains the fat-digesting enzyme lipase	No DHA. Doesn't adjust to infant's needs. No cholesterol. Not completely absorbed. No lipase	The most important nutrient in breastmilk; the absence of cholesterol and DHA may predispose a child to adult heart and CNS diseases. Leftover, unabsorbed fat accounts for unpleasant smelling stools in formula-fed babies
Protein		
Soft, easily digestible whey. More completely absorbed; higher in the milk of mothers who deliver preterm. Lactoferrin for intestinal health. Lysozyme, an antimicrobial. Rich in brain- and body-building protein components. Rich in growth factors. Contains sleep-inducing proteins	Harder-to-digest casein curds. Not completely absorbed, so more waste, harder on kidneys. Little or no lactoferrin. No lysozyme. Deficient or low in some brain and body-building proteins. Deficient in growth factors. Contains fewer sleep-inducing proteins	Infants aren't allergic to human milk proteins
Carbohydrates		
Rich in oligosaccharides, which promote intestinal health	No lactose in some formulas. Deficient in oligosaccharides	Lactose is important for brain development
Immune-boosters		
Millions of living white blood cells, in every feeding. Rich in immunoglobulins	No live white blood cells or any other cells. Has no immune benefit	Breastfeeding provides active and dynamic protection from infections of all kinds. Breastmilk can be used to alleviate a range of external health problems such as nappy rash and conjunctivitis

(Continued)

Breastmilk	Formula	Comments
Vitamins & Minerals		
Better absorbed	Not absorbed as well	Nutrients in formula are poorly absorbed. To compensate, more nutrients are added to formula, making it harder to digest
Iron is 50–75 per cent absorbed	Iron is 5–10 per cent absorbed	
Contains more selenium (an antioxidant)	Contains less selenium (an antioxidant)	
Enzymes & Hormones		
Rich in digestive enzymes such as lipase and amylase. Rich in many hormones such as thyroid, prolactin and oxytocin. Taste varies with mother's diet, thus helping the child acclimatise to the cultural diet	Processing kills digestive enzymes. Processing kills hormones, which are not human to begin with. Always tastes the same	Digestive enzymes promote intestinal health; hormones contribute to the biochemical balance and wellbeing of the baby
Cost		
Around £350/year in extra food for mother if she was on a very poor diet to begin with	Around £650/year. Up to £1300/year for hypoallergenic formulas. Cost for bottles and other supplies. Lost income when parents must stay home to care for a sick baby	In the UK, the NHS spends £35 million each year just treating gastroenteritis in bottlefed babies. In the US, insurance companies pay out $3.6 billion for treating diseases in bottlefed babies

For all of these reasons, formula cannot be considered even 'second best' compared with breastmilk. Officially, the World Health Organization (WHO) designates formula milk as the last choice in infant-feeding: Its first choice is breastmilk from the mother; second choice is the mother's own milk given via cup or bottle; third choice is breastmilk from a milk bank or wet nurse and, finally, in fourth place, formula milk.

And yet, breastfed babies are becoming an endangered species. In the UK, rates are catastrophically low and have been that way for decades. Current figures suggest that only 62 per cent of women in Britain even attempt to breastfeed (usually while in hospital). At six weeks, just 42 per cent are breastfeeding. By four months, only 29 per cent are still breastfeeding and, by six months, this figure drops to 22 per cent.

These figures could come from almost any developed country in the world and, it should be noted, do not necessarily reflect the ideal of 'exclusive' breastfeeding. Instead, many modern mothers practice mixed feeding—combining breastfeeding with artificial baby milks and infant foods. Worldwide, the WHO estimates that only 35 per cent of infants are getting any breastmilk at all by age four months and, although no one can say for sure because research into exclusive breastfeeding is both scarce and incomplete, it is estimated that only 1 per cent are exclusively breastfed at six months.

Younger women in particular are the least likely to breastfeed, with over 40 per cent of mothers under 24 never even trying. The biggest gap, however, is a socioeconomic one. Women who live in low-income households or who are poorly educated are many times less likely to breastfeed, even though it can make an enormous difference to a child's health.

In children from socially disadvantaged families, exclusive breastfeeding in the first six months of life can go a long way towards cancelling out the health inequalities between being born into poverty and being born into affluence. In essence, breastfeeding takes the infant out of poverty for those first crucial months and gives it a decent start in life.

So Why Aren't Women Breastfeeding?

Before bottles became the norm, breastfeeding was an activity of daily living based on mimicry, and learning within the family and community. Women became their own experts through the trial and error of the experience itself. But today, what should come more or less naturally has become extraordinarily complicated—the focus of global marketing strategies and politics, lawmaking, lobbying support groups, activists and the interference of a well-intentioned, but occasionally ineffective, cult of experts.

According to Mary Smale, it's confidence and the expectation of support that make the difference, particularly for socially disadvantaged women.

'The concept of 'self efficacy'—in other words, whether you think you can do something—is quite important. You can say to a woman that breastfeeding is really a good idea, but she's got to believe various things in order for it to work. First of all, she has to think it's a good idea—that it will be good for her and her baby. Second, she has to think: 'I'm the sort of person who can do that'; third—and maybe the most important thing—is the belief that if she does have problems, she's the sort of person who, with help, will be able to sort them out.

'Studies show, for example, that women on low incomes often believe that breastfeeding hurts, and they also tend to believe that formula is just as good. So from the start, the motivation to breastfeed simply isn't there. But really, it's the thought that if there were any problems, you couldn't do anything about them; that, for instance, if it hurts, it's just the luck of the draw. This mindset is very different from that of a middle-class mother who is used to asking for help to solve things, who isn't frightened of picking up the phone, or saying to her midwife or health visitor, 'I want you to help me with this'.'

Nearly all women—around 99 per cent—can breastfeed successfully and make enough milk for their babies to not simply grow, but to thrive. With encouragement, support and help, almost all women are willing to initiate breastfeeding, but the drop-off rates are alarming: 90 per cent of women who give up in the first six weeks say that they would like to have continued. And it seems likely that long-term exclusive breastfeeding rates could be improved if consistent support were available, and if approval within the family and the wider community for breastfeeding, both at home and in public, were more obvious and widespread.

Clearly, this social support isn't there, and the bigger picture of breastfeeding vs bottlefeeding suggests that there is, in addition, a confluence of complex factors—medical, socioeconomic, cultural and political—that regularly undermine women's confidence, while reinforcing the notion that feeding their children artificially is about lifestyle rather than health, and that the modern woman's body is simply not up to the task of producing enough milk for its offspring.

'Breastfeeding is a natural negotiation between mother and baby and you interfere with it at your peril,' says Professor Mary Renfrew, Director of the Mother and Infant Research Unit, University of York. But, in the early years of the last century, people were very busy interfering with it. In terms of the ecology of breastfeeding, what you have is a natural habitat that has been disturbed. But it's not just the presence of one big predator—the invention of artificial milk—that is important. It is the fact that the habitat was already weakened by other forces that made it so vulnerable to disaster.

'If you look at medical textbooks from the early part of the 20th century, you'll find many quotes about making breastfeeding scientific and exact, and it's out of these that you can see things beginning to fall apart.' This falling apart, says Renfrew, is largely due to the fear and mistrust that science had of the natural process of breastfeeding. In particular, the fact that a mother can put a baby on the breast and do something else while breastfeeding, and have the baby naturally come off the breast when it's had enough, was seen as disorderly and inexact. The medical/scientific model replaced this natural situation with precise measurements—for instance, how many millilitres of milk a baby should ideally have at each sitting—which skewed the natural balance between mother and baby, and established bottlefeeding as a biological norm.

Breastfeeding rates also began to decline as a consequence of women's changed circumstances after World War I, as more women left their children behind to go into the workplace as a consequence of women's emancipation—and the loss of men in the 'killing fields'—and to an even larger extent with the advent of World War II, when even more women entered into employment outside of the home.

'There was also the first wave of feminism,' says Renfrew, 'which stamped into everyone's consciousness in the 60s, and encouraged women get away from their babies and start living their lives. So the one thing that might have helped—women supporting each other—actually created a situation where even the intellectual, engaged, consciously aware women who might have questioned this got lost for a while. As a consequence, we ended up with a widespread and declining confidence in breastfeeding, a declining understanding of its importance and a declining ability of health professionals to support it. And, of course, all this ran along the same timeline as the technological development of artificial milk and the free availability of formula.'

Medicalised Birth

Before World War II, pregnancy and birth—and, by extension, breastfeeding— were part of the continuum of normal life. Women gave birth at home with the assistance and support of trained midwives, who were themselves part of the community, and afterwards they breastfed with the encouragement of family and friends.

Taking birth out of the community and relocating it into hospitals gave rise to the medicalisation of women's reproductive lives. Life events were transformed into medical problems, and traditional knowledge was replaced with scientific and technological solutions. This medicalisation resulted in a cascade of interventions that deeply undermined women's confidence in their abilities to conceive and grow a healthy baby, give birth to it and then feed it.

The cascade falls something like this: Hospitals are institutions; they are impersonal and, of necessity, must run on schedules and routines. For a hospital to run smoothly, patients must ideally be sedate and immobile. For the woman giving birth, this meant lying on her back in a bed, an unnatural position that made labour slow, unproductive and very much more painful.

To 'fix' these iatrogenically dysfunctional labours, doctors developed a range of drugs (usually synthetic hormones such as prostaglandins or syntocinon), technologies (such as forceps and vacuum extraction) and procedures (such as episiotomies) to speed the process up. Speeding up labour artificially made it even more painful and this, in turn, led to the development of an array of pain-relieving drugs. Many of these were so powerful that the mother was often unconscious or deeply sedated at the moment of delivery and, thus, unable to offer her breast to her newborn infant.

All pain-relieving drugs cross the placenta, so even if the mother were conscious, her baby may not have been, or may have been so heavily drugged that its natural rooting instincts (which help it find the nipple) and muscle coordination (necessary to latch properly onto the breast) were severely impaired.

While both mother and baby were recovering from the ordeal of a medicalised birth, they were, until the 1970s and 1980s, routinely separated. Often, the baby wasn't 'allowed' to breastfeed until it had a bottle first, in case there was something wrong with its gastrointestinal tract. Breastfeeding, when it took place at all, took place according to strict schedules. These feeding schedules—usually on a three- or four-hourly basis—were totally unnatural for human newborns, who need to feed 12 or more times in any 24-hour period. Babies who were inevitably hungry between feeds were routinely given supplements of water and/or formula.

'There was lots of topping up,' says Professor Renfrew. 'The way this 'scientific' breastfeeding happened in hospital was that the baby would be given two minutes on each breast on day one, then four minutes on each breast on day two, seven minutes on each on day three, and so on. This created enormous anxiety since the mother would then be watching the clock instead of the baby. The babies would then get topped-up after every feed, then topped-up again throughout the night rather than brought to their mothers to feed. So you had a situation where the babies were crying in the nursery, and the mothers were crying in the postnatal ward. That's what we called 'normal' all throughout the 60s and 70s.'

Breastmilk is produced on a supply-and-demand basis, and these topping-up routines, which assuaged infant hunger and lessened demand, also reduced the mother's milk supply. As a result, women at the mercy of institutionalised birth experienced breastfeeding as a frustrating struggle that was often painful and just as often unsuccessful.

When, under these impossible circumstances, breastfeeding 'failed', formula was offered as a 'nutritionally complete solution' that was also more 'modern', 'cleaner' and more 'socially acceptable'.

At least two generations of women have been subjected to these kinds of damaging routines and, as a result, many of today's mothers find the concept of breastfeeding strange and unfamiliar, and very often framed as something that can and frequently does not 'take', something they might 'have a go' at but, equally, something that they shouldn't feel too badly about if it doesn't work out.

Professional Failures

The same young doctors, nurses and midwives who were pioneering this medical model of reproduction are now running today's health services. So, perhaps not surprisingly, modern hospitals are, at heart, little different from their predecessors. They may have TVs and CD players, and prettier wallpaper, and the drugs may be more sophisticated, but the basic goals and principles of medicalised birth have changed very little in the last 40 years—and the effect on breastfeeding is still as devastating.

In many cases, the healthcare providers' views on infant-feeding are based on their own, highly personal experiences. Surveys show, for instance, that the most important factor influencing the effectiveness and accuracy of a doctor's breastfeeding advice is whether the doctor herself, or the doctor's wife, had breastfed her children. Likewise, a midwife, nurse or health visitor formulated her own children is unlikely to be an effective advocate for breastfeeding.

More worrying, these professionals can end up perpetuating damaging myths about breastfeeding that facilitate its failure. In some hospitals, women are still advised to limit the amount of time, at first, that a baby sucks on each breast, to 'toughen up' their nipples. Or they are told their babies get all the milk they 'need' in the first 10 minutes and sucking after this time is unnecessary. Some are still told to stick to four-hour feeding schedules. Figures from the UK's Office of National Statistics show that we are still topping babies up. In 2002, nearly 30 per cent of babies in UK hospitals were given supplemental bottles by hospital staff, and nearly 20 per cent of all babies were separated from their mothers at some point while in hospital.

Continued inappropriate advice from medical professionals is one reason why, in 1991, UNICEF started the Baby Friendly Hospital Initiative (BFHI)—a certification system for hospitals meeting certain criteria known to promote successful breastfeeding. These criteria include: training all healthcare staff on how to facilitate breastfeeding; helping mothers start breastfeeding within one hour of birth; giving newborn infants no food or drink other than breastmilk, unless medically indicated; and the hospital not accepting free or heavily discounted formula and supplies. In principle, it is an important step in the promotion of breastfeeding, and studies show that women who give birth in Baby Friendly hospitals do breastfeed for longer.

In Scotland, for example, where around 50 per cent of hospitals are rated Baby Friendly, breastfeeding initiation rates have increased dramatically in recent years. In Cuba, where 49 of the country's 56 hospitals and maternity facilities are Baby Friendly, the rate of exclusive breastfeeding at four months almost tripled in six years—from 25 per cent in 1990 to 72 per cent in 1996. Similar increases have been found in Bangladesh, Brazil and China.

Unfortunately, interest in obtaining BFHI status is not universal. In the UK, only 43 hospitals (representing just 16 per cent of all UK hospitals) have achieved full accreditation—and none are in London. Out of the approximately 16,000 hospitals worldwide that have qualified for the Baby Friendly designation, only 32 are in the US. What's more, while Baby Friendly hospitals achieve a high initiation rate, they cannot guarantee continuation of breastfeeding once the woman is back in the community. Even among women who give birth in Baby Friendly hospitals, the number who exclusively breastfeed for six months is unacceptably low.

The Influence of Advertising

Baby Friendly hospitals face a daunting task in combatting the laissez-faire and general ignorance of health professionals, mothers and the public at large. They are also fighting a difficult battle with an acquiescent media which, through politically correct editorialising aimed at assuaging mothers' guilt if they bottlefeed and, more influentially, through advertising, has helped redefine formula as an acceptable choice.

Although there are now stricter limitations on the advertising of infant formula, for years, manufacturers were able, through advertising and promotion, to define the issue of infant-feeding in both the scientific world (for instance, by providing doctors with growth charts that established the growth patterns of bottlefed babies as the norm) and in its wider social context, reframing perceptions of what is appropriate and what is not.

As a result, in the absence of communities of women talking to each other about pregnancy, birthing and mothering, women's choices today are more directly influenced by commercial leaflets, booklets and advertising than almost anything else.

Baby-milk manufacturers spend countless millions devising marketing strategies that keep their products at the forefront of public consciousness. In the UK, formula companies spend at least £12 million per year on booklets, leaflets and other promotions, often in the guise of 'educational materials'. This works out at approximately £20 per baby born. In contrast, the UK government spends about 14 pence per newborn each year to promote breastfeeding.

It's a pattern of inequity that is repeated throughout the world—and not just in the arena of infant-feeding. The food-industry's global advertising budget is $40 billion, a figure greater than the gross domestic product (GDP) of 70 per cent of the world's nations. For every $1 spent by the WHO on preventing the diseases caused by Western diets, more than $500 is spent by the food industry to promote such diets.

Since they can no longer advertise infant formulas directly to women (for instance, in mother and baby magazines or through direct leafleting), or hand out free samples in hospitals or clinics, manufacturers have started to exploit other outlets, such as mother and baby clubs, and Internet sites that purport to help busy mothers get all the information they need about infant-feeding. They also occasionally rely on subterfuge. Manufacturers are allowed to advertise follow-on milks, suitable for babies over six months, to parents. But, sometimes, these ads feature a picture of a much younger baby, implying the product's suitability for infants.

The impact of these types of promotions should not be underestimated. A 2005 NCT/UNICEF study in the UK determined that one third of British mothers who admitted to seeing formula advertisements in the previous six months believed that infant formula was as good or better than breastmilk. This revelation is all the more surprising since advertising of infant formula to mothers has been banned for many years in several countries, including the UK.

To get around restrictions that prevent direct advertising to parents, manufacturers use a number of psychological strategies that focus on the natural worries that new parents have about the health of their babies. Many of today's formulas, for instance, are conceived and sold as solutions to the 'medical' problems of infants such as lactose intolerance, incomplete digestion and being 'too hungry'—even though many of these problems can be caused by inappropriately giving cow's milk formula in the first place.

The socioeconomic divide among breastfeeding mothers is also exploited by formula manufacturers, as targeting low-income women (with advertising as well as through welfare schemes) has proven very profitable.

When presented with the opportunity to provide their children with the best that science has to offer, many low-income mothers are naturally tempted by formula. This is especially true if they receive free samples, as is still the case in many developing countries.

But the supply-and-demand nature of breastmilk is such that, once a mother accepts these free samples and starts her baby on formula, her own milk supply will quickly dry up. Sadly, after these mothers run out of formula samples and money-off coupons, they will find themselves unable to produce breastmilk and have no option but to spend large sums of money on continuing to feed their child with formula.

Even when manufacturers 'promote' breastfeeding, they plant what Mary Smale calls 'seeds of 'conditionality' that can lead to failure.' Several years ago, manufacturers used to produce these amazing leaflets for women, encouraging women to breastfeed and reassuring them that they only need a few extra calories a day. You couldn't fault them on the words, but the pictures which were of things like Marks & Spencer yoghurt and whole fish with their heads on, and wholemeal bread—but not the sort of wholemeal bread that you buy in the corner shop, the sort of wholemeal bread you buy in specialist shops.

The underlying message was clear: a healthy pregnancy and a good supply of breastmilk are the preserve of the middle classes, and that any women who doesn't belong to that group will have to rely on other resources to provide for her baby.

A quick skim through any pregnancy magazine or the 'Bounty' pack—the glossy information booklet with free product samples given to new mothers in the UK—shows that these subtle visual messages, which include luxurious photos of whole grains and pulses, artistically arranged bowls of muesli, artisan loaves of bread and wedges of deli-style cheeses, exotic mangoes, grapes and kiwis, and fresh vegetables artistically arranged as crudités, are still prevalent.

Funding Research

Manufacturers also ply their influence through contact with health professionals (to whom they can provide free samples for research and 'educational purposes') as middlemen. Free gifts, educational trips to exotic locations and funding for research are just some of the ways in which the medical profession becomes 'educated' about the benefits of formula.

According to Patti Rundall, OBE, policy director for the UK's Baby Milk Action group, which has been lobbying for responsible marketing of baby food for over 20 years, 'Throughout the last two decades, the baby-feeding companies have tried to establish a strong role for themselves with the medical profession, knowing that health and education services represent a key marketing opportunity. Companies are, for instance, keen to fund the infant-feeding research on which health policies are based, and to pay for midwives, teachers, education materials and community projects.'

They are also keen to fund 'critical' NGOs—that is, lay groups whose mandate is to inform and support women. But this sort of funding is not allowed by the International Code of Marketing of Breastmilk Substitutes (see below) because it prejudices the ability of these organisations to provide mothers with independent information about infant feeding. Nevertheless, such practices remain prevalent—if somewhat more discreet than in the past—and continue to weaken health professionals' advocacy for breastfeeding.

Fighting Back

When it became clear that declining breastfeeding rates were affecting infant health and that the advertising of infant formula had a direct effect on a woman's decision not to breastfeed, the International Code of Marketing of Breastmilk Substitutes was drafted and eventually adopted by the World Health Assembly (WHA) in 1981. The vote was near-unanimous, with 118 member nations voting in favour, three abstaining and one—the US—voting against. (In 1994, after years of opposition, the US eventually joined every other developed nation in the world as a signatory to the Code.)

The Code is a unique instrument that promotes safe and adequate nutrition for infants on a global scale by trying to protect breastfeeding and ensuring the appropriate marketing of breastmilk substitutes. It applies to all products marketed as partial or total replacements for breastmilk, including infant formula, follow-on formula, special formulas, cereals, juices, vegetable mixes and baby teas, and also applies to feeding bottles and teats. In addition, it maintains that no infant food may be marketed in ways that undermine breastfeeding. Specifically, the Code:

- Bans all advertising or promotion of these products to the general public
- Bans samples and gifts to mothers and health workers
- Requires information materials to advocate for breastfeeding, to warn against bottlefeeding and to not contain pictures of babies or text that idealises the use of breastmilk substitutes
- Bans the use of the healthcare system to promote breastmilk substitutes
- Bans free or low-cost supplies of breastmilk substitutes
- Allows health professionals to receive samples, but only for research purposes
- Demands that product information be factual and scientific
- Bans sales incentives for breastmilk substitutes and direct contact with mothers
- Requires that labels inform fully on the correct use of infant formula and the risks of misuse
- Requires labels not to discourage breastfeeding.

This document probably couldn't have been created today. Since the founding of the World Trade Organization (WTO) and its 'free trade' ethos in 1995, the increasing sophistication of corporate power strategies and aggressive lobbying of health organisations has increased to the extent that the Code would have been binned long before it reached the voting stage.

However, in 1981, member states, corporations and NGOs were on a somewhat more equal footing. By preventing industry from advertising infant formula, giving out free samples, promoting their products in healthcare facilities or by way of mother-and-baby 'goody bags', and insisting on better labelling, the Code acts to regulate an industry that would otherwise be given a free hand to peddle an inferior food product to babies and infants.

Unfortunately . . .

Being a signatory to the Code does not mean that member countries are obliged to adopt its recommendations wholesale. Many countries, the UK included, have adopted only parts of it—for instance, the basic principle that breastfeeding is a good thing—while ignoring the nuts-and-bolts strategies that limit advertising and corporate contact with mothers. So, in the UK, infant formula for 'healthy babies' can be advertised to mothers through hospitals and clinics, though not via the media.

What's more, formula manufacturers for their part continue to argue that the Code is too restrictive and that it stops them from fully exploiting their target markets. Indeed, Helmut Maucher, a powerful corporate lobbyist and honorary chairman of Nestlé—the company that claims 40 per cent of the global baby-food market—has gone on record as saying: 'Ethical decisions that injure a firm's ability to compete are actually immoral.'

And make no mistake, these markets are big. The UK baby milk market is worth £150 million per year and the US market around $2 billion. The worldwide market for baby milks and foods is a staggering $17 billion and growing by 12 per cent each year. From formula manufacturers' point of view, the more women breastfeed, the more profit is lost. It is estimated that, for every child exclusively breastfed for six months, an average of $450 worth of infant food will not be bought. On a global scale, that amounts to billions of dollars in lost profits.

What particularly worries manufacturers is that, if they accept the Code without a fight, it could set a dangerous precedent for other areas of international trade—for instance, the pharmaceutical, tobacco, food and agriculture industries, and oil companies. This is why the focus on infant-feeding has been diverted away from children's health and instead become a symbolic struggle for a free market.

While most manufacturers publicly agree to adhere to the Code, privately, they deploy enormous resources in constructing ways to reinterpret or get round it. In this endeavour, Nestlé has shown a defiance and tenacity that beggars belief.

In India, for example, Nestlé lobbied against the Code being entered into law and when, after the law was passed, it faced criminal charges over its labelling, it issued a writ petition against the Indian government rather than accept the charges.

Years of aggressive actions like this, combined with unethical advertising and marketing practices, has led to an ongoing campaign to boycott the company's products that stretches back to 1977.

The Achilles' heel of the Code is that it does not provide for a monitoring office. This concept was in the original draft, but was removed from subsequent drafts. Instead, monitoring of the Code has been left to 'governments acting individually and collectively through the World Health Organization'.

But, over the last 25 years, corporate accountability has slipped lower down on the UN agenda, far behind free trade, self-regulation and partnerships. Lack of government monitoring means that small and comparatively poorly funded groups like the International Baby Food Action Network (IBFAN), which has 200 member groups working in over 100 countries, have taken on the job of monitoring Code violations almost by default. But while these watchdog groups can monitor and report Code violations to the health authorities, they cannot stop them.

In 2004, IBFAN's bi-annual report *Breaking the Rules, Stretching the Rules*, analysed the promotional practices of 16 international baby-food companies, and 14 bottle and teat companies, between January 2002 and April 2004. The researchers found some 2,000 violations of the Code in 69 countries.

On a global scale, reinterpreting the Code to suit marketing strategies is rife, and Nestlé continues to be the leader of the pack. According to IBFAN, Nestlé believes that only one of its products—infant formula—comes within the scope of the Code. The company also denies the universality of the Code, insisting that it only applies to developing nations. Where Nestlé, and the Infant Food Manufacturers Association that it dominates, leads, other companies have followed, and when companies like Nestlé are caught breaking the Code, the strategy is simple, but effective—initiate complex and boring discussions with organisations at WHO or WHA level about how best to interpret the Code in the hopes that these will offset any bad publicity and divert attention from the harm caused by these continual infractions.

According to Patti Rundall, it's important not to let such distractions divert attention from the bottom line: 'There can be no food more locally produced, more sustainable or more environmentally friendly than a mother's breastmilk, the only food required by an infant for the first six months of life. It is a naturally renewable resource, which requires no packaging or transport, results in no wastage and is free. Breastfeeding can also help reduce family poverty, which is a major cause of malnutrition.'

So perhaps we should be further simplifying the debate by asking: Are the companies who promote infant formula as the norm simply clever entrepreneurs doing their jobs or human-rights violators of the worst kind?

Not Good Enough

After more than two decades, it is clear that a half-hearted advocacy of breastfeeding benefits multinational formula manufacturers, not mothers and babies, and that the baby-food industry has no intention of complying with UN recommendations on infant-feeding or with the principles of the International Code for Marketing of Breastmilk Substitutes—unless they are forced to do so by law or consumer pressure or, more effectively, both.

Women do not fail to breastfeed. Health professionals, health agencies and governments fail to educate and support women who want to breastfeed.

Without support, many women will give up when they encounter even small difficulties. And yet, according to Mary Renfrew, 'Giving up breastfeeding is not something that women do lightly. They don't just stop breastfeeding and walk away from it. Many of them fight very hard to continue it and they fight with no support. These women are fighting society—a society that is not just bottle-friendly, but is deeply breastfeeding-unfriendly.'

To reverse this trend, governments all over the world must begin to take seriously the responsibility of ensuring the good health of future generations. To do this requires deep and profound social change. We must stop harassing mothers with simplistic 'breast is best' messages and put time, energy and money into reeducating health professionals and society at large.

We must also stop making compromises. Government health policies such as, say, in the UK and US, which aim for 75 per cent of women to be breastfeeding on hospital discharge, are little more than paying lip service to the importance of breastfeeding.

Most of these women will stop breastfeeding within a few weeks, and such policies benefit no one except the formula manufacturers, who will start making money the moment breastfeeding stops.

To get all mothers breastfeeding, we must be prepared to:

- Ban all advertising of formula including follow-on milks
- Ban all free samples of formula, even those given for educational or study purposes

- Require truthful and prominent health warnings on all tins and cartons of infant formula
- Put substantial funding into promoting breastfeeding in every community, especially among the socially disadvantaged, with a view to achieving 100-per-cent exclusive breastfeeding for the first six months of life
- Fund advertising and education campaigns that target fathers, mothers-in-law, schoolchildren, doctors, midwives and the general public
- Give women who wish to breastfeed in public the necessary encouragement and approval
- Make provisions for all women who are in employment to take at least six months paid leave after birth, without fear of losing their jobs.

Such strategies have already proven their worth elsewhere. In 1970, breast-feeding rates in Scandinavia were as low as those in Britain. Then, one by one, the Scandinavian countries banned all advertising of artificial formula milk, offered a year's maternity leave with 80 per cent of pay and, on the mother's return to work, an hour's breastfeeding break every day. Today, 98 per cent of Scandinavian women initiate breastfeeding, and 94 per cent are still breastfeeding at one month, 81 per cent at two months, 69 per cent at four months and 42 per cent at six months. These rates, albeit still not optimal, are nevertheless the highest in the world, and the result of a concerted, multifaceted approach to promoting breastfeeding.

Given all that we know of the benefits of breastfeeding and the dangers of formula milk, it is simply not acceptable that we have allowed breastfeeding rates in the UK and elsewhere in the world to decline so disastrously.

The goal is clear—100 per cent of mothers should be exclusively breast-feeding for at least the first six months of their babies' lives.

Hanna Rosin　　　　　　　　　　　　　　　　　　➡ **NO**

The Case Against Breast-Feeding

One afternoon at the playground last summer, shortly after the birth of my third child, I made the mistake of idly musing about breast-feeding to a group of new mothers I'd just met. This time around, I said, I was considering cutting it off after a month or so. At this remark, the air of insta-friendship we had established cooled into an icy politeness, and the mothers shortly wandered away to chase little Emma or Liam onto the slide. Just to be perverse, over the next few weeks I tried this experiment again several more times. The reaction was always the same: circles were redrawn such that I ended up in the class of mom who, in a pinch, might feed her baby mashed-up Chicken McNuggets.

In my playground set, the urban moms in their tight jeans and over-size sunglasses size each other up using a whole range of signifiers: organic content of snacks, sleekness of stroller, ratio of tasteful wooden toys to plastic. But breast-feeding is the real ticket into the club. My mother friends love to exchange stories about subversive ways they used to sneak frozen breast milk through airline security (it's now legal), or about the random brutes on the street who don't approve of breast-feeding in public. When Angelina Jolie wanted to secure her status as America's ur-mother, she posed on the cover of *W* magazine nursing one of her twins. Alt-rocker Pete Wentz recently admitted that he tasted his wife, Ashlee Simpson's, breast milk ("soury" and "weird"), after bragging that they have a lot of sex—both of which must have seemed to him markers of a cool domestic existence.

From the moment a new mother enters the obstetrician's waiting room, she is subjected to the upper-class parents' jingle: "Breast Is Best." Parenting magazines offer "23 Great Nursing Tips," warnings on "Nursing Roadblocks," and advice on how to find your local lactation consultant (note to the childless: yes, this is an actual profession, and it's thriving). Many of the stories are accompanied by suggestions from the ubiquitous parenting guru Dr. William Sears, whose Web site hosts a comprehensive list of the benefits of mother's milk. "Brighter Brains" sits at the top: "I.Q. scores averaging seven to ten points higher!" (Sears knows his audience well.) The list then moves on to the dangers averted, from infancy on up: fewer ear infections, allergies, stomach illnesses; lower rates of obesity, diabetes, heart disease. Then it adds, for good measure, stool with a "buttermilk-like odor" and "nicer skin"—benefits, in short, "more far-reaching than researchers have even dared to imagine."

In 2005, *Babytalk* magazine won a National Magazine Award for an article called "You *Can* Breastfeed." Given the prestige of the award, I had hoped the article might provide some respite from the relentlessly cheerful tip culture of the parenting magazines, and fill mothers in on the real problems with nursing. Indeed, the article opens with a promisingly realistic vignette, featuring a theoretical "You" cracking under the strain of having to breast-feed around the clock, suffering "crying jags" and cursing at your husband. But fear not, You. The root of the problem is not the sudden realization that your ideal of an equal marriage, with two parents happily taking turns working and raising children, now seems like a farce. It turns out to be quite simple: You just haven't quite figured out how to fit "Part A into Part B." Try the "C-hold" with your baby and some "rapid arm movement," the story suggests. Even Dr. Sears pitches in: "Think 'fish lips,'" he offers.

In the days after my first child was born, I welcomed such practical advice. I remember the midwife coming to my hospital bed and shifting my arm here, and the baby's head there, and then everything falling into place. But after three children and 28 months of breast-feeding (and counting), the insistent cheerleading has begun to grate. Buttermilk-like odor? Now Dr. Sears is selling me too hard. I may have put in fewer parenting years than he has, but I do have *some* perspective. And when I look around my daughter's second-grade class, I can't seem to pick out the unfortunate ones: "Oh, poor little Sophie, whose mother couldn't breast-feed. What dim eyes she has. What a sickly pallor. And already sprouting acne!"

I dutifully breast-fed each of my first two children for the full year that the American Academy of Pediatrics recommends. I have experienced what the *Babytalk* story calls breast-feeding-induced "maternal nirvana." This time around, *nirvana* did not describe my state of mind; I was launching a new Web site and I had two other children to care for, and a husband I would occasionally like to talk to. Being stuck at home breast-feeding as he walked out the door for work just made me unreasonably furious, at him and everyone else.

In Betty Friedan's day, feminists felt shackled to domesticity by the unreasonably high bar for housework, the endless dusting and shopping and pushing the Hoover around—a vacuum cleaner being the obligatory prop for the "happy housewife heroine," as Friedan sardonically called her. When I looked at the picture on the cover of Sears's *Breastfeeding Book*—a lady lying down, gently smiling at her baby and *still in her robe*, although the sun is well up—the scales fell from my eyes: it was not the vacuum that was keeping me and my 21st-century sisters down, but another sucking sound.

Still, despite my stint as the postpartum playground crank, I could not bring myself to stop breast-feeding—too many years of Sears's conditioning, too many playground spies. So I was left feeling trapped, like many women before me, in the middle-class mother's prison of vague discontent: surly but too privileged for pity, breast-feeding with one hand while answering the cell phone with the other, and barking at my older kids to get their own organic, 100 percent juice—the modern, multitasking mother's version of Friedan's "problem that has no name."

And in this prison I would have stayed, if not for a chance sighting. One day, while nursing my baby in my pediatrician's office, I noticed a 2001 issue of the *Journal of the American Medical Association* open to an article about breast-feeding: "Conclusions: There are inconsistent associations among breastfeeding, its duration, and the risk of being overweight in young children." Inconsistent? There I was, sitting half-naked in public for the tenth time that day, the hundredth time that month, the millionth time in my life—and the associations were *inconsistent*? The seed was planted. That night, I did what any sleep-deprived, slightly paranoid mother of a newborn would do. I called my doctor friend for her password to an online medical library, and then sat up and read dozens of studies examining breast-feeding's association with allergies, obesity, leukemia, mother-infant bonding, intelligence, and all the Dr. Sears highlights.

After a couple of hours, the basic pattern became obvious: the medical literature looks nothing like the popular literature. It shows that breast-feeding is probably, maybe, a *little* better; but it is far from the stampede of evidence that Sears describes. More like tiny, unsure baby steps: two forward, two back, with much meandering and bumping into walls. A couple of studies will show fewer allergies, and then the next one will turn up no difference. Same with mother-infant bonding, IQ, leukemia, cholesterol, diabetes. Even where consensus is mounting, the meta studies—reviews of existing studies—consistently complain about biases, missing evidence, and other major flaws in study design. "The studies do not demonstrate a universal phenomenon, in which one method is superior to another in all instances," concluded one of the first, and still one of the broadest, meta studies, in a 1984 issue of *Pediatrics*, "and they do not support making a mother feel that she is doing psychological harm to her child if she is unable or unwilling to breastfeed." Twenty-five years later, the picture hasn't changed all that much. So how is it that every mother I know has become a breast-feeding fascist?

Like many babies of my generation, I was never breast-fed. My parents were working-class Israelis, living in Tel Aviv in the '70s and aspiring to be modern. In the U.S., people were already souring on formula and passing out No NESTLÉ buttons, but in Israel, Nestlé formula was the latest thing. My mother had already ditched her fussy Turkish coffee for Nescafé (just mix with water), and her younger sister would soon be addicted to NesQuik. Transforming soft, sandy grains from solid to magic liquid must have seemed like the forward thing to do. Plus, my mom believed her pediatrician when he said that it was important to precisely measure a baby's food intake and stick to a schedule. (To this day she pesters me about whether I'm *sure* my breast-fed babies are getting enough to eat; the parenting magazines would classify her as "unsupportive" and warn me to stay away.) Formula grew out of a late-19th-century effort to combat atrocious rates of infant mortality by turning infant feeding into a controlled science. Pediatrics was then a newly minted profession, and for the next century, the men who dominated it would constantly try to get mothers to welcome "enlightenment from the laboratory," writes Ann Hulbert in *Raising America*. But now and again, mothers would fight back. In the U.S., the rebellion against formula began in the late '50s, when a group of moms from the Chicago suburbs got together to form a breast-feeding support group they called La Leche League. They were Catholic mothers, influenced by the Christian Family Movement, who spoke of breast-feeding as "God's plan for mothers and babies." Their role model was the biblical Eve ("Her baby came. The milk came. She nursed her baby," they wrote in their first, pamphlet edition of *The Womanly Art of Breastfeeding*, published in 1958).

They took their league's name, La Leche, from a shrine to the Madonna near Jacksonville, Florida, called Nuestra Señora de La Leche y Buen Parto, which loosely translates into "Our Lady of Happy Delivery and Plentiful Milk." A more forthright name was deemed inappropriate: "You didn't mention *breast* in print unless you were talking about Jean Harlow," said co-founder Edwina Froehlich. In their photos, the women of La Leche wear practical pumps and high-neck housewife dresses, buttoned to the top. They saw themselves as a group of women who were "kind of thinking crazy," said co-founder Mary Ann Cahill. "Everything we did was radical."

La Leche League mothers rebelled against the notion of mother as lab assistant, mixing formula for the specimen under her care. Instead, they aimed to "bring mother and baby together again." An illustration in the second edition shows a woman named Eve—looking not unlike Jean Harlow—exposed to the waist and caressing her baby, with no doctor hovering nearby. Over time the group adopted a feminist edge. A 1972 publication rallies mothers to have "confidence in themselves and their sisters rather than passively following the advice of licensed professionals." As one woman wrote in another league publication, "Yes, I want to be liberated! I want to be free! I want to be free to be a woman!"

In 1971, the Boston Women's Health Book Collective published *Our Bodies, Ourselves*, launching a branch of feminism known as the women's-health movement. The authors were more groovy types than the La Leche League moms; they wore slouchy jeans, clogs, and bandanas holding back waist-length hair. But the two movements had something in common; *Our Bodies* also grew out of "frustration and anger" with a medical establishment that was "condescending, paternalistic, judgmental and non-informative." Teaching women about their own bodies would make them "more self-confident, more autonomous, stronger," the authors wrote. Breasts were not things for men to whistle and wink at; they were made for women to feed their babies in a way that was "sensual and fulfilling." The book also noted, in passing, that breast-feeding could "strengthen the infant's resistance to infection and disease"—an early hint of what would soon become the national obsession with breast milk as liquid vaccine.

Pediatricians have been scrutinizing breast milk since the late 1800s. But the public didn't pay much attention until an international scandal in the '70s over "killer baby bottles." Studies in South America and Africa showed that babies who were fed formula instead of breast milk were more likely to die. The mothers, it turned out, were using contaminated water or rationing formula because it was so expensive. Still, in the U.S., the whole episode turned breast-feeding advocates and formula makers into Crips and Bloods, and introduced the take-no-prisoners turf war between them that continues to this day.

Some of the magical thinking about breast-feeding stems from a common misconception. Even many doctors believe that breast milk is full of maternal antibodies that get absorbed into the baby's bloodstream, says Sydney Spiesel, a clinical professor of pediatrics at Yale University's School of Medicine. That is how it works for most mammals. But in humans, the process is more pedestrian, and less powerful. A human baby is born with antibodies already in place, having absorbed them from the placenta. Breast milk dumps another layer of antibodies, primarily secretory IgA, directly into the baby's gastrointestinal tract. As the baby is nursing, these extra antibodies provide some added protection against infection, but they never get into the blood.

Since the identification of sIgA, in 1961, labs have hunted for other marvels. Could the oligosaccharides in milk prevent diarrhea? Do the fatty acids boost brain development? The past few decades have turned up many promising leads, hypotheses, and theories, all suggestive and nifty but never confirmed in the lab. Instead, most of the claims about breast-feeding's benefits lean on research conducted outside the lab: comparing one group of infants being breast-fed against another being breast-fed less, or not at all. Thousands of such studies have been published, linking breast-feeding with healthier, happier, smarter children. But they all share one glaring flaw.

An ideal study would randomly divide a group of mothers, tell one half to breast-feed and the other not to, and then measure the outcomes. But researchers cannot ethically tell mothers what to feed their babies. Instead they have to settle for "observational" studies. These simply look for differences in two populations, one breast-fed and one not. The problem is, breast-fed infants are typically brought up in very different families from those raised on the bottle. In the U.S., breast-feeding is on the rise—69 percent of mothers initiate the practice at the hospital, and 17 percent nurse exclusively for at least six months. But the numbers are much higher among women who are white, older, and educated; a woman who attended college, for instance, is roughly twice as likely to nurse for six months. Researchers try to factor out all these "confounding variables" that might affect the babies' health and development. But they still can't know if they've missed some critical factor. "Studies about the benefits of breast-feeding are extremely difficult and complex because of who breast-feeds and who doesn't," says Michael Kramer, a highly respected researcher at McGill University. "There have been claims that it prevents everything—cancer, diabetes. A reasonable person would be cautious about every new amazing discovery."

The study about obesity I saw in my pediatrician's office that morning is a good example of the complexity of breast-feeding research—and of the pitfalls it contains. Some studies have found a link between nursing and slimmer kids, but they haven't proved that one causes the other. This study surveyed 2,685 children between the ages of 3 and 5. After adjusting for race, parental education, maternal smoking, and other factors—all of which are thought to affect a child's risk of obesity—the study found little correlation between breast-feeding and weight. Instead, the strongest predictor of the child's weight was the mother's. Whether obese mothers nursed or used formula, their children were more likely to be heavy. The breast-feeding advocates' dream—that something in the milk somehow reprograms appetite—is still a long shot.

In the past decade, researchers have come up with ever more elaborate ways to tease out the truth. One 2005 paper focused on 523 sibling pairs who were fed differently, and its results put a big question mark over all the previous research. The economists Eirik Evenhouse and Siobhan Reilly compared rates of diabetes, asthma, and allergies; childhood weight; various measures of mother-child bonding; and levels of intelligence. Almost all the differences turned out to be statistically insignificant. For the most part, the "long-term effects of breast feeding have been overstated," they wrote.

Nearly all the researchers I talked to pointed me to a series of studies designed by Kramer, published starting in 2001. Kramer followed 17,000 infants born in Belarus throughout their childhoods. He came up with a clever way to randomize his study, at least somewhat, without doing anything unethical. He took mothers who had already started nursing, and then subjected half of them to an intervention strongly encouraging them to nurse exclusively for several months. The intervention worked: many women nursed longer as a result. And extended breast-feeding did reduce the risk of a gastrointestinal infection by 40 percent. This result seems to be consistent with the protection that sIgA provides; in real life, it adds up to about four out of 100 babies having one less incident of diarrhea or vomiting. Kramer also noted some reduction in infant rashes. Otherwise, his studies found very few significant differences: none, for instance, in weight, blood pressure, ear infections, or allergies—some of the most commonly cited benefits in the breast-feeding literature.

Both the Kramer study and the sibling study did turn up one interesting finding: a bump in "cognitive ability" among breast-fed children. But intelligence is tricky to measure, because it's subjective and affected by so many factors. Other recent studies, particularly those that have factored out the mother's IQ, have found no difference at all between breast-fed and formula-fed babies. In Kramer's study, the mean scores varied widely and mysteriously from clinic to clinic. What's more, the connection he found "could be banal," he told me—simply the result of "breast-feeding mothers' interacting more with their babies, rather than of anything in the milk."

The IQ studies run into the central problem of breast-feeding research: it is impossible to separate a mother's decision to breast-feed—and everything that goes along with it—from the breast-feeding itself. Even sibling studies can't get around this problem. With her first child, for instance, a mother may be extra cautious, keeping the neighbor's germy brats away and slapping the nurse who gives out the free formula sample. By her third child, she may no longer breast-feed—giving researchers the sibling comparison that they crave—but many other things may have changed as well. Maybe she is now using day care, exposing the baby to more illnesses. Surely she is not noticing that kid No. 2 has the baby's pacifier in his mouth, or that the cat is sleeping in the crib (trust me on this one). She is also not staring lovingly into the baby's eyes all day, singing songs, reading book after infant book, because she has to make sure that the other two kids are not drowning each other in the tub. On paper, the three siblings are equivalent, but their experiences are not.

What does all the evidence add up to? We have clear indications that breast-feeding helps prevent an extra incident of gastrointestinal illness in some kids—an unpleasant few days of diarrhea or vomiting, but rarely life-threatening in developed countries. We have murky correlations with a whole bunch of long-term conditions. The evidence on IQs is intriguing but not all that compelling, and at best suggests a small advantage, perhaps five points; an individual kid's IQ score can vary that much from test to test or day to day. If a child is disadvantaged in other ways, this bump might make a difference. But for the kids in my playground set, the ones whose mothers obsess about breast-feeding, it gets lost in a wash of Baby Einstein videos, piano lessons, and the rest. And in any case, if a breast-feeding mother is miserable, or stressed out, or alienated by nursing, as many women are, if her marriage is under stress and breast-feeding is making things worse, surely that can have a greater effect on a kid's future success than a few IQ points.

So overall, yes, breast is probably best. But not so much better that formula deserves the label of "public health menace," alongside smoking. Given what we know so far, it seems reasonable to put breast-feeding's health benefits on the plus side of the ledger and other things—modesty, independence, career, sanity—on the minus side, and then tally them up and make a decision. But in this risk-averse age of parenting, that's not how it's done.

In the early '90s, a group of researchers got together to revise the American Academy of Pediatrics' policy statement on breast-feeding. They were of the generation that had fought the formula wars and had lived through the days when maternity wards automatically gave women hormone shots to stop the flow of breast milk. The academy had long encouraged mothers to make "every effort" to nurse their newborns, but the researchers felt the medical evidence justified a stronger statement. Released in 1997, the new policy recommended exclusive breast-feeding for six months, followed by six more months of partial breast-feeding, supplemented with other foods. The National Organization for Women complained that this would tax working mothers, but to no avail. "The fact that the major pediatric group in the country was taking a definitive stance made all the difference," recalls Lawrence Gartner, a pediatrician and neonatologist at the University of Chicago, and the head of the committee that made the change. "After that, every major organization turned the corner, and the popular media changed radically."

In 2004, the Department of Health and Human Services launched the National Breastfeeding Awareness Campaign. The ads came out just after my second child was born, and were so odious that they nearly caused me to wean him on the spot. One television ad shows two hugely pregnant women in a logrolling contest, with an audience egging them on. "You wouldn't take risks before your baby is born," reads the caption. "Why start after?" The screen then flashes: "Breastfeed exclusively for 6 months." A second spot shows a pregnant woman—this time African American—riding a mechanical bull in a bar while trying to hold on to her huge belly. She falls off the bull and the crowd moans.

To convey the idea that failing to breast-feed is harmful to a baby's health, the print ads show ordinary objects arranged to look like breasts: two dandelions (respiratory illness), two scoops of ice cream with cherries on top (obesity), two otoscopes (ear infections). Plans were made to do another ad showing rubber nipples on top of insulin syringes (suggesting that bottle-feeding causes diabetes), but then someone thought better of it. The whole campaign is so knowing, so dripping with sexual innuendo and condescension, that it brings to mind nothing so much as an episode of *Mad Men*, where Don Draper and the boys break out the whiskey at day's end to toast another victory over the enemy sex.

What's most amazing is how, 50 years after La Leche League's founding, "enlightenment from the laboratory"—judgmental and absolutist—has triumphed again. The seventh edition of *The Womanly Art*, published in 2004, has ballooned to more than 400 pages, and is filled with photographs in place of the original hand drawings. But what's most noticeable is the shift in attitude. Each edition of the book contains new expert testimony about breast milk as an "arsenal against illness." "The resistance to disease that human milk affords a baby cannot be duplicated in any other way," the authors scold. The experience of reading the 1958 edition is like talking with your bossy but charming neighbor, who has some motherly advice to share. Reading the latest edition is like being trapped in the office of a doctor who's haranguing you about the choices you make.

In her critique of the awareness campaign, Joan Wolf, a women's-studies professor at Texas A&M University, chalks up the overzealous ads to a new ethic of "total motherhood." Mothers these days are expected to "optimize every dimension of children's lives," she writes. Choices are often presented as the mother's selfish desires versus the baby's needs. As an example, Wolf quotes *What to Expect When You're Expecting*, from a section called the "Best-Odds Diet," which I remember quite well: "Every bite counts. You've got only nine months of meals and snacks with which to give your baby the best possible start in life. . . . Before you close your mouth on a forkful of food, consider, 'Is this the best bite I can give my baby?' If it will benefit your baby, chew away. If it'll only benefit your sweet tooth or appease your appetite put your fork down." To which any self-respecting pregnant woman should respond: "I am carrying 35 extra pounds and my ankles have swelled to the size of a life raft, and now I would like to eat some coconut-cream pie. So you know what you can do with this damned fork."

About seven years ago, I met a woman from Montreal, the sister-in-law of a friend, who was young and healthy and normal in every way, except that she refused to breast-feed her children. She wasn't working at the time. She just felt that breast-feeding would set up an unequal dynamic in her marriage—one in which the mother, who was responsible for the very sustenance of the infant, would naturally become responsible for everything else as well. At the time, I had only one young child, so I thought she was a kooky Canadian—and selfish and irresponsible. But of course now I know she was right. I recalled her with sisterly love a few months ago, at three in the morning, when I was propped up in bed for the second time that night with my new baby (note the *my*). My husband acknowledged the ripple in the nighttime peace with a grunt, and that's about it. And why should he do more? There's no use in both of us being a wreck in the morning. Nonetheless, it's hard not to seethe.

The Bitch in the House, published in 2002, reframed *The Feminine Mystique* for my generation of mothers. We were raised to expect that co-parenting was an attainable goal. But who were we kidding? Even in the best of marriages, the domestic burden shifts, in incremental, mostly unacknowledged ways, onto the woman. Breast-feeding plays a central role in the shift. In my set, no husband tells his wife that it is her womanly duty to stay home and nurse the child. Instead, both parents together weigh the evidence and then make a rational, informed decision that she should do so. Then other, logical decisions follow: she alone fed the child, so she naturally knows better how to comfort the child, so she is the better judge to pick a school for the child and the better nurse when the child is sick, and so on. Recently, my husband and I noticed that we had reached the age at which friends from high school and college now hold positions of serious power. When we went down the list, we had to work hard to find any women. Where had all our female friends strayed? Why had they disappeared during the years they'd had small children?

The debate about breast-feeding takes place without any reference to its actual context in women's lives. Breast-feeding exclusively is not like taking a prenatal vitamin. It is a serious time commitment that pretty much guarantees that you will not work in any meaningful way. Let's say a baby feeds seven times a day and then a couple more times at night. That's nine times for about a half hour each, which adds up to more than half of a working day, every day, for at least six months. This is why, when people say that breast-feeding is "free," I want to hit them with a two-by-four. It's only free if a woman's time is worth nothing.

That brings us to the subject of pumping. Explain to your employer that while you're away from your baby, "you will need to take breaks throughout the day to pump your milk," suggest the materials from the awareness campaign. Demand a "clean, quiet place" to pump, and a place to store the milk. A clean, quiet place. So peaceful, so spa-like. Leave aside the preposterousness of this advice if you are, say, a waitress or a bus driver. Say you are a newspaper reporter, like I used to be, and deadline is approaching. Your choices are (a) leave your story to go down to the dingy nurse's office and relieve yourself; or (b) grow increasingly panicked and sweaty as your body continues on its merry, milk-factory way, even though the plant shouldn't be operating today and the pump is about to explode. And then one day, the inevitable will happen. You will be talking to a male colleague and saying to yourself, "Don't think of the baby. Please don't think of the baby." And then the pump *will* explode, and the stigmata will spread down your shirt as you rush into the ladies' room.

This year alone I had two friends whose babies could not breast-feed for one reason or another, so they mostly had to pump. They were both first-time mothers who had written themselves dreamy birth plans involving hot baths followed by hours of intimate nursing. When that didn't work out, they panicked about their babies' missing out on the milky elixir. One of them sat on my couch the other day hooked up to tubes and suctions and a giant deconstructed bra, looking like some fetish ad, or a footnote from the Josef Mengele years. Looking as far as humanly possible from Eve in her natural, feminine state.

In his study on breast-feeding and cognitive development, Michael Kramer mentions research on the long-term effects of mother rats' licking and grooming their pups. Maybe, he writes, it's "the physical and/or emotional act of breastfeeding" that might lead to benefits. This is the theory he prefers, he told me, because "it would suggest something the formula companies can't reproduce." No offense to Kramer, who seems like a great guy, but this gets under my skin. If the researchers just want us to lick and groom our pups, why don't they say so? We can find our own way to do that. In fact, by insisting that milk is some kind of vaccine, they make it less likely that we'll experience nursing primarily as a loving maternal act—"pleasant and relaxing," in the words of *Our Bodies, Ourselves* and more likely that we'll view it as, well, dispensing medicine.

I continue to breast-feed my new son some of the time—but I don't do it slavishly. When I am out for the day working, or out with friends at night, he can have all the formula he wants, and I won't give it a second thought. I'm not really sure why I don't stop entirely. I know it has nothing to do with the science; I have no grandiose illusions that I'm making him lean and healthy and smart with my milk. Nursing is certainly not pure pleasure, either; often I'm tapping my foot impatiently, waiting for him to finish. I do it partly because I can get away with breast-feeding part-time. I work at home and don't punch a clock, which is not the situation of most women. Had I been more closely tied to a workplace, I would have breast-fed during my maternity leave and then given him formula exclusively, with no guilt.

My best guess is something I can't quite articulate. Breast-feeding does not belong in the realm of facts and hard numbers; it is much too intimate and elemental. It contains all of my awe about motherhood, and also my ambivalence. Right now, even part-time, it's a strain. But I also know that this is probably my last chance to feel warm baby skin up against mine, and one day I will miss it.

POSTSCRIPT

Is Breastfeeding the Best Way to Feed Babies?

Most authorities believe that breastfeeding provides optimal nutrition for infants and is associated with a decreased risk of infant mortality. Breastfed babies may have less allergies, less ear infections, and higher IQs. Nursing mothers are more likely to lose weight gained during pregnancy and may have a reduced risk of breast and other cancers. Breast milk is also less costly than formula. There are, however, women who should not breastfeed. For instance, women who use and/or abuse alcohol, nicotine, and other drugs should choose formula feeding. Alcohol enters breast milk and can affect its production, volume, and composition and overwhelm a baby's ability to break down the alcohol. Drug abusers can take drugs in such high doses that their babies can become addicted via breast milk. Smoking mothers produce less milk and milk with abnormal fat levels. As a result, their infants gain weight more slowly than those of nonsmoking mothers. Nursing mothers who smoke also transfer nicotine and other harmful substances in their milk as well as expose their babies to secondhand smoke.

Other contraindications to breastfeeding include environmental contaminants. A woman may hesitate to nurse because of warnings about contaminants in water, freshwater fish, or other foods that may enter her milk and have a negative effect on her child. Although some contaminants enter breast milk, others may be filtered out. Formula-fed infants may also be exposed to contaminants in the water used to dilute the formula. For further reading on contaminants in breast milk, see "Benefits of Breastfeeding Outweigh Risk of Infant Exposure to Environmental Chemicals in Breast Milk," *Women's Health Weekly* (January 1, 2009) and "Contaminants in Human Milk," *Environmental Health Perspectives* (October 2008).

If a woman has a minor illness such as a head cold, she can continue nursing without worry. If she has certain other illnesses, breastfeeding is contraindicated. Active, untreated tuberculosis is an example along with HIV/AIDS. The virus responsible for causing AIDS can be transmitted from an infected mother to her infant during pregnancy, at the time of birth, or via breastfeeding, particularly during the early months of life. Overall, women who have tested positive for HIV should not breastfeed their babies. See "Human Milk, Breastfeeding, and Transmission of Human Immunodeficiency Virus Type 1 in the United States," *Pediatrics* (vol. 112, 2003).

Although there are contraindications to breastfeeding, experts generally agree that there are significant benefits, especially in infancy. The long-term benefits are less clear. In "Breast Is Best: The Evidence" (*Early Human Development*,

November 2010), the author discusses the benefits of breastfeeding in reducing illness and death from gastrointestinal and respiratory infections and sudden infant death syndrome. Although these benefits are well established, long-term health effects are less clear. The evidence is controversial concerning the effect of breastfeeding in protecting against child obesity, elevated cholesterol, hypertension, and type 2 diabetes. Cognitive development has been associated with breastfeeding in many studies, although doubts remain about the results due to cognitive and behavioral differences between mothers who breastfeed (or those who breastfeed for a longer duration or more exclusively) and those who do not. In "What Research Does and Doesn't Say about Breastfeeding: A Critical Review" (*Early Child Development & Care*, July 2010), the authors review the research literature on breastfeeding benefits. It appears that although nursing offers many advantages to infants and mothers, the authors deduce that breastfeeding promotion initiatives sometimes exaggerate or misrepresent what the research actually supports. Psychological or cognitive benefits, particularly for full-term healthy infants, may be overemphasized. In some studies, variables such as income, education, and mother's IQ are not adequately taken into account. Studies that do address these variables often find little or no relationship between breastfeeding and cognitive outcomes except in the case of premature or low-birthweight infants. That view is not completely shared by the authors of "The Risks and Benefits of Infant Feeding Practices for Women and Their Children" (*Journal of Perinatology*, March 2010). They have determined that infant feeding decisions impact both mother and child health outcomes. The decision to bottle-feed can harm maternal health by increasing the risk of premenopausal breast cancer, ovarian cancer, type 2 diabetes, hypertension, elevated cholesterol, and cardiovascular disease. Practitioners' advise to pregnant women about the health impact of infant feeding and evidence-based care to enhance successful breastfeeding can maximize both the short-term and the long-term health of both mothers and babies.

Internet References . . .

The American Dietetic Association

This home page offers FAQs about nutrition and dieting, nutrition and dieting resources, and "hot topics." Good and valid information.

http://www.eatright.org

Ask Dr. Weil

The "Ask Dr. Weil" site is a question-and-answer forum on a variety of medical and nutritional topics.

http://www.drweil.com/drw/ecs/index.html

Organic Consumers Association

Official site of the consumer advocate group supporting the labeling of genetically engineered food. They also promote organic food and sustainable agriculture.

http://www.organicconsumers.org/

Consumer Health

A shift is occurring in medical care toward informed self-care. People are starting to reclaim their autonomy, and the relationship between doctor and patient is changing. Many patients are asking more questions of their physicians, considering a wider range of medical options, and becoming more educated about what determines their health. This unit addresses consumer issues: the threat posed by multiple chemical sensitivities and the validity of a low-carbohydrate weight loss diet. Finally, are organic foods worth the additional cost? Are they really healthier for consumers?

- Is It Safe to Consume Genetically Engineered Foods?
- Does Obesity Cause a Decline in Life Expectancy?

ISSUE 20

Is It Safe to Consume Genetically Engineered Foods?

YES: Henry I. Miller and Gregory Conko, from "Scary Food," *Policy Review* (June/July 2006)

NO: Mark Schapiro, from "Sowing Disaster: How Genetically Engineered American Corn Has Altered the Global Landscape," *The Nation* (October 28, 2002)

ISSUE SUMMARY

YES: Authors Henry I. Miller and Gregory Conko defend biotechnology used in genetically modifying crops and foods and believe they bring many advantages.

NO: Reporter Mark Schapiro argues that the impact of genetically engineered products include the emergence of potential allergens that could trigger reactions in humans, the rising resistance of pests to the Bt toxin, and the crossing of new genes into wild relatives.

Genetically modified foods involve changing the characteristics of an animal, plant, or microorganism by rearranging, adding, or replacing genes in its DNA. Currently in the United States, many different types of genetically modified foods are already under cultivation including soybeans and corn. Approximately three-fourths of the American soybean crop has been genetically modified to make it resistant to a weed killer. About one-third of the corn crop carries genes for resistance to herbicides or pests. Other crops that are genetically modified are canola, alfalfa, squash, and papayas. Animals that are used to produce meal or milk can also be cloned using genetic material from one animal to create a "twin." Since they were introduced in 1996, genetically modified foods have become common throughout the United States. Many consumer items are manufactured using genetically modified organisms and include oils, salad dressings, nuts, and soft drinks.

The U.S. Department of Agriculture oversees and regulates genetically modified crops. These modified crops have a number of desirable traits that benefit both grower and consumer. For example, these plants can withstand drought and exposure to herbicides, resist insect infestation, and provide enhanced nutrition. Many growers endorse this technology because it allows them to produce food with less pesticide applications. This can benefit farm workers by helping to prevent pesticide-related health concerns. These crops also lessen the amount of insecticides that can end up in water, soil, and the food chain. For consumers, genetically modified foods offer lower prices and less pesticide residues. Scientists also believe there are potential benefits such as developing peanuts that are less likely to cause allergies. Genetically modified crops also might reduce the effects of global warming and resulting drought. Some regions of the world support a limited number of crops due to low rainfall. One solution might be to plant modified crops that would thrive on little water. This could provide more available food and help reduce malnutrition in some areas.

Despite the apparent benefits of genetically modifying crops, safety concerns exist. No one has any idea about the long-term effects of these foods on the environment or on consumers. Since these products have only been available since 1996, long-term data are not available. Gene manipulation could increase levels of naturally occurring allergens or toxins, permanently alter the gene pool thus reducing biodiversity, and encourage the rise of populations of pesticide-resistant insects. Growers have found that keeping genetically modified products separated from conventional crops is difficult due to cross-pollination and contamination during processing.

Based on data from the National Academy of Sciences, genetically modified foods appear to be safe. However, it seems prudent that studies, particularly to assess long-term effects, continue. Labeling is an additional issue. The Food and Drug Administration requires a food label to indicate the presence of genetically modified food only when a food's composition is altered significantly or when a known allergen is added to a food.

In the following articles, Henry I. Miller and Gregory Conko defend biotechnology used in genetically modifying crops and foods and believe they bring many advantages. Reporter Mark Schapiro argues that the impact of genetically engineered products includes the emergence of potential allergens that could trigger reactions in humans, the rising resistance of pests to the Bt toxin, and the crossing of new genes into wild relatives.

YES ↵

Henry I. Miller and
Gregory Conko

Scary Food

Like a scene from some Hollywood thriller, a team of U.S. Marshals stormed a warehouse in Irvington, New Jersey, last summer to intercept a shipment of evildoers from Pakistan. The reason you probably haven't heard about the raid is that the objective was not to seize Al Qaeda operatives or white slavers, but $80,000 worth of basmati rice contaminated with weevils, beetles, and insect larvae, making it unfit for human consumption. In regulation-speak, the food was "adulterated," because "it consists in whole or in part of any filthy, putrid, or decomposed substance, or if it is otherwise unfit for food."

Americans take food safety very seriously. Still, many consumers tend to ignore Mother Nature's contaminants while they worry unduly about high technology, such as the advanced technologies that farmers, plant breeders, and food processors use to make our food supply the most affordable, nutritious, varied, and safe in history.

For example, recombinant DNA technology—also known as food biotechnology, gene-splicing, or genetic modification (GM)—is often singled out by critics as posing a risk that new allergens, toxins, or other nasty substances will be introduced into the food supply. And, because of the mainstream media's "if it bleeds, it leads" approach, news coverage of food biotech is dominated by the outlandish claims and speculations of anti-technology activists. This has caused some food companies—including fast-food giant McDonald's and baby-food manufacturers Gerber and Heinz—to forgo superior (and even cost-saving) gene-spliced ingredients in favor of ones the public will find less threatening.

Scientists agree, however, that gene-spliced crops and foods are not only better for the natural environment than conventionally produced food crops, but also safer for consumers. Several varieties now on the market have been modified to resist insect predation and plant diseases, which makes the harvested crop much cleaner and safer. Ironically (and also surprisingly in these litigious times), in their eagerness to avoid biotechnology, some major food companies may knowingly be making their products less safe and wholesome for consumers. This places them in richly deserved legal jeopardy.

Don't Trust Mother Nature

Every year, scores of packaged food products are recalled from the American market due to the presence of all-natural contaminants like insect parts, toxic

From *Policy Review*, June/July 2006, pp. 61–69. Copyright © 2006 by Henry I. Miller and Gregory Conko. Reprinted by permission of Policy Review/Hoover Institution/Stanford University and Henry I. Miller and Gregory Conko.

molds, bacteria, and viruses. Because farming takes place out-of-doors and in dirt, such contamination is a fact of life. Fortunately, modern technology has enabled farmers and food processors to minimize the threat from these contaminants.

The historical record of mass food poisoning in Europe offers a cautionary tale. From the ninth to the nineteenth centuries, Europe suffered a succession of epidemics caused by the contamination of rye with ergot, a poisonous fungus. Ergot contains the potent toxin ergotamine, the consumption of which induces hallucinations, bizarre behavior, and violent muscle twitching. These symptoms gave rise at various times to the belief that victims were possessed by evil spirits. Witch-hunting and persecution were commonplace—and the New World was not immune. One leading explanation for the notorious 1691–92 Salem witch trials also relates to ergot contamination. Three young girls suffered violent convulsions, incomprehensible speech, trance-like states, odd skin sensations, and delirious visions in which they supposedly saw the mark of the devil on certain women in the village. The girls lived in a swampy meadow area around Salem; rye was a major staple of their diet; and records indicate that the rye harvest at the time was complicated by rainy and humid conditions, exactly the situation in which ergot would thrive.

Worried villagers feared the girls were under a spell cast by demons, and the girls eventually named three women as witches. The subsequent panic led to the execution of as many as 20 innocent people. Until a University of California graduate student discovered this link, a reasonable explanation had defied historians. But the girls' symptoms are typical of ergot poisoning, and when the supply of infected grain ran out, the delusions and persecution likewise disappeared.

In the twenty-first century, modern technology, aggressive regulations, and a vigorous legal liability system in industrialized countries such as the United States are able to mitigate much of this sort of contamination. Occasionally, though, Americans will succumb to tainted food picked from the woods or a backyard garden. However, elsewhere in the world, particularly in less-developed countries, people are poisoned every day by fungal toxins that contaminate grain. The result is birth defects, cancer, organ failure, and premature death.

About a decade ago, Hispanic women in the Rio Grande Valley of Texas were found to be giving birth to an unusually large number of babies with crippling and lethal neural tube defects (NTDS) such as spina bifida, hydrocephalus, and anencephaly—at a rate approximately six times higher than the national average for non-Hispanic women. The cause remained a mystery until recent research revealed a link between NTDS and consumption of large amounts of unprocessed corn like that found in tortillas and other staples of the Latino diet.

The connection is obscure but fascinating. The culprit is fumonisin, a deadly mycotoxin, or fungal toxin, produced by the mold *Fusarium* and sometimes found in unprocessed corn. When insects attack corn, they open wounds in the plant that provide a perfect breeding ground for *Fusarium*. Once molds get a foothold, poor storage conditions also promote their post-harvest growth on grain.

Fumonisin and some other mycotoxins are highly toxic, causing fatal diseases in livestock that eat infected corn and esophageal cancer in humans. Fumonisin also interferes with the cellular uptake of folic acid, a vitamin that is known to reduce the risk of NTDS in developing fetuses. Because fumonisin prevents the folic acid from being absorbed by cells, the toxin can, in effect, induce functional folic acid deficiency—and thereby cause NTDS—even when the diet contains what otherwise would be sufficient amounts of folic acid.

The epidemiological evidence was compelling. At the time that the babies of Hispanic women in the Rio Grande Valley experienced the high rate of neural tube defects, the fumonisin level in corn in that locale was two to three times higher than normal, and the affected women reported much higher dietary consumption of homemade tortillas than in women who were unaffected.

Acutely aware of the danger of mycotoxins, regulatory agencies such as the U.S. Food and Drug Administration and Britain's Food Safety Agency have established recommended maximum fumonisin levels in food and feed products made from corn. Although highly processed cornstarch and corn oil are unlikely to be contaminated with fumonisin, unprocessed corn or lightly processed corn (e.g., cornmeal) can have fumonisin levels that exceed recommended levels.

In 2003, the Food Safety Agency tested six organic cornmeal products and twenty conventional cornmeal products for fumonisin contamination. All six organic cornmeals had elevated levels—from nine to 40 times greater than the recommended levels for human health—and they were voluntarily withdrawn from grocery stores.

A Technical Fix

The conventional way to combat mycotoxins is simply to test unprocessed and processed grains and throw out those found to be contaminated—an approach that is both wasteful and dubious. But modern technology—specifically in the form of gene-splicing—is already attacking the fungal problem at its source. An excellent example is "Bt corn," crafted by splicing into commercial corn varieties a gene from the bacterium *Bacillus thuringiensis*. The "Bt" gene expresses a protein that is toxic to corn-boring insects but is perfectly harmless to birds, fish, and mammals, including humans.

As the Bt corn fends off insect pests, it also reduces the levels of the mold *Fusarium,* thereby reducing the levels of fumonisin. Thus, switching to the gene-spliced, insect-resistant corn for food processing lowers the levels of fumonisin—as well as the concentration of insect parts—likely to be found in the final product. Researchers at Iowa State University and the U.S. Department of Agriculture found that Bt corn reduces the level of fumonisin by as much as 80 percent compared to conventional corn.

Thus, on the basis of both theory and empirical knowledge, there should be potent incentives—legal, commercial, and ethical—to use such gene-spliced grains more widely. One would expect public and private sector advocates of public health to demand that such improved varieties be cultivated and used for food—not unlike requirements for drinking water to be chlorinated and fluoridated. Food producers who wish to offer the safest and best products to their customers—to say nothing of being offered the opportunity to advertise "New and Improved!"—should be competing to get gene-spliced products into the marketplace.

Alas, none of this has come to pass. Activists have mounted intractable opposition to food biotechnology in spite of demonstrated, significant benefits, including reduced use of chemical pesticides, less runoff of chemicals into waterways, greater use of farming practices that prevent soil erosion, higher profits for farmers, and less fungal contamination. Inexplicably, government oversight has also been an obstacle, by subjecting the testing and commercialization of gene-spliced crops to unscientific and draconian regulations that have vastly increased testing and development costs and limited the use and diffusion of food biotechnology.

The result is jeopardy for everyone involved in food production and consumption: Consumers are subjected to avoidable and often undetected health risks, and food producers have placed themselves in legal jeopardy. The first point is obvious, the latter less so, but as described first by Drew Kershen, professor of law at the University of Oklahoma, it makes a fascinating story: Agricultural processors and food companies may face at least two kinds of civil liability for their refusal to purchase and use fungus-resistant, gene-spliced plant varieties, as well as other superior products.

Food for Thought

In 1999 the Gerber foods company succumbed to activist pressure, announcing that its baby food products would no longer contain any gene-spliced ingredients. Indeed, Gerber went farther and promised it would attempt to shift to organic ingredients that are grown without synthetic pesticides or fertilizers. Because corn starch and corn sweeteners are often used in a range of foods, this could mean changing Gerber's entire product line.

But in its attempt to head off a potential public relations problem concerning the use of gene-spliced ingredients, Gerber has actually increased the health risk for its baby consumers—and, thereby, its legal liability. As noted above, not only is gene-spliced corn likely to have lower levels of fumonisin than conventional corn; organic corn is likely to have the highest levels, because it suffers greater insect predation due to less effective pest controls.

If a mother some day discovers that her "Gerber baby" has developed liver or esophageal cancer, she might have a legal case against Gerber. On the child's behalf, a plaintiff's lawyer can allege liability based on mycotoxin contamination in the baby food as the causal agent of the cancer. The contamination would be considered a *manufacturing defect* under product liability law because the baby food did not meet its intended product specifications or level of safety. According to Kershen, Gerber could be found liable "even though all possible care was exercised in the preparation and marketing of the product," simply because the contamination occurred.

The plaintiff's lawyer could also allege a *design defect* in the baby food, because Gerber knew of the existence of a less risky design—namely, the use of gene-spliced varieties that are less prone to *Fusarium* and fumonisin contamination—but deliberately chose not to use it. Instead, Gerber chose to use non-gene-spliced, organic food ingredients, knowing that the foreseeable risks of harm posed by them could have been reduced or avoided by adopting a reasonable alternative design—that is, by using gene-spliced Bt corn, which is known to have a lower risk of mycotoxin contamination.

Gerber might answer this design defect claim by contending that it was only responding to consumer demand, but that alone would not be persuasive. Product liability law subjects defenses in design defect cases to a risk-utility balancing in which consumer expectations are only one of several factors used to determine whether the product design (e.g., the use of only non-gene-spliced ingredients) is reasonably safe. A jury might conclude that whatever consumer demand there may be for non-biotech ingredients does not outweigh Gerber's failure to use a technology that is known to lower the health risks to consumers.

Even if Gerber was able to defend itself from the design defect claim, the company might still be liable because it failed to provide adequate instructions or warnings about the potential risks of non-gene-spliced ingredients. For example, Gerber could label its non-gene-spliced baby food with a statement such as: "This product does not contain gene-spliced ingredients. Consequently, this product has a very slight additional risk of mycotoxin contamination. Mycotoxins can cause serious diseases such as liver and esophageal cancer and birth defects."

Whatever the risk of toxic or carcinogenic fumonisin levels in non-biotech corn may be (probably low in industrialized countries, where food producers generally are cautious about such contamination), a more likely scenario is potential liability for an allergic reaction.

Six percent to 8 percent of children and 1 to 2 percent of adults are allergic to one or another food ingredient, and an estimated 150 Americans die each year from exposure to food allergens. Allergies to peanuts, soybeans, and wheat proteins, for example, are quite common and can be severe. Although only about 1 percent of the population is allergic to peanuts, some individuals are so highly sensitive that exposure causes anaphylactic shock, killing dozens of people every year in North America.

Protecting those with true food allergies is a daunting task. Farmers, food shippers and processors, wholesalers and retailers, and even restaurants must maintain meticulous records and labels and ensure against cross-contamination. Still, in a country where about a billion meals are eaten every day, missteps are inevitable. Dozens of processed food items must be recalled every year due to accidental contamination or inaccurate labeling.

Fortunately, biotechnology researchers are well along in the development of peanuts, soybeans, wheat, and other crops in which the genes coding for allergenic proteins have been silenced or removed. According to University of California, Berkeley, biochemist Bob Buchanan, hypoallergenic varieties of wheat could be ready for commercialization within the decade, and nuts soon thereafter. Once these products are commercially available, agricultural processors and food companies that refuse to use these safer food sources will open themselves to products-liability, design-defect lawsuits.

Property Damage and Personal Injury

Potato farming is a growth industry, primarily due to the vast consumption of french fries at fast-food restaurants. However, growing potatoes is not easy, because they are preyed upon by a wide range of voracious and difficult-to-control pests, such as the Colorado potato beetle, virus-spreading aphids, nematodes, potato blight, and others.

To combat these pests and diseases, potato growers use an assortment of fungicides (to control blight), insecticides (to kill aphids and the Colorado potato beetle), and fumigants (to control soil nematodes). Although some of these chemicals are quite hazardous to farm workers, forgoing them could jeopardize the sustainability and profitability of the entire potato industry. Standard application of synthetic pesticides enhances yields more than 50 percent over organic potato production, which prohibits most synthetic inputs.

Consider a specific example. Many growers use methamidophos, a toxic organophosphate nerve poison, for aphid control. Although methamidophos is an EPA-approved pesticide, the agency is currently reevaluating the use of organophosphates and could ultimately prohibit or greatly restrict the use of this entire class of pesticides. As an alternative to these chemicals, the Monsanto Company developed a potato that contains a gene from the bacterium *Bacillus thuringiensis* (Bt) to control the Colorado potato beetle and another gene to control the potato leaf roll virus spread by the aphids. Monsanto's NewLeaf potato is resistant to these two scourges of potato plants, which allowed growers who adopted it to reduce their use of chemical controls and increase yields.

Farmers who planted NewLeaf became convinced that it was the most environmentally sound and economically efficient way to grow potatoes. But after five years of excellent results it encountered an unexpected snag. Under pressure from anti-biotechnology organizations, McDonald's, Burger King, and other restaurant chains informed their potato suppliers that they would no longer accept gene-spliced potato varieties for their french fries. As a result, potato processors such as J.R. Simplot inserted a nonbiotech-potato clause into their farmer-processor contracts and informed farmers that they would no longer buy gene-spliced potatoes. In spite of its substantial environmental, occupational safety, and economic benefits, NewLeaf became a sort of contractual poison pill and is no longer grown commercially. Talk about market distortions.

Now, let us assume that a farmer who is required by contractual arrangement to plant nonbiotech potatoes sprays his potato crop with methamidophos (the organophosphate nerve poison) and that the pesticide drifts into a nearby stream and onto nearby farm laborers. Thousands of fish die in the stream, and the laborers report to hospital emergency rooms complaining of neurological symptoms.

This hypothetical scenario is, in fact, not at all far-fetched. Fish-kills attributed to pesticide runoff from potato fields are commonplace. In the potato-growing region of Prince Edward Island, Canada, for example, a dozen such incidents occurred in one 13-month period alone, between July 1999 and August 2000. According to the UN's Food and Agriculture Organization, "normal" use of the pesticides parathion and methamidophos is responsible for some 7,500 pesticide poisoning cases in China each year.

In our hypothetical scenario, the state environmental agency might bring an administrative action for civil damages to recover the cost of the fish-kill, and a plaintiff's lawyer could file a class-action suit on behalf of the farm laborers for personal injury damages.

Who's legally responsible? Several possible circumstances could enable the farmer's defense lawyer to shift culpability for the alleged damages to the contracting food processor and to the fast-food restaurants that are the ultimate purchasers of the potatoes. These circumstances include the farmer's having planted Bt potatoes in the recent past; his contractual obligation to the potato processor and its fast-food retail buyers to provide only nonbiotech varieties; and his demonstrated preference for planting gene-spliced, Bt potatoes, were it not for the contractual proscription. If these conditions could be proved, the lawyer defending the farmer could name the contracting processor and the fast-food restaurants as cross-defendants, claiming either contribution in tort law or indemnification in contract law for any damages legally imposed upon the farmer client.

The farmer's defense could be that those companies bear the ultimate responsibility for the damages because they compelled the farmer to engage in higher-risk production practices than he would otherwise have chosen. The companies chose to impose cultivation of a non-gene-spliced variety upon the farmer although they knew that in order to avoid severe losses in yield, he would need to use organophosphate pesticides. Thus, the defense could argue that the farmer should have a legal right to pass any damages (arising from contractually imposed production practices) back to the processor and the fast-food chains.

Why Biotech?

Companies that insist upon farmers' using production techniques that involve foreseeable harms to the environment and humans may be—we would argue, *should* be—legally accountable for that decision. If agricultural processors and food companies manage to avoid legal liability for their insistence on nonbiotech crops, they will be "guilty" at least of externalizing their environmental costs onto the farmers, the environment, and society at large.

Food biotechnology provides an effective—and cost-effective—way to prevent many of these injurious scenarios, but instead of being widely encouraged, it is being resisted by self-styled environmental activists and even government officials.

It should not fall to the courts to resolve and reconcile what are essentially scientific and moral issues. However, other components of society—industry, government, and "consumer advocacy" groups—have failed abjectly to fully exploit a superior, life-enhancing, and life-saving technology. Even the biotechnology trade associations have been unhelpful. All are guilty, in varying measures, of sacrificing the public interest to self-interest and of helping to perpetuate a gross public misconception—that food biotechnology is unproven, untested, and unregulated.

If consumers genuinely want a safer, more nutritious, and more varied food supply at a reasonable cost, they need to know where the real threats lie. They must also become better informed, demand public policy that makes sense, and deny fringe anti-technology activists permission to speak for consumers.

 **NO**

Sowing Disaster?
How Genetically Engineered
American Corn Has Altered
the Global Landscape

It's an hour-and-a-half drive over switchbacks from the southern Mexican city of Oaxaca to the village of Capulalpan, a settlement of some 1,500 people nestled in the Sierra Norte Mountains. The thick forest and remoteness of this mountainous region has long enabled the local Zacateca Indians to maintain their cultural integrity and, to a great extent, write their own rules. When Mexican clocks were turned back for daylight saving time in the spring, the Zacatecans refused to make the adjustment, insisting that they live in "God's time," not in what they derisively call "Fox time," referring to President Vicente Fox in far-off Mexico City. Carlos Castaneda wrote about this region as a center for natural transcendence in his book *Journey to Ixtlan*. But over the past year, this tiny puebla among the cedars and the wild mustard of the Sierra Norte has been unwillingly thrust into the center of a worldwide controversy over something quite different than the quality of its peyote: genetically engineered corn.

Last winter a team of plant scientists from the University of California, Berkeley, published a paper in the journal *Nature* asserting that the genes from genetically altered corn had been discovered in the local varieties of corn grown here in Capulalpan. The news traveled quickly. The biotechnology industry has long claimed that genetic engineering is predictable: that the genes end up where they are put, and that their presence in the environment can be controlled. But the discovery of genetically engineered (GE) corn in Capulalpan appeared to defy those claims. In 1998 the Mexican government outlawed the planting—although not the eating—of GE corn, in order to protect the genetic diversity of the crop that is the country's most important food supply.

Preserving the rich genetic diversity of Capulalpan's corn is a matter of more than sentimental significance. When disaster strikes corn anywhere in the world—disease, too much rain, not enough rain, a new pest—plant scientists traditionally come to this region, which stretches from the Sierra Norte Mountains down to the southernmost state of Chiapas and into Guatemala, for the germ plasm to rejuvenate beleaguered domestic varieties. Genetic diversity is what provides a hedge against unanticipated environmental changes. In the state of Oaxaca alone, corn grows in sixty different varieties, in shades of blue, black, purple and white, as well as the yellow that we have come to associate with our most widely grown crop.

"This is the world's insurance policy," says Mauricio Bellon, director of the economics programs at the International Maize and Wheat Improvement Center (CIMMYT), the world's foremost public research facility for corn. "The diversity of these land races, these genes, is the basis of our food supply. We'll have great science, we'll have great breeding, but at the end of the day, the base [of this crop] is here. We need this diversity to cope with the unpredictable. . . . The climate changes, new plant diseases and pests continue to evolve. Diseases we thought we had controlled come back. We don't know what's going to happen in the future, and so we need to keep our options open. And this," says Bellon, in the middle of a Oaxacan cornfield, "is what keeps our options open."

The villagers in Capulalpan had no idea what genetic engineering was until they found the errant genes in their fields. Genetic engineering involves introducing genes from a separate organism into corn—or any of a number of other food crops—in order to express a desired trait. Olga Maldonado, the first villager in Capulalpan to discover transgenic elements in her corn, found the very concept bewildering. "Maybe it comes from some other plant," she said, "or animal—it has another ingredient that's different from corn."

Americans, too, might be blindsided by such a revelation, even though most of us eat genetically engineered products practically every day. Walk through your local supermarket, and you'll find it in breakfast cereals, canned drinks, processed foods of every sort. Unless it's duly labeled, chances are anything with processed soy or corn has been genetically modified. The most popular sweetener today is not sugar, but corn syrup—and most corn syrup is made from genetically modified corn. GE corn and soybeans are fed to animals, so it's in our beef, our pork, our chicken and our milk. Over the past five years, the products of genetic engineering have slipped almost unnoticed into the American food system. Though there is no hard evidence that these products are harmful to human health, foreign and domestic scientists and activists are questioning their long-term impact on the environment, whether their much-heralded benefits are actually coming true and whether the introduction of what is, in essence, a new living organism into the ecosystem can be so easily controlled. And now here these organisms were in Mexico—which had banned the planting of genetically engineered crops four years ago. If the genetic traces could make their way all the way to tiny Capulalpan, where else are they going to go?

❦

I am walking through Olga Maldonado's field in Capulalpan. A Zacateca Indian with a broad, weathered face, Olga now approaches her field, where her ancestors have farmed for centuries, with a new diffidence and uncertainty. "I only know that I am afraid," she says.

Her field is on a hillside over the town, with a sweeping view of the Sierra valleys below. The field itself is a patch of perhaps 200 plants; you can walk from one end to the other in about a minute. But it's enough to produce food for her, her husband and their young children for most of the year.

The problems surfaced when Olga first discerned that some of the corn in her field did not have the hardiness to which she was accustomed. Several others in the village were having similar problems: nothing devastating, just that their yields were off, and in an area where corn is central to the region's economic and cultural life, that registers as a significant event.

How could transgenic crops have made it into the fields in this remote location in Mexico? In Capulalpan, Olga herself remembers buying some corn from the local store, where imported kernels are sold by the crate (and are, legally, only supposed to be ground up for food). She didn't know about the government ban on planting, and she figured she'd try some of it out in her fields. "I planted that corn out of curiosity," she says. "I bought it at the government store and planted it to see if it was better than ours. And because there was more corn in each plant."

But later, when the corn had problems maturing, she had her plants tested at a small laboratory located on the cusp of a hillside overlooking the Sierra valley, in the town of La Trinidad. There, the UC Berkeley microbiologist Ignacio Chapela had helped to establish a genetic testing facility as part of a successful effort to demonstrate to Japanese buyers that the large, brimmed fungi that grow wild at the foot of the trees in the surrounding forest and look like shiitake mushrooms actually are shiitake mushrooms. Every month traders make the trek to Capulalpan to purchase mushrooms, which are flown express to Japan, providing much-needed cash to the community. This time, however, the lab discovered something it didn't want: Within the genome of Olga's corn kernels—varieties that have grown here for centuries—was, suddenly, evidence of genetic manipulation. The lab ultimately found that fifteen of the twenty-two corn samples it tested from the surrounding mountain communities also had traces of transgenes.

❧

Genetic engineering has transformed American agriculture: In just six years, 34 percent of our corn, 75 percent of our soy, 70 percent of our cotton and 15 percent of our canola is genetically engineered. Genetically engineered potatoes, tomatoes and wheat are also headed toward mass production. The critical forces behind the development of the technology itself are just five companies—Dow, DuPont, Syngenta, Aventis and Monsanto—which control three out of every four patents issued over the past ten years for genetically modified crops. And fully 90 percent of the genetically modified seed technology planted around the world is either owned by or licensed by one company, Monsanto, according to the ETC Group (erosion, technology and concentration), a sustainable-agriculture NGO that has followed changes in the seed industry over the past two decades. According to an assessment by *Chemical and Engineering News*, just two companies—DuPont (owner of Pioneer and other smaller seed companies) and Monsanto—control nearly three-quarters of the US corn-seed market. These companies are now anxious to export the rapid advances the technology has made across America.

But the very idea of manipulating the genetic structure of a living organism has caused unease around the world. While I and a production crew from the PBS newsmagazine show *NOW with Bill Moyers* (which aired a version of this story on October 4) were visiting Olga Maldonado in Mexico last summer, half a world away, two southern African countries, Zambia and Zimbabwe, were refusing to accept American donations of genetically engineered corn to help them contend with a food crisis that was sending tens of thousands of people into starvation. The European Union was facing down a possible US challenge at the World Trade Organization over European restrictions on imports of genetically engineered food. In countries as far afield as France, India and New Zealand, the new technology was sparking anti-American demonstrations. The release of genetically modified organisms (GMOs) into the environment would later emerge as one of the most contentious issues to be discussed at the Earth Summit in Johannesburg, South Africa. Altogether, more than thirty countries have imposed either a total ban or heavy restrictions on GMO imports from the United States.

The news from Mexico stoked fears around the world that genetic engineering is out of control. While Ignacio Chapela and his graduate student David Quist's discovery ignited a firestorm of controversy by scientists who criticized their work, in August a study commissioned by Mexico's National Institute of Ecology confirmed their findings: Transgenic corn genes were in Oaxacan corn. "What is most important about these findings," Exequiel Ezcurra, president of the institute, told the newspaper *La Jornada*, "is that transgenic creations move quickly into the environment and that it's time to reconsider ways of insuring our bio-security."

Nobody knows for sure what precise variety of transgenes wound up in Capulalpan corn. Dr. Norman Ellstrand, professor of genetics at the University of California, Riverside, and one of the country's foremost experts on corn genetics, says that the corn in Capulalpan could contain any number of characteristics that have been engineered into American corn. Since corn is openly pollinated, he explains, pollen from one plant can blow or be transported in some other way to fertilize another plant. "And if just 1 percent of [American] experimental pollen escaped into Mexico, that means those land races could potentially be making medicines or industrial chemicals or things that are not so good for people to eat. Right now, we just don't know what's in there."

Chances are good, however, according to Ellstrand, that the genes are from Bt corn, a popular US corn variety genetically engineered to produce its own toxins against a pest known as the European corn borer. The borer presents a sporadically serious threat to US and European cornfields but is rare in Mexico. Ellstrand says there would likely be no immediate damaging effects from the presence of Bt corn in Mexico, but what frightens him is how much we don't know: This year, he is researching how long transgenes will persist in native varieties—whether, in fact, they can ever be bred out of the population. This is a question that until now has not even been studied.

At least for the foreseeable future, then, here in the heart of the world's reservoir for genetic diversity of corn will be transgenes developed for the vast rolling flatlands of American corn country—where, in just six years, Bt corn has moved from laboratory petri dishes into one of every five acres of cornfield.

꧁⟡꧂

Frank McLain shifts the gears on his 1982 pickup as we drive through his family's cornfields in central Iowa. This land has been in his family for five generations, since it was homesteaded in 1862. "What they passed on to me is the feeling that this land is not just a hunk of dirt that you use and sell," he says, "that a piece of ground is something that should be kept for the next generation; that you're just a steward and you're not just to use it as a tool or as a doormat."

Frank is the first in his family to plant transgenic crops. On the left side of the road, we're passing a field of Bt corn; on the right, Roundup Ready soybeans. Monsanto's Bt corn contains a gene inserted from a bacteria that prompts the plant to produce its own insecticide; when the corn borer eats it, the plant's toxins go to work in its digestive tract, literally blowing up its stomach. It means that Frank has cut in half the amount of pesticides he used to have to apply to his corn. And Monsanto's Roundup Ready soybean seeds have been genetically altered—using a gene from a bacterium—in a way that enables them to resist the application of Monsanto's own herbicide, Roundup. "When I was a kid you'd see grass or other weeds poking up in these fields, and we'd have to go through and chop them out with hoes or shovels or whatever to clean them up manually or mechanically as best we could," Frank explains. "Now it's pretty easy to come in here with a [Roundup] sprayer and accomplish the same thing."

Frank's experience with genetic engineering illustrates both the allure and the potential dangers of the new technology. For many American farmers, genetically engineered crops offer a level of predictability in a business that can rise or fall with a few degrees Fahrenheit each season.

꧁⟡꧂

Twenty years a go I visited Frank and his father, Fred, while reporting a story on the American seed industry. At the time, the industry was undergoing rapid consolidation as regionally based seed companies were being bought out by large multinational pesticide and pharmaceutical companies. Hundreds of locally bred seed varieties were being phased out in favor of hybrids that could be grown in broad swaths of land across America.

I talked with the McLains then about what effect this consolidation would have on genetic diversity. They had lived through the infamous corn blight of 1970, a year in which 15 percent of the US corn crop was devastated by a blight that attacked a single hybridized corn variety that had been planted in one out of four acres from Florida to the Midwest. Meat prices shot up that year, as most of the lost corn was being grown as cattle feed. The reason for the blight was subsequently identified by the National Academy of Sciences as genetic uniformity: Corn seed across the country was, the academy reported, "as alike as identical twins." Fred told me how he watched as his plants became black and shriveled under the corrosive effects of the blight. When scientists quickly raced another slew of corn varieties onto the market for the following season, they relied on genetic material contained in traditional corn varieties, whose roots could be traced back to those land races around Oaxaca.

I hadn't seen the McLains since the summer of 1982, except once the following year, during a cross-country trip when Fred and his wife, Donnie, graciously laid out a lunch for me when I pulled into their farm, located just off Highway 30. At the time, Monsanto had just announced the creation of the first transgenic plant, launching the technology that would later evolve into fullscale genetic engineering. Few understood what that would mean.

Today, Fred has retired, and Frank, 50, is running the farm. I have a vivid memory of when I last saw Frank, sitting with him in a cramped tractor cab listening to the Rolling Stones' *Exile on Main Street* at full volume as we churned fertilizer into the soil. Now, on a sweltering July day, we're rumbling along the dirt road past those same fields, past acre upon acre of corn plants of identical height, a perfect crop. Frank points out the window of his pickup to a field of seed corn almost five feet high. In addition to his fields of Bt feed corn, he is growing experimental seed for Monsanto, the nation's largest producer of genetically engineered crops. "They're wanting to see how it will do maybe one last time before putting it out in large acreage," he says. Growing the experimental seed pays a premium and insulates him from the rollicking prices of commodity feed corn, enabling him to make a comfortable living from farming—an increasing rarity for American family farmers.

Frank, like many American family farmers, is struggling to keep the farm afloat in an era when hundreds of farms a month are thrown into bankruptcy by the twin forces of low commodity prices and the rising cost of inputs, like seed and agricultural chemicals. He needs to obtain an ever-rising production from his 1,400 acres just to stay alive as a farmer. Through careful tailoring, the new crops shrink, by at least a bit, the immense workload involved in running a family farm, and add, at least a bit, to the reliability of being able to make a livelihood off the land.

But like most farmers, he is now deeply dependent on the multinational agribusiness enterprises that dominate the US food production system. To grow transgenic seeds, Frank has to agree to Monsanto's conditions. Every year Frank signs a contract with Monsanto for its patented Bt corn and Roundup Ready soy, agreeing not to replant it the following season—which means Monsanto gets to resell it to him the following year. Frank sees himself as entrenched on the conveyor belt of American industrial agriculture. "My job," he says, "is the production end of this assembly line. We're just a small little cog in the wheel. . . . What we're concerned with is production agriculture. To most of us that means our five or ten miles that we were born and raised and will probably die in."

But whether he likes to think about it or not, Frank's fate is entwined with that of Olga Maldonado and other farmers like her. Indeed, it's even possible, among infinite possibilities, that Frank is growing the same type of corn that surfaced in Capulalpan. Ultimately, it is questions of control and predictability that lie at the heart of the controversy over genetically modified crops. In the farmer's fields, it is a question of control over corn's freefloating means of insemination—those tassels you see feathering the air in corn country are like a plant's version of a peacock's tail, there to produce and release "male" pollen to be carried to the "female" silks. And inside the corn plant itself is the issue of whether genetic manipulations might have unforeseen effects. These are questions that bedevil even the scientists who are engineering the changes.

Some twenty miles from Frank McLain's farm, in Ames, the Iowa State University campus spreads out amid leafy oak trees and pleasant, low-slung buildings. The university hosts one of the nation's leading plant-science research institutions for agricultural biotechnology.

Dr. Mike Lee, a plant biologist, is in the agronomy department's plant-transformation center doing genetic engineering. Lee is at work on a research project to increase the nutritional value of corn by inserting the most nutritious part of a hog—the gene for hog's milk—into a corn embryo. A lab technician has inserted a petri dish of corn embryos onto the lower shelf of what Lee calls "the gene gun"—a critical tool of today's genetic engineers, actually a rectangular box made from thick plastic. On the top shelf the technician places a petri dish containing genetic information from a female hog's milk onto a thin layer of gold pellets—which serve as the "bullets." She flicks a switch, and as a meter measuring air pressure per square inch marches quickly upward, there's a notable "pop": The bullet is fired. Lee explains:

"You just accelerate those particles inside that chamber at a very high speed. High enough so that it can crash through the cell walls, get into the nucleus and then somehow, by a process that is not completely understood, the DNA that's coating those gold particles gets integrated into the corn chromosomes. They'll start to form roots and shoots and a new plant emerges, hopefully a plant that carries those genes now in their chromosomes." This is genetic engineering in action, mixing the genetic material from two organisms that would never ordinarily mix in nature. It's been done with flounder genes in strawberries, mice genes in potatoes, cow genes in sugarcane and soy, chicken genes in corn. And now, as Lee explains, he hopes to increase the nutritional value of corn with genes from hog's milk.

For Mike Lee, like many other scientists, this technology has huge potential to increase yields, make food more nutritious, and develop new varieties of crops that are better adapted to climatic and pest conditions that threaten food production. "That's why I got into this business," Lee says, "to create new versions of existing plant species that are just a little bit more beneficial to the needs and wants of society."

Lee has a scientist's natural curiosity and excitement about the new technology, but he is also willing to acknowledge that considerable uncertainties accompany it. "We're not just changing carburetors on cars or parts on a machine," he says. "When you introduce a new DNA sequence into a chromosome it has a new function for the plant. Well, that function doesn't operate in a vacuum. It operates in the context of a complex organism growing in a complex dynamic environment."

❧

It is those uncertainties that provoke ire among critics, aghast at the hubris of genetic manipulation. More to the point, perhaps, is the fact that people like Mike Lee are not the ones driving the development of this technology. Public universities are significantly outgunned in resources by private research labs, which are looking, increasingly, for blockbuster products to be used where they have the biggest markets; even the gene gun used by Dr. Lee is available through an annual leasing arrangement from DuPont, which owns the patent on the technology. Lee's public-spirited ambitions for the technology, and his willingness to entertain doubts while forging ahead with his research in the controlled environment of a publicly funded laboratory, are an anomaly in an arena dominated by a handful of corporations.

The reality is that agricultural biotechnology has little to do with idealism, and far more with the financial imperatives of the biotechnology industry. "If you ask why these are the technologies that are on the market," says Dr. Chuck Benbrook, former executive director of the Board on Agriculture of the National Academy of Sciences, "the reason is that the companies that had invested so heavily in the technology and in buying up the seed industry had to have product on the market."

Monsanto alone poured at least a billion dollars into biotech research, according to NPR technology correspondent Daniel Charles in his book *Lords of the Harvest*, "before it had a single genetically engineered plant to sell." Other companies—DuPont, Dow, Aventis and Syngenta—spent billions more on research and on a seed-company buying spree that lasted well into the 1990s. The stakes for these companies are huge.

❧

Few studies assessing the long-term impact of genetically engineered products on the environment or human health were conducted before they were rushed into mass production. As Benbrook explains, "Promoters of the technology and certainly the federal government in the early 1990s embraced biotechnology so enthusiastically that there was just no patience, no interest in, no serious investigation of those potential problems. It was sort of a don't look, don't see policy. As a result, there really was no serious science done in the United States for most of the 1990s on the potential risks of biotechnology."

Those risks, as documented by scientists writing in the *American Journal of Botany* and the *International Journal of Food Science and Technology*, and at the Weed Science Society of America, the British Environment Ministry and the Pasteur Institute in Paris, include the emergence of potential allergens that could trigger reactions in humans; the rising resistance rates of pests to the Bt toxin; the persistence of Bt toxins in sediment, threatening nontarget insect populations; lingering residues from Roundup Ready herbicides left behind in the soil, which could injure subsequent seasons of crops; and the crossing of new genes into wild relatives. Unintended environmental consequences are surfacing around the world. In Canada, Bt toxins produced by Bt corn were discovered in the sediment of the St. Lawrence River—which could potentially affect the river soil and marine life. In Switzerland a scientist demonstrated that in Bt corn the "lignin" content—the material that keeps the stalk erect—is tougher than in non-GE varieties, a physiological change with as-yet-unknown consequences. According to an assessment by the US Department of Agriculture's own Economic Research Service last spring, yields from GE crops are no higher than yields from conventional crops, and are already starting to decline—largely because of the extra energy it takes the plant to produce its own insecticide.

Even the industry's spokesman in Washington, Dr. Mike Phillips, executive director of the food and agriculture department of the industry trade group BIO, concedes that industry studies have only followed the trajectory of impact of genetically engineered organisms "for eight or nine generations." That's not a lot of time in evolutionary terms. But once a transgenic crop is introduced, the evolutionary dynamics of living organisms insure that ripple effects will continue for hundreds of years—in fact, they're virtually unstoppable once loose in the environment.

Ten years ago the government's position toward the new technology was expressed by then–Vice President Dan Quayle, who declared that no new "unnecessary regulation" was needed to oversee the genetic engineering of food crops. Genetically engineered crops were, as was later enunciated by USDA policy, not "significantly different" from previously existing means of breeding new types of plants. That principle has provided the foundation of the government's position ever since.

The result has been inattention to potential risks and sporadic regulation by the government. The USDA apportioned just $1.6 million out of a $250 million budget for all biotech-related programs to inquire into risk assessment. (By statute, just 1 percent of the total USDA research budget on agricultural biotechnology is allocated to risk assessments. Ohio Congressman Dennis Kucinich fought the biotech industry last spring and succeeded in raising that figure to 2 percent, which will double the budget for USDA risk assessments next year.)

The USDA issues use permits for experimental trials of new genetic varieties of crops, but once they enter commercial production, the agency has no mandate to oversee them. For ten years, the FDA has engaged in what it calls "voluntary safety consultations" with biotech companies, reviewing safety data supplied by the companies; not once over the past ten years has it refused to permit development of new GE crop varieties to move forward.

❧

The Environmental Protection Agency has responsibility for any new variety producing its own insecticide—which the Bt gene does for corn, cotton and potatoes. But it relies on the companies to submit studies as to the potential for environmental harm; nor is it required by law to do follow-up inspections or independent monitoring. In August of last year, top officials from each of the EPA's ten regional offices sent an internal memorandum to their superiors in Washington expressing concern about the agency's lack of regulatory authority. A year later the agency still has no rules supporting long-term monitoring of these crops in the field. According to the EPA website, twenty "Experimental or Conditional Use" permits were granted for trial runs of new varieties of Bt corn between November 1998 and June 2002. Not one had been inspected until this past August, when officials from the EPA's Region IX office decided to pay a visit to two experimental plots of Bt corn being grown by Dow Chemical's Mycogen seed division and DuPont's seed subsidiary Pioneer in Hawaii. Both were found to be in violation, and on August 5 were cited for defying requirements intended to protect surrounding fields from the drift of genetically altered pollen from its experimental plots.

Michael Hanson, who follows genetic engineering for the Consumers Union, says that while there are abundant regulations governing the technology on paper, in reality "the lack of legal authority to pursue independent investigations, to do follow-up on producer assertions or to conduct independent assessments of safety claims means that in practice, the biotech industry has been given a free ride."

Lax regulation, however, is only part of the story. The industry received its most important historical spur from Congress, which passed the Plant Variety Protection Act in 1980, giving patentlike, proprietary protection to the developers of new plant varieties. These protections made the seed industry an attractive investment for chemical and pharmaceutical companies. And genetic engineering made patent protection far simpler to enforce; by inserting genetic "markers" alongside the new genes, the proprietary genes inside the plant become clearly identifiable. If Frank McLain, for example, were to defy his agreement with Monsanto and replant the seed he purchases from them every year, the company would be able to tell that its gene was inside his plants. Thus, genetic engineering also serves as a sort of branding mechanism—the brand is imprinted in the very biology of the plant—strengthening the proprietary hold of corporate patentholders over their creations, and giving them an ever-tighter grip on the farmer.

◦◦◉◦◦

A hundred miles east of the McLain farm, Laura Krause is standing amid her fields of corn, which sway with a refreshing summer breeze. Krause is one of Iowa's 500 organic farmers. Wearing a straw hat, with a sun-reddened face and lively eyes, Krause appears the very icon of the American farmer from the last century. Her farm is tiny; she farms a hundred acres of corn, broccoli, potatoes, kale and carrots, all of them certified organic.

Krause's cornfield varies wildly, with plants from four feet to others over six feet tall, a notable contrast from most of the corn in Iowa, which seems to spread for miles in tight walls of plants of identical height. Her field crackles with insects, and birds swooping in and out to eat them. Krause bought the farm here ten years ago, and has kept growing her home-grown seed, a variety developed by the owner of this land a century ago, by replanting it every year. She sells the seed to other organic farmers.

But not this year. In February, she sent her seed to a local lab for routine tests: Because she's certified organic, her customers want to know if there are transgenes in her corn. And sure enough, she discovered that genetically modified genes were in there. The test didn't tell her which variety they were, but she says they were most likely from Yield Guard, Monsanto's variety of Bt corn, which is widely grown in her area of Iowa. She lost her certification, and the price she received for her corn dropped by half—from $3.50 a bushel to $1.75 a bushel.

Now, like Olga Maldonado in Oaxaca, Laura Krause has transgenes in her corn whether she wants them or not. "There's no way for me to go into that field and look for the plants that contain the transgenes and deselect them," Krause says. "There's no way for me to sort them out, because they all look exactly alike. I can't get my business back, because I don't have any way to remove this gene from this [corn] population."

How did it get there? Corn pollen containing the transgene could have come from the local combine operator, who is supposed to clean out his machinery before visiting organic farms, or—most likely, she thinks—it came from pollen that blew in from a neighbor's field. All it takes is a handful of loose pollen to land on one of her silks, and transgenes enter the genetic mix.

But Krause does not want to sue her neighbor. Besides, corn pollen is known to travel as far as six miles by the wind, so it could have come from anywhere within striking distance in this corn-filled corner of the state. And there is as yet no legal precedent establishing liability for the financial damage caused by genetically engineered crops. Ron Rosmann, president of the board of the Organic Farming Research Foundation, whose own cornfields in southern Iowa were contaminated with Bt genes, says that cases like Krause's are only going to increase "as they release more and more genetically engineered seeds. . . . What we're unfortunately coming to is that zero contamination for corn is impossible." Organic farmers in Nebraska, Minnesota and elsewhere in Iowa, Rosmann says, have also experienced contamination similar to that on Laura Krause's farm.

Companies retain the legal right to enforce their patent-holder prerogatives over unlicensed use of their seed. And if their pollen happens to escape and fertilize crops in another field such as Krause's, there is no legal means for farmers to enforce the purity of their own varieties. Laura Krause, and thousands of farmers like her, are finding themselves in a legal black hole.

In response, a group of farmers in Iowa has crafted a state bill that would establish an indemnity fund to be paid out in instances of GE contamination with the hope that the bill will be introduced in this coming legislative session. In Congress, Kucinich has introduced a bill that would establish firm lines of liability for the companies that produce the "contaminating" seed, but at this stage it has little chance of passing. And next month, state residents in

Oregon will be voting on an initiative that would require labeling of all foods containing GE ingredients.

⋅◉⋅

As for Mexico, the biotech industry itself no longer even disputes Chapela's assertions that transgenic corn made its way over that "ironclad wall" into Oaxaca. Rather, according to Dr. Phillips of BIO, the fact that GE crops are in Mexico's soil now, despite the government planting ban, should be an invitation to let more in. "If you're the government of Mexico," he says, "hopefully you've learned a lesson here and that is that it's very difficult to keep a new technology from entering your borders, particularly in a biological system. . . . It really is incumbent upon the Mexican government to step up the process and get their regulatory system in place so that [they] can begin accepting these products and give farmers the opportunity to choose."

American farmers, both those growing organic and non-GMO conventional corn, have paid a heavy price for the porousness of that "biological system." The American Corn Growers Association, representing corn producers in twenty-eight states, estimates that US corn farmers have lost more than $814 million in foreign sales over the past five years as a result of restrictions on genetically modified food imports imposed by Europe, Japan and other world buyers. That enormous figure doesn't even account for the depressed prices farmers now receive for their corn as a result of an oversupply (of unexported corn) on the domestic market—with a deleterious effect on farmers' livelihood that the recent farm bill attempts to address with up to $20 billion in subsidies. For every American taxpayer, that amounts to a personal subsidy to the agricultural biotech industry.

Defying evolution by customizing traits that would never appear in nature holds out the dream of new markets—and premium prices—in the evergreen enterprise of food production. But the dream, even according to the USDA's own assessments, is turning sour. While promoting agricultural biotechnology with one hand, the department's Economic Research Service is reporting, with the other, that not only are yields not coming anywhere near expectations, but that genetically engineered corn and soybeans have not meant an overall improvement in the financial status of farmers.

Still, the horizons of agricultural biotechnology continue to expand. I am driving in a van with Dr. Kan Wang, an agronomist at Iowa State University in Ames. We turn off a country lane onto a dirt road and into the woods. A student of Dr. Wang's unlocks a gate, and we continue driving on the dirt road through the woods until we reach an extraordinary sight: a tiny cornfield, set amid a large soybean field, in the middle of the woods. This is where the next generation of genetic engineering is unfolding: Dr. Wang is conducting research into the development of vaccines in corn.

In the field a hundred or so corn plants are surrounded by an electric fence. Each tassel is capped by a brown paper bag, what Wang jokingly refers to as a "corn condom." I am here to witness corn sex, or, really, safe sex for corn. The reason? Wang is experimenting with a vaccine in this corn that will prevent diarrhea in baby pigs: When pigs eat the corn, she wants them to be immunized against a disease that is costing hog farmers millions of dollars in losses each year. And they don't want the corn pollen flowing anywhere they don't want it to go; nor do they want any outside pollen fertilizing these special plants. Thus the corn condoms. Right now, Wang is testing the corn to insure that it's not also developing potential allergens for the pigs. And if it works for pigs, says Wang, "it could work for humans too."

This is the future of agricultural biotechnology. One might have some measure of confidence with the prospect of corn vaccines in the hands of Dr. Wang, the only scientist in the country working exclusively with public funding to explore the possibilities—and risks—of breeding medicines into corn. She has taken extreme precautions with this field: It is miles away from any neighboring corn, and is surrounded by soybeans and woods, with which corn has no chance of cross-pollinating.

But Dr. Ellstrand, the plant geneticist, fears what might happen when the pharmaceutical industry, which is now testing corn as a vehicle for antibiotics and vaccines, starts putting such medicines into mass production. "Corn produces a lot of pollen," he says. "And once there's a little bit of contamination, there's the potential for releasing pharmaceutical corn genes into food crops."

Thus far, the record has not been reassuring. Farmers like Laura Krause and Olga Maldonado have already, through the various routes that a living organism may travel, been the recipients of unwanted transgenes propelled beyond the barriers of control.

Standing in his Berkeley, California, greenhouse, Ignacio Chapela, the scientist who ignited the controversy in Mexico, comments: "The genie is out of the bottle. What we are confronted with now is just thousands of very different genies that are still in their bottles, and the question is this: Do we want to keep those bottles closed or are we opening them?"

POSTSCRIPT

Is It Safe to Consume Genetically Engineered Foods?

In Europe, many people are wary of consuming genetically engineered foods. Europeans seem to want more confirmation that these foods are truly safe for human consumption and for the environment. Many European countries have more stringent labeling laws than the United States has. In addition, approval of genetically engineered items is required before they can enter the European Union's (EU) food supply. In 2006, some rice imports from the United States were contaminated with an organism not approved by the EU and were rejected. Japan immediately banned all imports of U.S. rice following the EU's ban.

In the United States, however, reactions to genetically modified foods are not as strong. One reason may be that many Americans are unaware that most grocery stores sell genetically modified food products and only one-fourth realize that they likely eat these foods on a daily basis. Americans may be unaware of the presence of these ingredients because they are not listed on the food label. In a recent poll, one-third of people thought genetically modified foods were completely safe and 29 percent believed they were not. And though 43 percent think eating food products from clones is dangerous, the Food and Drug Administration has tentatively approved meat and milk from clones for sale in the United States.

Why are Europeans and some Americans concerned over the use of genetically modified crops? According to "Seeds of Concern" (*Scientific American Special Edition*, December 2006), author Kathryn Brown claims 8.5 million farmers in 21 countries grow these crops. The United States led the way with 55 percent, followed by Argentina, Brazil, Canada, and China. These countries are committed to growing genetically engineered crops and believe the benefits outweigh the negatives. In China, a seven-year study was completed in July of 2006. Farmers planted cotton modified with a gene from the soil bacterium *Bacillus thuringiensis* (Bt). This gene directs cells to manufacture a protein that is toxic to certain insects, especially caterpillars and beetles that eat crops, but does not harm other organisms. Farmers planting engineered cotton designed to repel the leaf-eating bollworm initially did well, reducing pesticide use by 70 percent. By the seventh year, however, secondary insects moved in, replacing the bollworm as the main pest, forcing farmers to go back to normal spraying levels.

While the scientists debate the merits and disadvantages of engineered seed, politicians also seem to be at odds. In 2005, 117 legislative items related to agricultural technology were introduced. Many state legislatures tried to halt local efforts to ban or limit modified seeds and crops. Of the 23 state bills that passed during 2005, 67 percent supported this technology. It appears that modified seed and crops will increase in the future despite concerns over long-term safety. For a debate on whether or not the world would benefit from modified seed, see "Does the World Need GM Foods? YES" (*Scientific American Special Edition,* December 2006) and "Does the World Need GM Foods? NO" (*Scientific American Special Edition,* December 2006). Many other writers expressed concern over modified foods. These include "What's Happening to Your Food?" (*Current Health,* April/May 2007); "Playing with Our Food" (*Better Nutrition,* April 2007); and "Seeds for the Future" (*Library Journal,* March 1, 2007). For a balanced view of the issue, see "Genetically Modified Foods Benefits, Risks, and Global Marketing" (*International Debates,* March 2006).

ISSUE 21

Does Obesity Cause a Decline in Life Expectancy?

YES: Samuel H. Preston, from "Deadweight? The Influence of Obesity on Longevity," *New England Journal of Medicine* (March 17, 2005)

NO: Paul Campos, from "The Weighting Game: Why Being Fat Isn't Bad for You," *The New Republic* (January 13, 2003)

ISSUE SUMMARY

YES: Samuel H. Preston maintains that obesity negatively affects a person's longevity and has become a major public health problem for Americans.

NO: Law professor and writer Paul Campos disagrees and claims that the health consequences of obesity are not as dire as some health officials claim.

$\mathbf{T}$he number of Americans who are overweight and obese has been steadily climbing. Currently, about two-thirds are overweight, including more than one-third who are classified as obese. This is almost 20 percent more than 20 years ago. Obesity can double mortality and can reduce life expectancy by 10 to 20 years. If current trends continue, the average American's life expectancy will actually begin to decline by five years. Obesity is linked to unhealthy blood fat levels including cholesterol and heart disease. Other health risks associated with obesity include high blood pressure, some cancers, diabetes, gallbladder and kidney disease, sleep disorders, arthritis, and other bone and joint disorders. Obesity is also linked to complications of pregnancy, stress incontinence, and elevated surgical risk. The risks from obesity rise with its severity, and they are much more likely to occur among people more than double their recommended body weight. Obesity can impact psychological as well as physical well-being. Being obese can contribute to psychological problems including depression, anxiety, and low self-esteem. Overweight is defined as total body weight above the recommended range for good health. Obesity is a more serious degree of overweight measured by various means including height–weight charts, body composition analyses, and body mass index (BMI). BMI is a measure of height–weight ratios used to classify the health risks of body weight in the absence of more sophisticated methods. It is based on the concept that weight should be proportional to height. While it's not a perfect way to assess weight status, it is a fairly accurate way to assess weight in relationship to health risks. A BMI between 18.5 and 24.9 is considered healthy, between 25 and 29.9 is considered overweight, and over 30 is classified as obese. For example, a normal weight range for a 5'5" woman is from 114 to 144 pounds. She is classified as overweight if her weight ranges from 150 to 174 pounds, and obese if her weight is 180 to 235 pounds.

Since 1990, the prevalence of overweight and obesity has been rising in the United States. Despite public health campaigns, the trend shows little sign of changing. A 2006 study conducted by Ogden et al. ("Prevalence of Overweight and Obesity in the U.S. 1999–2004," *JAMA,* vol. 295, 2006) reported that during the six-year period from 1999 to 2004, the prevalence of overweight in children and adolescents increased significantly, as did the prevalence of obesity in men. Along with these rising rates of obesity come increased rates of obesity-related health issues. There has been a 60 percent rise in type 2 diabetes since 1990. Inactivity and overweight may be responsible for as many as 112,000 premature deaths each year in the United States, second only to smoking-related deaths.

According to the USDA, the average American has increased his/her caloric intake by more than 500 calories per day, while levels of physical activity have decreased. This is related to more meals eaten away from the home, which typically are higher in calories, fat, sugar, and salt. Restaurants also tend to serve larger portions than home-cooked meals. Many Americans are also sleep deprived. Lack of sleep appears to trigger weight gain. Finally, Americans are more engaged in sedentary activities and less likely to engage in physical activity on a regular basis. Whatever the cause of obesity, its incidence and prevalence appear to be rising and it is linked to health concerns that may affect longevity.

The following two selections address whether obesity contributes to a decline in longevity. Samuel H. Preston maintains that obesity negatively affects a person's longevity and has become a major public health problem for Americans. Writer Paul Campos disagrees and claims that the health consequences of obesity are not as dire as some health officials claim.

YES ↵

Deadweight?—The Influence of Obesity on Longevity

Obesity has clearly become a major personal and public health problem for Americans; it affects many aspects of our society. In this issue of the *Journal*, Olshansky et al.[1] make an important contribution to national discussions of the future of longevity by calling attention to the very substantial increase in the prevalence and severity of obesity since 1980 and its consequences on health and mortality. They estimate that the current life expectancy at birth in the United States would be one third to three quarters of a year higher if all overweight adults were to attain their ideal weight.

Although Olshansky et al. put obesity in the foreground of their vision of the future, the background for their vision is at least as bleak. They argue that past gains in life expectancy were largely a product of saving the young, which is unrepeatable. They claim that advances in life expectancy at older ages will be much smaller than in previous decades and that demographers and actuaries fail to recognize the disjunction and blindly continue to extrapolate the past into the future. They add to this concern that AIDS, antibiotic-resistant pathogens, and influenza pandemics represent additional threats to health. In their scenario, our children may have lives shorter than our own.

I believe that these background elements are excessively gloomy. Decreases in the rate of death at older ages have been the principal force driving American longevity for at least half a century, and they show no signs of abating. Sixty percent of the 9.23-year increase in life expectancy at birth between 1950 and 2002 is attributable to decreases in mortality among persons above 50 years of age.[2] Although improvements in life expectancy among women have slowed in the past decade, improvements among men have accelerated. The mean of male and female life expectancies at 65 years of age grew by 0.081 year per calendar year between 1950 and 1990, and by an identical 0.081 year per year between 1990 and 2002, the last year for which official U.S. life tables have been prepared.[3]

Demographers and actuaries use extrapolation to project the future of life expectancy because it seems to work better than any alternatives.[4-6] The biggest mistake, which has been made repeatedly in projections of mortality in the past, is to assume that life expectancy is close to a biologic maximum.[7] Confidence in the use of extrapolation is increased by the very steady behavior of mortality trends themselves. The mean of life expectancies at birth in 21 high-income

From *The New England Journal of Medicine*, March 17, 2005, pp. 1135–1137. Copyright © 2005 by Massachusetts Medical Society. All rights reserved. Reprinted by permission.

countries shows a nearly perfect fit (a coefficient of determination, R^2, of 0.994) to a linear time trend during the period from 1955 to 1996.[8]

The effect of an increase in the prevalence and severity of obesity on the longevity of U.S. citizens is already embedded in extrapolated forecasts made in recent periods. In fact, these forecasts implicitly assume that the severity of obesity will continue to worsen, and the prevalence will rise, since it is the rate of change in the determinants of mortality, rather than the level, that drives projected changes in life expectancy. Hundreds of factors affect a population's rate of death in any particular period, and it is their combined effect that establishes the trend.

Although Olshansky et al. cite threats to future improvements in life expectancy, it is important to recognize that many factors are at work to maintain a steady pace of advance. These include medical research organizations whose products have, for example, been responsible for much of the massive decrease in the rates of death from cardiovascular causes during the past four decades.[9] Public support for the National Institutes of Health remains very strong, and private companies will continue to have incentives to develop new products that enhance health and longevity. Longevity seems to have a strong genetic component,[10] which holds out the possibility that genetic engineering may, sometime within the 75-year projection of the Social Security Administration, begin to enhance longevity.

Other positive influences on longevity are embodied in cohorts of young persons who are approaching the ages at which death occurs most commonly and who will presumably enjoy greater protection from many diseases than will the people who have already reached those ages. Younger cohorts are better educated than older cohorts, and mortality is profoundly influenced by education. In 1998, life expectancy at age 25 was 7.1 years higher for men with some college education than for men with only a high-school education. For women, the discrepancy was 4.2 years.[11]

Younger cohorts have had lives less scarred by infectious diseases, which influence the development of many chronic diseases of adulthood.[12,13] Younger cohorts have consumed fewer cigarettes at a given age than older cohorts, and the effect of smoking is clearly manifested in the rates of death of the general population. In fact, a large fraction of the decrease in the rate of the decline in mortality among older women in recent years is a result of the rising rate of death from lung cancer in this group, which is a reflection of the delayed uptake of smoking among women in comparison with men.[14,15] Significant "cohort effects" have been demonstrated in the prevalence of cardiovascular disease, emphysema, and arthritis, suggesting that younger cohorts will have lower morbidity from these conditions as they age.[16]

Another reason to expect the longevity of U.S. citizens to continue to increase is that some populations have achieved life spans far longer than those of people in the United States, thus demonstrating what is possible even with no further technological advances. Japan has achieved a life expectancy of nearly 82 years, 4.5 years higher than that achieved by the United States and higher than that projected by the Social Security Administration for the United States for 2055.[17,18] Some researchers have used a wide variety of data to suggest that within the United States, subgroups with the healthiest lifestyles may have already achieved life expectancies of 90 years or more.[19]

But let me be clear. The rising prevalence and severity of obesity are capable of offsetting the array of positive influences on longevity. How likely is that to happen? One promising observation is that the recent increase in the levels of obesity was produced by relatively few excess calories in the typical daily diet. The consumption of a median of 30 excess calories a day produced the observed increase in weight during an eight-year period for Americans 20 to 40 years of age.[20] At the 90th percentile of weight gain, the excess consumed was about 100 calories a day. Reversing the increase in body mass might be accomplished through small behavioral changes that fit relatively easily into most people's lifestyles. The food and restaurant industries would be valuable allies in this effort, and there are recent indications of their willingness to cooperate.[21]

The fact that the U.S. population has already shown the ability to shift to healthier lifestyles is encouraging. Forty-two percent of U.S. adults were smokers in 1965, as compared with 23 percent in 2001.[14] The percentage of Americans 20 to 74 years of age with high levels of serum cholesterol fell from 33 percent in 1961 to 18 percent in 1999 and 2000.[14] Primarily because of behavioral changes, the incidence of AIDS has fallen by nearly 50 percent since 1992.[22] The percentage of fatal crashes involving drunk drivers declined from 30 percent in 1982 to 17 percent in 1999.[23] Each of these improvements in risk factors was facilitated by national campaigns that warned of the hazards of particular behaviors.[23]

The time has come to consider another major campaign. Even though the requisite behavioral changes may be small, they may be difficult to accomplish. The fact that most health-related behaviors have improved while obesity has worsened may be an indication of just how daunting the prospect of reducing levels of obesity may be. The rising prevalence and severity of obesity are already reducing life expectancy among the U.S. population. A failure to address the problem could impede the improvements in longevity that are otherwise in store.

Notes

I am indebted to John Wilmoth and Mitch Lazar for suggestions and assistance.

From the Population Studies Center, University of Pennsylvania, Philadelphia.

1. Olshansky SJ, Passaro D, Hershow R, et al. A potential decline in life expectancy in the United States in the 21st century. N Engl J Med 2005;352:1138–45.

2. Arias E. United States life tables, 2002. National vital statistics reports. Vol. 53. No. 6. Hyattsville, Md.: National Center for Health Statistics, 2002:25, 29. (DHHS publication no. (PHS) 2005–1120 PRS 04-0554.)

3. *Idem.* United States life tables, 2002. Vol. 53. No. 6. Hyattsville, Md.: National Center for Health Statistics, 2002:29. (PHS) 2005-1120 PRS 04–0554.

4. Lee R, Miller T. Evaluating the performance of the Lee-Carter method for forecasting mortality. Demography 2001;38:537–49.

5. Rosenberg M, Luckner W. Summary of results of survey of seminar attendees. North Am Actuarial J 1998;2:64–82.

6. Tuljaparkar S, Boe C. Mortality change and forecasting: how much and how little do we know? North Am Actuarial J 1998;2:13–47.

7. Oeppen J, Vaupel JW. Broken limits to life expectancy. Science 2002;296: 1029–31.

8. White K. Longevity advances in high income countries, 1955–96. Popul Dev Rev 2002;28:59–76.

9. Cutler D. Your money or your life: strong medicine for America's health care system. New York: Oxford University Press, 2004.

10. Perls TT, Wilmoth J, Levenson R, et al. Life-long sustained mortality advantage of siblings of centenarians. Proc Natl Acad Sci U S A 2002;99:8442–7.

11. Molla MT, Madans JH, Wagener DK. Differentials in adult mortality and activity limitation by education in the United States at the end of the 1990s. Popul Dev Rev 2004;30:625–46.

12. Costa DL. Understanding the twentieth-century decline in chronic conditions among older men. Demography 2000;37:53–72.

13. Zimmer C. Do chronic diseases have an infectious root? Science 2001; 293:1974–7.

14. Freid VM, Prager K, MacKay AP, Xia H. Health, United States, 2003: with chartbook on trends in the health of Americans. Washington, D.C.: Government Printing Office, 2003:169, 212, 228. (DHHS publication no. 2003–1232.)

15. Pampel FC. Declining sex differences in mortality from lung cancer in high-income nations. Demography 2003;40:45–66.

16. Reynolds SL, Crimmins EM, Saito Y. Cohort differences in disability and disease presence. Gerontologist 1998;38:578–90.

17. OECD health data 2004. Paris: Organisation for Economic Co-operation and Development, 2004.

18. Board of Trustees. Federal old-age and survivors insurance and disability insurance trust funds: 2004 annual report. Baltimore, Md.: U.S. Social Security Administration, 2004.

19. Manton KG, Stallard E, Tolley DH. Limits to human life expectancy: evidence, prospects, and implications. Popul Dev Rev 1991;17:603–37.

20. Hill JO, Wyatt HR, Reed GW, Peters JC. Obesity and the environment: where do we go from here? Science 2003;299:853–8.

21. Carpenter D. Food industry push: cater to health needs. Press release of the Associated Press, New York, January 18, 2005.

22. Jaffe H. Whatever happened to the U.S. AIDS epidemic? Science 2004;305: 1243–4.

23. Cutler DM. Behavioral health interventions: what works and why? In: Anderson NB, Bulatao RA, Cohen B, eds. Critical perspectives on racial and ethnic differences in health in late life. Washington, D.C.: National Academies Press, 2004:643–74.

Paul Campos   ➡ **NO**

The Weighting Game

Perhaps America's most common New Year's resolution is to lose weight. This week, as we push ourselves away from the increasingly guilty pleasures of the holiday table, we will be bombarded with ads imploring us to slim down with the help of health club memberships, exercise equipment, or the latest miracle diet. Yet, however common it may be, the resolution to lose weight appears to be a particularly ineffective one: The latest figures indicate that 65 percent of the adult population—more than 135 million Americans—is either "overweight" or "obese." And government officials are increasingly eager to declare America's burgeoning waistline the nation's number-one public health problem. The Surgeon General's recent Call to Action to Prevent and Decrease Overweight and Obesity labels being fat an "epidemic" that kills upward of 300,000 Americans per year. Such declarations lend our obsession with being thin a respectable medical justification. But are they accurate? A careful survey of medical literature reveals that the conventional wisdom about the health risks of fat is a grotesque distortion of a far more complicated story. Indeed, subject to exceptions for the most extreme cases, it's not at all clear that being overweight is an independent health risk of any kind, let alone something that kills hundreds of thousands of Americans every year. While having a sedentary lifestyle or a lousy diet—both factors, of course, that can contribute to being overweight—do pose health risks, there's virtually no evidence that being fat, in and of itself, is at all bad for you. In other words, while lifestyle is a good predictor of health, weight isn't: A moderately active fat person is likely to be far healthier than someone who is svelte but sedentary. What's worse, Americans' (largely unsuccessful) efforts to make themselves thin through dieting and supplements are themselves a major cause of the ill health associated with being overweight—meaning that America's war on fat is actually helping cause the very disease it is supposed to cure.

The most common way researchers determine whether someone is overweight is by using the "body mass index" (BMI), a simple and rather arbitrary mathematical formula that puts people of varying heights and weights on a single integrated scale. According to the government, you're "overweight" (that is, your weight becomes a significant health risk) if you have a BMI figure of 25 and "obese" (your weight becomes a major health risk) if your BMI is 30 or higher. A five-foot-four-inch woman is thus labeled "overweight" and "obese" at weights of 146 pounds and 175 pounds, respectively; a five-foot-ten-inch man crosses those thresholds at weights of 174 pounds and 210 pounds.

Such claims have been given enormous publicity by, among other government officials, former Surgeons General C. Everett Koop—whose Shape Up America foundation has been a leading source for the claim that fat kills 300,000 Americans per year—and David Satcher, who in 1998 declared that America's young people are "seriously at risk of starting out obese and dooming themselves to the difficult task of overcoming a tough illness." And the federal government is beginning to put its money where its mouth is: Last April, the Internal Revenue Service announced that diet-related costs could henceforth be deducted as medical expenses, as long as such expenses were incurred in the course of treating the "disease" of being fat—a ruling that will create a multibillion dollar per year public subsidy for the weight-loss industry.

Yet, despite the intense campaign to place fat in the same category of public health hazards as smoking and drug abuse, there is in fact no medical basis for the government's BMI recommendations or the public health policies based on them. The most obvious flaw lies with the BMI itself, which is simply based on height and weight. The arbitrariness of these charts becomes clear as soon as one starts applying them to actual human beings. As *The Wall Street Journal* pointed out last July, taking the BMI charts seriously requires concluding that Brad Pitt, George Clooney, and Michael Jordan are all "overweight," and that Sylvester Stallone and baseball star Sammy Sosa are "obese." According to my calculations, fully three-quarters of National Football League running backs—speedy, chiseled athletes, all of whom, it's safe to say, could beat the world's fastest obesity researcher by a wide margin in a 100-yard dash—are "obese."

To be sure, even if the BMI categories can be spectacularly wrong in cases such as those involving professional athletes, they're often a pretty good indicator of how "fat" most people are in everyday life. The real question is whether being fat—as determined by the BMI or by any other measure—is actually a health risk. To answer this question, it's necessary to examine the epidemiological evidence. Since the measurable factors that affect whether someone contracts any particular disease or condition can easily number in the hundreds or thousands, it's often difficult to distinguish meaningful data from random statistical noise. And, even where there are clear correlations, establishing cause and effect can be a complicated matter. If researchers observe that fat people are more prone to contract, say, heart disease than thin people, this fact by itself doesn't tell them whether being fat contributes to acquiring heart disease. It could easily be the case that some other factor or set of factors—i.e., being sedentary or eating junk food or dieting aggressively—contributes both to being fat and to contracting heart disease.

Unfortunately, in the world of obesity research these sorts of theoretical and practical complications are often dealt with by simply ignoring them. The most cited studies purporting to demonstrate that fat is a major health risk almost invariably make little or no attempt to control for what medical researchers refer to as "confounding variables." For example, the research providing the basis for the claim that fat contributes to the deaths of 300,000 Americans per year—a 1999 study published in the Journal of the American Medical Association (JAMA)—did not attempt to control for any confounding variables other than age, gender, and smoking.

And, even among studies—such as the JAMA one—that ignore variables such as diet or activity levels, there is tremendous disagreement: For every study that indicates some sort of increased health risk for people with BMI figures between 25 and 30 (a category that currently includes more than one out of every three adult Americans), another study indicates such people enjoy lower overall health risks than those whom the government and the medical establishment have labeled "ideal-weight" individuals (i.e., people with BMI figures between 18.5 and 24.9). Perhaps the most comprehensive survey of the literature regarding the health risks of different weight levels is a 1996 study by scientists at the National Center for Health Statistics and Cornell University. This survey analyzed data from dozens of previous studies involving more than 600,000 subjects. It concluded that, for nonsmoking men, the lowest mortality rate was found among those with BMI figures between 23 and 29, meaning that a large majority of the healthiest men in the survey would be considered "overweight" by current government standards. For nonsmoking women, the results were even more striking: The authors concluded that, for such women, the BMI range correlating with the lowest mortality rate is extremely broad, from about 18 to 32, meaning that a woman of average height can weigh anywhere within an 80-pound range without seeing any statistically meaningful change in her risk of premature death.

What accounts for the conflict between studies that claim being "overweight" is a significant health risk and those that suggest such weight levels might actually be optimal? The biggest factor is that researchers fail to point out that, in practical terms, the differences in risk they are measuring are usually so small as to be trivial. For example, suppose that Group A consists of 2,500 subjects and that over the course of a decade five of these people die from heart attacks. Now suppose that Group B consists of 4,000 subjects and that five members of this group also die from heart attacks over the same ten-year span. One way of characterizing these figures is to say that people in Group A are subject to a (implicitly terrifying) 60 percent greater risk of a fatal heart attack than those in Group B. But the practical reality is that the relevant risk for members of both groups is miniscule. Indeed, upon closer examination, almost all studies that claim "overweight" people run significantly increased health risks involve this sort of interpretation (or, less generously, distortion) of their data.

This phenomenon is in part a product of the fact that studies that purport to find significant elevations of mortality risk associated with different weight levels usually focus on mortality rates among relatively young adults. Since these studies typically involve very small numbers of deaths among very large numbers of subjects, it isn't surprising to see what appear to be large oscillations in relative risk across different studies. Indeed, one often observes large, apparently random oscillations in risk even within studies. Lost in the uproar over the JAMA study's 300,000 deaths figure is the peculiar fact that the report actually found that supposedly "ideal-weight" individuals with a BMI of 20 had essentially the same mortality risk as "obese" persons with BMI figures of 30 and that both groups had a slightly higher mortality risk than "overweight" people with BMI figures of 25.

In short, the Cornell survey of the existing literature merely confirmed what anyone who actually examines the data will discover: In a decided majority of studies, groups of people labeled "overweight" by current standards are found to have equal or lower mortality rates than groups of supposedly "ideal-weight" individuals. University of Virginia professor Glenn Gaesser has estimated that three-quarters of all medical studies on the effects of weight on health between 1945 and 1995 concluded either that "excess" weight had no effect on health or that it was actually beneficial. And again, this remains the case even before one begins to take into account complicating factors such as sedentary lifestyle, poor nutrition, dieting and diet drugs, etc. "As of 2002," Gaesser points out in his book *Big Fat Lies*, "there has not been a single study that has truly evaluated the effects of weight alone on health, which means that 'thinner is healthier' is not a fact but an unsubstantiated hypothesis for which there is a wealth of evidence that suggests the reverse."

As we have seen, most of the people the government and the health establishment claim are too fat—those categorized as "overweight" or "mildly obese"—do not in fact suffer from worse health than supposedly "ideal-weight" individuals. It is true that some groups of fat people—generally those with BMI figures well above 30—are less healthy than average, although not nearly to the extent the anti-fat warriors would have you believe. (Large-scale mortality studies indicate that women who are 50 or even 75 pounds "overweight" will on average still have longer life expectancies than those who are 10 to 15 pounds "underweight," a.k.a. fashionably thin.) Yet there is considerable evidence that even substantially "obese" people are not less healthy because they're fat. Rather, other factors are causing them to be both fat and unhealthy. Chief among these factors are sedentary lifestyle and diet-driven weight fluctuation.

The most comprehensive work regarding the dangers of sedentary lifestyle has been done at the Cooper Institute in Dallas. The institute's director of research, Steven Blair, is probably the world's leading expert on the relationship between activity levels and overall health. For the past 20 years, the Cooper Institute has maintained a database that has tracked the health, weight, and basic fitness levels of tens of thousands of individuals. What Blair and his colleagues have discovered turns the conventional wisdom about the relationship between fat and fitness on its head. Quite simply, when researchers factor in the activity levels of the people being studied, body mass appears to have no relevance to health whatsoever—even among people who are substantially "obese." It turns out that "obese" people who engage in moderate levels of physical activity have radically lower rates of premature death than sedentary people who maintain supposedly "ideal-weight" levels.

For example, a 1999 Cooper Institute study found the highest death rate to be among sedentary men with waist measurements under 34 inches and the lowest death rate to be among physically fit men with waist measurements of 40 inches or more. And these results do not change when the researchers control for body-fat percentage, thus dispensing with the claim that such percentages, rather than body mass itself, are the crucial variables when measuring the health effects of weight. Fat people might be less healthy if they're fat because of a sedentary lifestyle. But, if they're fat and active, they have nothing to worry about.

Still, even if it's clear that it's better to be fat and active than fat and sedentary—or even thin and sedentary—isn't it the case that being thin and active is the best combination of all? Not according to Blair's research: His numerous studies of the question have found no difference in mortality rates between fit people who are fat and those who are thin.

Of course, in a culture as anti-fat as ours, the whole notion of people who are both fat and fit seems contradictory. Yet the research done by Blair and others indicates that our belief that fatness and fitness are in fundamental tension is based on myths, not science. "Fitness" in Blair's work isn't defined by weight or body-fat percentage but rather by cardiovascular and aerobic endurance, as measured by treadmill stress tests. And he has found that people don't need to be marathon runners to garner the immense health benefits that follow from maintaining good fitness levels. Blair's research shows that to move into the fitness category that offers most of the health benefits of being active, people need merely to engage in some combination of daily activities equivalent to going for a brisk half-hour walk. To move into the top fitness category requires a bit more—the daily equivalent of jogging for perhaps 25 minutes or walking briskly for close to an hour. (Our true public health scandal has nothing to do with fat and everything to do with the fact that 80 percent of the population is so inactive that it doesn't even achieve the former modest fitness standard.)

Other researchers have reached similar conclusions. For instance, the Harvard Alumni Study, which has tracked the health of Harvard graduates for many decades, has found the lowest mortality rates among those graduates who have gained the most weight since college while also expending at least 2,000 calories per week in physical activities. Such work suggests strongly that when obesity researchers have described the supposed health risks of fat, what they have actually been doing is using fat as a proxy—and a poor one at that—for a factor that actually does have a significant effect on health and mortality: cardiovascular and metabolic fitness. As Blair himself has put it, Americans have a "misdirected obsession with weight and weight loss. The focus is all wrong. It's fitness that is the key."

If fat is ultimately irrelevant to health, our fear of fat, unfortunately, is not. Americans' obsession with thinness feeds an institution that actually is a danger to Americans' health: the diet industry.

Tens of millions of Americans are trying more or less constantly to lose 20 or 30 pounds. (Recent estimates are that, on any particular day, close to half the adult population is on some sort of diet.) Most say they are doing so for their health, often on the advice of their doctors. Yet numerous studies—two dozen in the last 20 years alone—have shown that weight loss of this magnitude (and indeed even of as little as ten pounds) leads to an increased risk of premature death, sometimes by an order of several hundred percent. By contrast, over this same time frame, only a handful of studies have indicated that weight loss leads to lower mortality rates—and one of these found an eleven-hour increase in life expectancy per pound lost (i.e., less than an extra month of life in return for a 50-pound weight loss). This pattern holds true even when studies take into account "occult wasting," the weight loss that sometimes accompanies a serious but unrelated illness. For example, a major American Cancer Society study published in 1995 concluded in no uncertain terms that healthy "overweight" and "obese" women were better off if they didn't lose weight. In this study, healthy women who intentionally lost weight over a period of a year or longer suffered an all-cause increased risk of premature mortality that was up to 70 percent higher than that of healthy women who didn't intentionally lose weight. Meanwhile, unintentional weight gain had no effect on mortality rates. (A 1999 report based on the same data pool found similar results for men.) The only other large study that has examined the health effects of intentional weight loss, the Iowa Women's Health Study, also failed to find an association between weight loss and significantly lower mortality rates. In fact, in this 42,000-person study, "overweight" women had an all-cause mortality rate 5 to 10 percent lower than that of "ideal-weight" women.

One explanation for the ill effects of intentional weight loss is diet drugs (others include the binge eating to which chronic dieters are especially prone). The havoc wrought by drugs such as Redux and fen-phen is well-known and has resulted in billions of dollars' worth of legal liability for their manufacturers. What has been less publicized is that other diet drugs are being discovered to have similarly devastating effects: For example, a recent Yale University study indicates that women between the ages of 18 and 49 who use appetite suppressants containing phenylpropanolamine increase their risk of hemorrhagic stroke by 1,558 percent. (This over-the-counter drug was used by approximately nine million Americans at any given time during the late '90s. The Food and Drug Administration, which is in the process of formally banning the drug, has requested that in the interim manufacturers remove it from the market voluntarily.)

The grim irony lurking behind these statistics is that, as numerous studies have demonstrated, people who lose weight via dieting and diet drugs often end up weighing a good deal more than people of similar initial weight who never diet. The explanation for this perverse result can be found in the well-documented "set-point" phenomenon—that is, the body's tendency to fight the threat of starvation by slowing its metabolism in response to a caloric reduction. For example, obesity researcher Paul Ernsberger has done several studies in which rats are placed on very low-calorie diets. Invariably, when the rats are returned to their previous level of caloric intake, they get fat by eating exactly the same number of calories that had merely maintained their weight before they were put on diets. The same is true of human beings. "Put people on crash diets, and they'll gain back more weight than they lost," Ernsberger has said.

The literature on the health effects of dieting and diet drugs suggests that, as Gaesser pointed out, what most studies that find a correlation between higher mortality and higher body mass really demonstrate is a correlation between higher mortality and higher rates of dieting and diet-drug use. Under these circumstances, advising fat people to diet for the sake of their health is tantamount to prescribing a drug that causes the disease it's supposed to cure.

What is it about fat that renders so many otherwise sensible Americans more than a little bit crazy? The war on fat is based on many things: the deeply neurotic relationship so many Americans have developed toward food and their bodies, the identification of thinness with social privilege and of fat with lower-class status, the financial interests of the diet industry, and many other factors as well. Ultimately, the fundamental forces driving our national obsession with fat fall into two broad and interrelated categories: economic interest and psychological motivation.

Obesity research in the United States is almost wholly funded by the weight-loss industry. For all the government's apparent interest in the fat "epidemic," in recent years less than 1 percent of the federal health research budget has gone toward obesity-related research. (For example, in 1995, the National Institutes of Health spent $87 million on obesity research out of a total budget of $11.3 billion.) And, while it's virtually impossible to determine just how much the dieting industry spends on such research, it is safe to say that it is many, many times more. Indeed, many of the nation's most prominent obesity researchers have direct financial stakes in companies that produce weight-loss products. (When they are quoted in the media, such researchers routinely fail to disclose their financial interests in the matters on which they are commenting, in part because journalists fail to ask them about potential conflicts.) And the contamination of supposedly disinterested research goes well beyond the effects of such direct financial interests. As Laura Fraser points out in her book *Losing It: False Hopes and Fat Profits in the Diet Industry*, "Diet and pharmaceutical companies influence every step along the way of the scientific process. They pay for the ads that keep obesity journals publishing. They underwrite medical conferences, flying physicians around the country expense-free and paying them large lecture fees to attend."

This situation creates a kind of structural distortion, analogous to that which takes place in the stock market when analysts employed by brokerage houses make recommendations to clients intended to inflate the price of stock issued by companies that in return send their business to the brokerages' investment-banking divisions. In such circumstances, it's easy for all the players to convince themselves of the purity of their motives. "It isn't diabolical," eating-disorders specialist David Garner told Fraser. "Some people are very committed to the belief that weight loss is a national health problem. It's just that, if their livelihood is based in large part on the diet industry, they can't be impartial." Fraser writes that when she asked one obesity researcher, who has criticized dieting as ineffective and psychologically damaging, to comment on the policies of one commercial weight-loss program, he replied, "What can I say? I'm a consultant for them."

What makes this structural distortion particularly insidious is that, just as Americans wanted desperately to believe that the IPO bubble of the '90s would never burst—and were therefore eager to accept whatever the experts at Merrill Lynch and on *The Wall Street Journal's* editorial page had to say about the "New Economy"—they also long to believe that medical experts can solve the problem of their expanding waistlines. The reason for this can be summed up in six words: Americans think being fat is disgusting. That psychological truth creates an enormous incentive to give our disgust a respectable motiva-tion. In other words, being fat must be terrible for one's health, because if it isn't that means our increasing hatred of fat represents a social, psychological, and moral problem rather than a medical one.

The convergence of economic interest and psychological motivation helps ensure that, for example, when former Surgeon General Koop raised more than $2 million from diet-industry heavyweights Weight Watchers and Jenny Craig for his Shape Up America foundation, he remained largely immune to the charge that he was exploiting a national neurosis for financial gain. After all, "everyone knows" that fat is a major health risk, so why should we find it disturbing to discover such close links between prominent former public health officials and the dietary-pharmaceutical complex?

None of this is to suggest that the war against fat is the product of some sort of conscious conspiracy on the part of those whose interests are served by it. The relationship between economic motives, cultural trends, social psy-chology, and the many other factors that fuel the war on fat is surely far more complex than that. But it does suggest that the conventional wisdom about fat in the United States is based on factors that have very little to do with a disinterested evaluation of the medical and scientific evidence, and therefore this conventional wisdom needs to be taken for what it is: a pervasive social myth rather than a rational judgment about risk.

So what should we do about fat in the United States? The short answer is: nothing. The longer answer is that we should refocus our attention from people's waistlines to their levels of activity. Americans have become far too sedentary. It sometimes seems that much of American life is organized around the principle that people should be able to go through an average day without ever actually using their legs. We do eat too much junk that isn't good for us because it's quick and cheap and easier than taking the time and money to prepare food that is both nutritious and satisfies our cravings.

A rational public health policy would emphasize that the keys to good health (at least those that anyone can do anything about—genetic factors remain far more important than anything else) are, in roughly descending order of importance: not to smoke, not to be an alcoholic or drug addict, not to be sedentary, and not to eat a diet packed with junk food. It's true that a more active populace that ate a healthier diet would be somewhat thinner, as would a nation that wasn't dieting obsessively. Even so, there is no reason why there shouldn't be millions of healthy, happy fat people in the United States, as there no doubt would be in a culture that maintained a rational attitude toward the fact that people will always come in all shapes and sizes, whether they live healthy lives or not. In the end, nothing could be easier than to win the war on fat: All we need to do is stop fighting it.

POSTSCRIPT

Does Obesity Cause a Decline in Life Expectancy?

Although genetics and metabolism may elevate the risk for overweight and obesity, they don't explain the rising rate of obesity seen in the United States. Our genetic background has not changed significantly in the past 40 years, during which time the rate of obesity among Americans more than doubled. The causes can be linked to changing eating habits and a decline in physical activity. Whatever the reason, there appears to be a relationship between obesity and longevity. For further reading, see "9 Keys to Living to a Healthy 85+" (*Tufts University Health & Nutrition Letter*, February 2007). This article suggests that one of the important risk factors to a long life is maintaining a lean body weight. A study published in the *Gerontologist* estimated the effect of obesity on both the length of life and the length of nondisabled life for older Americans ("The Impact of Obesity on Active Life Expectancy in Older American Men and Women," August 2005). They found that although obesity didn't have much impact on longevity for those over 70, it did correlate with a greater likelihood of becoming disabled. Also see "Obesity & Longevity" (*Total Health*, January/February 2007). The article "Longevity Olympics: We're Losing" (*Prevention*, June 2006), indicates that 28 countries have a higher life expectancy than that in the United States and that American obesity rates is the reason.

However, several researchers question the relationship between obesity and reduced longevity. University of Chicago political scientist J. Eric Oliver, author of *Fat Politics*, and University of Colorado law professor Paul Campos, author of *The Diet Myth*, both address this question. And they both argue that except for certain conditions associated with BMIs over 40, there is little evidence that extra pounds per se cause health problems and disease. Even though obesity may be correlated with illness, it is mostly because obesity is related to poor nutrition and a sedentary lifestyle. These two factors independently elevate the risk of hypertension, type 2 diabetes, certain cancers, and heart disease. Obese individuals are also less likely to get regular exercise and eat healthy foods such as fruits, vegetables, and whole grains. They are, unfortunately, more likely to consume more unhealthy foods including those with high amounts of sugars and unhealthy fats. The authors say these habits, which are more likely to occur among obese individuals, are the primary problem. Both Campos and Oliver question why the medical case against obesity is pushed so aggressively since it's so weak. Patrick Johnson agrees with Oliver and Campos. In "The Obesity Myth" (*Skeptic*, 2005), Johnson talks about compelling scientific evidence that indicates obesity by itself may not pose a significant threat to our health.

It is instead poor diet and lack of exercise that pose the biggest concern. Most of the attention given to the obesity epidemic by popular media outlets and most health care professionals is focused on scare tactics. A significant problem lies in the fact that the evidence is not completely clear and that the issue is emotionally charged, which results in the proponents of both sides of the argument engaging more in bias than scientific reasoning.

Another article that makes a similar case is "A 'Few Extra Pounds'—Fewer Years, or *More* Years? (*Health at Every Size*, Winter 2007). Glenn Gaesser maintains that most studies stress that overweight individuals, especially men, had a slight advantage from the standpoint of avoiding premature death. In "But It's Not So Bad to Be Fat (*New Scientist*, January 20, 2007), Gregg Fonarow of the University of California at Los Angeles and his colleagues looked at the records of more than 100,000 patients hospitalized because their heart failure was worsening. They found that the fatter the person, the less likely they were to die during a week-long hospital stay. Fonarow suggests that overweight individuals may cope better with heart failure because they have more metabolic reserves to draw on when the heart isn't pumping blood fast enough to meet the body's needs.

It appears that the relationship between obesity and longevity is a complex issue. For additional readings on the topic, see "An American Epidemic" (*Economist*, February 17, 2007); "The Expanding Obesity Problem" (*State Legislatures*, January 2007); "Overweight, Obesity, and Mortality in a Large Prospective Cohort of Persons 50 to 71 Years Old" (*The New England Journal of Medicine*, vol. 355, 2006); "The Obesity Epidemic and Its Cardiovascular Consequences" (*Current Opinions in Cardiology*, vol. 21, 2006); and "The Health and Cost Consequences of Obesity among the Future Elderly" (*Health Affairs*, 2005).

Contributors to This Volume

EDITOR

EILEEN L. DANIEL, a registered dietitian and licensed nutritionist, is a professor in the Department of Health Science and associate vice provost for academic affairs at the State University of New York College at Brockport. She received a B.S. in nutrition and dietetics from the Rochester Institute of Technology in 1977, an M.S. in community health education from SUNY College at Brockport in 1978, and a Ph.D. in health education from the University of Oregon in 1986. A member of the American Dietetics Association, the New York State Dietetics Society, and other professional and community organizations, she has published more than 40 articles in professional journals on issues of health, nutrition, and health education. She is the editor of *Annual Editions: Health.*

AUTHORS

PAUL ANTHONY is the chief medical officer at the Pharmaceutical Research and Manufacturers of America.

EMILY BAZELON is a senior editor at *Slate* and frequently writes about the law and science.

DEENA BERKOWITZ is an assistant professor of pediatrics at George Washington University School of Medicine and Health Sciences in Washington, DC.

CARL BLOICE is a freelance writer based in San Francisco.

PHYLLIDA BROWN is a science writer based in the UK.

PAUL CAMPOS is a professor of law at the University of Colorado–Boulder and author of *The Last American Diet*.

R. ALTA CHARO teaches law and bioethics at the University of Wisconsin Law and Medical Schools.

GREGORY CONKO is the director of food safety policy at the Competitive Enterprise Institute.

CYNTHIA DAILARD was a senior public policy associate at the Guttmacher Institute and a NFPRHA Board member.

JESSE DALLERY is an associate professor in the behavior analysis program, Department of Psychology, University of Florida, Gainesville, Florida.

GREGORY MICHAEL DORR is a visiting assistant professor at Amherst College and a visiting scholar at the Center for the Study of Diversity at MIT.

KEVIN DRUM is a political columnist and blogger.

GREGG EASTERBROOK is an editor at the *National Review*.

EZEKIEL J. EMANUEL, M.D., Ph.D., is the director of the Clinical Bioethics Department at the U.S. National Institutes of Health.

MARC-ANDRÉ GAGNON is an assistant professor in the School of Public Policy and Administration at Carleton University, Ottawa, Ontario, Canada.

IAN GENTLES is the vice president of the deVeber Institute for Bioethics and Social Research in Ontario, Canada, and a visiting professor of history at Tyndale College, Toronto, Ontario, Canada.

INDUR M. GOKLANY is the assistant director of science and technology policy at the U.S. Department of the Interior.

LAWRENCE O. GOSTIN is an associate dean, a Linda D. and Timothy J. O'Neil Professor of Global Health Law, the faculty director of the O'Neil Institute for National and Global Health Law, and the director of the Center for Law and the Public's Health at Georgetown University Law Center in Washington, DC.

JEFFREY HART is a senior editor of the *National Review*.

RONALD B. HERBERMAN is a physician and the director of the Pittsburgh Cancer Institute, Pittsburgh, PA.

CONN HALLINAN is a foreign policy analyst for Foreign Policy in Focus and a lecturer in journalism at UC Santa Cruz.

MICHAEL IDOV is a contributing editor at *New York Magazine* and the author of the novel *Ground Up*.

GAIL JAVITT is the law and policy director at the Genetics and Public Policy Center in Washington, DC. She is also a research scientist in the Berman Institute of Bioethics at Johns Hopkins University in Baltimore, Maryland.

DAVID S. JONES is an associate professor of the history of science at MIT, where he directs the Center for the Study of Diversity, and a lecturer in social medicine at Harvard Medical School.

ROBERT F. KENNEDY JR., an environmentalist, is the president of Waterkeeper Alliance.

BERNARD LEIKIND is a physicist and board member of *Skeptic* magazine.

ALAN I. LESHNER is the director of the National Institute on Drug Abuse at the National Institutes of Health.

JOEL LEXCHIN is a physician and professor in the School of Health Policy and Management at York University and an associate professor in the Department of Family and Community Medicine at the University of Toronto.

JOHN A. MENGES is a licensed pharmacist.

HENRY I. MILLER, M.D., is a fellow at Hoover Institution, Stanford University.

JULIA MOSKIN is a reporter for *The New York Times*.

MATTHEW NORMAND is an assistant professor of psychology at the University of the Pacific.

RAMESH PONNURU is a senior editor at the *National Review*.

SAMUEL H. PRESTON is a professor at the University of Pennsylvania.

JAMES RIDGEWAY is a senior Washington correspondent for *Mother Jones*.

MARION E. ROBERTS is a psychologist with the Institute of Psychiatry, Department of Psychological Medicine and Psychiatry, Section of Eating Disorders, King's College London, UK.

HANNA ROSIN is a senior editor for *The Atlantic Magazine*.

SALLY L. SATEL is a practicing psychiatrist in Washington, DC, and a lecturer in psychiatry at Yale University School of Medicine.

MARK SCHAPIRO is a reporter with the Center for Investigative Reporting and was the correspondent for *NOW with Bill Moyers*.

JOHN R. SEFFRIN is the president of the American Cancer Society.

MICHAEL SHERMER is a science writer and the editor-in-chief of *Skeptic*.

PETER SINGER is an Australian philosopher who is a professor of bioethics at Princeton University and a laureate professor at the Centre for Applied Philosophy and Public Ethics at the University of Melbourne, Australia.

REYNOLD SPECTOR is a physician and clinical professor of medicine at the Robert Wood Johnson Medical School in New Jersey.

FRED SCHWARZ is a journalist who writes for the *National Review*.

JANET L. TREASURE is a physician with the Institute of Psychiatry, Department of Psychological Medicine and Psychiatry, Section of Eating Disorders, King's College London, UK.

ELIZABETH R. WACK is a psychologist with the Institute of Psychiatry, Department of Psychological Medicine and Psychiatry, Section of Eating Disorders, King's College London, UK.